JOURNAL FOR THE STUDY OF THE OLD TESTAMENT SUPPLEMENT SERIES
298

Sheffield Academic Press

Paradisal Love

Johann Gottfried Herder and
the Song of Songs

John D. Baildam

Journal for the Study of the Old Testament
Supplement Series 298

Copyright © 1999 Sheffield Academic Press

Published by
Sheffield Academic Press Ltd
Mansion House
19 Kingfield Road
Sheffield S11 9AS
England

Typeset by Sheffield Academic Press
and
Printed on acid-free paper in Great Britain
by Biddles
Guildford, Surrey

British Library Cataloguing in Publication Data

A catalogue record for this book is available
from the British Library

ISBN 1-84127-022-9

CONTENTS

PREFACE

This work claims to be the first comprehensive published study of the preoccupation of Johann Gottfried Herder (1744–1803) with the Song of Songs; it considers the work's importance in his thinking, and examines in detail his commentaries and translations of 1776 and 1778. The book argues that, despite Herder's claims to the contrary, his own cultural position is revealed in his translations and in his unique interpretation of the work as the voice of pure, paradisal love.

The Introduction states the need for this study, and describes the methodology used. Chapter 1 examines Herder's interest in the Song of Songs between 1765 and 1778. Chapter 2 puts his reflections into the wider context of his relativistic views on the nature of poetry, on contemporary German culture, and on the importance of primitive poetry in general and the poetry of the Bible in particular. Chapter 3 considers certain current literary-critical theories which have implications for Herder's translations of these 'Lieder der Liebe' ('Songs of Love'), as he entitled his published translation of 1778. Herder's theories of language and translation are discussed, using other German translation theories as a touchstone. Chapter 4 discusses Herder's reading of the book as the most primitive, natural and sublime example of Hebrew poetry, placing it in the context of earlier and contemporary interpretations. His opinion of other translations is examined, including the Middle High German text appended to his own work. Chapter 5 appraises Herder's commentaries, analysing how the points which emerge reflect his overall concept of the work. Chapter 6 focuses on his translations, comparing them with each other, with the Lutheran text to which Herder ultimately directed his readership, and with the Hebrew text. Where appropriate, Goethe's translation is referred to as one example of several contemporary translations. The Conclusion examines the reception of Herder's work. The three appendices consist of a parallel presentation of Herder's translations of 1776 and 1778, Luther's translation of 1545, and Goethe's translation of 1775.

Given that the original dissertation used as a basis for this study was prepared within the discipline of German Literature rather than Old Testament Studies, all quotations from German were given in the original language only, maintaining the orthography used by the relevant author.[1] As this present work is intended for a readership wider than those with an interest in Germanic Studies, I have endeavoured to provide my own English translations of all German quotations used. Nevertheless, I have also insisted on maintaining the original throughout, both in order to satisfy the Germanist, and as otherwise the argument would be weakened linguistically. My translations are in no way intended to be definitive or of literary value, but are there merely to aid the reader.[2] I am well aware that I run the risk of being accused—like Herder—of translating according to my own reader response and my own cultural background, but the point of my translations is purely to be supportive of the reader. Indeed, if any reader is offended by my translations, then permit me to adopt Luther's challenge concerning his own translation of the New Testament: 'Es ist niemand verboten, ein bessers zu machen. Wer's nicht lesen will, der laß es liegen.'[3]

Unless a supporting footnote has proved necessary, my translations of quotations of approximately one line or less are included parenthetically within the body of the text. My translations of longer quotations and block quotations are given in a footnote. It is hoped that this method will facilitate reading. I have not translated the Appendices, which contain translations of the Song of Songs by Herder, Luther and Goethe, nor have I translated the Lutheran text used on a verse-by-verse basis to aid presentation in Chapter 6.

1.   Readers of German should bear this point in mind when noting differences between current orthography and that of Luther and Herder, for example.

2.   In this regard, I look for support from Ernest A. Menze and Karl Menges who maintain that 'for a translator Herder's prose is treacherous ground with spiked pitfalls. His style of expression seems at times to defy English rendering' (*Johann Gottfried Herder: Selected Early Works 1764–1767. Addresses, Essays, and Drafts; 'Fragments on Recent German Literature'* [trans. Ernest A. Menze with Michael Palma; University Park, PA: Pennsylvania State University Press, 1992], p. viii). I suspect that Herder's poetry represents no less treacherous ground.

3.   'Nobody is forbidden from making a better one. Whoever does not wish to read it, let him leave it be.' Quoted in Douglas Robinson, *The Translator's Turn* (Baltimore: The Johns Hopkins University Press, 1991), p. 72. Interestingly, as we shall see in Chapter 1 of this study, Herder encouraged his readers to turn to Luther should they find his own translation of the Song of Songs inadequate.

References throughout this study to *Herders Sämmtliche Werke*, edited by Bernhard Suphan (*SWS*), are to volume and page numbers. They are given parenthetically within the body of the text after the abbreviation as listed for the appropriate work, where to omit it would be unclear. I have maintained the orthography of *SWS*, except in Appendix A which follows MS(3) of 1776 and the published translation of 1778.

ACKNOWLEDGMENTS

This monograph is based on a dissertation which was accepted in 1994 by the University of London for the degree of PhD in German. Thanks and appreciation are due to many individuals, all of whom in one way or another made a contribution towards the writing of the dissertation; I mention just a few. Deep gratitude is due to Mrs Dorothy Reich, formerly of Royal Holloway and Bedford New College, University of London, who was so willing to interrupt her retirement to act as my supervisor until ill-health forced her to relinquish the task in the autumn of 1991. Her enthusiasm greatly supported my own interest in the topic. I wish to express particular appreciation to Mrs Joyce Crick, formerly of University College London, who agreed so readily to assume the responsibilities of supervisor. I have learned much from her and hope that something of that learning is reflected in the following pages. Special thanks go to Dr Kenneth Newport, of Liverpool Hope University, for his constant interest and encouragement. I would also like to thank Professor Bill Jones of Royal Holloway and Bedford New College, University of London, for his encouragement and support. Over a number of years I have also appreciated greatly the constant encouragement and support of friends and colleagues at Newbold College, Bracknell. Finally, my loving thanks go to my wife Lynda, who, patiently, and without complaint, spent countless lonely hours selflessly permitting me to devote my thoughts to another.

ABBREVIATIONS

Works by Herder

The works below are cited from Bernhard Suphan (ed.), *Herders Sämmtliche Werke* (33 vols.; Berlin: Weidmann, 1877–1913), abbreviated throughout to *SWS*. These abbreviations are always given with the appropriate *SWS* volume and page references.

AD	*Adrastea* (1801–1802)
AK	*Von deutscher Art und Kunst* (1773)
AM	*Fragmente zu einer Archäologie des Morgenlandes* (1769)
AP	*Auch eine Philosophie der Geschichte zur Bildung der Menschheit* (1774)
ÄU	*Älteste Urkunde des Menschengeschlechts* (1774–76)
AV	*Alte Volkslieder* (1774)
BH	*Briefe zu Beförderung der Humanität* (1793–97)
BL	*Fragment über die beste Leitung eines jungen Genies zu den Schätzen der Dichtkunst* (1795)
BT	*Briefe an Theophron* (1780)
DL	*Über die neuere deutsche Litteratur. Fragmente* (1767)
DR	Recension of Johann N.C. Michael Denis's *Die Gedichte Ossians eines alten celtischen Dichters, aus dem Englischen übersetzt* (1771)
EE	*Vom Erkennen und Empfinden der menschlichen Seele. Bemerkungen und Träume* (1778)
EP	*Vom Geist der Ebräischen Poesie* (1782–83)
FS	*Ueber den Fleiß in mehreren gelehrten Sprachen* (1764)
HR	Recension of Christian Gottfried Hase's *Versuch einer richtigern Auslegung des Hohenliedes Salomonis, worin das zuverläßige, schöne und göttliche dieses heiligen Buchs gezeiget wird* (1765)
IP	*Ideen zur Philosophie der Geschichte der Menschheit* (1784–91)
JR	*Journal meiner Reise im Jahre 1769* (1769)
KW	*Kritische Wälder* (1769)
LD	*Versuch einer Geschichte der lyrischen Dichtkunst* (1764)
LL	*Lieder der Liebe* (1778)
TB	*Briefe, das Studium der Theologie betreffend* (1780–81)

TS	*Terpsichore* (1795–96)
UG	*Ursachen des gesunknen Geschmacks bei den verschiednen Völkern, da er geblühet* (1775)
US	*Abhandlung über den Ursprung der Sprache* (1772)
VÄ	*Von Ähnlichkeit der mittlern englischen und deutschen Dichtkunst* (1777)
VL	*Volkslieder* (1778–79)
WD	*Ueber die Würkung der Dichtkunst auf die Sitten der Völker in alten und neuen Zeiten* (1778)
ZB	*Zerstreute Blätter* (1785–97)

Journals

DVjs	*Deutsche Vierteljahrsschrift für Literaturwissenschaft und Geistesgeschichte*
GLL	*German Life and Letters*
GR	*Germanic Review*
JEGP	*Journal of English and Germanic Philology*
JHI	*Journal of the History of Ideas*
MLQ	*Modern Language Quarterly*
MLR	*Modern Language Review*
MP	*Modern Philology*
PMLA	*Publications of the Modern Language Association of America*
VT	*Vetus Testamentum*

Others

AB	Anchor Bible
ADB	*Allgemeine Deutsche Bibliothek*
GNB	Good News Bible
IB	*Interpreter's Bible*
KJV	King James Version
NEB	*New English Bible*
PG	J.-P. Migne (ed.), *Patrologia cursus completus… Series graeca* (166 vols.; Paris; Petit-Montrouge, 1857–83)
PL	J.-P. Migne (ed.), *Patrologia cursus completus… Series prima [latina]* (221 vols.; Paris; J.-P. Migne, 1844–65)
RSV	Revised Standard Version
WKG	Martin Luther, *Werke: Kritische Gesamtausgabe* (64 vols.; Weimar: Böhlau, 1883–; repr. Weimar: Böhlau; Graz: Akademische Druck- und Verlagsanstalt, 1964–)
WKGB	Martin Luther, *Werke: Kritische Gesamtausgabe—Die Deutsche Bibel* (12 vols.; Weimar: Böhlau, 1906–61)
WW	Johann Wolfgang von Goethe, *Werke* (50 vols.; Weimar: Böhlau, 1887–1900)

INTRODUCTION

Purpose and Methodology

Hermann Hettner claims that Herder's *Lieder der Liebe* represents 'das Zarteste, was Herder jemals geschrieben hat. Nie betätigt sich die feine dichterische Nachempfindung und Nachbildung Herders herrlicher als hier in dieser Übersetzung der tiefempfundenen altmorgenländischen Minnegesänge'.[1] Yet, although work had been done on Herder's views on language and poetry, as well as on his work as a biblical scholar, my dissertation upon which this book is based, submitted in the two-hundred-and-fiftieth anniversary of Herder's birth, was the first critical and analytical consideration of any substance that had been given to his interest in the Song of Songs. Secondary writers such as Hettner had hinted briefly *en passant* at the importance of his *Lieder der Liebe*, but nobody had yet produced a comprehensive study of it. This is surprising, given Herder's view that the Song of Songs was the epitome of that poetry which he regarded as representing God's foremost revelation to mankind, and given the regard in which he held it in his endeavours to use it as a catalyst for the improvement of his own native poetry.

Apart from various manuscript drafts in Herder's *Nachlaß* ('unpublished works'), the major base texts used in this study are the unpublished *Lieder der Liebe. Ein Biblisches Buch. Nebst zwo Zugaben* of 1776 (reprinted by Carl Redlich in *SWS*, VIII, pp. 589-658), and the version published in Leipzig in 1778 as *Lieder der Liebe. Die ältesten und schönsten aus Morgenlande. Nebst vier und vierzig alten Minneliedern* (reprinted by Redlich in *SWS*, VIII, pp. 485-588).

After examining Herder's preoccupation with the Song of Songs

1. 'The tenderest thing that Herder ever wrote. Nowhere are Herder's delicate poetic sympathy and imitation manifested more splendidly than here in this translation of deeply experienced ancient Oriental love songs.' *Geschichte der deutschen Literatur im achtzehnten Jahrhundert* (2 vols.; Berlin: Aufbau-Verlag, 1961), II, p. 35.

between 1765 and 1778, I place his *Lieder der Liebe* within the well-known context of his views on poetry in general and German poetry in particular. I then undertake an examination of certain current literary critical theories, as well as Herder's own theories of language and translation, thus providing a new theoretical context for an understanding of Herder's work on the Song of Songs.

The study then provides a new analysis of Herder's interpretation within the context of other earlier and contemporary readings of the Song of Songs, before presenting for the first time an analysis of his commentaries. This is of particular importance, if we accept the premise that translation and interpretation (for such is commentary) are inextricably linked. It is, of course, usual for translators to translate without providing a commentary of any kind. If one is given, it is almost invariably separate from the translation itself. Possibly Herder was unique in arbitrarily dividing his translations into sections and interspersing them with paragraphs of commentary, thereby acknowledging the dependence of translation upon interpretation.

This study further underlines Herder's abundant use in his commentaries of the travel-writers of his age, and represents a careful reading of the original editions to which Herder specifically referred in *Lieder der Liebe*. Although reference is made to these writers in Ulrich Gaier's edition commented upon below, this is the first time that Herder's borrowings have been used extensively as analytic tools.

Although Herder claimed to have attempted to leave the Song of Songs within its own *Sitz im Leben*,[2] I seek in this study to demonstrate that, despite his insistence on the difference and distinction of Oriental poetry, Herder's commentaries and translations were inevitably coloured by the poetic idiom of his own time and place. They were imbued with the emotional attitudes which belong to 'Empfindsamkeit' ('sentimentality') and 'Sturm und Drang' ('Storm and Stress'), with elements of folk-song,[3] and an idealizing, chaste view of love.[4] In other words,

---

2.   This expression is used in theological writing when referring to the original historical, geographical and cultural significance of a text. Given Herder's claims that he attempted to leave the Song of Songs within its own original context, this theological expression is most appropriate, even in a literary study, and I use it throughout.

3.   Francis Landy notes the repetition typical of folk-song in the Song of Songs, commenting particularly on the folkloristic associations of the repetition in the little foxes poem (Song 2.15). See *Paradoxes of Paradise: Identity and Difference in the*

although Herder argued that each culture was unique, yet may be pene-trated by 'Einfühlung' or empathy—a key notion of his hermeneutics—and a thorough knowledge of the cultural background, his own cultural position is revealed by the choices he made in his interpretation and translations, and by his own overt reading of the original text.

This study also provides the first detailed comparison with each other of Herder's attempts to translate the Song of Songs in 1776 and 1778. Furthermore, it represents the first detailed comparison between the translations of Herder and that of Martin Luther, to whom Herder ulti-mately pointed his readers.[5] Herder praised Luther's translation, indi-cating that, in the last resort, his own efforts failed to satisfy him as much, yet he was breaking new ground in challenging Luther's text. For this reason, we must consider the details of Luther's translation as a touchstone, examining the extent to which Herder was dependent upon it in his own translations.

This study also claims to be the first to include comparisons between the Hebrew text and the German translations under discussion, wher-ever it is illuminating or decisive to do so. This will additionally afford an opportunity to consider the extent to which Herder followed the original poetry in his translations.

I have selected Goethe's translation as a contemporary one deserving comparison, since his development as a lyric poet was hastened by his reception of Herder's teaching about the nature of poetry and poetic language. He was driven to put Herder's theories into practice, and thus

Song of Songs (Sheffield: Almond Press, 1983), p. 48-49 and p. 289 n. 59.

4.   See Edward Said's view in *Orientalism: Western Conceptions of the Orient* (Harmondsworth: Penguin Books, 1991) that European images of the Orient are ideologically loaded (see especially pp. 278, 279, 308-309 and 321-25). Said's examples, of course, are taken mainly from writing later than that of Herder.

5.   Luther's translations *Das Hohe Lied Salomo* (1524), and *Das Hohelied Salomo* (1545), are in *WKGB*, X/2, pp. 134-47. A printing of the translation entitled '…Stark wie der Tod' ('As Strong as Death') is given in Hermann Timm (ed.), *Das Hohe Lied Salomos: Nachdichtungen und Übersetzungen aus sieben Jahrhunderten* (Frankfurt am Main: Insel Verlag, 1982), pp. 67-77. Luther's Latin commentary, *Vorlesung über das Hohelied: In Cantica Canticorum brevis, sed admodum di-lucida enarratio*, is in *WKG*, XXXI/2, pp. 586-769, and an English translation by Ian Siggins, *Lectures on the Song of Solomon: A Brief but Altogether Lucid Com-mentary on the Song of Songs*, is in Jaroslav Pelikan and Helmut T. Lehmann (eds.), *Luther's Works* (55 vols.; St Louis: Concordia Publishing House, vols. 1–29; and Philadelphia: Fortress Press, vols. 30–54, n.d.), XV, pp. 189-264.

I have used his translation—or version?—as a point of reference. I also give consideration throughout to the mediaeval translation of the Song of Songs which Herder prized as springing from a stage in the development of German poetry and poetic language comparable with the flowering of Hebrew poetry in the time of Solomon.

Both the final unpublished draft translation of 1776 and the published translation of 1778 are printed side by side in columns in Appendix A. This will facilitate comparison of the two versions, allowing the reader also to note the importance of the differing appearance of each translation on the page. Appendix B reproduces Luther's translation of 1545 and Appendix C reproduces Goethe's translation of 1775.

The extensive Bibliography provides full details of those works which provide general biographical information about Herder, as well as those which document his preoccupation with folk-song, poetry, translation and biblical criticism. Such works demonstrate that many have referred very briefly to Herder's work on the Song of Songs, but such was not the major thrust of their contribution.

Apart from such brief comments in the many studies of Herder, and excluding those who have edited *Lieder der Liebe* per se, those who discuss Herder and the Song of Songs in any detail are Rudolf Haym in his two-volume biography of 1877–85; Paul Haupt in 1907; Robert T. Clark in 1946 and 1955; Andreas F. Kelletat in 1984; and Helmut Mueller-Sievers and Emil Adler in 1990. Full details are given in the Bibliography.

The title of Haupt's work, *Biblische Liebeslieder: Das sogenannte Hohelied Salomos unter steter Berücksichtigung der Übersetzungen Goethes und Herders* ('Biblical Love Songs: The So-called Song of Solomon, with Constant Reference to the Translations of Goethe and Herder') would suggest some overlap with this study, but in fact Haupt's main purpose was to produce his own heavily annotated translation of the Song of Songs, at the end of which he sought to include a commentary to rationalize his own renderings. He certainly makes occasional references to Goethe and Herder, but these hardly represent the 'stete Berücksichtigung' ('constant reference') of the full title. Comments on Haupt will be made where appropriate.

I shall also consider Clark's work at various points below, although I do not accept all his findings. Indeed, although his work is of general contextual interest, Clark claimed no competence to judge the relative linguistic merits of the translations of Herder and Luther.[6]

Our attention now turns to those who have edited *Lieder der Liebe*. Apart from the publication of 1778 and the subsequent reprint in 1781, the work was placed in the fourth volume of works on religion and theology in Johann Georg Müller's edition of Herder's works in 1778. It then disappeared until Redlich's contribution in the eighth volume of Suphan's edition in 1892. This is the base edition for this study.

One year later Heinrich Meyer's ten-volume edition of Herder's *Werke* was published in the series Deutsche National-Litteratur, edited by Joseph Kürschner (Stuttgart: Union Deutsche Verlagsgesellschaft, 1893). The very first volume of Herder's works (vol. LXXIV/1 of the whole series) contains *Lieder der Liebe*. After an introduction, Meyer (pp. 31-118) gives the published version of 1778. In an appendix (pp. 119-34) he includes only the translation of the 1776 version given by Redlich, omitting the commentary. Meyer's aim was to illustrate the development of Herder's style and art of poetic reproduction. He regretted being unable to offer pieces from the oldest rhyming versions, but included also Herder's translations of Psalms 8, 18, 23, 72, 121 and 126, and the Song of Lamech. He also omitted the Middle High German translation, except for the first four poems included in his introduction (pp. 7-10).

Just as we note great interest in the Song of Songs around the time of Herder's own preoccupation with it, we find recent interest in the editing of Herder's work, demonstrated by the appearance of three editions between 1987 and 1992. After a gap of almost a century, an edition of *Lieder der Liebe* appeared in 1987, 'herausgegeben von Johann Gottfried Herder' ('edited by Johann Gottfried Herder') and published by the Franz Greno Verlag in Nördlingen. With some modernization of orthography, all three parts of the 1778 publication are reproduced. There is a very brief introduction by an anonymous sub-editor, and the bibliography includes just 12 titles, the most recent of which is Emil Adler's *Herder und die deutsche Aufklärung* (Vienna and Frankfurt am Main: Europa Verlag, 1968).

The most important edition of *Lieder der Liebe* since Meyer's edition of 1893 is without doubt that of Ulrich Gaier. This forms part of *Volkslieder, Übertragungen, Dichtungen*, edited by Gaier (Bibliothek deutscher Klassiker, 60; Frankfurt am Main: Deutscher Klassiker Verlag,

---

6. See 'Herder, Percy, and the *Song of Songs*', *PMLA* 61 (1946), pp. 1087-1100 (1099).

1990). It represents the third volume in a ten-volume edition of Herder's *Werke*, edited by Martin Bollacher and others.

Gaier (p. 1209) states that his text 'folgt dem Druck Leipzig 1778: Abweichungen zur Korrektur von Druckfehlern (wobei ich Redlich nicht immer folge) sind im Kommentar vermerkt'.[7] In fact, Gaier has modernized the orthography considerably (for example, 'Zeder' for 'Ceder', 'süß' for 'süss' and 'sei' for 'sey'); one four-line stanza is given as two couplets; and there is a misreading of the text which I comment on below. Gaier reproduces Herder's text (pp. 431-521), although he does not include any of the material from 1776 examined in this study, nor does he include the Middle High German translation which formed the final part of Herder's publication.[8]

Gaier's editorial comments (pp. 1199-263) are more copious and informative than those given by Redlich, but it must be stressed that Gaier's is merely an important *edition*. It is replete with information, and as such is helpful. However, by no means does it offer the interpretative and critical analysis of this present study, nor does it offer a comparative study of the translations.

Gaier's edition contains information which is readily accessible elsewhere, although his strength is that he has synthesized it relevantly. Necessary points of information will be repeated in this work too, although this is inevitable given their fundamental importance to the area of study. For example, various exponents of the allegorical interpretation (see Chapter 4 of this study) are mentioned in Gaier too, although without analysis. Much of Gaier's information is of the kind already available for the English reader in Clark, for example, or for the German reader in Haym. It is not analysed, criticized nor contextualized.

---

7.   'Follows the Leipzig printing of 1778: departures from the correction of printing errors (where I do not always follow Redlich) are noted in the commentary.'

8.   Claiming lack of space as his reason for omitting the section of *Lieder der Liebe* containing the mediaeval text, Gaier regrets that 'unberücksichtigt mußte auch die interessante 1. Fassung von 1776 bleiben' ('the interesting first draft of 1776 also had to be disregarded'). It is possible that Gaier assumed this to be the complete 1776 version used by Redlich, although, as will emerge below, there are three unpublished manuscripts dating from 1776, the last of which was used by Redlich. Gaier's use of the term '1. Fassung' ('first draft') is thus at least ambiguous.

Arguably many of Gaier's notes tend to be banal or patronizing, especially as they are intended for the native speaker of German.[9] His chosen point of reference is the *Neue Jerusalemer Bibel: Einheitsübersetzung mit dem Kommentar der Jerusalemer Bibel*, edited by A. Deissler and A. Vögtle (Freiburg: Herder, 1985). Many of his notes compare Herder's renderings with this version, although without further analysis. Gaier gives no motivation for his (strange) choice.

Without documentation, Gaier suggests that Herder used the Greek Septuagint as an aid, although there would appear to be no real internal or external evidence for this. I comment on this claim further in Chapter 6 of this study.

Consideration will be given later to Herder's division of the Song of Songs into seven sections. However, as Hugh Barr Nisbet points out in his review of Gaier's edition,[10] there is no evidence for Gaier's view (pp. 1204 and 1251) that these divisions underpin Herder's sevenfold mystical hieroglyph theory as set out in his consideration of the first chapter of Genesis in *Älteste Urkunde des Menschengeschlechts*.

In his review, Nisbet claims that Herder's 'translation of, and commentary on, the Song of Songs are [...] admirably elucidated; the depth and originality of his scholarship in this area have never before been so fully explored' (p. 796). On the other hand, it does not explore as deeply or widely—or indeed in the same areas—as this study. Nisbet's comments serve to underline my proposition that no work of any substance had been done before 1990 in the area of Herder's preoccupation with the Song of Songs. Gaier's work is an informative edition—for, laudable as it is, it is no more than that—of a selected part of Herder's

---

9.　Five examples will suffice:

'*Unwillig]* Gegen ihren Willen' (p. 1213) ('*Unwillingly]* against her will').

'*Mit Pünktchen Silber gesprengt]* Herders dem Text nach richtige Vorstellung scheint, daß in das Gold der Kette Silberpünktchen eingelassen sind' (p. 1215). ('*Sprinkled with dashes of silver]* Herder's notion, which is correct according to the text, seems to be that dashes of silver are worked into the gold of the chain').

'*An Ihm, nicht am Schmucke]* Sie denkt an ihn, nicht an Schmuck' (p. 1216) ('*Of him rather than jewellery]* she thinks about him rather than jewellery').

'*Tadel]* Makel, etwas, das zu tadeln wäre' (p. 1226) ('*Blemish]* something to find fault with').

'*Stimmhammer]* Gerät, das beim Stimmen von Tasteninstrumenten verwendet wird' (p. 1248) ('*Tuning key]* tool used to tune keyboard instruments').

10.　Untitled review, *MLR* 88.3 (1993), pp. 795-99 (796).

work on the Song of Songs. As such it increases rather than diminishes the need for the present study.

The most recent edition of *Lieder der Liebe* is that by Regine Otto (Zürich: Manesse, 1992). This contains all three parts of the 1778 publication, and the text follows the published version more closely than does that of Gaier, although the use of 'Umlaut' is consistently modernized. A very short 'Nachwort' ('epilogue') completes the edition.

Where appropriate, I acknowledge, support or take issue with the above-mentioned writers and editors throughout.

For this study I have used Suphan's edition for all Herder references unless otherwise stated. In the light of *Der handschriftliche Nachlaß Johann Gottfried Herders in Berlin* (Wiesbaden: Harrassowitz, 1979), the catalogue of Herder's *Nachlaß* prepared by Hans Dietrich Irmscher and Emil Adler, Nisbet points out in his review of Gaier that 'the task of preparing a satisfactory critical edition of Herder's complete works seems even more daunting than before, and no such edition is contemplated at present' (p. 795). The Suphan edition, then, is generally regarded as the most authoritative, and I shall show below, for example, that Redlich's reprinting of *Lieder der Liebe* is reliable.[11]

Apart from the base texts, other texts by Herder which have been particularly important in the preparation of this study are listed below in chronological order and with the relevant reference in *SWS*:

1764   *Ueber den Fleiß in mehreren gelehrten Sprachen*, I, pp. 1-7 and
        XXX, pp. 7-14.

---

11. Irmscher too accepts that the historical-critical Suphan edition is the most complete and reliable one available. However, from his cataloguing of Herder's *Nachlaß*, he argues that generally *SWS* is inadequate in many places, and its quality is only high in comparison with other editions available. The edition is complete for those works published in Herder's lifetime, but not for sketches, drafts and fragments written in the early years of his life, to which, of course, Herder's first drafts of *Lieder der Liebe* belong. Irmscher claims that Emil Gottfried Herder's *Lebensbild* of 1846 is almost as good in respect of early works. Parts of the text of *SWS* lack dependability, partly because Suphan never catalogued the manuscripts in the *Nachlaß*, and partly because he left Berlin in 1887 to become Director of the Goethe-und-Schiller Archiv in Weimar, leaving it to men such as Redlich to edit the remaining volumes. As a result, the coordination of the individual volumes suffered, as did the production of an error-free text. For more detail, see H.D. Irmscher, 'Mitteilungen aus Herders Nachlaß', *Euphorion: Zeitschrift für Literaturgeschichte* 54 (1960), pp. 281-94, and B. Suphan, 'Meine Herder-Ausgabe', *Revue germanique* 3 (1907), pp. 233-40.

1764 *Versuch einer Geschichte der lyrischen Dichtkunst*, XXXII, pp. 85-140.

1765 *Versuch einer richtigern Auslegung des Hohenliedes Salomons, worin das Zuverläßige, Schöne und Göttliche dieses H. Buchs gezeigt wird von M. Christian Gottfried Hase.* Recension of 18 October in *Die Königsbergschen Gelehrten und Politischen Zeitungen*, 83tes Stück, I, pp. 89-91.

1766 *Über die neuere deutsche Litteratur: Eine Beilage zu den*
and *Briefen, die neueste Litteratur betreffend*, 1. Auflage, I,
1767 pp. 131-531.

1768 *Über die neuere deutsche Litteratur*, 2. Auflage, II, pp. 1-248.

1769 *Journal meiner Reise im Jahre 1769*, IV, pp. 343-461.

1771 *Die Gedichte Ossians eines alten celtischen Dichters, aus dem Englischen übersetzt von M. Denis.* Recension from *Die Allgemeine Deutsche Bibliothek*, V, pp. 322-30.

1772 *Abhandlung über den Ursprung der Sprache*, V, pp. 1-154.

1773 *Von deutscher Art und Kunst*, V, pp. 159-257.

1774 *Alte Volkslieder*, 1. Theil, XXV, pp. 1-60.

1774 *Alte Volkslieder*, 2. Theil, XXV, pp. 61-126.

1775 *Ursachen des gesunknen Geschmacks bei den verschiednen Völkern, da er geblühet*, V, pp. 595-655.

1777 *Von Ähnlichkeit der mittlern englischen und deutschen Dichtkunst*, IX, pp. 522-35.

1778 *Vom Erkennen und Empfinden der menschlichen Seele. Bemerkungen und Träume*, VIII, pp. 165-333.

1778 *Ueber die Würkung der Dichtkunst auf die Sitten der Völker in alten und neuen Zeiten*, VIII, pp. 334-436.

1778 *Volkslieder*, 1. Theil, XXV, pp. 127-310.

1778 *Volkslieder*, 2. Theil, XXV, pp. 311-645.

1782 *Vom Geist der Ebräischen Poesie. Eine Anleitung für die Liebhaber derselben, und der ältesten Geschichte des menschlichen Geistes*, 1. Theil, XI, pp. 213-466.

1783 *Vom Geist der Ebräischen Poesie*, 2. Theil, XII, pp. 1-302.

1795 *Fragment über die beste Leitung eines jungen Genies zu den Schätzen der Dichtkunst*, IX, pp. 541-44.

1796 *Eine Rechenschaft des Uebersetzers*, in *Terpsichore*, 3. Theil, XXVII, pp. 274-82.

The State of the Manuscripts

The research for this study included a study of the various drafts and fragments of *Lieder der Liebe* in the Staatsbibliothek Preußischer Kulturbesitz in Berlin, where Herder's *Nachlaß* is currently housed. The manuscripts are contained in Kapsel VI Konvolute 1-24, 59, 61, and 62, and Kapsel XX Konvolute 120-23, as denoted by Irmscher and Adler in their catalogue (see *Der Handschriftliche Nachlaß*, pp. 18-22 and p. 161).[12] I have proposed the sigla used below:

MS(1)

VI 1 contains what appears to be the earliest rejected draft translation and commentary, consisting of 100 manuscript sheets, and henceforth referred to as MS(1).[13] It cannot be dated earlier than 1776, since reference is made in it to the work of Friedrich Esaias von Pufendorf which was published that year in Bremen.[14] Significantly, the title on the cover originally began 'Die ältesten Minnelieder' ('The Most Ancient Minnelieder' [Minnelieder were mediaeval love songs]), but Herder crossed out 'Minnelieder' in favour of 'Lieder der Liebe' ('Songs of Love') which he wrote above his deletion. The resulting title is therefore *Die ältesten Lieder der Liebe. Ein Biblisches Buch* ('The Most Ancient Songs of Love. A Biblical Book').

---

12. In his article 'Probleme der Herder-Forschung', *DVjs* 37 (1963), pp. 266-317, Irmscher describes thus the mass of Herder material (now moved to Berlin from the depository of the Preußische Staatsbibliothek in the library of the University of Tübingen): 'Das auf 45 Kapseln verteilte Material umfaßt etwa 3200 Stücke: Manuskripte zu Herders Schriften, ferner Auszüge, Entwürfe (in zahlreichen Studienbüchern), Abschriften und Nachschriften' ('The material, which is divided into 45 cases, comprises some 3200 items: manuscripts of Herder's writings, as well as extracts, drafts [in numerous notebooks], copies and transcripts').

13. See *SWS*, VIII, p. xiv, where Redlich draws attention to the fact that parts of MS(1) are included in VIII, p. 594 n. 1, and VIII, p. 680, note to p. 643. Irmscher argues that these initial attempts in no way mirror the ultimate contents of the first manuscript, but rather reflect the interest of the editor (see 'Probleme der Herder-Forschung', p. 298). I discuss this further in Chapter 4.

14. The title of the work was *Umschreibung des Hohenliedes, oder die Gemeinde mit Christo und den Engeln im Grabe, nebst andern biblischen Erklärungen*, and it was edited by Konrad Heinrich Runge. It has proved impossible to trace a copy of the book.

At the bottom of the title page there is a comment in Herder's hand claiming that 'der alte Minnemann soll hinten an geschoben auch alles noch umgearbeitet werden' ('the ancient minnesinger is to be placed at the end, and everything is to be reworked'), a remark which Herder must have intended for a reader of the manuscript. This would suggest that it was this version that he sent to Goethe, for with a letter to Charlotte von Stein dated Sunday 20 April and Monday 21 April 1777, Goethe sent her 'Herders Hohes Lied und ein paar neuere' ('Herder's Song of Songs and a few more recent items').[15]

Although Herder's promise here of a revision unquestionably suggests that he did not intend this manuscript for publication, MS(1) clearly shows the extent to which his view that the Song of Songs was a collection of single songs was dependent on the Minnelieder of David Gottfried Schöber (1696–1778), a merchant who was also Bürgermeister of Gera (*SWS*, VIII, p. xiv). In the summer of 1777 Herder had requested the Minnelieder from the library of Friedrich der Weise in Jena.[16] These Minnelieder were a Middle High German translation of the Song of Songs written about 1300 CE.[17] The 44 songs were

15. Julius Petersen (ed.), *Briefe an Charlotte von Stein* (2 vols.; Leipzig: Insel-Verlag, 1923), Letter 151, I/1, p. 65.

16. See Herder's letter to Hamann on 20 March 1778, in Otto Hoffmann (ed.), *Briefe an Hamann/Herders Briefwechsel mit Nicolai* (Berlin: Gaertner, 1889; repr. Hildesheim and New York: Olms, 1975), p. 135. Herder also acknowledged here his debt to Basilius Wiedeburg, who had described the collection of Minnelieder in his *Ausführliche Nachricht von einigen alten teutschen poetischen Manuscripten aus dem dreyzehenden und vierzehenden Jahrhunderte welche in der Jenaischen akademischen Bibliothek aufbehalten werden* (Jena: Melchiors, 1754). In 1793 Herder further acknowledged his debt in *Zerstreute Blätter*, where he stated that 'in der Jenaischen Universitätsbibliothek liegt ein nicht unbekannter, schätzbarer Codex, von dem Wiedeburg vor fast vierzig Jahren Nachricht gegeben [...] hat' ('in the library of the University of Jena there is a not unknown, valuable manuscript to which Wiedeburg drew attention almost 40 years ago') (XVI, p. 215).

17. The title page of Herder's copy read: *Das Hohelied Salomonis aus zwoen alten deutschen Handschriften, deren Eine in zerschiedenen Stücken deutscher Reime über dasselbe, die Andere in einer altdeutschen Uebersetzung davon, bestehet; mit vorläufiger Nachricht von diesen beiden Handschriften, und angehängter kurzen Umschreibung des ersten Cap. des Hohenliedes, dem Drucke übergeben von D.G.S. Augsburg, verlegt bey Philipp Ludwig Klaffschenkels sel. Wittib. 1752.* The work is printed as 'Des Minnesangs Erzvater' ('The Patriarch of Minnesang') in Timm (ed.), *Das Hohe Lied Salomos*, pp. 15-61. Unlike Herder, Timm has omitted poem 43, believing it to have been included erroneously.

published ultimately in the third section of Herder's *Lieder der Liebe* of 1778 (given also in VIII, pp. 559-86). They are certainly appropriate to Herder's reading of the Song of Songs, for he would seem to have ascribed the work to the genre of Minnelied. Although he does not explicitly state this in the text, it is implicitly clear in his choice of title that for him the Song of Songs consisted of *'Lieder der Liebe'* ('Songs of Love'). Indeed, as we shall see, in certain of his translations Herder presented the Song of Songs in the form and idiom of the Minnelied.

It is clear from Herder's comment on the title page of MS(1) that he intended the mediaeval songs ultimately to form an appendix, but in this draft 41 of the 44 songs form the basis of the work. They are interspersed throughout with commentary and translation attempts of Herder's own.[18] They appear in MS(1) in a different order from that given in the 1778 version, and Herder chose to give them German rather than Latin titles.[19] In MS(1) they follow the order of Luther's text, whereas Schöber's text shows a more arbitrary division. There are many orthographical differences between the two versions of the songs, since in MS(1) Herder chose to modernize the mediaeval text, for example giving 'har' as 'Haar' ('hair'), 'kus' as 'Kuß' ('kiss') and 'uf sten' as 'aufstehn' ('arise'). He opted to use the original orthography in his final version, however, doubtless considering that it thus lent his own work more original authority.

Herder divided the various translation attempts in MS(1) into 22 sections, each with an arabic number and a title. In the first few sections he reproduced the individual mediaeval version first before attempting a draft of his own. As he became more confident, he began to give his own translation of a section first, followed by the corresponding mediaeval song. Later he occasionally gave his own translation only, preferring to offer groups of as many as nine mediaeval songs together without comment. It is apparent from this progression that Herder was

18. Redlich claimed that the three missing songs are those numbered in the 1778 appendix as 13, 20 and 36 (VIII, p. xiv). However, a study of MS(1) shows that he was not quite correct, for number 13 is used, while number 17 is missing.

19. These do not necessarily correspond. For example, the second song in MS(1), entitled 'Das braune Landmädchen' (literally 'The brown country girl'), is given in 1778 as song 26 with the title 'Nigra sum sed formosa' ('I am black but beautiful'). Similarly the fourth song in MS(1), entitled 'Liebe im Grünen' ('Love in the countryside'), is given in 1778 as song 37 with the title 'Ecce tu pulcra' ('Behold, you are beautiful').

moving towards his goal of placing the mediaeval songs all together at the end, an aim finally achieved in 1778.

It is very clear from MS(1) that the mediaeval poems acted as a catalyst for Herder's own work on the Song of Songs, although this draft also demonstrates his growing confidence in his own work as he became more independent of them. Although MS(1) is different from all the other manuscripts, it is closer in essence, presentation and effect to MSS(2) and (3), discussed below, than to the definitive version of 1778. The final part of the introduction is given by Redlich in his reprinting of MS(3) in VIII, pp. 594-95 n. 1. I use relevant examples from MS(1) in Chapters 5 and 6 of this study.

MS(2)

VI 3 contains a second draft translation and commentary, consisting of 59 manuscript sheets, and henceforth referred to as MS(2). The translation covers the whole of the Song of Songs and is divided into 16 songs, each with a roman number and a title. The draft contains an (incomplete) 'erste Zugabe' ('first supplement'), its numerical designation suggesting that a second was planned. Almost certainly this would have contained the mediaeval text promised in MS(1). Although the commentary is incomplete, MS(2) as a whole is so similar to MS(3) discussed below—indeed, much is identical—that it is surprising that Herder abandoned it in favour of beginning yet again.[20] I give relevant examples in Chapters 5 and 6 below.

MS(3)

VI 6 contains a third draft translation and commentary, a 'Reinschrift' ('final copy') consisting of 72 manuscript sheets, and henceforth referred to as MS(3). It is entitled *Lieder der Liebe. Ein Biblisches Buch. Nebst zwo Zugaben* ('Songs of Love. A Biblical Book. Including Two Supplements'), although the second appendix is missing. This seems to be the most fixed—or least fluid—version of the translation which Herder in the event did not appear to consider final or appropriate enough for publication. This most definitive of the unpublished drafts represents one of the two main objects of this study, for arguably

---

20. The introductions in both drafts finish at the same point, and hence Redlich's reprinting of the end of the introduction of MS(1) mentioned above. The commentary of MS(2) roughly corresponds to that of MS(3) up to the end of the first paragraph of VIII, p. 647.

it supersedes MSS(1) and (2). Moreover, whereas the earlier drafts are not printed anywhere, MS(3) is accessible to the reader of this study, since it is reproduced fully and accurately by Redlich (VIII, pp. 589-658), with just minor differences such as in orthography, spacing or punctuation.[21] The 1776 translation reproduced in Appendix A below follows exactly that given by Herder in MS(3). For ease of reference, however, quotations from the commentary of MS(3) are from Redlich throughout.

After an introduction, Herder's translation follows in 22 sections, each with a roman number and a title. As in the earlier drafts, it is in rhyming verse. Comments on the text follow each song, adding aesthetic illumination to its thought, structure and artistic form. An epilogue follows without warning (VIII, pp. 628-41). The first of the promised appendices, *Erläuterung einzelner Stellen des Hohenliedes* ('Commentary on Individual Portions of the Song of Songs') (VIII, pp. 642-56), discusses single verses and expressions which concern the climate and customs of the Orient. These comments serve to show how widely read Herder was, especially in travel literature. A 'Nachschrift' ('postscript') contains variant readings of Psalms 45, 72 and 127, and the end of the book of Proverbs, as set out in the published version of 1778. Undoubtedly the second (missing) appendix would have consisted of Schöber's Minnelieder as they appear in the third part of the 1778 publication. Calling on Herder's statement in MS(2) that 'die letzte Zugabe enthält einen Minnesinger' ('the final supplement contains a Minnesinger') (VIII, p. xiv), Redlich too confirmed that 'diese sollte ohne Zweifel aus den Schöberschen Minneliedern bestehen, die im Druckmanuskript ebenfalls fehlen, weil nach seiner eigenhändigen Notiz Herder die Schöberschen Bogen selbst als Druckvorlage geschickt hat' (VIII, p. 658 n. 1).[22]

---

21. In fact, Redlich also gave the number XVI to poems XVI *and* XVII, an error not present in MS(3). Irmscher and Adler award the letter A to the reprinting of the manuscript in Redlich, denoting that it was 'vollständig und dem Inhalt nach genau gedruckt' ('printed in its entirety and, as far as the content goes, accurately') (*Der Handschriftliche Nachlaß*, p. xxviii and p. 18).

22. 'Indubitably this was to consist of Schöber's Minnelieder which likewise are missing from the printed manuscript, because according to a note in his own hand, Herder himself sent the Schöber pages as part of the original copy.'

MS(a)

VI 8 contains the Druckmanuskript of *Lieder der Liebe: Die ältesten und schönsten aus Morgenlande. Nebst vier und vierzig alten Minne-liedern* ('Songs of Love: The Most Ancient and Most Beautiful from the Orient. Including 44 Ancient Minnelieder') (Leipzig: Weygand, 1778), henceforth referred to as MS(a). It consists of pages 1-98 and 103-16, with pages 99-102 missing.[23] As already promised in MS(1), MS(a) shows considerable reworking from its predecessors. The first of the three parts, entitled *Salomons Hohes Lied*, is now the translation itself. Whereas Herder gives a fairly lengthy introduction in MS(3), a motto from Martin Luther is his sole introduction in MS(a).[24] He then begins immediately with the first part of his translation, which is now in free verse, with the rhymes of the earlier manuscripts showing through only occasionally. In many places where the text is almost identical, the rhyme or assonance has been intentionally eliminated. The translation is altogether less florid, starker and more minimalist. It is closer to an interlinear translation than are the earlier paraphrases. In Chapter 6 I compare and contrast in detail this translation and that of MS(3).

23. Inside the folder is a sheet dated 4 June 1891 and signed by Redlich to confirm that even then the manuscript was 'vollständig bis auf S. 99-102' ('complete except for pp. 99-102'). On the front cover of the folder Irmscher has confirmed that '4 Seiten fehlen schon zu Suphans Zeit' ('even in Suphan's time four pages were missing'), a point reiterated on the inside of the folder. These missing pages are given by Redlich in VIII, pp. 552-54, presumably from the published version. (See p. 552 n. 1 for exact references.)

24. 'Hunc librum suscepimus enarrandum, non studio ostentandae eruditionis, sicut quidam qui omnem operam ponunt in obscuros libros, quod scilicet et ad laudem ingenii faciat, ausum esse ea attingere, quae alii propter obscuritatem fugiunt, et in obscuris cuique liberum sit diuinare, ac speculationibus seu propriis cogitationibus indulgere, sed ut repulsis ineptis opinionibus, quibus hactenus libel-lus hic obscuratus est, aliam commodiorem sententiam ostenderemus' (see VIII, p. 487). This is taken from the beginning of Luther's *Vorlesung über das Hohelied*. Ian Siggins's English translation reads: 'We take up this book for exposition not from any fondness for display of erudition, like some who lavish every effort upon the obscure books because, of course, on the one hand it provokes praise for their cleverness to have dared address subjects which others flee on account of their obscurity and on the other hand because in the obscure books each of them is freer to make divinations and to indulge in speculations or private musings; rather, we take it up in order that after the absurd opinions which have so far obscured this little book have been rejected, we may demonstrate another, more suitable view' (Pelikan and Lehmann [eds.], *Luther's Works*, XV, p. 194).

The songs follow the order of the Song of Songs, but are divided differently from before. The numbers and titles evident in the earlier manuscripts do not figure here. It may be that Herder's ultimate decision not to number or name the songs was in order to stress the thread running through them as well as the arbitrary nature of their division. Indeed, he claimed in MS(3) that 'an Zahl und Ueberschrift liegt nichts' ('number and title are of no consequence') (VIII, p. 628).

The second part is the treatise *Ueber den Inhalt, die Art und den Zweck dieses Buchs in der Bibel* ('On the Contents, Nature and Aim of this Book in the Bible'). The first section corresponds to the 'Vorrede' ('Preface') of MS(3), although the five paragraphs of the latter are expanded to twelve in the 1778 version. The second section contains relatively new material, while the last section corresponds to the epilogue of MS(3).

MS(a) does not include the actual Schöber text, reprinted by Redlich in VIII, pp. 559-86. Herder stopped on p. 112 of the manuscript after 'Gera' (see VIII, p. 559), made several notes for the printer which were unconnected with the mediaeval text, and continued on p. 113 with the final section of his own commentary, reproduced by Redlich in VIII, pp. 586-88.

While Herder wrote all his manuscripts in black ink, in MS(a) the translation per se is marked throughout with a red line down the left-hand side. Stanza divisions are denoted by a short red line between each stanza.

MS(a) of *Lieder der Liebe* was published anonymously by Weygand at the Michaelismesse in Leipzig in 1778, significantly at about the same time as the 1778 version of the *Volkslieder*. This version, reprinted in 1781, represents the other major object of this study. As with MS(3), it is given accurately and completely by Redlich (VIII, pp. 485-588), again with similar very minor exceptions.[25]

A comparison of MS(a) with the first printing confirms Redlich's view that the publication was fairly free of error, 'abgesehen von den orthographischen Willkürlichkeiten des Weygandschen Korrektors' ('apart from the orthographical arbitrariness of Weygand's proofreader') (VIII, p. xiii).[26] One problem—although not serious—is as

---

25. As with Redlich's printing of MS(3), Irmscher and Adler (*Der handschriftliche Nachlaß*, p. 18) likewise award the letter A to his reprinting of MS(a) to confirm its accuracy.

26. For example, the published version commences each line with an upper-case

follows. In MS(a), p. 53, Herder translates with 'Präge mich Ein Siegel' (literally 'stamp me a seal'), adding the numbers 3, 4, 1 and 2 above each of the four words respectively, resulting in the definitive inverted 'ein Siegel präge mich auf dein Herz' (literally 'a seal stamp me upon your heart'). Yet the printing of 1778 has the incorrect word order 'Präge Ein Siegel', although one of the two *corrigenda* on the last page (p. 216) acknowledges the error with 'S. 81 Z. 17. Präge Ein Siegel l. Ein Siegel präge' (literally 'p. 81 line 17. For "stamp a seal" read "a seal stamp"'). Strangely, the second edition of 1781 was not corrected, nor was the appropriate *corrigendum* appended. Redlich ensured that his printing in *SWS*, VIII was corrected in this regard, and Regine Otto's edition (*Lieder der Liebe*, p. 63) likewise follows Herder's version. However, it would appear that both Herder's manuscript alteration and the correction in the published work were missed by Meyer (*Werke*, p. 79) and Gaier (*Lieder der Liebe*, p. 478) whose editions have 'präge Ein Siegel mich' (literally 'stamp a seal me').[27]

The third part (omitted by Herder in MS(a), by Meyer just one year after Redlich's edition, and by Gaier in 1987) is entitled *Von Uebersetzungen des Buchs, insonderheit Einer in alten Minneliedern* ('Of Translations of the Book, especially One in Ancient Minnelieder'). Herder here reproduced Schöber exactly, including very little original material of his own apart from an epilogue.

The section closes as the whole work begins, namely with a quotation from Luther.[28] Claus V. Bock has made a valid point when he suggests

letter, whereas MS(a) is inconsistent, commencing many lines with a lower-case letter.

27. The second of the two 'official' *corrigenda* is 'S. 57 Z. 12. Naturwiz l. Naturreiz' ('p. 57 line 12. For "natural wit" read "natural charm"'). Although the change was likewise not made in the 1781 reprint, the word is rendered correctly by Gaier (*Lieder der Liebe*, p. 463).

28. Significantly Herder omitted that part informing the reader that Luther understood the Song of Songs to be about Solomon's state. This would have interfered with his rejection of an allegorical interpretation. The quotation is taken from the end of Luther's *Vorlesung über das Hohelied*. With the relevant words bracketed, it reads: 'Ad hunc modum ego hunc librum intelligo <de Politia Salomonis>. Quodsi erro, veniam meretur primus labor: nam aliorum cogitationes longe plus absurditatis habent' (see *SWS*, VIII, p. 588). Ian Siggins's English translation reads: 'In this way I understand this book <to be about Solomon's state>. If I am wrong about this, a first effort deserves lenience. The musings of others have a much larger share of absurdity!' (Pelikan and Lehmann [eds.], *Luther's Works*, XV, p. 264).

that 'it is a fair indication of the boldness and novelty of what Herder
had to say that he should have felt it advisable to anchor his text
securely both at the opening and at the end to quotations from Luther's
more authoritative commentary'.[29] Arguably Herder realized that
Luther was poetically superior—and had the theological authority—and
he wanted to attain a higher poetic value for the Song of Songs than his
own work might have allowed. Indeed, it was Clark's claim that the
substantial changes in phrasing since MS(3) were all in the direction of
Luther,[30] a view which I shall consider in detail in Chapter 6.

The 1778 translation provided in Appendix A below is that of the
definitive published version rather than MS(a) or Redlich. For ease of
reference, however, quotations from the commentary are from Redlich
throughout.

Apart from these four main manuscripts, the *Nachlaß* contains a number of shorter related drafts and fragmentary translation variants. These
have been accurately catalogued by Irmscher and Adler (*Der handschriftliche Nachlaß*, pp. 18-22 and p. 161), and I give relevant
examples in Chapter 6 of this study.

It will suffice here to draw attention to the following:

VI 2 contains four sheets with only half a side of writing. As Irmscher has it, this is either a rejected opening section to MS(1) or it was
written very soon after MS(1).

VI 4 contains another version of sheet 6 of MS(2), promising that the
mediaeval text will be appended to the translation and commentary.[31]

VI 7 contains three sheets of rejected material which is very close to
songs XV, XVI and XVII, as given in MS(3) in VIII, pp. 617-21.

VI 11 contains a fragment virtually identical to the first part of the
translation of MS(3), going as far as 'der Mein' ist hin!' ('mine [i.e. my
vineyard] has gone') in song II (see *SWS*, VIII, p. 597). Irmscher holds
that this fragment was written presumably some time between MSS(2)
and (3).

29. 'A Tower of Ivory?', an inaugural lecture delivered at Westfield College
(University of London), 30 April 1970, p. 18.

30. *Herder: His Life and Thought* (Berkeley: University of California Press,
1955), p. 257.

31. We have already noted Redlich's reference to the paragraph in MS(2) in
which Herder promised that 'die letzte Zugabe enthält einen Minnesinger' ('the
final supplement contains a Minnesinger') (VIII, p. xiv).

VI 12 contains a fragment of a translation as far as the end of song I in MS(3), although closer to MS(a) and presumably therefore claimed by Irmscher to date from just before the published version.

VI 13 contains a fragment with two further attempts at song I, both on one sheet, although the fragment consists of a double sheet with one blank page.

VI 14 contains a fragment showing attempts at songs I, II and III only.

VI 15 contains an attempt on one side at song I only.

VI 16 principally represents an attempt at songs I, II and III only.

VI 17 contains a fragment rightly claimed by Irmscher to consist of two sheets, although the second one is blank.

VI 24 contains a fragment consisting of Herder's transliteration of the Hebrew text in Latin letters, beginning 'Schir haschirim aschèr lischlomoh. (Inschakéni minschikot pihu).' It is just over three very small sides long, ends as early as Song 2.12 (KJV) with 'hanitzanim nir,u' ('the flowers appear'), and contains very few lines indeed of (marginal and abbreviated) translation attempts.[32] Although it proves Herder's familiarity with Hebrew, it is hardly the interlinear translation claimed by Clark, who asserts that 'other drafts of the work exist, including a word-for-word translation of Canticles from the Hebrew'.[33] This view

---

32. The following example will illustrate the point:

Schwarz bin ich und doch bin ich schön
Ihr T.J.m
Wie die Zelte Kedars
------- Decken Sal.
Schaut mich nicht an, daß so schwarz ich bin
Mich brannte die Sonne an

('I am black and yet I am beautiful
You d(aughters) of J(erusale)m
As the tents of Kedar
-------- curtains of Sol(omon)
Do not stare at me because I am so black
The sun has burned me')

33. *Herder: His Life and Thought*, p. 254. Nine years earlier, Clark wrote that 'parts of his interlinear version [...] still exist in manuscript in the *Nachlaß* (if the *Nachlaß* still exists)' ('Herder, Percy, and the *Song of Songs*', p. 1098). One possible explanation for the latter comment is that after the ravages of war the existence of the *Nachlaß* itself must have been in doubt. By 1955 Clark would have learned that it had survived.

is based almost certainly on a misreading of Redlich's reference to this fragment, for Redlich mentioned rather than reproduced it, claiming that the intonation of the translations here sought to copy the intonation of the original Hebrew text (VIII, pp. xiii-xiv).

VI 61 consists of a very tiny fragment with a translation of the beginning of song II on the reverse which Irmscher may have missed, as he does not mention it in his catalogue.

Judging by the handwriting, Redlich held that these translation attempts most probably dated from the Bückeburg period (VIII, p. xiii). This was from the end of April 1771 to the end of September 1776, and if Redlich was right, it could explain Herder's offerings to his future wife Caroline Flachsland in 1772. It is difficult, however, to accept Redlich's premise unconditionally, for surely Herder's handwriting did not change so quickly that it can be maintained categorically that some of these fragments were not written earlier, possibly during his time with Goethe in Strasbourg. Whatever the case, the many translation variants contained in the *Nachlaß* clearly demonstrate how Herder struggled with parts of his translation as he searched for a definitive version before publishing MS(a) in 1778.

Herder and the Hebrew Text

Doubtless the study of Hebrew was a required part of a Protestant pastor's education. Although it cannot be established with certainty how Herder learned Hebrew, Hans Joachim Kraus has reminded us of Herder's use both of Johannes Reuchlin's *Rudimenta linguae Hebraicae* which had appeared in 1506, and of the work of the greatest eighteenth-century Hebrew scholar, Albert Schultens (1686–1750), whose *Clavis mutationis elementorum, qua dialecti linguae hebraeae ac praesertim arabica dialectus ab hebraea deflectunt* appeared in 1733.[34] Nevertheless, Johann Heinrich Michaelis wrote various Hebrew

---

34. See 'Herders alttestamentliche Forschungen', in J.G. Maltusch (ed.), *Bückeburger Gespräche über Johann Gottfried Herder 1971* (Schaumburger Studien, 33; Bückeburg: Grimme, 1973), pp. 59-75 (63). Kraus also draws attention to Herder's use of Johann Andreä Eisenmenger's *Entdecktes Judentum* (1700) and Johann Christoph Wagenseil's *Benachrichtigung über einige Jüdische Sachen* (1705). Kraus further notes that Herder 'skizzierte und kritisierte den Forschungsgang der hebräischen Grammatik' ('delineated and criticized the methods of researching Hebrew grammar') (p. 63), and refers to *SWS*, XIV, p. 442.

grammars, and it is highly probable that the young Herder had access to his *Erleichterte hebräische Grammatica: Richtige Anführung zur hebräischen Sprache zu mehrerem Nutzen der Jugend in teutscher Sprache [...]*, possibly the eighth edition (Halle: Waysenhaus Verlag, 1745).[35]

Likewise, it is unclear which was Herder's source text for his work on the Song of Songs, so we can do little more than conjecture. The Hebrew text of the Old Testament is based on the Masora, the textual tradition of the Jewish scholars known as the Masoretes. The Second Rabbinic Bible of Jacob ben Chayyim, printed by Daniel Bomberg in Venice (1524–25), and known as Bombergiana, was based on late mediaeval manuscripts. This remained the standard printed text of the Hebrew Old Testament until the twentieth century, and it is just possible that Herder used this. Indeed, Ernst Würthwein has reminded us that Christian Ginsburg wrote in 1897 that it represented the only Masoretic recension, and that any modern editor of the Hebrew text must show conclusive evidence for introducing any deviation from it.[36] In Herder's time, however, the most likely available text was the edition of Johann Heinrich Michaelis known as *Biblia Hebraica ex aliquot manuscriptis et compluribus impressis codicibus, item Masora tam edita, quam manuscripta aliisque hebraeorum criticis diligenter recensita [...]*, which was published in Halle in 1720.[37]

The General Context

John W. Draper noted that the eighteenth century inherited a tradition of free translations, of translations not for their own sake, but for the enrichment of the vernacular as well as for the cultivation of good manners, of propriety and decorum.[38] Herder's work as a translator must be seen in the context of the very striking development of the art of translation which took place during the eighteenth century. The age was one

35. Johann Heinrich Michaelis (1668–1738), a prominent Pietist, was a Protestant theologian and orientalist in Halle.

36. *Der Text des Alten Testaments: Eine Einführung in die Biblia Hebraica* (Stuttgart: Württembergische Bibelanstalt, 4th edn, 1973), p. 42.

37. Michaelis's edition followed mainly the text of Daniel E. Jablonski's edition of 1699 (see Würthwein, *Der Text des Alten Testaments*, p. 43).

38. 'The Theory of Translation in the Eighteenth Century', *Neophilologus* 6 (1921), pp. 241-50.

of many translations, especially due to the susceptibility of Europe at the time to foreign influence, and the interest in Oriental literature was served through them. Translations bore witness to changes which had a fundamental influence on currents of feeling about life and art. In the second half of the eighteenth century the idea of a universal, timeless criterion of excellence gradually gave way to an awareness of and respect for the distinctions between civilizations produced by diverse locations in time and place. The 'garment of thought and feeling', as Edna Purdie has it[39]—the unique form and language in which these are clothed—became an increasingly important aspect of works of literature, and Herder came to recognize environment as an integral part of a particular culture. Capturing the characteristic tone of an original, especially in sound and rhythm, was all-important, and the works which Herder chose to translate were those which he saw as expressing a spontaneous, vivid response to powerfully felt experience and emotion. They were above all the often-anonymous products of primitive poets or the works of original genius. These he regarded as representing the most fruitful stimulus to his contemporaries.

In the case of folk-songs or the songs of Shakespeare, Herder was often the first to translate poems which had been little appreciated. In the case of other, often-translated material, the inspiration came from the need to retranslate work seen in a fresh light. The most striking example of the latter is undoubtedly the Song of Songs. The task facing Herder was a singularly daunting one in an age still dominated by conventional faith, when acceptance of change in the presentation of a familiar text could by no means be counted on. It was, however, a task for which Herder, as a trained theologian, biblical scholar and practising clergyman, as well as an historian, linguist, critic and man of letters, was well qualified.

Herder's *Ueber die Würkung der Dichtkunst auf die Sitten der Völker in alten und neuen Zeiten*, the *Volkslieder* and *Lieder der Liebe* typify his relativistic attitude towards the historical background and individual geographical, cultural and climatic conditions under whose influence a work of art is produced. In *Ueber die Würkung [...]*, Herder sought to justify his *Volkslieder*, a work that was offensive to courtly culture and the Enlightenment, which found such literature too spontaneous and

---

39. *Studies in German Literature of the Eighteenth Century: Some Aspects of Literary Affiliation* (London: Athlone Press, 1965), p. 124.

primitive.[40] *Lieder der Liebe* was thus a practical demonstration of Herder's theories, using as an illustration a biblical text that was widely known and accepted as being of high literary value. Herder's desire to spark a revival of pure German poetry, and his conclusion that the primitive poetry of the Orient could not be imitated, led him to believe that such a revival could only be instigated by that poetry which, through Luther's translation, already had had such an impact on Germany's language and history, namely the poetry of the Bible. Herder thus defended Hebrew poetry against the charge of primitiveness levelled at it by the Aufklärer, and he hoped that German poetry could once again become a similarly spontaneous, organic expression of its national character.

Compared with the views of the time on biblical poetry in general and the Song of Songs in particular, Herder's was a lone voice. Before him, the book had been regarded as either pornography or allegory, so the allegorical interpretation of the Song of Songs represented an implicit rejection of the pornographic reading. Herder stood out from his own background within the Christian tradition by insisting that the Song of Songs was not allegorical, yet he also stood out within the deist non-Christian background, arguing that the Song was still revelatory and had something to say about God. Herder thus opposed both traditions in his mission to rescue the Song of Songs and thereby Germany's own poetry. He was able to throw out the allegorical approach yet find something of benefit for the Christian church. In this, he mixed the human and the divine. Thus, while some regarded the Song of Songs as allegory and others regarded it as a piece of lewd literature, Herder's position was unique.

From the outset, Herder emphatically rejected the allegorical interpretations of the Song of Songs which had made its acceptance into the canon possible for most of his predecessors. In order to understand his approach, we must realize that he saw the Bible as reflecting directly all the experiences of mind and body with which God had endowed mankind. Of these experiences the most important was love, the prime bond between mankind and God, and between human beings. For Herder the sole theme of the Song of Songs was human love between a

---

40. Unfortunately, *Ueber die Würkung [...]* was published too late to lay the critical-theoretical groundwork for the *Volkslieder* of 1778, although doubtless it was originally intended to serve such a purpose. Although written in 1778, it was not published in the *Abhandlungen* of the Bavarian Academy until 1781.

man and a woman, love perhaps of the kind which the young Herder was experiencing himself at the time of his main preoccupation with his interpretation and translation. He was well aware that the unfamiliar setting of the poems and their frank sensuality could give offence to some, but the tone of the whole was to him so patently innocent as to be inspiring to true morality. Indeed, this approach—strangely naïve for a young man in love—was the hallmark of Herder's distinctive reading of the work, as will become clear in more detail in Chapters 5 and 6.

Communication of what Herder regarded as the essential character of the Song of Songs through the medium of poetic language and verse to the literary public and general readership of the day posed special problems to the translator. Recapturing the unique note of any great lyric poetry is difficult enough, but love poems—and, above all, *these* '*Lieder der Liebe*'—presented a supreme challenge. For all his intuitive genius as a literary critic, Herder himself did not possess the original poetic gift which the occasion demanded, nor did he yet live in an age which had shaped a poetic tradition on language adequate to the task.[41] However, he worked to produce these prerequisites for a renaissance of German poetry, and, if nothing more, his translations of the Song of Songs were a contribution to their production.

41. See Eric A. Blackall, *The Emergence of German as a Literary Language 1700–1775* (Ithaca, NY: Cornell University Press, 2nd edn, 1978).

Chapter 1

HERDER'S PREOCCUPATION WITH THE SONG OF SONGS

The first sign of Herder's informed interest in the Song of Songs can be seen in his recension of Christian Gottfried Hase's *Versuch einer richtigern Auslegung des Hohenliedes Salomonis, worin das zuverläßige, schöne und göttliche dieses heiligen Buchs gezeiget wird* (Leipzig: J.W. and J.S. Halle, 1765), an exegesis with a verse translation.[1] Herder's review, dated 18 October 1765, was published in the *Anzeigen aus den Königsbergschen Gelehrten und Politischen Zeitungen* and it is reproduced in *SWS*, I, pp. 89-91. Here we find clear hints of his later critical work, in which he regarded the Song of Songs primarily as poetry—and as culture-specific folk-poetry at that—rather than as theological allegory. For this reason, it seems appropriate that the points made by

1.   Hase became Rector in Tangermünde in 1755, and later became Pastor at St Paul's in Brandenburg, as well as a teacher of philosophy in Halle. He wrote a Hebrew textbook in 1750, and he also wrote *Erläuterung der Gedanken im Hohen Liede überhaupt*, although no date of publication is given. His *Versuch einer richtigern Auslegung des Hohenliedes Salomonis* begins with a short introduction, followed by the first part, namely the 'Einleitung in das Hohelied Salomonis, um den rechten Verstand dieses heiligen Buches überhaupt zu bestimmen' ('introduction to the Song of Songs in order to determine the correct understanding of this holy work'). This is subdivided into sections discussing such matters as the title, author, date and contents of the book. The second part is the 'Auslegung des Hohenliedes selbst' ('interpretation of the Song of Songs itself'). The Song of Songs is divided into an introduction (corresponding to Song 1.2-4), 'das Hauptlied in fünf Gesängen' ('the main song in five sections'), then a conclusion (corresponding to Song 8.11-14). Each section is divided into two or three verses of translation in blank verse, followed by a section of interpretation and notes. From examples it is clear that Hase considered the Hebrew text, and the final page (p. 346) contains a 'Verzeichniß der vornehmsten ebräischen Wörter, welche nebst andern änlichen besonders erläutert und näher untersucht worden sind' ('an index of the principal Hebrew words which, along with other similar words, have been specifically commented upon and closely examined').

Herder in his review should form the basis of this chapter.

Given the considerable debate at the time concerning the place of the Song of Songs in the biblical canon and the tradition of allegorical interpretation, Herder's opening comment is immediately significant:

> Jeder Liebhaber der Lieder des Alterthums muß sich freuen, daß das Hohelied Salomons, das Lied der Lieder, welches Rabbinen, Epikuräer und Naturalisten für höher als alle Stücke Theokrits, Virgils und Katulls halten, in unserer Zeit so viele und so mancherley Hände beschäftigt. Evremond, Voltaire und die Rabbinen—drey Namen, die man selten zusammen findet—erschöpfen sich im Lobe dieses unvergleichlichen Gedichts, und die Gottesgelehrten—(etwas was beynahe noch seltner ist)—stimmen diesem Lobe bey (*HR*, I, p. 89).[2]

Herder's allusion to the 'Liebhaber der Lieder des Alterthums' implies that he considered the Song of Songs as just another (although very fine) example of the songs of antiquity. Even the use of the plural 'Lieder' ('songs') suggests his view that the Song of Songs was a collection of poems rather than a single unit. It is also significant that Herder referred to the work as an 'unvergleichliches Gedicht' ('incomparable poem')—a work to be regarded as beautiful poetry.

Herder's high regard for the Song of Songs was clearly rooted in his belief that it arose naturally from the culture in which it was written. According to him, the writers of the Old Testament had no literary pretensions. Their work was natural and naïve, as was the poetry of the Orient in general, stemming as it did from the childhood of the human race. Such naturalness and naïveté were to him the hallmark of all true, genuine poetry. This was the poetry of Nature—'Volkslied' ('folk-song'), vastly superior to the polished, imitative art form of the poetry of the time. Herder regarded simple folk-poetry as in no way inferior to the classical poetry of Greece or Rome which was held in such high regard by his contemporaries. By showing that three distinct groups, namely Rabbis, Epicureans and Naturalists, compared the Song of

---

2.	'Every lover of the songs of antiquity must rejoice that the Song of Solomon, the Song of Songs, which Rabbis, Epicureans and Naturalists consider to be greater than all the works of Theocritus, Virgil and Catullus, is keeping so many and such diverse hands busy in our own day. Evremond, Voltaire and the rabbis—three names which we rarely find together—exhaust themselves in praising this incomparable poem, and the theologians agree with this praise—something which is almost even rarer.'

Songs favourably with the literature of Theocritus, Virgil and Catullus, he was able to bolster his claim. By doing so, Herder was already hinting at his later views on primitive poetry. It was his thesis that important literature existed prior to and concurrently with that of the Greeks, for instance, and that the Greeks were therefore not 'die Väter aller Litteratur in Europa' ('the fathers of all literature in Europe') (*DL*, II, p. 112). They were merely the fathers of that culture which influential contemporary critics viewed as the only culture worthy of emulation.

Herder's naming of these three diverse groups is significant. In the discussion of allegorical interpretation below, we shall note that Herder had no time whatsoever for those who allegorized the Song of Songs. Although the Rabbis generally interpreted the book allegorically, it was important to Herder that some of the religious leaders of that culture which gave birth to it were also able to regard it simply as poetry. The followers of Epicurus, the Athenian philosopher, were devoted both to the practice of virtue as the highest good, and to the pursuit of refined sensuous enjoyment. Herder saw the Song of Songs as a paean of pure, virtuous love and sensuality. It is therefore fitting that he should refer to the Epicureans. The Naturalists believed that the world operated by natural rather than supernatural or spiritual laws. This leads us to reflect on Herder's non-allegorical approach to the Song of Songs, and also to note his future efforts to place it in its natural setting and to comment where necessary on those aspects which would otherwise be obscure to the European reader. We have noted above that in his *Lieder der Liebe* Herder attempted to leave every line of the poems within its own *Sitz im Leben*.

In order to underline here the universal appeal of the Song, Herder claimed that the eighth-century French theologian Evremond,[3] Voltaire and the Rabbis—unusual bed-fellows indeed—were united in their praise of the Song of Songs. With a jibe at the members of his own later profession, Herder noted with a certain sarcasm that even theologians were in agreement here. However, while attempting to place Hase's work in context, Herder stated in his review that he had no time for the earlier exegeses of Johann Gerhard and Hugo Grotius,[4] and he commented cynically on those of his contemporaries Robert Lowth (1710–

---

3.   Evremond (died c. 720 CE), is reputed to have founded the Monastery of Fontenay-les-Louvets in the diocese of Sées, where he became abbot.

4.   See Grotius's 'Annotata ad Canticum Canticorum', in *idem*, *Annotata ad Vetus Testamentum* (3 vols.; Paris: S. and G. Cramoisy, 1644), I, pp. 541-48.

87), and the Neologists Johann David Michaelis (1717–91), Peter Hanssen (1686–1760),[5] Friedrich Eberhard Boysen (1720–1800)[6] and Pellegrino Niccola Celotti.[7] Their interpretations had been partly poetical and partly exegetical, partly natural and partly mystical, in Herder's view all without success.

Herder noted Hase's appearance 'mit einer richtigern Erklärung' ('with a more accurate interpretation')[8] in which he hoped to ascertain the reliability, beauty and divinity of the Song of Songs. There is a hint of scepticism in Herder's stress on the word 'richtiger' ('more accurate'), given his dismissive reception of other interpretations of the work. He clearly suspected that Hase's work was unlikely to please him more, although Hase's title would suggest his own disagreement with previous work on the Song of Songs. Yet Herder considered that the translation itself was moving in the right direction, namely away from the neo-classical model. We must doubt, however, that Hase was moving towards a relativistic view, given Herder's criticism of his interpretation as 'unnatural'.

Herder remarked scornfully that not every biblical interpreter was at the same time a linguist, poet and theologian. His criticism here is ironic, for surely he himself was later to attempt to unite all three approaches in his own work. Andreas F. Kelletat supports this view, claiming that 'an kaum einem anderen Text läßt sich [...] Herders eigene Umsetzung seiner in den *Fragmenten*, den *Kritischen Wäldern* und den Rezensionen der sechziger und siebziger Jahre erhobenen Forderungen an einen guten Übersetzer so detailliert studieren wie an den *Liedern der Liebe*'.[9]

---

5. I have been unable to locate Hanssen's work on the Song of Songs.

6. Boysen's views on the Song of Songs are undoubtedly in his *Kritische Erläuterungen des Grundtextes der Heiligen Schriften Altes Testaments* (Halle: Hemmerde, 1760–64). Herder must also have known Boysen's *Beyträge zu einem richtigen System der hebräischen Philologie [...]* (Leipzig and Chemnitz: Stössel, 1762–63).

7. It is unclear which work Herder had in mind here.

8. This is presumably an adaptation of Hase's title *Versuch einer richtigern Auslegung*.

9. 'In scarcely any text [...] other than his *Lieder der Liebe* can we study in such detail Herder's own realization of his demands of a good translator which he had put forward in his *Fragmente*, his *Kritische Wälder*, and his critical reviews of the 1760s and 1770s.' *Herder und die Weltliteratur: Zur Geschichte des Übersetzens im achtzehnten Jahrhundert* (Europäische Hochschulschriften, Series I, 760;

Despite Herder's scepticism, his comments on Hase's work were not entirely negative. For example, he praised a well-written introduction, Hase's knowledge of literature and his ability to use his sources. The fact that Herder could comment in this way shows how widely read and knowledgeable he himself was at such a young age. Perhaps prophetically, as far as his own work was concerned, he noted Hase's disagreement with Michaelis and Boysen, describing Hase's translation as accurate, beautiful and much to be preferred to Boysen's. To be able to comment in this way on the translation, Herder must have compared it closely with the original. Even by 1765, then, he must have spent some time working on the problems of translation from the Hebrew text.

Yet while Herder approved of Hase's translation and his scholarly notes per se, he found the interpretation too unnatural, mystical and tedious—in short, 'das Werk eines Predigers, der über jeden Vers eine erbauliche Predigt gehalten, die wir ungern hören möchten, noch weniger lesen wollen' (I, p. 90).[10] Although later to be a pastor himself, Herder always rejected the didactic approach, and his thinking was already clear in this comment.[11]

Thus Herder's view of Hase's work was not unequivocal. While very much in favour of the translation, he was not so enamoured with Hase's 'mystical' exegesis. It is not surprising, then, that Herder wished that Hase had not published his detailed interpretation along with his translation and notes. His exegesis would have been better published separately 'für erbauende und zu erbauende Gläubige' ('for believers who encourage and those who need encouraging') (I, p. 90) who would not look too much at the notes anyway. Arguably Herder implied here the possibility of a dichotomy between translation and interpretation, a view which cannot be accepted unconditionally. Indeed, when he came to translate the Song of Songs himself, Herder not only included a

Frankfurt am Main: Peter Lang, 1984), p. 59.

10. 'The work of a clergyman who delivers on each verse a devotional sermon which we would rather not listen to, let alone read.'

11. In this regard, it is ironic that Rudolf Haym, referring to Herder's later query as to why the Song of Songs should be in the Bible (see *SWS*, VIII, pp. 543 and 628), claimed that 'die Frage wie die Antwort ist nicht mehr des poetischen Auslegers, sondern des Theologen' ('the question, like the answer, is no longer that of the poetic interpreter, but rather that of the theologian'). *Herder nach seinem Leben und seinen Werken dargestellt* (2 vols.; Berlin: Gaertner, 1877–85), II, p. 87.

commentary as part of his overall interpretation, but also mingled it with the translations themselves.

In his review Herder had encouraging words for Hase's promise of a poetic translation which would attempt to transpose the beauties of the Hebrew into 'Deutsche Formen und Empfindungen' ('German forms and feelings') (I, p. 90). He insisted, however, that Hase should avoid what Herder termed the Icarus-like fate 'eines Wilhelmi' ('of a Wilhelmi'),[12] who, in his attempts to surpass Johann David Michaelis's translation of Ecclesiastes, translated the Song of Songs into 'Deutsche Lobwasserreime' ('German Lobwasser verses')[13] (I, p. 90). Significantly, the criterion for Herder's scorn of Wilhelmi's translation was not its measure of fidelity to the original text, but Herder's view that it offended against his own native German language. We must bear this in mind when considering Herder's proposed rejection of his own translation in favour of Luther's in an attempt to do justice to it as poetry in his own tongue. He was always more concerned with the quality of the German and with how far the translator had succeeded in creating a poetic equivalent in terms of the resources of the German language, rather than with literal fidelity to the original text—although I shall demonstrate in Chapter 6 that his published translation of the Song of Songs was closer to the Hebrew than were his earlier drafts. Herder's poetic translations—particularly those from Hebrew—were primarily to be used as examples whereby the language of German poetry could be advanced.

André Lefevere has argued that one of the historical functions of translations is to introduce changes into a national literary system,[14] and Herder's preoccupation with the Song of Songs seems to be a splendid example of what he is referring to. Suphan underlined this point in his introduction to Herder's *Archäologie des Morgenlandes*: 'Es ist ander-

12. It is not clear from his review to whom Herder was referring here, although in his preface Hase drew attention to 'die neueste Uebersetzung in Reimen von dem Herrn Pastor Wilhelmi 1764 zu Leipzig' ('the latest translation in rhyming verse by Pastor Wilhelmi in 1764 in Leipzig'). This was probably the theologian Wilhelm W. Wilhelmi (1735–90).

13. This is undoubtedly a reference to the work of Ambrosius Lobwasser (died 1585 CE), the famous translator of the Psalms.

14. See 'Theory and Practice—Process and Product', *Modern Poetry in Translation* 41–42 (1981), pp. 19-27 (particularly 22-23).

wärts[15] schon darauf aufmerksam gemacht worden, wie unter den Versuchen Herders, der deutschen Sprache Bildsamkeit an der Poesie aller Völker zu erproben und sie so zum Organ einer Weltpoesie geschickt zu machen, seine Übertragungen aus dem Hebräischen voranstehen' (VI, p. xx).[16] Here we have the reason why Herder offered poetry rather than theology, and we can see from his comments on Hase's work that he was aware of this as early as 1765.

Herder did not want yet another mystical paraphrase, but rather a poetical interpretation which might enhance the literary reputation of the Song of Songs in Germany: 'Der Autor schreibe als Philolog und Poet: so daß man auch seinem Deutschen Liede der Lieder das zuruffen könne, was der Sohar vom Ebräischen Hohenliede sagt: An dem Tage, der dies Lied der Welt offenbarte, ist die Vollkommenheit aller Dinge erfunden' (I, pp. 90-91).[17] Already he was adopting the same point of view that he was later to espouse in his *Lieder der Liebe*, rejecting a mystical interpretation, and demanding instead one which was informed by the poetic practice as well as the linguistic knowledge of the translator. In other words, the 'und' ('and') must be stressed in the phrase 'Philolog *und* Poet' ('philologist *and* poet'). The tension in Herder between the philological, the aesthetic and the theological was already apparent.

Thus many of Herder's ideas, including his dynamic view of literature and culture, were found in embryonic form in his review of Hase. Perhaps most important was his insistence that a translation of the Song of Songs should be a 'living' translation. He pleaded for one to which

15. Suphan refers in a note here to his own comments in XII, pp. 408ff.

16. 'It has already been pointed out elsewhere how, among Herder's efforts to test out the flexibility of the German language on the poetry of all nations and thus skilfully to make it a voice of world poetry, his translations from Hebrew are the most felicitous.'

17. 'Let the author write as a philologist and poet, so that even his German Song of Songs may be applauded with what the Zohar says of the Hebrew Song of Solomon: On the day upon which this Song was revealed to the world, the perfection of all things was discovered.' According to Jewish mystics, the Zohar contains divine revelations given to Rabbi Simeon ben Yohai and his son Eleazer while hiding from the Romans in the second century CE. Modern critics, however, claim that the Zohar was written by Moses de Leon in about 1280 CE. (See David Goldstein, 'On Translating God's Name', in William Radice and Barbara Reynolds [eds.], *The Translator's Art: Essays in Honour of Betty Radice* [Harmondsworth: Penguin Books, 1987], pp. 72-80.)

the reader could respond in his own situation, although one which did not betray its own cultural flavour. Arguably it is not possible for a translation to retain its original *Volksgeist*, that is, faithfulness to the spirit and colour of the text within its original culture, and at the same time to be able to claim to be a 'living' translation. There was thus a possible tension here in Herder's aims.

For Herder, philological fidelity to the written text was not as important as aesthetic fidelity to the original *Volksgeist*, and this became a main beam of his thinking. Given this view, we can more readily understand Herder's various attempts to translate the Song of Songs without easily arriving at a definitive version. His was an attempt to stress the spirit and colour of the work rather than produce a faithful translation, even though his published translation of 1778 shows considerable fidelity to the original text. Equally important were Herder's views that Hebrew poetry should be regarded in no way as inferior to that of the Greeks, that his own native poetry was unnecessarily imitative, and that it should stem naturally, as did that of the Hebrews, from within its own cultural and linguistic group—that is, it should be bound to its own *Sitz im Leben*.

It is apparent, then, that by 1765 Herder was already quite well acquainted with both the original Song of Songs and some recent translations and studies of it. What is more, he had given these studies considerable thought. We know that Herder attended the Mohrunger Stadtschule until 1760, and then worked for Sebastian Friedrich Trescho, Deacon of the Stadtkirche, until 1762 when he went to Königsberg. During this two-year period, Herder studied classical and contemporary literature, teaching himself with the aid of books borrowed from Trescho's private library. With a little justifiable guesswork, therefore, we may conjecture that Herder's interest in the Song of Songs began in about 1761. This date is, of course, open to some doubt, but, in the light of the evidence laid out above, it would seem to be about right. Certainly the date could not be moved by more than a year or so either way.

Accepting that it is not easy, therefore, to establish absolutely the beginnings of Herder's passive interest in the Song of Songs, we now turn from Herder's mere interest in it to his actually translating it. During his courtship of his future wife, Caroline Flachsland, Herder seemed to find particularly appropriate inspiration for his work on the Song of Songs. In a letter addressed to Caroline and dated 21 March 1772, a year after he became Pastor in Bückeburg, Herder wrote: 'Ich kann Ihnen, wenn Sie wollen, noch mehr schicken, [...]. Falls Sie Appetit haben, den *Hiob* und das *Hohelied Salomons*.'[18] Here is the first evidence that Herder was actually working on a translation himself. Although it was to go through a number of versions and revisions, it would seem, then, that his earliest active work on the Song of Songs dates from late 1771 or early 1772. Herder was greatly encouraged by the interest Caroline shared with him in the beauties of primitive poetry: 'Sie können nicht glauben, wie innig ichs fühle, daß Ihnen diese Stücke in aller ihrer rohen Einfalt so gefallen.'[19] This is important, given that Herder was less concerned with the place of the Song of Songs in the Bible than with its intrinsic poetic values.

Although Herder's translation of the Song of Songs from this period is no longer extant, his rhyming translations of Job are.[20] According to Redlich, however, it is clear from the form in which it appeared in the earlier drafts that Herder tried to translate the Song of Songs in the same rhyme as Job. Indeed, Redlich believed it possible that an even earlier draft may have existed (VIII, p. vii). Whatever the case, by 1772 the kernel of the later *Lieder der Liebe* was already formed. This view was broadly confirmed by Herder in the second edition of the first part of his *Theologische Briefe* (1785), where he stated that he had already been contemplating his work on the Song of Songs at least ten years previously, that is, before 1775 (*TB*, X, p. 132). In a note, Herder further claimed that the work had in fact been written some years earlier than its eventual publication date of 1778 (*TB*, X, p. 132).

18. 'If you wish, I can send you even more, [...]. If you like, Job and the Song of Solomon.' *Briefwechsel mit seiner Braut Caroline Flachsland*, in Heinrich Düntzer and Ferdinand Gottfried Herder (eds.), *Aus Herders Nachlaß: Ungedruckte Briefe* (3 vols.; Frankfurt am Main: Meidinger, 1856–57), III, p. 205.

19. 'You cannot believe how much it means to me that these items in all their raw simplicity please you so much.' *Briefwechsel mit seiner Braut Caroline Flachsland*, pp. 205-206.

20. There are several translation attempts in the *Nachlaß*: Kapsel VII 61 and 62 contain *Hiob. Entwurf des Buchs als Composition betrachtet* (1781–82) (see *SWS*, XI, pp. 316-20); Kapsel VII 130-40 contain translations of various chapters and verses of Job (1771); there are further translation attempts from Job in Kapseln XX 85 and 134 (no date), XXII 129 and 130 (1781), and XXV 31 (no date); Kapsel XXIX 2, fol.y^{r}f., contains a translation and commentary on Job 1–14 (no date); and Kapsel XXX 1, fol.74^v, contains a translation of Job's curse (*Metrische Bearbeitung der Selbstverfluchung Hiobs*) (c. 1764).

Herder married Caroline Flachsland on 2 May 1773. During the early years of the marriage, the Song of Songs seemed to disappear among Herder's other preoccupations, both literary and marital, although we can see from the manuscript of the *Volkslieder*, dating from 1774, that his original intention was to include among them samples of his work on the Song of Songs, together with other pieces of Hebrew poetry, for, as Haym put it, 'vom *Volksliede* redete Herder, wenn er von dem allgemeinen Wesen und wenn er von dem lebendigen Quell aller Dichtung reden wollte'.[21]

In the event, the 1774 version of the *Volkslieder* was not published, and had in any case been filled with a preponderance of English and German folk-songs, leaving no room for those from the South or the Orient. In fact, by 1778, when the *Volkslieder* were finally published, *Lieder der Liebe* had already become a separate work on a larger scale than Herder had perhaps originally intended. Thus we find nothing of the Song of Songs in the *Volkslieder*, but plenty of what Herder regarded as folk-songs in *Lieder der Liebe*, including Schöber's Minnelieder. They confirm Herder's purely human conception of the Song of Songs and his inclination to place literary works of different nations and times in parallel and to include them, as Meyer had it, 'unter Einem Gesichtspunkt [...], als Erzeugnis und Ausdruck Einer Menschheit, Einer Humanität'.[22]

While Herder's work on the Song of Songs apparently lay dormant, Goethe undertook his own translation—used as a point of reference in this study—in the autumn of 1775, when he was 26: 'Ich hab das Hohelied Salomons übersezt welches ist die herrlichste Sammlung liebes Lieder die Gott erschaffen hat.'[23] As I have shown above, Herder may

21. 'Herder spoke of *folk-song* whenever he wanted to speak of the general character and of the living source of all poetry.' *Herder*, II, p. 88.

22. 'Within one framework [...], as the product and expression of one human race, of one humanity.' *Werke*, p. 15.

23. 'I have translated the Song of Songs which is the most magnificent collection of love songs which God has created.' Goethe to Johann Heinrich Merck on 7 October 1775 (*Briefe* [4 vols.; Hamburg: Wegner, 1962–67], I, p. 196). Haupt (*Biblische Liebeslieder: Das sogenannte Hohelied Salomos unter steter Berücksichtigung der Übersetzungen Goethes und Herdes* [Leipzig: J.C. Hinrichs; Baltimore, MD: The Johns Hopkins University Press, 1907, p. vi) maintained that the letter was written on 8 October. Goethe's translation 'Das Hohelied Salomons' was first published by Gustav von Loeper in *Briefe Goethes an Sophie von La Roche und Bettina Brentano mit dichterischen Beilagen* (Berlin: Hertz, 1879), p. 130, and is in

have given Goethe single parts of the Song of Songs during the winter of 1770-71 in Strasbourg, possibly in written form and almost certainly orally.

It would appear that Herder returned fully to the Song of Songs in 1776, for MSS(1), (2) and (3) in the *Nachlaß* date back to this time. Indeed, they could not be earlier than this date, because of the comment on Pufendorf mentioned above in the Introduction (see also *SWS*, VIII, pp. 589-91). Additionally we note Johann Kaspar Lavater's enquiry to Herder concerning his *Lieder der Liebe* on 19 October 1776.[24] In order to have elicited such an enquiry, it is clear that Herder must have mentioned his work on the Song of Songs to Lavater before this date, although how long it is clearly impossible to judge.

In a letter to Johann Georg Hamann dated 29 December 1778 and 2 January 1779, Herder gave two domestic reasons for the publication of his work in 1778. One reason was 'das Zureden meiner Frauen, weil es seit 4. Jahren dalag' ('my wife's encouragement, since it had been lying around for four years').[25] We have noted how Caroline's interest in Herder's work was a source of encouragement to him, and here is another example. The second reason given here was 'die Heurath meines Schwagers, der aber noch nichts davon weiß' ('the marriage of my brother-in-law, who nevertheless still knows nothing about it'). Apparently, Herder intended the work to be a wedding present to his brother-in-law Sigmund Flachsland on the occasion of his marriage to Christine Martin, which presumably took place early in 1779.

Herder's comment concerning his lack of work on the Song of Songs is important, for at first sight it suggests that he was at work on it in 1774. We have seen that he was active in 1772 and again in 1776, but nowhere else is it suggested that Herder was engaged in this project in 1774. Clearly he was referring back to 1776 when his wife apparently

---

WW, XXXVII, pp. 299-310. It is also printed as 'Liebliche Verwirrung' ('Delightful Entanglement') in Timm (ed.), *Das Hohe Lied Salomos*, pp. 121-29. Goethe followed Herder's view that the Song of Songs was a collection of songs rather than a single unit. Although he initially regarded the work as lyric poetry, he changed his view in 1820 after the appearance of Friedrich Wilhelm Carl Umbreit's translation and commentary (see Haupt, *Biblische Liebeslieder*, p. vi).

24. The simple enquiry 'Dein hohes Lied?' ('Your Song of Songs?') appears as a postscript to Lavater's letter to Herder in *Aus Herders Nachlaß: Ungedruckte Briefe*, II, Letter 47, p. 171.

25. Hoffmann (ed.), *Briefe an Hamann*, p. 136.

persuaded him to take up his work of 1772 again, leading to final publication in 1778. This would also explain Herder's considerable activity
in 1776.[26]

Apart from these personal reasons, there is another. We will see
below how Herder reacted to what he regarded as the clumsy, even frivolous rationalistic interpretation of the critic Johann David Michaelis,
who viewed the Song as 'ein Ehelied voll Orientalischer Liebesränke'
('a marriage song full of Oriental amorous intrigues') (*SWS*, VIII,
p. 532). For the moment it is sufficient to note Herder's claim that
Michaelis's omission of the Song of Songs from his Bible translation[27]
acted as a catalyst for the ultimate publication of his own translation in
1778: 'Und darf ich sagen, daß dies die Ursache war, warum ich [...]
unter andern vielleicht nothwendigern Arbeiten einige Stunden der Er-
holung dem öffentlichen Geschreibe über dieses Buch stahl?' (*SWS*,
VIII, p. 533).[28]

Despite considerable preoccupation with the subject over a number of
years, Herder wrote to Hamann in the letter cited above that 'mein
Schiff ist völlig auf dem Strande. Das Hohelied ist nicht der Rede
werth. [...] Weiß übrigens nicht, woher es kommt oder wohin es
gehet?'[29] Furthermore, in a letter to Johann Wilhelm Ludewig Gleim on

---

26. It would seem that Clark misunderstood this when referring to other work
being done in Germany on the Song of Songs 'while Herder's study and translation
lay unfinished (1774–78)' (*Herder: His Life and Thought*, p. 255). He further states
that Herder's text 'as printed in 1778 is not that of his interlinear version of 1774'
(p. 257). We have seen that there is no evidence for such a version as understood by
Clark. Still confused by his misunderstanding of Herder's comments and seemingly
desperate to make his dates fit, Clark maintains without corroboration that the first
draft of *Lieder der Liebe* was made in 1774 on the occasion of Sigmund Flachsland's *engagement* to Christine Martin (p. 254). (Clark makes no mention of a 1774
version in his 'Herder, Percy, and the *Song of Songs*'.) Yet we have seen in
Herder's remarks to Hamann that Flachsland still knew nothing about the work
right at the end of 1778. Clark further claims that the wedding took place in 1778
coincidentally with the publication of *Lieder der Liebe*, although Herder's comments suggest differently.

27. Michaelis's translation was published in Göttingen between 1773 and 1790
as *Johann David Michaelis deutsche Uebersetzung des Alten Testaments, mit
Anmerkungen für Ungelehrte* (Göttingen: Dieterich).

28. 'And may I state that it was for this reason that [...] despite other perhaps
more vital tasks I stole some hours of relaxation to write about this book publicly?'

29. 'My ship has been totally wrecked. The Song of Songs is not worth dis-

6 December 1778, Herder voiced concern about the reception of his work.[30] It would appear that Herder was experiencing one of his periods of insecurity and lack of self-confidence, yet it is perhaps not surprising that he should be so self-critical about his work on the Song of Songs—for his comment was surely not about the intrinsic value of the biblical book—after spending so long on it. Many of his works were abandoned or revised and published in new editions, and we have seen that *Lieder der Liebe* was no exception. Although still proud of his own cultural placing of the songs, Herder bowed to Luther's poetic superiority:

> Man verzeihe also meine Kühnheit, mein Stammlen: es war mir um Seele, Zweck, Geist des Buchs zu thun in jedem einzelnen Bilde und Liede. Hat man diese gefaßet, so gehe man zu Luthers Uebersetzung; sie ist uns, Trotz einzelner Fehler, noch immer unersetzt und unerreichbar an Süßigkeit und ungezwungener Einfalt, so wie an Stärke und Leben' (VIII, p. 535. See also VIII, p. 594).[31]

Indeed, in his *Theologische Briefe* Herder confessed: 'Damit ich mich nicht in Nebensachen verliefe, [...] hätte ich beynah Luthers Text gar hingesetzt' ('Lest I became lost in matters of secondary importance, I all but used Luther's text itself') (X, p. 132). Moreover, he referred in MS(2) to Schöber's mediaeval version as a 'Minnesinger, der an Süßigkeit und Einfalt die Mängel meiner Sprache ersetzet, bei mir siehe nur auf Sinn, Seele, Zweck und Ort dieses Buchs' (VIII, p. xiv).[32]

After the publication of *Lieder der Liebe*, Goethe sent a copy of it in October 1778 to Charlotte von Stein: 'Dafür schick ich Ihnen auch Lieder der Liebe von einem weisen Könige gesungen und einem weisen Mann kommentirt.'[33] We further know from their correspondence that

cussing. Nor do I know where it has come from or where it is heading.' Hoffmann (ed.), *Briefe an Hamann*, pp. 136-37.

30. Heinrich Düntzer and Ferdinand Gottfried Herder (eds.), *Von und an Herder: Ungedruckte Briefe aus Herders Nachlaß* (3 vols.; Leipzig: Dyk, 1861–62), I, p. 58.

31. 'Thus please forgive my audacity, my stuttering. It was my aim to draw attention to the soul, nature and spirit of the work in every single image and song. Once these have been grasped, then go to Luther's translation; despite individual errors, it remains irreplaceable and unsurpassable as far as sweetness, unaffected simplicity, strength and life are concerned.'

32. 'A Minnesinger, who with his sweetness and simplicity made up for the deficiencies of my own language; in my work, look merely at the meaning, aim and locus of this book.'

33. 'I am sending you also Lieder der Liebe as sung by a wise king and com-

Gleim received a copy from Herder on 3 November 1778.[34] Still lacking confidence as far as the initial reception of his own work was concerned, Herder informed Gleim in a letter of 22 March 1779 that 'man schreibt mir heut, daß mein Hohelied in den Zeitungen überall jämmerlich mitgenommen werde'.[35] The poet Matthias Claudius acknowledged receiving a copy of *Lieder der Liebe* in his letter to Herder of 21 June 1779.[36]

mented upon by a wise man.' Petersen (ed.), *Briefe*, I/1, Letter 279, p. 131. The letter is undated, but appears between those of 14 October and 31 October. It is in the same position in Jonas Fränkel's edition (*Briefe an Charlotte von Stein* [3 vols.; Berlin: Akademie Verlag, 1960]), I, p. 122. Haym claimed that the letter was written on 26 December 1778, although this would seem unlikely (see *Herder*, II, p. 83).

34. *Von und an Herder*, I, p. 54. Gleim acknowledged receipt of the work in a letter to Herder dated 16 November 1778 (p. 55), and six days later he sent his own verse translation for his friend to consider (p. 56). Before Herder had replied, Gleim sent him a second improved and enlarged edition on 29 November 1778. He was impatient for Herder's response, and planned to publish under the title *Dreißig Lieder der Liebe*, 'damit der Titul nicht ganz der Ihrige sei' ('so that the title should not be entirely your own') (p. 57). The work was to be dedicated to Herder, who finally replied on 6 December 1778, although his letter was not sent until 18 December. He acknowledged that Gleim's songs 'haben mich kindisch gefreut' ('delighted me childishly') (p. 58). It is clear that at this stage Herder planned a second printing of his own work of 1778, for in his letter he promised Gleim that he would consider making use of his translation on account of its 'Naivetät und Treuherzigkeit' ('naïveté and frankness'). He finally told him to publish on 26 December 1778 (p. 59). There would appear, therefore, to be little if any mutual influence. Wilhelm Körte first published Gleim's *Liebeslieder. Nach Salomon* in *Johann Wilhelm Ludewig Gleim's Lieder* (7 vols.; Halberstadt: Büreau für Literatur und Kunst, 1811), II, pp. 334-43. The translation is abridged, with a simple rhyme scheme throughout, and it is mainly iambic in metre.

35. 'I was told in writing today that my Song of Songs is being criticized wretchedly in the newspapers.' *Von und an Herder*, I, p. 63. Herder undoubtedly had in mind the recension of his work in *ADB* XXXVII/2 (1779), pp. 478-83. However, while this was not exactly appreciative of Herder's *Lieder der Liebe*, it was not particularly scathing either. Moreover, the *Gothaische gelehrte Zeitungen*, 89. Stück, 7 November 1778, pp. 729-31, ran a favourable review of *Lieder der Liebe*, quoting from VIII, pp. 529-30 and 535. (See Hans-Jürgen Gaycken, *Johann Gottfried Herder und seine zeitgenössischen Kritiker: Herderkritik in der Allgemeinen Deutschen Bibliothek* [Europäische Hochschulschriften, Series I, 853; Frankfurt am Main: Peter Lang, 1985], pp. 45-50.)

36. *Aus Herders Nachlaß*, Letter 45, I, p. 421.

It would thus appear that Herder was actively concerned with the Song of Songs between the very early 1760s and 1778, with particularly concentrated bouts of work between 1776 and 1778, when the published edition of his work appeared. There is no apparent reference by Herder to the subject after this date.

Chapter 2

HERDER'S APPROACH TO POETRY AND THE BIBLE:
ITS SIGNIFICANCE FOR THE SONG OF SONGS

Introduction

In an age which considered Hebrew poetry barbaric (see *EP*, XI, pp. 223-27, for example), Herder was unique with his plea that poetry in general was divine revelation, and that the Hebrew poetry of the Bible was the epitome of all poetry, the pinnacle of which was the Song of Songs.[1] In other words, Herder argued that a biblical book which was regarded as allegorical at best, and primitive and distasteful by most, should serve as a catalyst for the renaissance of German poetry. In this chapter I aim to highlight the importance of the Song of Songs to Herder in the context of his perception of the poverty of German poetry, his unfavourable comparison of that poetry with the works of well-known and positively received poets of other languages and cultures, and his views on poetry in general and biblical poetry in particular.

First, I review those intellectual currents which played such an important role in helping to shape Herder's ideas about poetry, and hence the Song of Songs. I then consider Herder's condemnation of the imitative nature of German poetry, contrasting this with his enthusiastic reception of Shakespeare, Ossian and Homer, and his interest in the original and primitive as the hallmarks of 'true' poetry as exemplified by the Song of Songs. I review Herder's demand for German poetry to emerge from within the culture of its own 'Volk'—as was the case with the Song of Songs—rather than to borrow from other cultures, and

---

1.   We find the first signs of Herder's innate poetical feeling, and his interest in (Hebrew) folk-poetry, in his first published work, *Gesang an den Cyrus von einem gefangenen Israeliten* (1762) (*SWS*, XXIX, pp. 3 and 4), a free translation from Isa. 44.27–45.8 which he intended as an ode to Peter III of Russia.

finally I outline his reception of the Bible and Hebrew poetry. An appraisal is made throughout of Herder's relativistic theories of literature, where Herder was influenced by Immanuel Kant's lectures on physical geography, and which were important for his work on the Song of Songs. This chapter must be necessarily selective rather than exhaustive, given that Herder's views on poetry are so well documented and pervade much of his writing.

Herder's Reception of Contemporary Philosophies

Whenever we study Herder's writings we must bear in mind that his work was always in flux. His was never a fixed, dogmatic system, and he may stand accused of constant repetition and lack of cohesion as his thoughts sprawl throughout his work. For example, we have seen that he was not satisfied with one translation of the Song of Songs, but produced several versions within a short space of time. His thinking ebbed and flowed, constantly developing, much like the intellectual world in which it matured. German thought in the middle of the eighteenth century was essentially eclectic in approach, yet there were three main movements which constantly overlapped; Rationalism, Empiricism, and Pietism. The strongest movement was Rationalism as inspired by Gottfried Wilhelm Leibniz and popularized by Christian Wolff. From this sprang two further movements: the Neologists in the field of theology and the 'Aufklärer' ('enlightened writers') in the field of philosophy. Neologism was an apologetic theological movement which aimed to disarm the critics of French Rationalism by interpreting even the revealed dogmas of Christianity in the light of rational truths. The Neologists were thus partly responsible for the instigation of historical research into biblical documents, a development of great importance for Herder. At about this time we note the increase of works of textual and historical criticism in biblical research, as well as the appearance of translations and paraphrases, commentaries, discussions concerning authorship and dating, and studies in comparative religion and church history. As John Rogerson puts it:

> The Neologist approach to the Old Testament was based upon exact grammatical and philological exegesis of the text. Exegesis was not subject to constraints imposed by traditional Christian doctrines, and the doctrinal formularies of the Church were not considered to be sacrosanct. [...] The context of exegesis was a knowledge of the ancient world in which the Old Testament had been written. A careful study was made of

the customs and institutions of the Old Testament, as they were illu-
mined by classical Greek and Latin authors, by reports of travellers to
the East, and by Jewish, Arabic and Syriac literature.[2]

According to Rogerson, the majority of Old Testament professors in
Germany at the end of the eighteenth century were either Neologists or
Rationalists.[3] The main figures contributing to this interest were Hermann Samuel Reimarus,[4] Johann Salomo Semler,[5] Johann Jacob Griesbach,[6] Gotthold Ephraim Lessing,[7] Johann David Michaelis and Johann
August Ernesti.[8] Up to this point, the Bible had been accepted un-
questioningly, apart from the occasional work such as the *Tractatus
theologico-politicus* of Benedictus de Spinoza.[9] Now, however, reason
asserted the right to conduct a thorough independent investigation into
the claims of the Bible, a trend which was most significant for Herder's

2.   *Old Testament Criticism in the Nineteenth Century: England and Germany*
(London: SPCK, 1984), pp. 16-17.
3.   Rogerson points to a useful outline of the main positions of the Neologists
provided by Anthony O. Dyson's 'Theological Legacies of the Enlightenment:
England and Germany', in Stephen W. Sykes (ed.), *England and Germany: Studies
in Theological Diplomacy* (Studien zur interkulturellen Geschichte des Christentums, 25; Frankfurt am Main: Peter Lang, 1982), pp. 45-62 (56, 57).
4.   See Richard J. Coggins and James L. Houlden, *A Dictionary of Biblical
Interpretation* (London: SCM Press, 1990), pp. 585-86.
5.   See Gottfried Hornig, *Die Anfänge der historisch-kritischen Theologie:
Johann Salomo Semlers Schriftverständnis und seine Stellung zu Luther* (Forschungen zur systematischen Theologie und Religionsphilosophie, 8; Göttingen:
Vandenhoeck & Ruprecht, 1961).
6.   Griesbach was the teacher of Wilhelm Martin Leberecht de Wette in Jena.
For further information on Griesbach and Semler, see Samuel Davidson, *Sacred
Hermeneutics Developed and Applied, Including a History of Biblical Interpretation from the Earliest of the Fathers to the Reformation* (Edinburgh: T. & T. Clark,
1843).
7.   Herder shared with Lessing many ideas which came to fruition in his own
thinking, such as the need for a national literature and the conception of religion as
something relative as opposed to something absolute in value. However, he did not
share Lessing's idea of a *progressive* religious revelation.
8.   See Charles H. Terrot, *Principles of Biblical Interpretation, Translated from
the Institutio Interpretis of J.A. Ernesti* (2 vols.; Edinburgh: T. & T. Clark, 2nd edn,
1843–48).
9.   The full title was *Tractatus theologico-politicus continens dissertationes
aliquot, quibus ostenditur libertatem philosophandi non tantum salva pietate, &
reipublicae pace posse concedi: sed eandem nisi cum pace reipublicae, ipsaque
pietate tolli non posse* (Hamburg: Künraht, 1670).

subsequent work in the field of biblical criticism and interpretation, particularly with regard to his work on the Song of Songs.

In addition to Rationalist thinking, the rise of Empiricism in Germany influenced literary and historical criticism, as well as scientific research. While Herder was a student in Königsberg, Empiricism began to gain a foothold with the writings of Hamann, the introduction of David Hume to Germany[10] and the publication in 1765 of Gottfried Wilhelm Leibniz's *Nouveaux essais sur l'entendement humain*. Once Empiricist philosophy had recognized that knowledge is impossible without factual observation, the way was cleared for a new, vigorous prosecution of scientific research as the only true basis of knowledge in every field. Empiricism banished all theological explanation, and acts of providence were eliminated from history and natural science. All phenomena were to be interpreted henceforth along causal lines. A new interest in geography and anthropology also resulted in the many works of travel literature which were so important to Herder. His reception of the travel writers of his time, vital for his particular interpretation of the Song of Songs, was arguably a legacy from his interest in both the Empiricists and the Neologists.

Pietism first appeared in Germany as a religious movement which recognized the place of emotion in the Christian faith. Its influence upon German cultural and intellectual life was considerable, and it became linked with that sentimental poetry which so influenced Friedrich Gottlieb Klopstock and Hamann, and helped to prepare the way for the more directly emotional literature of the 'Sturm und Drang', with Herder as the critical founder and Goethe as the leading representative. By the 1760s there was an increasing awareness of the emotional power of poetry. Herder's most formative period coincided with the revival of Shakespeare and the discovery of ancient poetry, particularly that of Ossian and the bardic movements.[11] The glorification of the Natural and

10. Hume's *Vermischte Schriften* were published by Grund in four volumes in Hamburg and Leipzig between 1754 and 1755.

11. Herder attempted to paraphrase Ossian in the free style of Klopstock, basing his work on the German prose translations of Engelbrecht and Wittenberg (see Alexander Gillies, *Herder und Ossian* [Arbeiten zur Geistesgeschichte der germanischen und romanischen Völker, NS 19; Berlin: Junker and Dünnhaupt, 1933], p. 79). Klopstock's free rhythms, or non-metrical lines, undoubtedly influenced Herder's early translations of the Song of Songs, as will become clear both from this chapter and Chapter 6.

the Primitive became a cult, yet although the resulting 'Sturm und Drang' movement was far removed from the rational world of the 'Aufklärung', contact was maintained with Empiricism through the realistic psychological approach,[12] the mystical interest in nature and in natural forces, and also the new interest in the Bible as the poetry and folk-lore of a primitive people. Thus there was an interweaving of varied strands of influence upon Herder's thinking which affected his reception of the Song of Songs.

Robert Lowth's *De sacra poesi Hebraeorum: praelectiones academicae*, first published in England in 1753, had a significant impact upon Herder. Lowth was the first to apply the principles of literary criticism conscientiously to the Old Testament, and, despite his reaction against Lowth's own exegesis of the work, Herder applauded him for initiating the poetic study of the Bible, vital to his own interest in the Song of Songs.[13] He was aware of the difference between poetry and logic, although he shared the common belief of the century that poetry should instruct while it delights. His work was devoted to showing the aesthetic beauties of primitive Hebrew, thus secularizing the Bible. However, his model of classical literature could not satisfy Herder, whose model was that of primitive oral poetry. Herder challenged Lowth's interpretation of the origin of Hebrew poetry.[14] Lowth maintained that arts other than poetry had started in miserable circumstances and had

---

12. See Rudolf Unger, *Hamann und die Aufklärung* (2 vols.; Halle: Niemeyer, 2nd edn, 1925), I, p. 127.

13. Even in *Adrastea*, published posthumously in 1804, we read of Lowth: 'Durch seine lateinische Vorlesungen über die heilige Poesie der Ebräer [...] gab er diesem Inhalt ein Ansehen, da sonst schwache Seelen in der Bibel keine Poesie finden wollten' ('By means of his Latin lectures on the holy poetry of the Hebrews [...], he gave this content some respect, since otherwise weak souls claim to find no poetry in the Bible') (XXIV, p. 355). See also Herder's recension of Johann Georg Sulzer's *Allgemeine Theorie der Schönen Künste*, V, pp. 398-99; *ÄU*, VII, p. 147; *BT*, XI, p. 171; *EP*, XI, p. 215; *Entwurf der Anwendung dreier Akademischer Jahre für einen jungen Theologen*, XXX, p. 409; and *Fragmente einer Abhandlung über die Ode*, XXXII, p. 70.

14. Although Herder praised Lowth for his intentions, he was not always positively critical of his work (see *KW*, III, p. 449; *BL*, IX, p. 541; *TB*, X, pp. 15, 28, and 29; and *LD*, XXXII, p. 94). Indeed, Herder pleaded that Luther was more informative on the Psalms than 'der schönlateinische Lowth über seine drei Klassen Oden' ('Lowth, with his beautiful Latin, on his three classes of odes') (see his recension of Klopstock's odes, V, p. 350).

worked upwards only after a long period of trial and error. The art of poetry, on the other hand—and here Lowth was referring specifically to the Old Testament—had sprung into being already fully-fledged. Lowth tried to prove his thesis with aesthetic arguments, claiming that both the content and form of the Old Testament were therefore divine. Herder attacked this argument with the weapon of historical relativism and with Lowth's own literary-critical arguments (see *LD*, XXXII, pp. 94-101).

However, although Lowth's work was a vital force in Herder's own thinking, it was Hamann's fusion of revelation and poetry and exaltation of the primitive which exerted the most decisive influence on him and prepared the way for his future work, particularly on the Song of Songs. While in Königsberg, Herder formed a close friendship with Hamann, who nurtured his interest in poetry and religion. Hamann had returned some four years previously from a visit to London, full of a new religious experience and with a new enthusiasm for the poetry of English literature, for Shakespeare and Homer, for primitive poetry in general, and for the Bible in particular. In fact, Hamann attempted a prose translation of the Song of Songs himself in 1762, yet whereas he wrote extensively in his letters about his other work, there is no mention of this translation.[15] As Herder apparently never mentioned it either, he was presumably unaware of its existence, although Josef Nadler notes that from this work 'alles das ausstrahlt, was Hamann und durch ihn Herder über Natur und Wesen urtümlicher Lyrik, über Rhythmen und Melodien gewußt und gesagt haben'.[16] Herder's friendship with Hamann was crucial. Through Hamann, he was able to accept the doctrine of sensualism, and to assimilate it into that poetico-religious experience which was to form the basis of his ideas. An understanding of this assimilative process is essential to a true interpretation of Herder's thinking.

Herder attempted to interpret the natural and historical, empirically observed, in terms of the religious and poetic. It was Hamann who taught him to see in nature and history a poetic, religious manifestation

15. Hamann's *Das Lied der Lieder* is printed in Josef Nadler (ed.), *Sämtliche Werke* (5 vols.; Vienna: Thomas-Morus-Presse im Verlag Herder, 1953), IV, pp. 251-56.

16. 'Everything emanates that Hamann, and through him, Herder knew and said about the nature and essence of original lyric poetry, and about rhythms and melodies.' *Sämtliche Werke*, IV, p. 486.

of God. For Hamann, nature formed a living whole, of which man was the crown: 'Endlich krönte Gott die sinnliche Offenbarung seiner Herrlichkeit durch das Meisterstück des Menschen.'[17] God revealed himself supremely in the creative activity of poets whom Hamann, perhaps quoting St Paul out of context, regarded as divine prophets: 'Paulus thut einem Dichter die Ehre an, ihn einen Propheten seines Volks zu nennen. Die wahre Poesie ist eine natürliche Art der Prophezeyung.'[18] For Hamann, the poet was of necessity both believer and prophet. Hamann laid great stress upon that poetry which was primitive and spontaneous rather than that which was reflective and rational. This was important for Herder, who sought to reject what he saw as the artificiality of the German poetry of his time. Hamann held that poetry was an expression of personal feeling rather than an expression of the truths of reason. It was God's revelation of himself to man. The true poet, then, was a creator who was inspired by God to express spiritual truth through poetry, thus reflecting, on a small scale, God's creative power. Poetic talent was a divine force, a creative urge which transcended the rules and traditional conventions of men and acknowledged no laws but its own. Here Hamann was accepting and developing the ideas of Shaftesbury (1671–1713)[19] and Edward Young (1683–1765),[20] but he went further than they did. For him, poetry was a natural, divine impulse which was the true speech of primitive man. It was the language used by a non-reflecting, childlike age, and, as we shall see, Herder embraced Hamann's

17. 'Finally God crowned the emblematic revelation of his majesty with his masterpiece, mankind.' 'Aesthetica in Nuce', from *Kreuzzüge des Philologen*, in Nadler (ed.), *Sämtliche Werke*, II, pp. 113-240 (198).

18. 'Paul does a poet the honour of calling him a prophet of his people. True poetry is a natural kind of prophecy.' *Biblische Betrachtungen eines Christen*, Nadler (ed.), *Sämtliche Werke*, I, pp. 7-249 (241). This refers to Tit. 1.12: 'One of themselves, even a prophet of their own, said, The Cretians are alway liars, evil beasts, slow bellies' (KJV). Apparently Hamann believed that Paul was the author of Titus, although generally Pauline authorship is denied.

19. On Kant's advice, Herder read the works of the English philosopher Anthony Ashley Cooper, third Earl of Shaftesbury. (See Irvin C. Hatch, *Der Einfluß Shaftesburys auf Herder* [Berlin: Duncker, 1901].)

20. Young's fame in Europe was augmented particularly in Germany by a prose work attracting comparatively little attention in England, namely his *Conjectures on Original Composition: In a Letter to the Author of Sir Charles Grandison* (London: A. Millar; R. and J. Dodsley, 1759), addressed to his friend Samuel Richardson.

theory of the four ages of the human race and language. 'Poesie ist die Muttersprache des menschlichen Geschlechts'[21] is perhaps Hamann's best-known aphorism, adopted by Herder (*TB*, X, p. 23), who spoke of folk-song whenever he wanted to speak of the general nature of all poetry and whenever he wanted to refer to its living source.

Herder learned from Hamann to regard the Bible and Shakespeare as spontaneous and primitive creations, and their relationship is the key to understanding his predilection for the Orient. In the works of poets such as Homer, Ossian and Shakespeare—and in the Song of Songs too—the thoughts and feelings of entire peoples and races were expressed, rather than simply those of individuals. Poetry, language and history were basically one and the same, and so the whole destiny, historical development and meaning of a nation could be found in its speech or poetry: 'In der Sprache jedes Volkes finden wir die Geschichte desselben.'[22] Hamann concluded that a study of the origins of speech, poetry and religion was the key to an understanding of all the problems of life and history. It was for this reason that Hamann, and subsequently Herder, investigated the problems of the origin of speech, various questions arising from the early records of the Hebrews and other primitive peoples, and the problems connected with the origin and growth of the folk-lore and folk-poetry of the various nations. Herder's interest in these subjects is manifest throughout his work, but particularly in his *Volkslieder*, of which, as we have observed, his work on the Song of Songs was essentially a part, even though finally it was not published in the same volume.

Hamann saw a close relationship between nature and poetry, each being related to the other as a specific means of divine revelation. This was reflected in Herder's earlier writings, where the underlying concept was of literature and poetry as manifestations, either in a nation or an individual, of the power of God working in and through human beings. For him, it was the essence of all true poetry that it should be inspired by God.

---

21. 'Poetry is the mother tongue of the human race.' 'Aesthetica in Nuce', p. 197.

22. 'In the language of every nation we find its history.' Letter of 3 August 1759 from Hamann to G.E. Lindner, in Friedrich Roth (ed.), *Schriften* (8 vols.; Berlin and Augsburg: Reimer, 1821–43), I, p. 449.

Led by his basic conception of revelation, Hamann came to see a vital relationship between poetry and religion. Like religious faith, poetry was not an intellectual exercise, 'kein Werk der Vernunft',[23] but rather came from the heart. True poetry was filled with true feeling and with religious faith, which was also of the heart. As was the case with the Song of Songs, it was a product of nature which developed organically according to the laws of growth and under the influence of external circumstances such as climate, location, time, and historical conditions. Herder developed this idea in his *Fragmente*, and was enthusiastically supported by Hamann, who subjected the Bible, as poetry, to those natural laws of culture which he believed to govern all art, and thus opened up a whole world of possibilities which Herder was to exploit.

For Hamann, the fusion of poetry and religion was mythology, for all great poetry was either mythological or religious. Since the Bible was the most religious of books, and also the most poetic, God spoke to man in the fullest way through its imagery and emotion, and it was here that he revealed himself most vividly. Yet religion and poetry were blended as revelation not only in the Bible, but also in the work of Homer, Ossian, Shakespeare and primitive folk-poetry. The poet expressed the reality and activity of God both mythologically and symbolically. Thus for Hamann, and subsequently for Herder, the aesthetic and the religious were one. Indeed, Herder denied a supernatural character to the Bible, rejecting the view that it contained any revelation different from that contained in other similar writings, or that it was inspired in any way that would set it apart from other works of literature. True revelation in nature, history and art was poetry, and true poetry—such as the Song of Songs—was revelation.

Herder's reception of Johann Joachim Winckelmann also reinforced this sense of art as revelation. Winckelmann argued that it was useless to imitate the externalities of ancient literature, but that it was necessary instead to attempt to recapture its creative spirit. Herder appealed for another Winckelmann who could open up to the Germans the temple of Greek poetry and wisdom in the same way that Winckelmann himself had revealed the secrets of the Greeks in the area of plastic art: 'Ein Winckelmann in Absicht auf die Kunst konnte blos in Rom aufblühen; aber ein Winckelmann in Absicht der Dichter kann in Deutschland auch hervortreten, mit seinem Römischen Vorgänger einen großen Weg

---

23. 'Not a work of reason.' *Sokratische Denkwürdigkeiten*, in Nadler (ed.), *Sämtliche Werke*, II, pp. 57-82 (74).

zusammen thun' (*DL*, I, pp. 293-94).[24] Although Winckelmann introduced the genetic principle into the study of Greek art, he clung to the
absoluteness of Greek culture as an eternal ideal and absolute standard.
Herder generally received Winckelmann enthusiastically, but, as we
shall see, he refused to accept his thesis of an absolute and timeless
ideal (*DL*, II, pp. 119-24). Indeed, his preoccupation with the Song of
Songs was intended to discount the universal and promote the national
and culture-specific.

Herder's shipwreck in 1769 was also important in his development,
for this experience threw him into an elemental world, virtually neglected by the 'philosophes' and Rousseau, for example, in which
Homer, Ossian and the Bible alone were sufficient. Other important
inspirations for Herder's thinking here were Johann Jakob Bodmer's
publication of Middle High German poetry, Klopstock's glorification of
the German past (in which he confused Germans, Norsemen and
Celts),[25] and the publication of specimens from the *Edda* which were
printed in the supplement to Paul Henri Mallet's *Introduction à l'histoire de Dannemarc, où l'on traite de la religion, des loix, des moeurs
et des usages des anciens Danois* (Copenhagen: Berling, 1755), which
was translated into German between 1765 and 1769 as *Geschichte von
Dänemark*. These influences all helped to shape Herder's thinking on
primitive poetry, and were thus significant for his reception of the Song
of Songs.

Herder saw new possibilities in Klopstock's free rhythm, a natural,
original rhythm typically demonstrating an irregular number and quality
of syllables in a line.[26] He criticized Lessing's term 'künstliche Prosa'
('synthetic prose'), enthusiastically greeted Klopstock's 'neue glückliche Versart' ('new auspicious poetic form') (*DL*, I, p. 208), and
praised his lyric which brought German poetry closer to the tone of the

---

24. 'As far as art goes, a Winckelmann could only blossom in Rome; but as far
as poets are concerned, a Winckelmann may also emerge in Germany and walk a
good part of the way with his Roman predecessor.'

25. See Frederick Adler, *Herder and Klopstock: A Comparative Study* (New
York: Stechert, 1914), and Dieter Lohmeier, *Herder und Klopstock: Herders Auseinandersetzung mit der Persönlichkeit und dem Werk Klopstocks* (Ars Poetica:
Texte und Studien zur Dichtungslehre und Dichtkunst, 4; Bad Homburg: Gehlen,
1968).

26. See Katrin Maria Kohl, 'The Origins and Structure of Klopstock's Early
"Hymns" in Free Rhythms' (doctoral dissertation, University of London, 1988).

Hebrew psalm, and thus to the Song of Songs. This could free the Germans from 'vielem Uebel [...] und viel Aufschluß und Bequemlichkeit bringen' ('much ill [...] and bring much instruction and comfort') (*DL*, I, p. 208). Herder was one of the most ardent collectors of Klopstock's poems,[27] circulating them in manuscript form among his friends and admirers.[28] Caroline Herder wrote: 'Aus Klopstoks Messias die schönsten menschlichen Scenen, aus Klopstoks Oden, aus Kleist (seinem und meinem Lieblingsdichter), aus den Minnesängern, las er uns vor.'[29] Herder read the odes in conjunction with the Minnesänger because in both he felt the breath of that spirit which he hoped to reawaken in German hearts, and it was significant that he published a mediaeval translation of the Song of Songs with his own work.[30] Herder considered Klopstock to be the first poet to give Germany an appreciation of the poetic merits of the Hebrew psalm, and it was his initial hope that Klopstock's lyrical genius would lead to the creation of a German poetry which would correspond in originality to that of the Hebrews, as typified by the Song of Songs (*EP*, XII, p. 227).[31] Apart from Luther's translation of the Bible, Klopstock's *Messias* was Germany's first classical work of literature, for he had recreated the poetic language of his native land (*AD*, XXIV, p. 221). Klopstock's preoccupation with biblical poetry thus acted as a vital catalyst on Herder's own thinking. Much later, in *Terpsichore*, Herder offered an appreciation of Klopstock's classical metres:

27. For a list of copies of Klopstock's odes in Herder's *Nachlaß*, and for a list of Klopstock editions in Herder's possession, see Lohmeier, *Herder und Klopstock*, pp. 203-205.

28. See Emil Gottfried Herder, *Johann Gottfried von Herder's Lebensbild: Sein chronologisch geordneter Briefwechsel*, (3 vols.; Erlangen: Bläsing, 1846), I, pp. 2 and 116, and III/1, pp. 157, 224, 276, 308 and 325.

29. 'He read aloud to us the most wondrous human scenes from Klopstock's *Messias*, as well as from Klopstock's odes, from Kleist (his and my favourite poet) and from the Minnesänger.' *Erinnerungen aus dem Leben Johann Gottfried's von Herder* (ed. Johann Georg Müller; 2 vols.; Tübingen: Cotta, 1820), I, p. 151 (see also *SWS*, XX–XXII).

30. Emil Gottfried Herder, *Lebensbild*, III, pp. 1, 89 and 157.

31. For more of Herder's views on Klopstock see also *DL*, I, pp. 165, 208, 210, and 258; *TS*, XXVII, p. 172; *BH*, XVIII, p. 118; *AD*, XXIV, p. 202; and Düntzer and Herder (eds.), *Aus Herders Nachlaß: Ungedruckte Briefe*, II, p. 14, and III, pp. 81, 125, 270, 344 and 458.

Er hat uns in diesen Gedanken- und Empfindungsweisen der Alten für unsre eigensten und reinsten Empfindungen gleichsam eine neue Sprache geschaffen, und damit dem innigsten Gemüth eine Bildung, der Seele eine Selbsterkenntniß, dem Herzen einen Ausdruck, der Sprache eine Zartheit, Fülle und Wohlklang verliehen, von der man vor ihm nicht träumte (XXVII, p. 172).[32]

However, although Herder initially regarded Klopstock's poetry as the most natural and original, he was also critical of his work as being, ultimately, an imitation of a foreign model: 'Aber zu viel Morgen-ländische, Biblische Sprache, als daß sie immer nach unsern Ideen bestimmt gnug seyn sollte: gewisse Morgenländische Wiederholungen, die statt zu seufzen jähnen machen' (*DL*, I, p. 268).[33]

Herder's whole stance stemmed from the power he saw in poetry and how impossible he believed it was to separate it from its own peculiar cultural background. He rejected the imitation of a foreign (Oriental) style in contemporary poetry, and consequently was unable to accept Klopstock's use of Oriental devices in his poetry (*DL*, I, pp. 277-84), for each work of art was 'national, ein Kind der Umstände, des Locals und der Zeiten' ('national, a child of its own particular circumstances, environment and age') (*AD*, XXIV, p. 229). It was of paramount impor-tance for the understanding of a text to be able to study and interpret it 'gesund, d.i. local und Zeitmäßig' ('soundly, that is, according to its own particular environment and age') (*AD*, XXIV, p. 352). By adopting such a procedure, it was Herder's hope that he could rescue the Bible, and thus the Song of Songs, from the mocking of those rationalists attached to the Enlightenment.

Herder's View of German Poetry

Herder's view of poetry was a cosmic one. He did not regard it as the monopoly of the cultured few. The *Edda*, Ossian, Homer, Shakespeare and the Old Testament were all divinely inspired records of the voice of

32. 'In these ancient ways of thinking and feeling, he created for us, as it were, a new language for our very own, purest feelings, and thus bestowed a refinement upon our innermost spirit, a self-knowledge upon our souls, an expression upon our hearts, and a tenderness, fullness and harmony upon our language which, before him, were unimaginable.'

33. 'But there is too much Oriental and biblical language, rather than it always being sufficiently determined according to our own ideas; particular Oriental repe-titions, which cause us to yawn rather than sigh.'

creative nature. German poetry could be revived only by emulating the originality of other literatures, that is, by basing itself on the memorials of its own native past, and the songs and legends of its own people. Yet Germany's literature was culturally subjected to Classical and French models:

> O das verwünschte Wort: Classisch! [...] Das Wort: Classisch! ists gewesen, das den Ausdruck vom Gedanken, und den Gedanken von der ihn erzeugenden Gelegenheit gesondert, das uns gewöhnet hat, nach Horaz Exercitien zu machen, und ihn in seiner Sprache übertreffen zu wollen. Dies Wort wars, das alle wahre Bildung nach den Alten, als nach lebenden Mustern, verdrängete. [...] Dies Wort hat manches Genie unter einen Schutt von Worten vergraben, seinen Kopf zu einem Chaos von fremden Ausdrücken gemacht, und auf ihn die Last einer toten Sprache, wie einen Mühlstein gewälzet: es hat dem Vaterlande blühende Fruchtbäume entzogen; da stehen sie nun auf fremdem Boden, und trauren mit halbverwelkter Blüthe und sinkenden Blättern: statt daß sie uns Bäume hätten seyn sollen, unter denen ihr Geschlecht wohnen könnte (*DL*, I, p. 412).[34]

A whole generation of German writers was imprisoned by the laws of the Greeks and Romans, and it was Herder's aim to demonstrate that these laws possessed no universal validity. He argued for the promotion of national culture instead, for literature must be judged in the light of historical development rather than by absolute standards. He loved that which was primitive and spontaneous, and such was his reading of the Song of Songs. He had a passion for things German, yet for him 'Teutonic' meant that which was native and spontaneous rather than racial or nationalistic:

> Genösse jede Nation, in ihre Gränzen eingeschlossen, und an den Boden ihres Landes geheftet, die Gaben der Natur aus dem Schoos ihrer Erde,

34. 'Oh that confounded word: Classical! [...] It is the word: Classical! which has separated the expression from the thought, and the thought from the occasion which engendered it, which has accustomed us to do exercises in the manner of Horace and to endeavour to surpass him in his own language. It was this word that drove out all true development in the manner of the ancients, as living examples. [...] This word has buried many a genius beneath the rubble of words, made his head into a confusion of foreign expressions, and laid upon him the burden of a dead language like a millstone. It has deprived the fatherland of blossoming fruit trees; there they now stand on foreign soil and grieve with half-withered bloom and falling leaves; instead of being trees beneath which their race might be able to dwell.'

ohne von andern Völkern den Tribut des Reichthums wiederrechtlich zu fodern; so würde vielleicht niemand das Bürgerrecht seines Vaterlandes gegen ausländische Vorzüge vertauschen dörfen (*FS*, I, p. 3).[35]

According to Herder, a nation's own tongue possessed charms surpassing those of other languages, and it was wrong for German writers to be shackled to foreign literatures at the expense of their own (*FS*, I, p. 5). This had clearly not been the case with the writers of Hebrew poetry, and hence the attraction for Herder of the Song of Songs: 'Die Homere, die Ciceronen, die Voltäre, die Popens—waren sie es in erlernten Sprachen?' ('The Homers, Ciceros, Voltaires and Popes— were they such in acquired languages?') (*FS*, I, p. 6). Indeed, he criticized as 'ein lächerlicher Allwisser' ('a ridiculous know-all') (*FS*, I, p. 7) the expert in foreign languages who hardly understood the poets of his own language.

Herder complained that in every German state, prose was the language of the writers, while poetry was an art form: 'Wir in unsrer matten, unbestimmten [...] Prose wiederholen und prosaisiren so lange, bis wir endlich nichts mehr sagen' (*JR*, IV, p. 460).[36] The more poetry became art, the further removed it became from nature (*DL*, I, p. 154). In other words, the language of poetry should be as close to nature as possible. It should not be logicized, rich, chaotic or rational, for thus it would lack poetic authenticity. Speaking of his own role, Herder claimed: 'Ich wäre nicht ein Tintenfaß von gelehrter Schriftstellerei, nicht ein Wörterbuch von Künsten und Wißenschaften geworden, die ich nicht gesehen habe und nicht verstehe: ich wäre nicht ein Repositorium voll Papiere und Bücher geworden, das nur in die Studierstube gehört' (*JR*, IV, p. 347).[37]

---

35. 'If every nation, confined within its borders and fixed to the earth of its own country, were to enjoy the gifts of nature from the womb of its own soil, without unlawfully demanding from other nations the tribute of wealth, then perhaps nobody would exchange the civic rights of his native land for any foreign advantages.'

36. 'In our dull-sounding, indistinct [...] prose, we repeat and write unimaginatively for so long, until finally we have nothing more to say.'

37. 'I would not have become an inkwell of erudite literary writing, nor a dictionary of arts and sciences which I have not seen and do not understand: I would not have become a repository full of papers and books which only belongs in the study.'

Doubtless influenced by the inversions prevalent in primitive poetry, particularly in Hebrew poetry and thus in Ossian, Herder regarded inversion as characteristic of that which was natural, primitive and poetic. Thus he discouraged the removal of inversion from true, natural poetry: 'Je mehr man [...] die Inversionen abschaffet, je mehr bürgerliche und abstrakte Wörter eingeführet werden, je mehr Regeln eine Sprache erhält: desto vollkommener wird sie zwar, aber desto mehr verliert die wahre Poesie' (*DL*, I, p. 154).[38] Each restriction placed on inversion lessened the charm of a language (*DL*, I, p. 155): 'Alle alte Sprachen, die ursprünglich sind, und das Gepräge der ersten sinnlichen Lebensart führen, sind voll Inversionen' ('All ancient languages, which are original and which bear the impression of the first sensual behaviour, are full of inversions') (*DL*, I, p. 192). Primitive man produced such poetry because he expressed his passions and feelings without inhibition: 'Jede Sprache hat ihren Eigensinn; [...] die Inversionen überhaupt' ('Every language has its own peculiar characteristics; [...] especially the inversions') (*DL*, I, p. 190). Inversion was important for Herder's own tricks of language, and I shall note in Chapter 6 that in his own translations of the Song of Songs he attempted to maintain many of the inversions found in the original Hebrew poetry. In all his critical works he asserted that inversion was characteristic of primitive poetry, and by using it he attempted to show that his modern German translation of the Song of Songs could be as primitively authentic as ancient poetry.

Compared with the ancients and their more primitive languages, the poetry of his time was more for reflection than for appealing to the senses and imagination (*DL*, I, p. 158). In contrast to the Enlightenment's view of poetry held, for example, by Moses Mendelssohn, it was Herder's contention that true poetry was a necessary and natural expression of the individual. Its real purpose was not to instruct, nor even to entertain, but it was essentially the immediate expression of feeling, a result of sensual, natural necessity. Original, primitive poetry represented the individuality of a nation, including the language and culture peculiar to it (*VL*, XXV, pp. 313-14).

German natural philosophy was tied to bookish learning, particularly Latin books (*DL*, I, p. 167). In Herder's view, Latin should remain the

38. 'The more one [...] does away with inversions, the more common and abstract words are introduced, the more rules a language contains, the more perfect it will indeed be, but the more does true poetry lose.'

tool of scholarship, but should not become the language of taste, of the arts or of beauty—for otherwise it would rob a whole nation of writers using their own mother tongue. It should not be the ruling language of poetry nor the language of those who intended to educate by means of their writings (*DL*, I, p. 413). Herder was of the opinion that bookish learning was a demoralizing snare. It was the result of rationalism ('Verstand'), but truth came from personal experience. Herder stressed the spontaneity of individual feeling and non-conformity to an objective pattern. He argued for the genuineness of experience, and underlined the necessity of empathy with another culture ('Einfühlung'), yet he condemned blatant imitation. It was his aim to penetrate into the inner-most spirit of foreign poetry, and thus to interpret to his own people the finest, the grandest and the most delicate productions of other nations. This is an important point as far as Herder's study of the Song of Songs is concerned.

The German language was restricted to the role of 'Büchersprache' ('bookish language') (*DL*, I, p. 167), but its poetry would gain nothing from the language of German philosophers. Just as the ancients could not have translated every nuance of eighteenth-century German texts with their 'Bücher- und Kathedersprache' ('bookish and professorial language'), so it was impossible for German writers to imitate truly the literatures of ages past (*DL*, I, p. 171). They should still learn from the ancients, however, for all ancient languages, like all ancient nations and their works of art in general, possessed 'mehr Charakteristisches als das, was neuer ist' ('more of that which is distinctive, than does that which is more recent') (*DL*, I, p. 173). Thus German must be able to learn more from them than from those with which it was more closely related.

Herder contrasted those epochs and places where 'die Natur Poesie spricht' ('nature speaks the language of poetry') with those where 'die Kunst Poesie ordnet' ('art regulates poetry') (*AM*, VI, p. 43). The Ger-man language was at a stage in its development where there was no separation between poetic and prosaic forms. Following Hamann, Herder divided language into four ages. Its inarticulate beginnings were the innocence and spontaneity of childhood which appealed to him. In its youth, the age of poetry, linguistic symbols became more ordered and rhythmical, and the first signs of abstract thought began to appear in the form of imagery and metaphor with the emotional basis still intact. Its manhood revealed itself as the age of prose, when poetry had

Paradisal Love

ceased to be a direct expression of nature and had rather become art, and its old age was the period of philosophy.[39] Herder complained that German literature was already in its period of manhood, having been denied the joy and freshness of the poetry of youth. Its native strength remained untapped. Herder desired the recapture of this age of youth, the age of the emotional and poetic, and he called for classical literature to be dislodged from its position of absolute authority. Poetry was the product of national culture and its peculiarities and customs, but it also helped to form them. It stemmed from one nation alone and was meant for that one nation only. Thus a people without a national poetry, such as the Germans, was a people almost without character (*TS*, XXVII, p. 180). National culture should be studied in the light of poetry rather than the other way round. It was for this reason that Herder chose to share with his fellow Germans the natural beauty of the Song of Songs as a prime example of that national poetry which could similarly arise from German roots.

Herder's Reception of Shakespeare and Ossian

Although Herder condemned Germany's own literature, he praised English literature, which, unlike Germany's, was so rich, spontaneous and original because it was based on its own folk-song heritage: 'Chaucer und Spenser, Shakespeare und Milton [...] waren Enthusiasten der alten Lieder, und der Beweis wäre nicht schwer, daß das Lyrische, Mythische, Dramatische und Epische, wodurch sich die Englische Dichtkunst national unterscheidet, aus diesen alten Resten alter Sänger und Dichter entstanden sey' (*AV*, XXV, p. 8).[40] Herder called for a German Chaucer, Spenser and Shakespeare to enable Germany to take similar advantage of its own folk-poetry (*VÄ*, IX, pp. 525-26). A German Shakespeare could only be born of German folk-song.

39. Compare Herder's four ages of language with the rabbinic view that Solomon wrote the Song of Songs in his youth, the book of Proverbs in his manhood and the book of Ecclesiastes in his old age.

40. 'Chaucer and Spenser, Shakespeare and Milton [...] were enthusiasts of ancient songs, and it would not be hard to prove that the lyrical, the mythical, the dramatic and the epic, which nationally distinguishes English poetry, arose from these old remnants of ancient singers and poets.'

English literature—like that of the Greeks or the Hebrews—was independent and original, imitating nothing outside of itself. Its origin and purpose were native to itself. Shakespeare was a poet of the people, expressing their thoughts and sentiments. True poetry must remain inextricably linked to the spirit of the nation and culture which gave it birth. Thus Herder's celebration of English national poetry not only pointed forward to a new German national poetry, but it also led back to an ancient Hebrew literature as epitomized by the Song of Songs.

Given that Herder classed Shakespeare's work alongside the Bible, it was fitting that in his Shakespeare essay he should refer to Shakespeare as 'Göttersohn' ('son of the gods') (*AK*, V, p. 218), 'Schöpfer' ('creator') (*AK*, V, p. 223) and 'dramatischer Gott' ('dramatic god') (*AK*, V, p. 227). For Herder, the function of the poet was to make known God's purpose, and to interpret the universe and nature by recreating them and making them live again. Shakespeare taught Herder that the role of the poet was to lead mankind to an understanding of the preordained plan of the world. Every literature must be judged in and for itself and was not answerable to any other. For example, Herder maintained that Shakespeare could only be understood against the background of his own age and country, 'nach [...] Geschichte, nach Zeitgeist, Sitten, Meinungen, Sprache, Nationalvorurtheilen, Traditionen, und Liebhabereien' ('according to [...] history, spirit of the age, customs, opinions, language, national prejudices, traditions and fancies') (*AK*, V, p. 217). Clearly the same was equally true of a Hebrew folk-literature. To compare Shakespeare and the Greeks and to judge the one by the other was to be guilty of folly and literary vandalism: 'Wie ist der Boden? worauf ist er zubereitet? was ist in ihn gesäet? was sollte er tragen können?' ('What is the soil like? Upon what has it been prepared? With what has it been sown? What should it be able to support?') (*AK*, V, p. 217). Herder thus demanded a return to the historical context of a work of literature, a significant point as far as the Bible and the Song of Songs were concerned.

Herder stressed the importance of taking into consideration the age which formed Homer (*KW*, III, p. 200). The same was true of Shakespeare, and thus, by extension, of the Song of Songs. The conditions in which Shakespeare wrote, for example, were unique to him and could not be reproduced: 'Nimm dieser Pflanze ihren Boden, Saft und Kraft, und pflanze sie in die Luft: nimm diesem Menschen Ort, Zeit, individuelle Bestandheit—du hast ihm Othem und Seele genommen' (*AK*,

V, p. 225).[41] With such a revolutionary approach to Shakespeare, Herder prepared the way for a new age of Shakespearean study and appreciation.

Herder argued that the English had rapaciously gathered, printed, used and read their own songs and melodies, and yet if the Germans, 'wir überfüllte, satte, klassische Deutsche' ('we overfilled, satiated, classical Germans'), were to print songs as Allan Ramsay and Thomas Percy had done, then 'höre, was unsre geschmackvolle, klassische Kunstrichter sagen!' ('listen to what our tasteful, classical critics would say!') (*VÄ*, IX, p. 527). All the poetry discovered by the English was, like the Song of Songs, 'voll lebendigen Geistes, im vollen Kreise des Volks entsprungen, unter ihnen lebend und würkend' ('full of living spirit, with its roots in the very midst of the people, living and functioning among them') (*VÄ*, IX, p. 531). Herder was particularly attracted to that literature which stemmed from the people, was part of their existence, and exerted considerable influence on them. In Germany such literature was still waiting to be found, and the Song of Songs was to be a catalyst for its discovery.

Similarly impressed by the Scottish poetry of Ossian, Herder wished that there were a Macpherson in the Tyrol or in Bavaria (*VÄ*, IX, p. 527): 'Der wichtigste Fund unsres Jahrhunderts [...] sind die alten Celtischen, Schottischen oder Hersischen Gedichte die Macpherson herausgegeben' ('The most important discovery of our century [...] is the old Celtic, Scottish or Hersic poems which were published by Macpherson') (*BL*, IX, p. 542). Although the works of Ossian were actually written by James MacPherson in the eighteenth century, and their publication as original Celtic poetry was nothing more than a hoax, it is of special importance to remember that Ossian was regarded by Herder initially as being from a culture which was as ancient as Greece and yet—unlike German poetry—was in no way indebted to its literature. Herder had no hesitation in asserting that Ossian was, in his own way and against the background of his own age, just as great and important as Homer.[42] Clearly the same was true of the Song of Songs. For a reading of Ossian, Herder recommended the English translation, or else Johann N.C. Michael Denis's German translation *Die Gedichte Ossians*

---

41. 'Take from this plant its soil, its sap and strength, and plant it in the air; take from this man environment, age, individual durability—and you have deprived him of breath and soul.'

42. See Gillies, *Herder und Ossian*, pp. 121-24.

eines alten celtischen Dichters (Vienna: von Trattrern, 1768–69), with Hugh Blair's *A Critical Dissertation on the Poems of Ossian, the Son of Fingal* (London: Becket and De Hondt, 1763) to hand. Herder was particularly impressed by the 'Stärke der Empfindung, Größe des Charakters und der Bilderdenkart' ('strength of feeling, greatness of character and imagination') of the poems (*BL*, IX, p. 543). He found them gentle, tender, simple and recurrent, but strong, true and relevant. Most of all, they exuded Nature. Ossian, thus conceived, provided an important point of reference for the Song of Songs, for Herder spoke of both in the same breath: 'Selbst Oßian, er mag nun ächt oder glücklich nachgeahmt seyn, singt, wie alle Liebeslieder einfältiger, unverkünstelter Völker in Töne des Hohenliedes' (VIII, p. 591).[43]

In *Vom Geist der Ebräischen Poesie*, written after *Lieder der Liebe*, Herder continued to bracket Ossian (and Homer) with the poetry of the Old Testament, thereby hoping to prove to the Germans the value of Hebrew poetry. That the poetry of the Hebrews was great because it was like Ossian may seem a strange argument, but it was one with which Herder hoped to convert aberrant rationalists to a proper respect for the Bible. Indeed, the Bible had provided Macpherson with his model for Ossian, and it is no surprise that Herder saw an affinity between the Bible and Ossian in brevity of style, inversion, parallelism, imagery, repetition, boldness of metaphor and irregular progression of ideas—devices all valid for the poetry of nature, and particularly for the biblical poetry which Macpherson had imitated and which Herder found so appealing.

For Herder, Ossian served to place the poetic beauties of the Bible in a clearer light, since he was well known in Germany at the time. People

---

43. 'Even Ossian, whether genuine or fortuitously imitated, sings in the manner of the Song of Songs, as do all love songs of simple peoples who lack artificiality.' Clark claims that Herder did not repeat this comment of 1776 in his *Lieder der Liebe* of 1778, probably for fear of being accused of extreme heterodoxy, and yet he argues that 'this deleted sentence is the key to Herder's real opinion in the matter'. He further asserts that the work of 1778 contains no mention of Ossian, although he accepts that his ghost is present in every sentence of the commentary ('Herder, Percy, and the *Song of Songs*', pp. 1097-98). Clark's comment is clearly due to a careless reading of the 1778 publication in which Herder actually maintained that 'selbst Oßian und alle Völker in der ersten Einfalt, singen sie Liebe, so ists immer, wie aus dem Hohenliede' ('even when Ossian and all peoples in their first stage of innocence sing of love, it is always as if from the Song of Songs') (VIII, p. 529). In essence, therefore, no sentence had been deleted, as Clark maintains.

of all ages would love the Bible as much as Ossian (or Homer) if only they knew what it contained (*EP*, XI, p. 241). By persuading people to read Ossian, Herder saw a means of promoting the Bible as poetry, bringing what he regarded as the epitome of natural, primitive folk-poetry closer to their thinking.

The importance for Herder of both Shakespeare and Ossian cannot be overestimated. Caroline Herder wrote that 'die Bekanntschaft mit diesem Dichter [Shakespeare] und mit Ossian entwickelte seine eigen-thümliche Sympathie und vorherrschende Liebe zur einfach-rührenden Natursprache der Volkslieder, deren Keim durch die morgenländische Poesie schon in früher Jugend in ihm geweckt geworden war'.[44] Genius was to express the 'original' feeling of an epoch and country, and as such Shakespeare was the supremely divine genius. Herder wanted to create the 'Gefühlsmensch' ('person of feeling') as opposed to the 'Vernunftmensch' ('person of reason'), and in Ossian and Shakespeare he saw a unity of poetic thought and expression in word and rhythm, and an experience genuinely felt.

In *Über die Ode*, it was Herder's plea that 'Shakespears Schriften und die Nordische Edda, der Barden und Skaldrer Gesänge müßen unsere Poesie bestimmen' ('Shakespeare's writings, the Nordic Edda, the songs of the bards and the skalds, must direct our own poetry') (XXXII, p. 69). German literature was to be rid of foreign influences. The poet was to be 'Schöpfer eines Volkes um sich: er gibt ihnen eine Welt zu sehen und hat ihre Seelen in seiner Hand, sie dahin zu führen' ('creator of a nation around him; he gives them a world to view, and he has their souls in his hand so that he can lead them to it') (*WD*, VIII, p. 433). In other words, he was to create within his own language and culture rather than to imitate others or to be imitated by them. A nation's human soul was bared most freely in poetry of imagination and feeling (*BH*, XVIII, p. 58). True poetry was inextricably linked to the nature of the poet, which in turn was conditioned by culture and nationality. Thus, only that poetry which was produced within a given cultural and national setting—such as the Song of Songs—could be genuine.

---

44. 'The acquaintance with this poet [Shakespeare] and with Ossian developed his peculiar sympathy with and prevailing love for the simple, moving natural lan-guage of folk-songs, the embryo of which had been awoken in his early youth by Oriental poetry.' *Erinnerungen*, I, p. 64.

Herder's View of Homer and the Greeks

The same appeal to national origins and national spirit occurred when Herder came to speak of the so-called classical models. In his essay *Homer und Ossian*, the difference between Klopstock, Ossian and Shakespeare on the one hand, and Pindar, Homer and Sophocles on the other, was related to their difference in climate and cultural background (XVIII, pp. 446-62).[45] Each poet expressed the culture, traditions, religion, history, manners, mythology, ideas and sentiments of his own age and time. After all, writing in *Vom Wunderbaren bei der Mosaischen Gesetzgebung und Reife* particularly of the poetry of the Hebrews, Herder enquired: 'Warum müßte zu jeder Zeit alles zugehen, wie es jetzt bei uns zugeht?' ('Why in every age should everything happen just as it does in our own time?') (XII, p. 312).

Those Germans who were still shackled to the Greek model as the perfect ideal were reminded by Herder that even the Greeks were once a primitive race. Even in the blossoming of their best literature there was far more of Nature than the classical scholars of the eighteenth century had found. Homer 'sang aus alten Sagen, und sein Hexameter war nichts als Sangweise der griechischen Romanze' ('sang from old sagas, and his hexameter was merely the style of Greek ballads') (*BL*, IX, p. 534). For Herder, Homer was the greatest 'Volksdichter' ('folk poet'). He did not follow the rules of Aristotle, but rather sang about what he had seen and heard. Unlike German poetry, his songs were not written down on pieces of paper and sold in bookshops. They were preserved in the hearts of the people. 'Homers Vers [...] ist kein Schulen- und Kunsthexameter' ('Homer's verse [...] is not an academic, artificial hexameter') (*VL*, XXV, p. 314), but rather was produced in the natural rhythm of the Greek language, and as such was loved by the people. Homer was 'immer hörbar und [...] immer verständlich: die Bilder treten vors Auge' ('always audible and [...] always intelligible; the images dance before our very eyes') (*VL*, XXV, p. 315). The same was true, in Herder's view, of the Song of Songs, and it was such spontaneity that German poetry should try to capture.

Herder saw poetry as the 'Blüthe der Cultur und Humanität nach Nationen und Zeiten' ('flowering of culture and humanity according to

---

45. This essay was originally published in Friedrich von Schiller (ed.), *Die Horen* (Tübingen: Cotta, 1795–97), Zehntes Stück, 1795, pp. 86-107.

nations and ages') (*BH*, XVIII, p. 6), containing the sum total of all human effort. It was universal in Greece and must become so once again, given that all poetry was essentially universal, as well as being essentially local:

> Wenn Poesie die Blüthe des menschlichen Geistes, der menschlichen Sitten, ja ich möchte sagen das Ideal unsrer Vorstellungsart, die Sprache des Gesammtwunsches und Sehnens der Menschheit ist: so, dünkt mich, ist der glücklich, dem diese Blüthe vom Gipfel des Stammes der auf-geklärtesten Nation zu brechen vergönnt ist (*BH*, XVIII, p. 57).[46]

Herder developed in his *Fragmente* a universal view of literature in which he attempted to overcome the primacy of the classical Greek and Latin poetic traditions, and to move away from the generally accepted imitation of such literature in Germany. Herder pleaded for something in German literature that would bear the universal character of poetry, thus achieving what he noted enviously had already been achieved by the Hebrews, the Greeks and the English. He wanted to make German literature self-conscious of its own poverty. Poetry was an outpouring of feeling by those not perverted by false values, and thus the art poetry of his time was not true poetry. It bore no relation to Nature, nor to the feelings and sufferings of mankind.

The claim that cultures were relative and national was a leading theme in Herder's works on literature and art, its underlying principle being that of organic growth. Prior to Herder's *Fragmente* and *Kritische Wälder*, critics had taken it for granted that there was an absolute in art. For them, this was usually found either in Greek art or in the new French Classicism. Innovators such as Voltaire never thought of over-throwing these rules, but simply sought to improve technique and to exploit new themes and situations within the rules. Although Lessing, for example, was opposed to French Classicism, he tried to justify Shakespeare by pleading that in his way and in spirit he had fulfilled the rules more perfectly than Racine or Corneille had done, and was there-fore the true successor of the Greeks.[47]

---

46. 'If poetry is the flowering of the human spirit, of human morals, indeed I would suggest the ideal of our imaginative abilities, the language of the collective desire and yearning of the human race; then it seems to me that the one who is per-mitted to pluck this blossom from the top of the stem of the most enlightened nation is indeed fortunate.'

47. See Lessing's *Briefe, die neueste Litteratur betreffend*, 1759–65, 17th Let-ter, 16 February 1759, in Karl Lachmann (ed.), *Sämtliche Schriften* (23 vols.; ed.

It was no coincidence that Herder published his *Lieder der Liebe* at about the same time—and through the same house—as he published his *Volkslieder*. Both works are examples of his plea that important literature existed before and at the same time as the Greeks, who, as we have noted above, were therefore not the fathers of all European literature, but merely of that culture which critics viewed as the only culture worth handing down by tradition (*DL*, II, p. 112). For Herder it was not true that no literature was as good as that of the Greeks. Primitive barbarians were just as capable of giving poetical expression to their sorrows, and Ossian—as well as Hebrew poetry—represented a new element to be added to the conception of the Greeks held by Lessing and Winckelmann, both of whom had said that the Greeks should be imitated—a position held by Herder to be undesirable, and even impossible.

Herder considered the Greeks in their historical perspective and no more. He was more interested in their natural creativity than the means which they used, shifting the emphasis from the intellect to the emotions, from conscious art to unconscious impulse. Spontaneity and lyricism were essential ingredients which, along with the cultivation and communication of passion, were to lead to the 'Sturm und Drang' movement. In his view, Greek culture was not to be regarded as an original creation, but as the bringing forth, under favourable conditions, of something already potentially present in the human spirit. He held that the seeds which bore such abundant fruit in Greece even arrived there from without: 'Daß Griechenlands Samenkörner der Kultur anders woher erhalten, ist […] unläugbar' ('It is […] undeniable that the seeds of Greece's culture were obtained from elsewhere') (*AP*, V, p. 498). It was Herder's wish to dethrone antiquity as the highest authority in poetry.

For Herder, the application of rational judgments to literature in accordance with some absolute was meaningless. All works of literature were natural phenomena and varied according to the genius which expressed itself and to the circumstances which had conditioned that expression. Speech and literature were living things and could not be mummified for posterity. It was Herder's view, for example, that people in the North tended to be harder than those in the South, although perhaps with a deeper sense of moral responsibility. The South made people livelier. In *Homer und Ossian*, we read: 'Dagegen aber bleiben

Franz Muncker; Leipzig: Göschen, 3rd edn, 1886–1907), VIII, pp. 41-44.

vielleicht auch Empfindungen unerweckt, die nur der nordische Himmel, einsame Geselligkeit, Noth und Gefahr ausbilden konnten' ('Yet on the other hand, maybe feelings remain dormant which could only be cultivated by the northern sky, solitary company, adversity and danger') (XVIII, p. 456). Thus Herder stressed that drama in Greece developed in a way that it could not possibly have developed in the North, and vice versa (*AK*, V, pp. 209-10).

Herder expanded his argument in a way particularly appropriate to the exotic poetry of the Song of Songs, arguing that the two main factors important for a correct understanding of any work of art were the temporal and physical conditions surrounding its execution, for culture sprang into being 'Ort- und Zeitmäßig' ('according to time and place') (*BH*, XVIII, p. 249). In order to make an adequate evaluation of a nation or culture, the critic must return to its own time, geographical position and peculiar way of thinking and feeling. He must observe how people are educated and how they live. He must see the objects they see and the things they love. He must consider the air, the sky, the physical build of the people, the way they dance and the kind of music they enjoy. Ultimately, 'man muß wieder ein Morgenländer werden, um es sinnlich zu fühlen' ('one must become an Oriental again in order to feel it sensually') (*AM*, VI, p. 12). Similarly, anyone translating from Greek literature should learn how to think and write like a Greek, 'mit starkem und innigem Gefühl des Schönen, nicht in dem süßen Geschmack unsrer Zeit' ('with a powerful, inner sense of the beautiful, not according to the sugared taste of our own age') (*DL*, II, p. 142), and the translator of Ossian 'sollte Celte geworden seyn!' ('ought to have become a Celt!') (*DR*, V, p. 325).[48] In this regard, we note how Goethe followed Herder's views in 1819:

> Wer das Dichten will verstehen
> Muß in's Land der Dichtung gehen

48. As Kraus puts it: 'Herder folgte dem Ruf *ad fontes*. [...] Denn Reuchlin hatte gelehrt, von den Juden müsse man lernen; jüdische Tradition müsse aufgenommen werden, wenn man das hebräische Alte Testament lesen und verstehen will: Mit den Juden ein Jude werden, um das Buch der Juden zu verstehen' ('Herder followed the call *ad fontes*. [...] For Reuchlin had taught that one should learn from the Jews; Jewish tradition must be absorbed if one wishes to read and understand the Hebrew Old Testament. With the Jews, become a Jew in order to understand the book of the Jews'), 'Herders alttestamentliche Forschungen', p. 63. This is an important point to bear in mind as far as the Song of Songs is concerned.

Wer den Dichter will verstehen
Muß in Dichters Lande gehen.[49]

It was Herder's belief that climate greatly affected the peculiarities and disposition of a nation. He argued that tastes changed according to where a people lived and the climate which it enjoyed,[50] for climate regulated a people's senses and formed the characteristics peculiar to it (*ZB*, XVI, p. 222): 'Der Morgenländer liebt, wie in Kleidern, so auch in Sprüchen, helle Farben; sein heiterer Himmel verlangt dieselbe' ('The Oriental loves bright colours, both in clothes and in sayings: his clear sky demands such') (*ZB*, XVI, p. 20). He also held that climate and landscape greatly influenced the kind of religion practised (*EP*, XI, p. 249, and *DL*, I, pp. 264 and 265). It should not surprise us, then, that Herder should allow for the influence of climate on language: 'Es schuffen sich tausend Sprachen nach dem Clima und den Sitten von tausend Nationen' ('A thousand languages arose from the climate and customs of a thousand peoples') (*FS*, I, p. 1). It was obvious from its sound, for example, that the German language developed beneath northern skies (*DL*, II, p. 31). In the development of language, Herder made allowance for external circumstances such as climate, diet and customs (*US*, V, pp. 125 and 131), for 'nichts folgt so sehr den Zeiten und Sitten, als Sprache und Tonkunst' ('nothing follows times and customs as much as do language and music') (*EP*, XII, p. 248).

Not only was the general shape of a language formed by climate, then, but even the different genres of literary art stemming from that language were influenced by it: 'Die Poesie jedes Volks richtet sich nach dem Clima, in dem sie ist gebildet worden' ('The poetry of every nation is guided by the climate in which it has been formed') (*EP*, XI, p. 247). Herder regarded the alliteration of old Germanic poetry as a result of the northern climate in which it was produced. Thus, the Greek idyll was formed according to the Greek climate, as well as the character, way of life and language of the people (*AD*, XXIII, p. 300). He argued that a particular climate produced its own particular works of art, which did not have the same effect when uprooted and moved to a

---

49. 'Whoever wants to understand poetry / Must go to the land of poetry / Whoever wants to understand the poet / Must go to the land of the poet.' *Noten und Abhandlungen zu besserem Verständniß des West-östlichen Divans*, *WW*, VII, p. 1.

50. See *Iduna oder der Apfel der Verjüngung* (XVIII, p. 499), also published in Schiller's *Die Horen*, Erstes Stück, 1796, pp. 1-28.

different environment. For example, Greek works of art were foreign to
the German climate (*BH*, XVII, p. 371), and it was the climate that hin-
dered the renaissance of Greek taste in Germany (*UG*, V, p. 650): 'Eine
Griechische Seele war gewiß von andrer Gestalt und Bauart, als eine
Seele, die unsre Zeit bildet' ('A Greek soul was certainly of different
form and build from a soul shaped by our own age') (*KW*, III, p. 199).
The poetry of the Greeks was conditioned by their sky, their constitu-
tional freedoms, their passions and their way of life, their government,
and their thought, as well as by the respect they had for their poets and
sages (*DL*, I, p. 294): 'Die Poesie richtet sich nach Zeiten und dem
Character des Dichters' ('Poetry is guided by the times and character of
the poet') (*EP*, XII, p. 100). It was impossible to carry Greek literature
over into eighteenth-century Germany with its very different customs
and language, although to attempt to do so was the tradition of the day
(*DL*, I, p. 178). It was a product of its own *Sitz im Leben*, as was also
the Song of Songs.

We have seen that Herder fully appreciated the excellence of Greek
art and culture, and yet he contended from the beginning that there can
be no absolutes in art. For him, culture was national, not international.
It existed in its own right and was therefore its own absolute. Whether it
was speech or literature, it sprang up as if from the ground. It was
spontaneous, and as such it did not accord with rules and standards.
Instead, it developed according to racial and individual character, geographical situation, and climate. True culture was natural, spontaneous,
national, individual and relative, producing works of art which must be
regarded as masterpieces in their own right.[51] It would indeed be most
strange 'wenn man ein Bild aus seinem Zusammenhange reissen, und
sein Kolorit, den Schatten einer zerpflückten Blume, mit dem Kolorit
eines Bildes, in einem Dichter ganz anderer Zeit, Nation, Sprache und
Dichtung vergleichen wollte' (*EP*, XII, p. 9).[52] Herder pleaded for

---

51. For example, Herder did not consider Shakespeare to be the successor of
Sophocles. Since English and Greek drama had nothing in common, it was impossible to measure one by the other, or to compare the two, either in origin or development. Shakespeare and Sophocles were both great creative artists, each was 'ein
Diener der Natur' ('a servant of nature') (*AK*, V, p. 222), and both worked with the
materials available to them.

52. 'If one were to rip an image from out of its context and compare its hue, the
shadow of a flower plucked to pieces, with that of an image in a poet of a quite different age, nation, language and poetic culture.'

individual methods of writing and ways of thinking. In the same way as Greek poetry—and the Song of Songs before it—was natural and primitive, so should German poetry be.

Herder's View of 'True' Poetry

For Herder, then, the only genuine poetry was that produced spontaneously by a specific people within a peculiar historical and social setting, and in a particular language. These themes came together in his use of the term 'Volk'. As used, for example, in the word 'Volkslieder',[53] the term was employed by Herder to refer to anything which expressed itself directly or spontaneously, as well as philosophically, provided the philosophy was common sense rather than subtle logic. A 'Volk' was a group of people identified with each other through linguistic links. It was not a political or genetic unit, although a political unit not corresponding to a 'Volk' was artificial. In Germany, for example, the aristocracy would be excluded, as their language and culture were French. Without its own language, a 'Volk' was an 'Unding' ('absurdity') (*DL*, I, p. 147). Such a premise was important for Herder's theories of translation.

According to Herder, language and 'Volk', language and national consciousness, were inseparably joined. It was his belief, for instance, that the mixing of Greek and Latin with Hebrew had resulted in linguistic decay which he compared to a withering plant (*KW*, IV, p. 212). He further regarded the use of Latin as the ruin of his own mother tongue, and intermixture with other nationalities was therefore to be avoided. Here we note an apparent paradox. Herder's cultural theory should, in its own terms, render translation impossible, yet he attempted to translate the Song of Songs, a work from a culture and language very different from his own. His apparent German chauvinism is explicable in terms of his overall theory that each nation—including his own—had its own distinctive culture which could be approached by way of the imaginative understanding outlined above. This he was quite remarkably able to appreciate. Thus it could be claimed with some justification

---

53. The term 'Volkslied' was first used by Herder in his Ossian essay. For Herder, 'Volkslied' applied to any song that could be sung and had something of the patina of older poetry about it. He included Minnelieder under the heading, and certain songs from Shakespeare's plays (see *VL*, XXV, p. 331)—as well as the various poems of the Song of Songs, of course.

that Herder made a good intermediary and hence translator, although it will be demonstrated that his own reading of the Song of Songs was coloured by his own culture.

The 'Volk', then, was the origin of all true values in art, literature and philosophy. Nature and people were diametrically opposed to 'Kunst' in the sense of 'artificiality', which was based on reason alone. For Herder, the terms 'Volk' ('people/nation'), 'Sprache' ('language') and 'Lied' ('Poesie') ('song' ['poetry']) were one.[54] Thus he denied the possibility of a national character in the absence of a folk-song tradition (*TS*, XXVII, p. 180). It should be stressed that Herder did not link the 'Volk' with the 'Pöbel auf den Gassen, der singet und dichtet niemals, sondern schreyt und verstümmelt' ('rabble in the streets who never sing or write poetry, but shriek and mutilate') (*VL*, XXV, p. 323). Folk-poetry was not the product of 'das dichtende Volk' ('the people writing poetry'), but rather the product of a poet who was a 'Naturgenie' ('natural genius'), forming the living experiences of the people into a dramatic poetic recitative: 'Je älter, je Volksmässiger, je lebendiger; desto kühner, desto werfender' ('The more ancient, the more popular, the more vivacious; the more audacious, the more vigorous') (*AK*, V, p. 187). Such a poet, however, was not necessarily of the common people: 'Zum Volksänger gehört nicht, daß er aus dem Pöbel seyn muß, oder für den Pöbel singt; so wenig es die edelste Dichtkunst beschimpft, daß die im Munde des Volkes tönet' (*VL*, XXV, p. 323).[55]

To Herder's mind, true (folk) poetry was the antithesis of the artificial poetry of his time which was written within the confines of literary rules and conventions:

> Je wilder, d.i. je lebendiger, je freiwürkender ein Volk ist, [...] desto wilder, d.i. desto lebendiger, freier, sinnlicher, lyrisch handelnder müßen auch, wenn es Lieder hat, seine Lieder seyn! Je entfernter von künstlicher, wißenschaftlicher Denkart, Sprache und Letternart das Volk ist: desto weniger müßen auch seine Lieder fürs Papier gemacht, und todte Lettern Verse seyn (*AK*, V, p. 164).[56]

---

54. See Herder's letter to Johann Georg Scheffner, dated 4 October 1766, in Regine Otto (ed.), *Herders Briefe in einem Band* (Bibliothek Deutscher Klassiker; Berlin and Weimar: Aufbau-Verlag, 1970), pp. 13-18.

55. 'It is not necessary for the folk-poet to be from the rabble, or to sing for the rabble, any more than it dishonours the noblest poetry if it sounds forth from the mouth of the people.'

56. 'The more primitive, i.e. the more vivacious and uninhibited a nation is,

True poetry was the outpouring of feeling by those not perverted by false values. Travel writers taught Herder that the ancients expressed themselves 'stark und fest, [...] sinnlich, klar, lebendig, [...] unmittelbar und genau fühlend' ('robustly and deeply, [...] sensuously, clearly, vivaciously, [...] with immediate and precise feelings') (*AK*, V, p. 181). Their literature contained almost no abstract ideas. It was spontaneous, whereas the pedants of Herder's time had to gather their ideas together first and then learn them by heart: 'Unsre Schulmeister, Küster, Halbgelehrte: [...] diese gelehrte Leute, was wären die gegen die Wilden?' ('Our schoolmasters, sacristans, semi-academics: [...] these educated people, what are they compared with primitive peoples?') (*A K*, V, p. 182). Poetry ought to be the 'stürmendste, sicherste Tochter der Menschlichen Seele' ('most turbulent, most reliable daughter of the human soul'), yet the Germans were almost unable to feel or see any more: 'Wir [...] denken und grüblen nur; wir [...] erkünsteln' ('We [...] just think and ponder; we [...] act artificially') (*AK*, V, p. 183).

Herder was interested in literature that could be read aloud rather than silently. For him mediaeval literature was an ideal, because the living sound of the spoken word was preserved in their poetry: 'Wohl den Schriftstellern unter uns, die da schreiben, als ob sie hören, die da dichten, als ob sie sängen' ('Happy are those among us who write as if they can hear, who compose poetry as if they were singing') (*DL*, II, p. 40). Herder regarded the ear as the most immediate of the sense organs (see also *KW*, III, p. 136), and speaking of Jacob Balde's lyrical poetry, Herder commented that 'nichts ist stärker, und ewiger, und schneller, und feiner, als Gewohnheit des Ohrs!' ('nothing is more powerful, more eternal, more rapid, and finer than the use of the ear!') (*AK*, V, p. 165). He spoke of the 'Ohr der Seele' ('ear of the soul') (*VL*, XXV, p. 333), claiming that 'nichts ist nationeller und individueller als das Vergnügen des Ohrs' ('nothing is more national and individual than the pleasure of the ear') (*EP*, XI, p. 231). In the same vein he asserted that 'nichts ist zarter, ja ekler und gebieterischer, als das hörende Ohr' ('nothing is more tender, or even more repulsive and irresistible, than the listening ear') (*TS*, XXVII, p. 169).

[...] the more primitively, vivaciously, freely, sensually, lyrically active must its songs be, if indeed it has songs! The more removed the nation is from artificial, scholarly thinking, language and letters, the less should its songs be prepared for paper, and its dead letters used as verses.'

Herder stressed the importance of the use of vowels and consonants, of imagery, of sentence construction and of rhythm. Reading aloud was obviously vitally important: 'Ehe der Knabe die Kunst zu schreiben lernen kann, muß er die Kunst zu lesen haben, und ehe er diese haben kann, muß er hören lernen. [...] Wer schätzt denn wohl die Kunst zu hören gnug [...]?' (*DL*, II, pp. 344 and 345).[57] Indeed, Herder wished he could read Homer in the same way as Klopstock: 'O sänge mir Homer, Pindar, und Sophokles vor' ('If only Homer, Pindar, and Sophocles could sing aloud for me') (*JR*, IV, p. 423). Indeed, whenever he read Homer, he stood in spirit in a crowded marketplace in Greece and imagined 'wie der Sänger [...] die Rhapsodien seines göttlichen Dichters mir vorsinget' (the singer [...] singing out loud for me the rhapsodies of his divine poet') (*DL*, I, p. 176). The Song of Songs too was intended to be read aloud, and Herder regarded the Hebrew language as 'Othem Gottes, wehende Luft, die das Ohr aufhaschete, und die todten Buchstaben [...] waren nur der Leichnam, der lesend mit Lebensgeist beseelet werden muste!' (*US*, V, p. 14).[58] Song must be sung, not just written and read silently. It must portray passion and feeling. It must be heard rather than seen, and it must be heard with the ear of the soul (*VL*, XXV, pp. 332-33).

The immediate spontaneity of primitive poetry appealed to Herder, for the ancients indulged the senses and the imagination: 'Nichts in der Welt (hat) mehr Sprünge und kühne Würfe, als Lieder des Volks' ('Nothing in the world [has] more leaps and bold bounds than the songs of the people') (*AK*, V, p. 186). Critics regarded these 'Sprünge und Würfe'[59] as 'Tollheiten der Morgenländischen Hitze' ('frenzied results

---

57. 'Before the boy can learn the art of writing he must possess the art of reading, and before he can have this, he must learn to hear. [...] Yet who appreciates sufficiently the art of hearing [...]?'

58. 'Breath of God, fluttering breeze, which were caught by the ear, and the dead letters [...] were merely the corpse which was to be brought to life through spirited reading.'

59. These are peculiar gaps and omissions in the narrative line and train of thought, particularly of old ballads, presumably resulting from an oral tradition over centuries. The reader's imagination is expected to fill in the missing parts. In 'The Marketing of Macpherson: The International Book Trade and the First Phase of German Ossian Reception', in Howard Gaskill (ed.), *Ossian Revisited* (Edinburgh: Edinburgh University Press, 1991), pp. 73-93, Uwe Böker claims that 'a literature which does not follow learnable rules but is open and pays attention to the realities of everyday form is characterized by those irregular "Sprünge und Würfe"

of the Oriental heat') and 'Enthusiasmus des Prophetengeistes' ('enthusiasm of the prophetic spirit') (*AK*, V, p. 197), so it is significant that Herder chose a piece of Oriental poetry, the Song of Songs, as the best example of the kind of natural, primitive, spontaneous poetry he was trying to promote in an attempt to rescue German literature from the direction in which it was heading. He regarded the original poetry of the Orient as 'eine Poesie der Einbildungskraft' ('a poetry of the powers of the imagination') (*JR*, IV, p. 352), and by juxtaposing it with the lifeless, artificial literature of Germany, he hoped to restore his native literature to its former state. His aim was to breathe new life into German literature by means of that poetry which demonstrated the unbroken unity of art and nature, of idea and reality. The poetry of the Orient, the land of beginnings, was diametrically opposed to that of eighteenth-century Germany. The Orient was man's first dwelling place (see *IP*, XIII, p. 35), as well as 'das erste Erziehungshause und Bildungsplatz der Völker' ('the initial locus for the education and development of the nations') (*IP*, XIII, p. 38. See also *ÄU*, VI, p. 360). Everything from the Orient was therefore original, and Oriental poetry was the origin and mother of all poetry. Herder intended the Song of Songs to be regarded as the noblest paradigm of that primitive, natural, 'true' poetry, whose essence German poets should emulate rather than imitate.

Herder's Call for a Renaissance of German Poetry

It was Herder's desire, then, that someone should show the Germans the true ideal of primitive poetry, so that they would no longer need to copy the Greeks, for example, but rather would be encouraged to adopt their own primitive literature as a paradigm instead (*DL*, I, p. 294). The literature of the day was too distant from its source, and Germans should find the way back to their original literary roots. Herder's path led him in the first instance by way of the natural, primitive poetry of the Orient. In all this, his main touchstones were Luther and Shakespeare, and we will note below the particular importance of his reception of Luther for his translation of the Song of Songs. Herder had high praise for Luther, for it was he who had awoken the German language,

---

(asyndetic "leaps and sallies") which are normally to be found in folk-song and ballads' (p. 86). See also Douglas Schumacher, 'Herder's Treatment of his English Sources in the Volkslieder' (masters thesis, University of London, 1937), p. 15.

a sleeping giant, and set it free: 'Er ists, der die Scholastische Wortkrämerei, wie jene Wechslertische, verschüttet' ('It was he who overturned academic verbiage, just like those moneychangers' tables') (*DL*, I, p. 372). Through his reformation, a whole nation had been led to think and feel, and as late as 1796 Herder still referred to Luther as 'der größeste Meister des Uebersetzens in unserer Sprache' ('the greatest master of translation in our own language') (*TS*, XXVII, p. 276).

Herder's thesis was that language and poetry were organically determined by environment as well as cultural, geographical, political and climatic conditions. Natural poetry signified the naïve, primitive, instinctive production of a poem which had emerged from the natural climatic, geographical, national and temporal conditions which had afforded it its own stamp of individuality. Because of the different situations in which they evolved, no two literatures could be alike. Any attempt to model one on the other, thus interfering with the free individual development of the other, was unnatural and even pernicious. German poetry, then, was to be based on its own past, just as Hebrew, Greek and English poetry had been. Herder exhorted Germans to return to their native sources of the Middle Ages and the sixteenth century, a daring suggestion given the prevailing view of the Middle Ages as barbaric and primitive (*AP*, V, p. 524).

In Herder's opinion, every culture was both a means and an end (*AP*, V, p. 546). The importance of the principle of relativism in Herder's historical view of world cultures was underlined in his *Auch eine Philosophie*. The civilizations of the world were stages of growth, each complete and justified in its own right, each attaining the perfection natural and peculiar to itself, and yet at the same time being a part of a larger whole: 'Was für ein Werk, zu dem so viel Schattengruppen von Nationen und Zeiten [...] gehören! [...] Was für ein Werk dies Ganze! [...] So viel Ordnung und so viel Wirrung!' (*AP*, V, p. 585).[60] No age and no achievement of any age was a final goal, but each was a part of an ultimate goal. History was a harmony of tones where one could hear now 'nur wenige Töne, oft nur ein verdrüßliches Stimmen von Mißtönen' ('only a few tones, often only a morose sound of discords') (*AP*, V, p. 560). For Herder, it was absurd to judge teleologically, according to an absolute, an ideal and a final purpose. It was also absurd to deny a

---

60. 'What an undertaking, to which so many shadow groups of nations and ages [...] belong! [...] What an undertaking this whole thing is! [...] So much order and so much chaos!'

measure of happiness and achievement to any individual age or race (*AP*, V, p. 510). Indeed, he made a special plea for the merits of the Gothic religion and culture of the Middle Ages as an 'ungeheures Gothisches Gebäude! überladen, drückend, finster, Geschmacklos—[...] aber wie groß! reich! überdacht! mächtig!' ('a vast Gothic building! Profusely adorned, heavy, dark, tasteless—[...] but how great! Opulent! Reasoned out! Mighty!') (*AP*, V, p. 522). He particularly condemned the lack of sympathy with the Middle Ages which was prevalent at the time, and his inclusion in *Lieder der Liebe* of a mediaeval translation of the Song of Songs was thus especially significant. Herder refused to deny independent achievement to any age. The true task of the critic or historian was not to judge, but rather to interpret and assess each age or culture in its own right.

Germans were to seek out their own national songs, which alone were genuine and characteristic. The imitation of foreign literatures was to give way to an appreciation only, and this would help native writers to produce native literature. Thus it was Herder's desire to spur German collectors on and infuse new life into German poetry:

> In mehr als einer Provinz sind mir Volkslieder, Provinziallieder, Bauerlieder bekannt, die an Lebhaftigkeit und Rhythmus, und Naivetät und Stärke der Sprache vielen derselben gewiß nichts nachgeben würden; nur wer ist der sie sammle? der sich um sie bekümmre? sich um Lieder des Volks bekümmre? auf Strassen, und Gassen und Fischmärkten? im ungelehrten Rundgesange des Landvolks? um Lieder, die oft nicht skandirt, und oft schlecht gereimt sind? wer wollte sie sammlen—wer für unsre Kritiker, die ja so gut Sylben zählen, und skandiren können, drucken lassen? (*AK*, V, p. 189)[61]

61. 'In more than one province I am aware of folksongs, songs in local dialect, and peasant songs, which in terms of vivacity, rhythm, naïveté, and strength of language would certainly in no way be inferior to many of those [i.e. Percy's]; yet who will collect them? Who will be concerned with them? Who will be concerned with the songs of the people? In streets, alleyways, and fish markets? In the uneducated roundelays of the country folk? With songs which often do not scan, and which rhyme badly? Who will collect them, who will have them printed for our critics, who, as we know, can count syllables so well, and are even able to scan!' See also Heinrich Lohre, *Von Percy zum Wunderhorn: Beiträge zur Geschichte der Volksliedforschung in Deutschland* (Palaestra: Untersuchungen aus der deutschen und englischen Philologie und Literaturgeschichte, 22; Berlin: Mayer & Müller, 1902), and Eugen Kühnemann, *Herder und das deutsche Wesen* (Munich: Beck, 1914), p. 64.

In his introduction to the *Alte Volkslieder* of 1774, Herder claimed
that whoever despised genuine folk-poetry was clearly so besotted with
copying foreign models that 'ihm das, was Körper der Nation ist,
unwerth und unfühlbar geworden' ('that which is the body of the nation
has to him become worthless and impalpable') (*AV*, XXV, p. 8). Folk-
songs—presumably like those contained in the Song of Songs—should
be collected and written down 'für Nation! Volk! einen Körper, der
Vaterland heißt!' ('for nation! People! A body known as Fatherland!')
(*AV*, XXV, p. 9). He appealed for the German people to arise from their
literary complacency and indifference, and to create a literature of their
own, as indeed the Hebrews had done: 'Großes Volk und Reich! oder
vielmehr Volk und Reich von zehn großen Völkern—du hast keine
Volkslieder? Und edles, Tugend- Schaam- und Sitte- so tief liebendes
Volk, du hast keine edlere, Gesang- Tugend- Sitte- und Inhaltvollere als
diese?' (*AV*, XXV, p. 9. See also *BL*, IX, pp. 528-30).[62] He deplored the
fate of Germany always to be the mother and yet the slave of foreign
powers, to be their regent, their law giver and the decider of their
destiny, and yet always to be their slave and nurse (*AV*, XXV, p. 10).
He despised Germany's flirtation with foreign voices and nations, pro-
stituting her own literature. In his view, Germans were simply regurgi-
tating what foreign writers had cast off, and he called for the discovery
of genuine pieces of national literature (*AV*, XXV, p. 11). The treasures
of German folk-poetry were there, hardly known, almost totally unused
and unread (*BL*, IX, p. 528). The remains 'aller lebendigen Volks-
denkart' ('of all living national thought process') were disappearing
into oblivion. Germany had no original national literature, and Herder
accused his people of being a 'Nachahmergeschlecht' ('race of imi-
tators') (*AV*, XXV, p. 11). He wrote with bitter cynicism of the Enlightenment:

> Schönes, erleuchtetes Jahrhundert […] voll schöner Worte, lieblicher
> Wendungen, aufgezählter Reime und herrlichkünstlicher Musikstanzen!
> herrliches Jahrhundert, wo es Hauptkunstgrif wird, die Seele ja unwein-
> erlich, Thränen- und Rührungslos, aber zur artigen Phrases- Licht- und

---

62. 'Great nation and empire! Or rather nation and empire of ten great nations—
do you have no folksongs? And noble nation, which so deeply loves virtue, chastity
and morality, do you have nothing more noble, nothing fuller in song, virtue,
morality and content than these?'

Vernunftseele zu machen: hast du an Inhalt, Kraft und daurender Glück-
seligkeit auf die Nachwelt gewonnen oder verlohren? (*AV*, XXV, pp. 12-
13).[63]

Man's original language was poetry, and his first encounters with
nature and life were expressed in folk-song, epic, myth, ballad, ode and
proverb. Truth was a personal, private experience, and the individual
was unique—whether a person, a language, a culture, a nation or an
age. In his *Ideen*, Herder set out to show the uniqueness of every nation
and age and to place it into the grand design of the whole. In his view
there was a chain of being in which one nation took over from another.
Germany should therefore learn from the past, but not imitate it.

For Herder, folk-songs (and he regarded the Song of Songs as such)
were historical documents interpreting national cultures in the widest
sense. They were the evidence of the superiority of early society and
simple folk over sophisticated civilization. They were examples of true
poetry upon which a new definition of the nature of poetry could be
built. Herder's championship of the folk-song was a revolt against the
culture of the educated and a defence of that of the common people. He
regarded folk-song as an impression of a nation's heart, a living grammar, the best dictionary. For Herder, every simple, singable song was
folk-song. His theoretical work on religion and poetry represented an
onslaught against those who thought that ideas and speculation were
truer and more real than feeling and sensuous certainty. Herder was
responsible for a new esteem for the culture of the common people, and
reversed much of the contempt of his age for the clumsiness and
coarseness of folk-poetry.

Primitive poetry arose from myths, therefore myths there must be if
German poetry were to be reborn:[64] 'Die alte wendische, schwäbische,
sächsische, holsteinische Mythologie [...] wäre wahrlich eine Fund-
grube für den Dichter und Redner seines Volks' ('The ancient Wendish,
Swabian, Saxon, Holstein mythology [...] really would be a treasure

---

63. 'Wonderful, enlightened century [...] full of beautiful words, delightful
phrases, countless rhymes and splendidly artful musical dances! Splendid century,
where it is the main artistic concept to render the soul naturally unprepared to weep,
without tears or emotion, but to make it a well-behaved soul of clichés, light and
reason: as far as content, strength and lasting happiness are concerned, for the world
to come, have you won or lost?'

64. See the section of the *Fragmente* entitled 'Vom neuern Gebrauch der
Mythologie' (I, pp. 426-47).

chest for the poet and orator of his people') (*VÄ*, IX, p. 525). Thus there was a tension between Herder the Christian and Herder the poet longing for ancient myths and gods, yet in his contributions to *Die Horen*, he urged the use by German writers of their own native mythology as well as the mythology of the Greeks.[65]

Herder's Reception of the Bible

For Herder, the Hebrews were the oldest and best example of a 'Volk' with a genuine national character. They were a simple, primitive nation, but 'die einfachsten Nationen haben an Naturbildern und Naturempfindung die erhabenste, rührendste Dichtkunst' ('the simplest nations have the most sublime, moving poetry as a result of natural imagery and natural feeling') (*EP*, XII, p. 8). He was drawn to the 'Schatten des Alterthums' ('shadow of antiquity') and acknowledged his inclination for the Hebrews as a nation (*JR*, IV, p. 439): 'Es gibt in den alten Zeiten der schönen Sinnlichkeit, insonderheit in den Morgenländern Spuren, daß ihre Seele gleichsam mehr Umkreis zu würken gehabt habe, als wir' (*JR*, IV, p. 454).[66]

Given Herder's views both on poetry and Hebrew culture, it should not be surprising that he was drawn to the poetry of ancient Israel as preserved in the Bible. This was a document which, in his estimation, was a product of the specific culture within which it was produced, although many of his contemporaries considered the scriptures to contain universally timeless, inspired truth. Herder spent much time reading, translating, and analysing the literature of the Old Testament. He valued the Bible highly as literature. It was an expression of the *Volksgeist* of the people who wrote it, and this, for Herder, was the mark of true poetry. It is in this light that we must consider his interest in the Song of Songs.

It was Herder's belief that the most characteristic feature of religion was its being completely human. This conviction influenced his belief in the Bible as a human and historical document which should be read

65. The mere span of the title of Herder's essay *Homer und Ossian* exemplifies his approach. For his contributions to *Die Horen* reproduced in *SWS*, see XVIII, pp. 404-502.

66. 'In those ancient times of wondrous sensuality, especially in the Orient, there are signs that their soul, so to speak, had more space in which to be effective than we do.'

and evaluated in terms of human values, and not be made an object of blind, uncritical worship. In his sermon *Ueber die Göttlichkeit und Gebrauch der Bibel* (1768), Herder contended that the Bible was a human book and must be read as such. While acknowledging the Bible as the word of God, he claimed that God revealed himself in human language. He could not speak as God, but had to speak in a human way, adopting the language and mode of thought of the people he was speaking to, with particular reference to the time and geographical situation in which they lived (XXXI, p. 106).

The Bible, then, was a book written by mankind for mankind: 'Menschlich ist die Sprache, menschlich die äussern Hülfsmittel, mit denen sie geschrieben und aufbehalten ist' ('The language is human, and human are the external aids with which it was written and maintained') (*TB*, X, p. 7). The Bible's whole meaning was human, as was its purpose and the use to which it should be put. Thus the more God's word was read in a human way, the closer the reader came to the purpose of its instigator, the one who created man in his own image and who acted as a human being wherever he revealed himself as God.

And so Herder denied any belief in the miraculous inspiration or authorship of the Bible, but demanded a philological interpretation and criticism. Since his time in Königsberg and Riga, Herder had ceased to regard the Bible as a book inspired by God in any special sense. In keeping with his relativism, he learned to study it against the background from which it had come and to compare it with other poetic books. Herder's relativistic principle extended in his thinking to culture and history, and thus it should not surprise us that the Bible itself was drawn, as poetry, into his general genetic interpretation, being considered simply as the expression of its own time, country and language (see *AM*, VI, p. 35). The Bible was a work which originated in the Orient, and which, by its very nature, could not have originated anywhere else.

For Herder, then, the Bible was ancient poetry and history, and was both human and divine (see *EP*, XII, p. 6). His reading of it was a kind of secularizing revelatory pantheism, poetic and humanistic. God, or 'die erste Offenbarung Gottes' ('the initial revelation of God'), was present in the whole history of humanity, and in poetry itself, which to Herder meant above all the true voice of primitive poetry. All things were revelation, so there was no need of a special, supernatural revelation. Within this view, especially as expressed in his essay *Vom Geist der Ebräischen Poesie*, *Lieder der Liebe* can be seen as the best example of Herder's thesis, given that this work teaches us that the Song of Songs is a purely human, although richly poetic, creation, and as such is the human expression of human emotions.

For Herder, the writers of the Old Testament had no literary pretensions or aims. Their work was natural and naïve, as was the poetry of the Orient in general; that is, during the childhood of the human race.[67] This, as we have seen, was the hallmark of all true, genuine poetry. The divine nature of the Bible was not totally denied, but the Bible was no more divine than any other work of poetry. For example, Herder insisted especially upon an understanding of and sympathy with the book of Genesis as pure poetry, the product of nature. He regarded it as 'keine scientifische Kosmogonie, sondern ein natürlicher erster Anblick des Weltalls' ('no scientific cosmogony, but rather a natural, initial view of the universe') (*TB*, X, p. 33). He studied Genesis not as literal history or even as allegory, but rather as divine truth in the form of a poetic child's fable (*ÄU*, VI, pp. 195-96, and VII, pp. 60-62). It was God who gave man poetic powers and language, and in this way the origin of all poetry was actually divine (*EP*, XII, p. 7). For Herder, the Bible was not simply a book of religion, but also a book of poetry containing the best poetry of the Hebrew people, the pinnacle of which he considered to be the Song of Songs. As Walter Dietze sums up:

> Die Epik der historischen Schriften, die Lyrik der Schlacht- und Siegeslieder, die Hymnik der Psalmen, die Elegik im Jeremias, die erotische Poesie im Hohen Lied. Für Herder gilt als ausgemacht, daß es sich hier um die 'älteste, einfachste, herzlichste Poesie der Erde' handle. Zweifellos nimmt dieses Bibel-Verständnis in der Geschichte der Theologie einen wichtigen Platz ein. Noch größere Bedeutung hat es allerdings für die Geschichte deutscher Literatur, weil es mit philologisch-historischer Akribie und feinstem Kunstverstand die ästhetischen Werte der Bibel aufschließt.[68]

---

67. See Herder's *Ideen*.

68. 'The epic poetry of the historical writings, the lyric poetry of the songs of battle and victory, the hymns of the Psalms, the elegies of Jeremiah, the erotic poetry of the Song of Songs. For Herder it goes without saying that here we have the 'most ancient, the simplest, the most heartfelt poetry on earth'. Undoubtedly, this understanding of the Bible occupies an important place in the history of theology. Yet it is of even greater importance for the history of German literature, because with scrupulous philological–historical exactitude, and the most delicate understanding of art, it unlocks the aesthetic values of the Bible.' *Johann Gottfried*

In Herder's attempts to rescue the Bible from the criticisms of the Rationalists, he claimed that unimaginative and pedantic criticism or reinterpretation of the Bible in the light of eighteenth-century knowledge was irrelevant and futile.[69] In his *Lieder der Liebe*, Herder treated the Song of Songs as a collection of love-songs without doctrinal or allegorical significance,[70] while in *Vom Geist der Ebräischen Poesie* the Old Testament was set against the background of Hebrew life and history, and sympathetically interpreted as the poetry and literature of the Hebrew race.

Vom Geist der Ebräischen Poesie did for the Old Testament what Winckelmann had done for the plastic art of the Greeks, and so arguably Herder was responding to his own call for someone to point the way in the literary arts. The very dialogic structure of the work was persuasive: Alciphron, a representative of the 'Aufklärung' ('Enlightenment') who had been compelled to learn Hebrew, must be convinced by Eutyphron[71] of the poetic value of the Old Testament. Alciphron has to be persuaded that the ancient barbarisms of the Old Testament are good poetry and valuable historical material. By easy stages, he is convinced of the primitive structure of the Hebrew language which, like Ossian, appeals directly to the ear, the most immediate sense organ, and expresses action through the inflection of the verbal root. He is also convinced of the sensuous imagery of the Old Testament. He can agree in general with Eutyphron's contention that all sublime and elevating poetry is celestial (*EP*, XI, p. 257), but needs to be convinced that Genesis, for example, is sublime and elevating. He is persuaded that his aversion to Old Testament poetry is a prejudice (a serious reproach to a

---

Herder: Abriß seines Lebens und Schaffens (Berlin and Weimar: Aufbau-Verlag, 1983), pp. 93-94.

69. For example, see Herder's harsh review of Michaelis's *Mosaisches Recht* in V, pp. 423-26. Significantly his *Erläuterungen zum Neuen Testament* and *Briefe zweener Brüder Jesu* were attempts first to relate the language and concepts of John's Gospel to an Asiatic religion and cultural background, especially to the Zoroastrian writings which had been recently discovered, translated and published by Anquetil du Perron (VII, pp. 337-470); and secondly to understand the letters of James and Jude in relation to that primitive circle of Judaistic Christianity from which they were seen to have sprung (VII, pp. 473-560).

70. That Herder regarded the Song of Songs as a collection of individual poems is an important point which will be discussed in more detail below.

71. Representing Herder, and therefore one who had learned Hebrew as a result of natural inclination rather than force.

representative of the Enlightenment), and allows himself to approach the document at least as interesting mythology.[72] Eutyphron draws more and more parallels between the books of the Old Testament and particularly that Greek poetry which was accepted as a model by the Enlightenment, for Herder regarded poetry and truth as one (*EP*, XII, pp. 15 and 16). Similarly, poetry and religion may be closely identified with each other, for Herder was not secularizing religion, but rather sanctifying poetry. In his earlier essays, there were suggestions of the link between poetry and religion, but in *Vom Geist der Ebräischen Poesie* the virtual identity of the two was stated clearly, if not emphasized.[73]

For Herder, then, the Old Testament was not a supernatural book without cultural origin, background or history, but it was simply the literature of the Hebrews. It could be studied in and for itself, as well as in relation to other literatures. It was a product of the same natural and cultural laws of which other works of poetry were also the product. As literature, the Bible did not lose its character as revelation or as an inspired book, but it was divinely inspired revelation only in the same way that all literature—and nature itself—was also divinely inspired revelation. To Herder, the poetry of the ancient Hebrews, as well as that of the ancient Greeks, and indeed the living poetry of all nations, must

72. It must be remembered that the use of mythology in poetry was a favourite topic of discussion in the critical journals of the Enlightenment (see *Die Horen*, for example).

73. Compare, for example, Herder's comment in the thirteenth of his *Provinzialblätter*: 'Dichtkunst, sie ist ursprünglich Theologie gewesen, und die edelste, höchste Dichtkunst wird wie die Tonkunst ihrem Wesen nach immer Theologie bleiben. Sänger und Propheten, die erhabensten Dichter des Alten Testaments schöpften Flammen aus heiligem Feuer' ('Poetry was originally theology, and, just like music, the noblest, highest form of poetry will in essence always remain theology. Singers and prophets, the most sublime poets of the Old Testament, created flames from sacred fire') (VII, p. 300). As Wulf Koepke puts it: 'Herder's presentation of poetry in the Old Testament and the Old Testament as poetry has commonly been understood as a secularizing view of the text of the Bible. But Herder was writing about "sacred poetry", a poetry which has the power to make God's presence evident to the senses. It was never far from his mind that the manifestation of the Holy should be the foremost task of poetry, as it was the case in ancient times, and a consideration of this, the highest function of poetry, would perhaps open an access to Herder's own generally neglected or ignored poetic works' (*Johann Gottfried Herder: Innovator through the Ages* [Modern German Studies, 10; Bonn: Bouvier, 1982], p. 139).

be regarded as inspired, because this entire body of language was primitive and therefore closer to the first revelation of God himself.

Herder complained that the greatest misuse of the Bible was when everything in it was ascribed to God, including those things pertaining to Satan. In *Briefe an Theophron*,[74] for example, he criticized those who misunderstood what they read merely because 'es steht ja [...] in der Bibel' ('after all, it's [...] in the Bible') (XI, p. 177). He brought out a similar point in his draft of *Lieder der Liebe* in 1776, where he claimed that the Song of Songs was the most misused book of all. Critics were unsure how to interpret it, for despite what Herder called 'klarer Wortverstand' ('clear literal meaning'), 'man [...] hat Allegorie, Mystik, zuletzt Zoten und Liebesränke drüber geschüttet—und das Alles aus lauter lieber Heiligkeit—es steht ja in der Bibel!' ('we [...] have heaped upon it allegory, mysticism and finally obscenities and amorous intrigues—and all that for reasons of pure holiness—after all, it's in the Bible!') (VIII, p. 589).[75]

As far as Herder was concerned, the Bible was one of God's books, just like nature itself. As the record of the human race, it contained both good and evil (*BT*, XI, p. 178). God's inspiration of the Bible rested upon the primitivity of the revelation. The Song of Songs was thus a valid revelation, along with Genesis and the Psalms, but also along with Homer, Ossian and other folk-songs of antiquity.

Herder's own folk-song collection, originally to have included the Song of Songs, was an attempt at a collection of folk-poetry similar to that of Percy's *Reliques of Ancient English Poetry*, a collection which Herder regarded, however, as 'besser, reicher und gesamleter' ('better, richer and more satisfactorily collected') (*AV*, XXV, p. 9). In Herder's mind, Homer, Ossian, Percy's *Reliques* and the latent primitivism of numerous travel-books, were all the bearers of a primitive revelation given by God to all mankind, although originally to the ancient Hebrews, most particularly through the Song of Songs. Herder's chief concern, then, was to present the Song of Songs as a primitive folk-song or anthology of folk-songs—in other words, an equivalent of

74. These letters were a continuation of *Briefe, das Studium der Theologie betreffend*, and were later developed into *Vom Geist der Ebräischen Poesie*.

75. The word 'Liebesränke' ('amorous intrigues') was aimed at Michaelis. This will be clarified in Chapter 4 as part of the discussion on Michaelis's view of the Song of Songs.

Percy's *Reliques*, although more glorious because it was both ancient and Hebrew.

Herder's 'Volkslied'-style versification of parts of the Old Testament was important, as this paved the way to his verse translation of the Song of Songs. Following Percy, Herder rewrote a few Bible stories, psalms and songs in Percy's ballad style, with all the attributes of the folk-song, including bold word formation, lack of rules in the rhyme, and enthusiasm of expression.[76] However, he was most attracted by Job and the Song of Songs.[77] His interpretation of the Bible was no longer dogmatic and theological, but rather according to feeling and experience.[78]

Herder's understanding of the term 'Natur' in the context of biblical poetry was the same as with all folk-poetry. As he so succinctly put it in the third of his *Theologische Briefe*:

> Poesie, wie sie in der Bibel ist, ist nicht zum Spaß, nicht zur entbehr-lichen, müßigen Gemüthsergötzung, noch weniger zu dem schändlichen Schlendrian erfunden, dazu wir sie jetzt zum Theil anwenden; fast sollte nicht Einerley Name so verschiedne Gattungen und Werke bezeichnen. Der poetische Ausdruck, die Art der Vorstellung und Wirkung war damals überall Natur; Erforderniß der Sprache und des Gemüths dessen, der sprach, so wie des Ohrs und Gemüthes derer, die hörten; Bedürfniß der Sache, der Zeit, des Zwecks, der Umstände (X, pp. 29-30).[79]

76. For his translations of Ps. 23, see XII, pp. 212-26 and 319-20. For Ps. 72, see VIII, pp. 536-38 and XII, pp. 275-76. For the end of Proverbs, see VIII, pp. 557-58 and XII, pp. 111-12. For his 'Schöpfungslied' see VI, pp. 72-74. For his 'Lied Lamechs', see VI, p. 178 (cf. XII, p. 409 n. 1). For his 'Worte des Königs Lemuels', see XII, pp. 110-11. Meyer too collated a number of Herder's Old Testament translations (*Werke*, pp. 135-50), and there are various Old Testament translations in *Vom Geist der Ebräischen Poesie* apart from those mentioned above.

77. For his translations of Job 4.12-21 and Job 38 and 39, see XII, pp. 321-28.

78. See Suphan's comments in XII, pp. 410-15.

79. 'As it stands in the Bible, poetry was not devised for pleasure, not for superfluous idle amusement of the spirit, and even less for shameful, familiar rou-tine, for which purpose we now use it in part; one single expression should almost not be used to designate so many different genres and works. The poetic expression, the birth of imagination and effect, was at that time everywhere nature—necessary for the language and spirit of the one who spoke, as well as for the ear and spirit of those who heard; a requirement of the matter, the age, the purpose, the circum-stances.'

Herder's technique of historical analysis was a valuable addition to the study of theology, which was threatening by 1780 to degenerate into rigid dogmatics on the one hand and into a shallow form of deism on the other. For Herder, the Bible contained the highest poetry of the human race, and no further proof of inspiration was necessary. After all, as Herder suggested, 'Poesie soll Eingebung seyn' ('poetry should be inspiration') (*WD*, VIII, p. 355).

Herder's conception of the Bible as such was perhaps his most original contribution to biblical exegesis. His was an uninhibited, purely human interpretation of the Bible. It is regrettable that many have noted Herder's enthusiasm for Homer and native German folk-songs, but have neglected too often the importance of his long preoccupation with the Old Testament and its poetry. He brought a secular, historical and sociopolitical interpretation to the whole subject of Hebrew poetry as embodied in the Bible. He also brought religious values to secular areas of scholarship, and secular values to religious ones. Mankind was not expected to treat his secular life with contempt, for nowhere did the Bible suggest that some hypothetical future life should spoil man's enjoyment of his present life: 'Hier auf Erden ist dein Ursprung, dein Geburtsland, deine Wohnung, dein Zweck, deine Bestimmung' ('Here on earth is your origin, your native land, your dwelling place, your purpose, your destiny') (*AM*, VI, p. 64). In a way, human beings were their own God here on earth. For a study of Herder's interpretation of the Song of Songs, this is a very important point.

Herder's Reception of Hebrew Poetry

In Herder's view of specifically Hebrew poetry, there is a major special instance of all he said in general terms about cultural distinctiveness (*Volksgeist*) and about poetry as the vehicle of divine revelation. Speaking of the poetry of the Hebrews, Herder claimed that if it were made into a universal abstraction, into something belonging to every age and every people, then it would cease to exist for any age or people (*WD*, VIII, p. 362).

Herder regarded the Hebrew (or Arabic) language as the oldest known to man (*DL*, I, pp. 166-71). It was the original language of nature, and the most primitive. It was the language closest to the creation of man, and as such was the language initially used by God for purposes of revelation. As we have seen, for Herder the more original a language, the less encumbered it was with abstract ideas and the fuller it was with feeling (*US*, V, p. 78). In his view, this earliest language was closely linked with the kind of primitive poetry he was trying to promote. It should not surprise us, then, that he should choose the language of the Bible to convey his ideas. It should surprise us even less that he should choose the Song of Songs as his vehicle, for he referred to the book as a collection of 'die zartesten duftendsten Blumen, die je auf diesem Boden wuchsen' ('the most delicate, sweet-smelling flowers which ever grew upon this earth') (*WD*, VIII, p. 351), and 'die zartesten geheimnißvollen Morgenrosen, die im Thale der Freuden je eine Königshand brach' ('the most delicate, mysterious morning roses which ever a royal hand gathered in the valley of delights') (*WD*, VIII, p. 354). It was Herder's opinion that the Orientals had a sharper sense of feeling and pleasure than Europeans. It was natural, then, that their poems of love and pleasure, of longing and hope—especially as embodied in the Song of Songs—should reflect this (*EP*, XI, p. 325).

Herder praised the imagery of Hebrew poetry, drawing attention to the images given to it by olive tree and vine, cedar and palm. Given the dearth of Hebrew pastoral literature, he argued that we must be satisfied with a single collection of such songs, namely those contained in the Song of Songs. These were songs 'die Rosenduft athmen und Turtel-taubengesang tönen' ('which breathe the fragrance of roses and sound of the song of turtle doves') (*EP*, XI, p. 272). They were simple and innocent, describing the pure, idyllic love of paradise itself (*EP*, XI, p. 328), written in language which Herder described as 'glänzend, [...] sinnreich und wohlgeründet' ('burnished, [...] witty and carefully sculpted') (*EP*, XI, p. 404).

For Herder, the Hebrew language was nothing but a collection of poetic elements. It was an imitation of nature itself (*US*, V, p. 56), the language of nature transformed into the sounds and images of activity, passion and interest (*US*, V, p. 57). This was the epitome of poetry, the language of the senses, for poetry was the language of the passions, of the imagination, of action, of memory, of joy and of pain (*WD*, VIII, p. 339): 'Je wahrer, [...] kenntlicher und stärker der Abdruck unsrer Empfindungen ist, [...] je mehr es wahre Poesie ist' ('The truer, [...] the more distinguishable, and the more powerful is the imprint of our feelings, [...] the more is it true poetry') (*WD*, VIII, p. 339). Hebrew poetry, 'die Morgenröthe der Aufklärung der Welt' ('the dawn of the enlightenment of the world') (*EP*, XI, p. 242), was replete with such action, description, passion, song and rhythm (*EP*, XI, p. 225), uniting beauty, truth and feeling (*EP*, XI, p. 271). In comparison with God's own poetry, or 'Tempelpoesie' ('temple poetry') (*EP*, XI, p. 457), the poetry of the Greeks—considered by Germans as an absolute to be copied—was merely decorative. Even the poetry of Herder's beloved Ossian, in comparison, seemed to him 'ohne Sonne, ohne Gott, ohne Zweck' ('sunless, godless, purposeless') (*EP*, XI, p. 398).

Herder maintained that a poetic language was one with a lot of expressive, descriptive verbs. The more a language was able to transform even nouns into verbs, the more poetic it was. The verb was the root of the whole Hebrew language, and thus Herder saw Hebrew as a language full of life and movement, lacking abstraction and replete with sensual description (*EP*, XI, pp. 227-28). As 'die sogenannte Göttliche, erste Sprache' ('the so-called divine, original language') (*US*, V, p. 13),[80] it was full of the spirit of God, leading mankind back to him (*WD*, VIII, p. 344).

It was Herder's contention that the Hebrews were innately and divinely poetic (*WD*, VIII, p. 347). Nobody could fail to sense the sublimity of their poetry, whether Jew, Christian or Muslim (*WD*, VIII, pp. 358-59),[81] for all sublime, uplifting poetry was divine (*EP*, XI, p. 257), and thus the interpreter of the nature of God and history itself (*WD*, VIII, p. 362). As Hebrew was a holy language, 'die Mutter unsrer edelsten Kenntniße' ('the mother of our most noble accomplishments') (*EP*, XI, p. 225), the very source of Hebrew poetry was holy (*WD*, VIII, p. 365).

Herder argued, then, that any study of poetry should begin with a study of Oriental poetry, the oldest, simplest and most sublime poetry ever written (*EP*, XI, p. 215. See also p. 221). He doubted, however, that anyone could still feel such poetry 'in all ihrem Leben, Rhythmus und Bildergeiste' ('in all its life, rhythm, and spirit of imagery') (*BL*, IX, p. 541). Homing in on the literature of the Hebrews, Herder pointed out that

> wenn die Biblischen Dichter von den Schneegüssen des Libanon; vom Thau des Hermon; von den Eichen Basans; vom prächtigen Libanon, und

---

80. Cf. V, p. 71, which reads 'die so genannte Göttliche Sprache' ('the so-called divine language').

81. Herder actually used the word 'Türke' ('Turk'), but in the context he was clearly referring to those of the Muslim faith. This implicit plea for religious tolerance was echoed in Lessing's *Nathan der Weise*.

angenehmen Carmel reden; so geben sie Bilder, die ihnen die Natur selbst vorgelegt hat: wenn unsre Dichter ihnen diese Bilder entwenden, so zeichnen sie nicht unsre Natur, sondern reden ihren Originalen einige Worte nach, die wir kaum nur halb verstehen (*DL*, I, pp. 258-59).[82]

In his view, if a poet referred to images which he had not been able to experience for himself, the result would be a 'prächtiges, neues, unge–wöhnliches—Unding' ('splendid, new, strange—absurdity'), regardless of how cleverly the poet used them (*DL*, I, p. 259). Poetry such as that of the Hebrews should not be imitated, but rather the unbroken unity between man and God, nature and art, should be closely considered:

Käme es nur erst so weit, daß niemand schriebe, was er nicht verstünde: befleißigten wir uns mehr, den Orient zu beschauen, die heiligen Gedichte zu verstehen und würklich erklären zu können: so würden wir es gewiß verlernen, mit Orientalischen Mastkälbern zu pflügen; wir würden uns, wenn wir ihre Kunst nur ganz einsehen, zu Schilderern unsrer eigenen Natur ausbilden (*DL*, I, p. 260).[83]

Herder claimed that Hebrew poetry possessed a rhythm which stemmed from the choruses and dances of triumph peculiar to that nation. It was impossible to convey this in a prosaic, philosophical language such as German, and unnatural to want to imitate songs in the German language which were originally intended for a vociferous chorus. It was foolish even to try to judge the language and imagery of the Hebrews by comparing them with the customs of the Germans (*EP*, XII, p. 100), or indeed of other races (*EP*, XII, p. 287). Indeed, in support of his own nation, Herder claimed that it was a violation of German to attempt to imitate Oriental poetry in poetic prose (*DL*, I, pp. 270-71). An urban way of life required 'daß unsre Poesie nicht Botanisch seyn kann, wie Michaelis die Morgenländische nennet' ('that our poetry

82. 'When the biblical poets speak of the torrents of snow on Mount Lebanon; of the dew on Mount Hermon; of the oaks of Bason; of the splendours of Mount Lebanon and the beauties of Mount Carmel; they are presenting images with which nature herself has provided them. When our poets borrow these images from them, they are not depicting our own nature, but they are repeating from their originals a few words which we are scarcely able to comprehend.'

83. 'If only we could reach the stage where nobody wrote what he did not understand: if we were to strive more to examine the Orient, to comprehend and really be able to explain the sacred poems; we would certainly then be able to forget how to plough with Oriental fatted calves; if we were to investigate fully their art, we would train ourselves to be depicters of our own nature.'

cannot be botanical, as Michaelis called that of the Orientals') (*DL*, I, p. 272). Oriental poetry was not there to be copied, but was there as a pattern for German literature to follow. With poetry such as that of the Song of Songs before him as a paradigm, the German poet could draw from his own primitive poetry the resources needed for the revitalization of his own literature, which had developed into the life-less, artificial, colourless poetry of the Enlightenment.

In this chapter I have confirmed the importance of Herder's specific preoccupation with the Song of Songs within the wider context of his views on poetry and the Bible. In the next chapter I shall seek to provide a theoretical backdrop for a detailed examination of Herder's interpretation of the Song of Songs.

Chapter 3

HERDER AS TRANSLATOR: A THEORETICAL CONTEXT
FOR *LIEDER DER LIEBE*

Introduction

In this chapter I aim first to analyse Herder's translation of the Song of
Songs in terms of certain modern literary-critical theories. I then consider translation theories prior to and contemporary with Herder in
order to provide categories of understanding for Herder's own theories.
After some observations on Herder's theories of language, I examine
his theories of translation and their importance for the Song of Songs.

Writing of his translation of the Song of Songs, Herder claimed that
'jedes Liedchen, jede Zeile sollte, soviel möglich, in ihrem Duft, in
ihrer Farbe seyn, nichts verschönert, verneut, verschmäckelt; so viel
möglich, nichts seinem Ort, seiner Zeit, seinem Lande entrißen werden—und wie schwer war das!' (*LL*, VIII, pp. 533-34).[1] In other words,
although he was an eighteenth-century Protestant German translating
and commenting on poetry from a totally different age and culture, he
was bold enough to presume that his response to the source language
and culture would not be affected by his own background, although
perhaps his 'soviel möglich' ('as far as possible') could be interpreted
as a disclaimer. His desire was not to adapt his source text to eighteenth-century German good taste. Edna Purdie points out that Herder's
revealing use here of the participles 'verschönert' ('embellished'), 'verneut' ('renewed') and 'verschmäckelt' ('distorted as far as taste is

---

1.   'As far as possible, each little song, every line was to be rendered in its own
fragrance and colour, with nothing embellished, nothing renewed, nothing distorted
as far as taste is concerned; as far as possible, with nothing torn from its own locale,
age or land—and how difficult that was!' Cf. p. 593, which similarly reads: 'Jedes
einzelne Lied erscheine an Stelle und Ort, in seinem Duft, in seiner eignen Farbe'
('Let each single song appear within its local context, in its own fragrance and
hue').

concerned') suggests his rejection of a main principle of translation current at the time.[2] Indeed, Herder's ironic use of the prefix 'ver-' produces a negative underpinning of a positive idea; it is almost one of those polarizations for which Herder was renowned. It was by seeking to improve upon an original text by moulding it into their own language, style and thought-processes, that translators of the time in fact destroyed its natural, primitive beauty. This was a principle to which Herder was opposed. Writing of folk-songs, Herder held that 'jedem stehets frei, sie, wie er will, zu übertragen, zu verschönern, zu feilen, zu ziehen, zu idealisiren, daß kein Mensch mehr das Original erkennet; es ist *seine* und nicht *meine* Weise, und dem Leser stehet frei, zu wählen' (*VL*, XXV, p. 329).[3] Indeed, as I shall explore more thoroughly below, it was vital that the original poetry of the Song of Songs should be presented as close to its original sense and form as possible, given Herder's attempts to use the work as a catalyst to show his countrymen what great literature could be formed from within the primitive spirit, culture and language of each individual nation. In this regard the fact that he made several attempts to translate the Song of Songs is important, and this study will consider how far Herder was influenced by his own cultural background in his reception of the Song of Songs.

Critical Approaches

Modern literary theory draws our attention to that school of German literary criticism known as reception theory or reception aesthetics ('Rezeptionsästhetik'), the most recent development of hermeneutics in Germany.[4] The work of disciples of this school in North America is known as reader-response criticism. In fact, Luanne Frank has argued that Herder was a trail-blazer of reception theory, and as such was a forerunner of Hans Robert Jauß, for whom the literary work exists only

---

2.   *Studies in German Literature of the Eighteenth Century*, p. 125. Cf. Purdie's 'Some Problems of Translation in the Eighteenth Century in Germany', *English Studies: A Journal of English Letters and Philology* 30 (1949), pp. 191-205 (201).

3.   'Others are at liberty to translate, embellish, refine, distort or idealize them so that nobody can recognize the original any more; it is *their* method rather than *mine*, and the reader is free to choose.'

4.   For an overview of the major theorists, see Robert C. Holub, *Reception Theory: A Critical Introduction* (New Accents Series; London: Methuen, 1984).

as the collective interpretation of successive generations of readers.[5] Every audience or readership responds to a literary work through the eyes of a particular set of conventions or rules.[6] Reader-response critics argue that it is difficult to talk about the meaning of a text without taking into account the reader's contribution to it. Susan Wittig's essay 'Theory of Multiple Meanings' places the emphasis not on the author, but on the reader.[7] Perhaps, then, the reader is the true writer, for reading is not a matter of discovering what a text means, but it is rather a process of experiencing what it does to one as the reader.[8] According to reader-response criticism, then, meaning is created by the reader construing the text. As Raman Selden has it, it is the reader who contributes something to the process of interpretation.[9] No reading is innocent or without prejudice or presupposition. Readers respond according to their social, historical and cultural backgrounds.

We shall need to consider Herder's claims to be as true as possible to the original text and the intentions of its author(s) in the light of this modern rejection of a historical-critical, quasi-scientific and documentary study of literature, that is, a study based on the belief that any sound interpretation must always start from the author's meaning. The text is the proper area of study, and the reader's response is paramount.

Writing specifically of the Gospel of Mark, Dan O. Via follows Wolfgang Iser's *The Act of Reading* thus:

---

5.   See 'Herder, Jauß, and the New Historicism: A Retrospective Reading', in Wulf Koepke (ed.), *Johann Gottfried Herder: Language, History, and the Enlightenment* (Studies in German Literature, Linguistics, and Culture, 52; Columbia, SC: Camden House, 1990), pp. 246-88.

6.   See Hans Robert Jauß, 'Literary History as a Challenge to Literary Theory', in Ralph Cohen (ed.), *New Directions in Literary History* (London: Routledge & Kegan Paul, 1974), pp. 11-41; *idem, Literaturgeschichte als Provokation* (Frankfurt am Main: Suhrkamp, 1970); and *idem, Toward an Aesthetic of Reception* (trans. Timothy Bahti; Brighton: Harvester Press, 1982), an English translation in book form of articles written by Jauß between 1969 and 1980.

7.   *Semeia* 9 (1977), pp. 75-103.

8.   See Stanley E. Fish, *Is There a Text in This Class? The Authority of Interpretive Communities* (Cambridge, MA: Harvard University Press, 1980), especially p. 3, and the sections entitled 'The Case for Reader-Response Analysis' (pp. 148-58) and 'Undoing the Case for Reader-Response Analysis' (pp. 158-67).

9.   See Raman Selden (ed.), *The Theory of Criticism: From Plato to the Present* (London: Longman, 1988), especially pp. 186-221.

> A text does not contain a formulated meaning but is a potential for mean-
> ing; the act of interpretation therefore is the production, performance, or
> assembling of this potential by the reader. The text itself has various
> qualities which summon the reader's participation in the constitution of
> its meaning. [...] What is missing—the gaps in the text—stimulates the
> reader to fill in the blanks with projections from the imagination. The
> text then brings the reader to the standpoint from which he or she con-
> structs its meaning. Therefore the text exercises some control, and the
> reader is not free to have it mean arbitrarily anything he or she wants it
> to mean. At the same time, the reader's subjectivity—experiences, deci-
> sions, and attitudes—comes to expression in the meaning he or she pro-
> jects. One must expect, then, a multiplicity of possible meanings.[10]

Terry Eagleton claims that significances vary throughout history, whereas meanings remain constant. The author puts in meanings, whereas it is the reader who assigns significances. For example, Eagleton proposes that his own account of what *Macbeth* might have meant in the cultural conditions of its time would still be *his* account, inescapably influenced by his own language and frames of cultural reference.[11] Hans-Georg Gadamer's aesthetic theory is based on Heidegger's philosophical ideas. For him, the meaning of a literary work is never exhausted by the intentions of its author. As the work passes from one cultural or historical context to another, new meanings may be culled from it which were perhaps never anticipated by its author or contemporary readership. All interpretation is situational, shaped and constrained by the historically relative criteria of a particular culture.[12] How, then, do these issues affect that peculiarly constrained mode of reading which issues in a translation, particularly of so heavily interpreted a text as a biblical book such as the Song of Songs?

Although agreeing that responses to forms of original language tend to be coloured by the mother tongue, Eugene Nida asserts that the so-called biblical culture has far more similarities with other cultures than maybe any other single culture in history. Thus he argues that the Bible is more easily translated in the many diverse cultures of the world than

10. *The Ethics of Mark's Gospel—in the Middle of Time* (Philadelphia: Fortress Press, 1985), pp. 4-5.

11. See *Literary Theory: An Introduction* (Oxford: Basil Blackwell, 1983), pp. 5 and 70.

12. See *Wahrheit und Methode: Grundzüge einer philosophischen Hermeneutik* (Tübingen: J.C.B. Mohr, 2nd edn, 1965).

most books which come out of our own Western culture.[13] Bible culture
is essentially similar to the cultures of so many different peoples, perhaps because so many derive from it. It is important to recall here that
Herder insisted on differences rather than similarities.

Nida insists that Bible translation consists of producing in the receptor language the closest natural equivalent to the message of the source
language, first in meaning and secondly in style, although he admits
that it is not always possible to have equivalence in both meaning and
style. If one must go, the translator must retain the meaning.[14] This puts
the weight on the meaning of the text, and not on the significances
ascribed to it by its (shifting) readership. It is important to note that
Nida pre-dates most reader-response theory, but in any case, texts (such
as the Bible) which claim truth present particular difficulties for reader-
response critics.

Robert C. Morgan underlines the importance of reader-response for
an understanding of biblical literature, although he points out that the
indeterminacy of deconstructive criticism, which denies to any text a
fixed and stable meaning, is hardly compatible with the ways in which
different religious communities use their scriptures as absolute authorities. Yet he pleads that an element of indeterminacy seems inseparable
from modern literary approaches:

> The Bible has meant and can mean somewhat different things to differ-
> ent people, and that is a condition of its capacity to speak of God to dif-
> ferent ages and cultures. [...] The written text is fixed, and sets limits to
> how it can rationally be read. It cannot mean anything the interpreter
> likes. On the other hand, in any act of interpretation the reader brings
> some pre-understanding, some aims, some interests—and these affect the
> way the text is read.[15]

Morgan admits that 'the most fundamental differences within biblical
interpretation have to do with the different possible reader responses

---

13. For an extensive bibliography of the large body of literature which exists on
the history of Bible translation, see Nida's *Toward a Science of Translating, with
Special Reference to Principles and Procedures Involved in Bible Translating*
(Leiden: E.J. Brill, 1964), pp. 265-320.

14. See 'Principles of Translation as Exemplified by Bible Translating', in
Reuben A. Brower (ed.), *On Translation* (Harvard Studies in Comparative Literature, 23; New York: Oxford University Press, 1966), pp. 11-31.

15. Robert C. Morgan, with John Barton, *Biblical Interpretation* (Oxford:
Oxford University Press, 1989), p. 257.

and the different interpretative communities'.[16] Presumably it would be possible for such interpretative communities to read the Bible as history, literature and religion, without making any assumptions which are specifically Christian.[17] This is an important point as far as Herder's work on the Song of Songs is concerned, for we shall see that his was an attempt at an historical, literary and even religious interpretation, although he attempted to offend neither Jew, nor Protestant, nor Catholic by being as religiously neutral as possible. In this regard, we may concur with Ulrich Simon that Herder's work on the Song of Songs 'is an enthusiastic rendering based upon a scholarly analysis', although we must reject his plea that 'it is meant to articulate a messianic, even Christian, union not only of individuals but also of church, state, and humanity'.[18] On the other hand, we can appreciate Simon's view that there is a tension between following modern critical theory, whereby the reader may be the interpreter, and pursuing the historical-critical approach advocated by Lowth and taken up by Herder. Writing specifically of the Song of Songs, Simon pleads that

> the hermeneutical problem inescapably raises a host of post-structural possibilities. One may proceed as if the text, and the text alone, hit our eyes and ears, irrespective of background material and possibly linking exclusively with our own world of passion, concubinage, pornography, disenchantment, in short with the erotic and sexual revolution of a post-biblical age. Or one may once again soberly re-examine the cultural background to the Song, even if its dating and exact locality remain uncertain. [...] The major thrust of these poems in the moral and the theological sense is often ignored.[19]

Arguably Simon's final complaint here results from an embracing of Herder's interpretation by those biblical scholars who subsequently refused to allow an allegorical approach.

If the reader (or translator) of a text is liberated from the shackles of the author's original intentions, the resulting multiplicity of meanings has serious implications for the interpretation of a document such as the Bible, especially for those of a fundamentalist persuasion who seek to impose a single set of beliefs upon their adherents. This means that the

16. *Biblical Interpretation*, p. 258.

17. See the section entitled 'Interpretive Communities' in Fish, *Is There a Text in This Class?*, pp. 167-73.

18. In Coggins and Houlden, *A Dictionary of Biblical Interpretation*, p. 281.

19. In Coggins and Houlden, *A Dictionary of Biblical Interpretation*, p. 644.

follower of reader-response criticism cannot accept the historical-critical approach advocated by Herder, and yet we shall observe that Herder
too was unable to provide the completely objective reading of the Song
of Songs which he demanded.

After this brief consideration of the implications of reader-response
criticism, let us now consider more fully the role of the translator within
this theoretical framework.

Approaches from Translation Theories

André Lefevere has claimed that translations are not transparent, but are
virtual rewrites in the cultural, intellectual and linguistic terms of the
translator.[20] Herder's translations of the Song of Songs provide an
excellent exemplification of this proposition, an argument which can be
supported both by a close reading of the translations themselves, and by
relating that to Herder's commentaries upon the Song of Songs.

First let us examine briefly those prior views on translation in Germany relevant to Herder, thus placing his work as a translator in context. It is important to remember that Herder pointed the reader of his
own translations of the Song of Songs to Luther, although as Chapter 6
will provide a fuller appraisal of Luther's work specifically as a Bible
translator, only a brief relevant comment is necessary here.

In Luther's view, 'übersetzen' ('translate') and 'verdeutschen' ('render into German') were virtual synonyms. Part of the translator's
responsibility was to help improve Germany's language and literature
so that they would not be inferior to foreign languages and literatures.
In other words, as Lefevere puts it, 'translation [...] becomes one of the
means by which a new nation "proves" itself, shows that its language is
capable of rendering what is rendered in more prestigious languages'.[21]
Such a point was essential to Herder's purpose in his work on the Song
of Songs, and, in this regard, Luther would have supported the rationale
behind his attempts to translate the book. Luther further held that the
Bible translator must change as little as possible of the original inspired
text, yet must adapt his text to the reader's understanding. He proposed
walking a tight-rope between the author's meaning and the reader's

20. See Susan Bassnett-McGuire and André Lefevere (eds.), *Translation, History and Culture* (London and New York: Pinter, 1990).
21. Bassnett-McGuire and Lefevere (eds.), *Translation, History and Culture*,
p. 8.

response. Nida points out Luther's shifts of word order, his use of modal auxiliaries, his use of connectives where required, his suppression of Greek or Hebrew terms without an acceptable equivalent in German, his use of whole phrases where necessary to translate single words, his shifts of metaphors to non-metaphors and vice versa, and his careful attention to exegetical accuracy and textual variants.[22]

Johann Christoph Gottsched's view of a text's universal transparency was the dominant one in Herder's day, yet one with which Herder particularly quarrelled. Gottsched held that the translation of foreign models would help translators to improve their skills and thus aid Germany's language and literature. By foreign models, Gottsched meant those works of literature which followed French neo-classical norms. He emphasized meaning rather than form, and, in contradiction to later theory, supported translation from one foreign language to another as well as into one's own mother tongue (although he stressed the importance of the mother tongue), a view which implied a degree of universalizing abstraction in his thinking. In this regard, Lefevere argues that translators should be bicultural rather than bilingual. Since language expresses culture and the translated text has a place in two cultures, consideration should be given to the relative function of the text in each of its two contexts.[23] We shall note below how opposed Herder was to the imitation of any foreign model as supported by Gottsched, and it is important to remember that, unlike Gottsched, Herder had a sense of cultural difference.[24]

Walter F.A. Fränzel points out that while German language societies of the eighteenth century accepted translations into German as works of German literature, Gottsched went so far as to include German imitations of foreign-language models.[25] Herder could not accept that foreign

22. Nida, *Toward a Science of Translating*, p. 15. See also Luther's *Ein Sendbrief von Dolmetschen* (1530), *WKG*, XXX/2, pp. 627-46, and *Summarien über die Psalmen und Ursachen des Dolmetschens* (1531–33), *WKG*, XXXVIII, pp. 1-69.

23. Bassnett-McGuire and Lefevere (eds.), *Translation, History and Culture*, pp. 11 and 12.

24. See Gottsched's *Ausführliche Redekunst, nach Anleitung der alten Griechen und Römer* (1743), in Joachim Birke, Brigitte Birke and P.M. Mitchell (eds.), *Ausgewählte Werke* (10 vols.; Berlin: W. de Gruyter, 1975), VII/1, VII/2 and VII/3, and *Versuch einer Critischen Dichtkunst* (1751) in Birke, Birke and Mitchell (eds.), *Ausgewählte Werke*, vols. VI/1 and VI/2.

25. Walter F.A. Fränzel, *Geschichte des Übersetzens im 18. Jahrhundert* (Beiträge zur Kultur und Universalgeschichte, 25; Leipzig: Voigtländer, 1914), p. 131.

models could become instances of original German literature, whether
by imitation or in translation, as they could not contain that characteristic national spirit which he found, for example, in the Song of Songs,
and which he was hoping to instil into his own literature. Indeed, Herder argued that changes in the original were necessary, for 'es gehörte
dies zur Gestalt unsrer Sprache' ('this pertained to the character of our
language') (*TS*, XXVII, p. 231). As early as 4 October 1766 Herder
wrote to Scheffner: 'Ein Übersetzer, der sich zur klassischen Höhe er-
heben will, muß den Gedanken einer fremden Sprache, den Stempel der
Eigenheit in der seinigen zu geben wissen.'[26]

While Jakob Bodmer (1698–1783) was the first to distinguish between translation as the interpretation of thought and content vis-à-vis
translation as the conveying of the formal and individual characteristics
of the original text, Johann Jacob Breitinger (1701–76) stressed that the
translator should treat meaning and form equally.[27] As we shall see,
Herder sought fidelity to form in his translation of the Song of Songs,
for example, by allowing the word order of the original to influence the
structure of his translation. It was Breitinger's view that the reader of
the translation must be affected in the same way as the reader of the
original. He demanded a high degree of empathy between the translator
and the original author. Unlike Gottsched, Breitinger rejected French
neo-classicism in favour of Milton as his paradigm, distinguishing
between translation and imitation.[28]

Herder's particularist view was to a large extent shared by Gotthold
Ephraim Lessing, who was opposed to the French neo-classical model,
and thus to Gottsched, for it was Gottsched's kind of universalizing abstraction that Herder, with his strong sense of the validity of individual
cultures, was attempting to refute precisely with his translation of the

26. 'A translator who wishes to rise to classical heights has to be able to lend to
the thoughts of a foreign language the stamp of idiom in his own language.' Otto
(ed.), *Herders Briefe*, p. 13.

27. See Anneliese Senger, *Deutsche Übersetzungstheorie im achtzehnten Jahrhundert* (Abhandlungen zur Kunst-, Musik- und Literaturwissenschaft, 97; Bonn:
Bouvier, 1971), p. 68. See also J. Bodmer and J.J. Breitinger's *Der Mahler der
Sitten* (2 vols.; Zürich: Orell, 1746; repr. Hildesheim: Georg Olms, 1972), especially the Ninety-Fourth Letter, II, pp. 512-24.

28. For Breitinger's views of translation, see his *Critische Dichtkunst*, especially
Section 4, 'Von der Kunst der Uebersetzung' (Deutsche Neudrucke, Reihe Texte
des 18. Jahrhunderts; ed. Paul Böckmann and Friedrich Sengle; 2 vols.; Zürich:
Orell; Leipzig: Gleditsch, 1740; repr. Stuttgart: Metzler, 1966), II, pp. 136-99.

Song of Songs. The specific nature of the original should be maintained in the translation, although the best kind of translation allowed the beauties of the original to shine through in a language for which they were not intended. By way of example Lessing cited Johann Nikolaus Meinhard's *Versuche über den Charakter und die Werke der besten italienischen Dichter* (3 vols.; Brunswick: Fürstliche Waysenhaus-Buchhandlung, 1774).[29] In other words, faithfulness to an original text was not equivalence between words, but an attempt to make the target text function in the target culture in the same way as the source text did in the source culture.[30] In this regard, Fränzel argues that Herder, along with Goethe, refused to rank his own translations with the greatness of the original text, publishing them not for their own sake, 'sondern [...] unter irgendeinem Vorwande, in irgendeinem größeren Zusammenhang' ('but [...] behind some pretext or other, within some greater context') such as is found, for example, in his work on Hebrew poetry in *Vom Geist der Ebräischen Poesie* and *Lieder der Liebe*.[31]

Herder passed on to Goethe the view that translation was penetration into the inner spirit of a work. Goethe held that there are three phases of translation—although, as these phases are recurrent, they may all be found in the same language system at the same time. The first phase acquaints the reader with foreign countries on his own terms, and Goethe cited Luther's Bible translation as an example. The second phase is one of appropriation through substitution and reproduction, where the translator absorbs the sense of a foreign work but reproduces it in his own terms. This, then, is the parodistic remaking of a work according to the cultural norms of the translator. As examples, Goethe pointed to Wieland and the French tradition of translating.[32] The third phase aims for perfect identity between the original text and the text in the target language. This is to be achieved through the fusing of the uniqueness of the original with the form and structure of the new language. This represents an 'interlinear version' in which the translator

---

29. For Lessing's views on translation, see his *Briefe, die neueste Literatur betreffend* (written 1759–65), in *Sämtliche Schriften* (ed. Karl Lachmann; 23 vols.; Leipzig: Göschen, 3rd edn [ed. Franz Muncker], 1886–1907), VIII, pp. 1-285.

30. See Bassnett-McGuire and Lefevere (eds.), *Translation, History and Culture*, p. 8.

31. *Geschichte des Übersetzens*, p. 141.

32. Cf. Herder's rejection of such 'Verschönerung' ('embellishment') noted above.

penetrates to the essence of the original through the close imitation of
the use of language. Goethe's example here was the translation of
Homer by Johann Heinrich Voß into German hexameters:[33]

> Eine Übersetzung, die sich mit dem Original zu identificiren strebt,
> nähert sich zuletzt der Interlinear-Version und erleichtert höchlich das
> Verständniß des Originals, hiedurch werden wir an den Grundtext hin-
> angeführt, ja getrieben, und so ist denn der ganze Cirkel abgeschlossen,
> in welchem sich die Annäherung des Fremden und Einheimischen, des
> Bekannten und Unbekannten bewegt.[34]

Lefevere writes of a hypothetical *tertium comparationis* which
hovers somewhere between two languages in some kind of air bubble,
ensuring that a word in the translation is the equivalent of a word in the
original. He points out that translations can never be produced in an air-
lock, where they and the original text can be checked against the *ter-*
tium comparationis in the purest possible lexical chamber, without the
influences of power, time or culture. Rather, translations are made to
respond not only to the demands of a given culture, but also to the
demands of various groups within that culture.[35]

Thus if a text such as the Bible embodies the fundamental beliefs of a
particular culture, that culture will demand the most literal translation
possible. If the text has little to do with the beliefs of the members of a
culture—as is the case with most literary texts—then that culture's
translators have more freedom. In this regard, we are reminded that
Herder was translating the Song of Songs as literature rather than
dogma, attempting to persuade representatives of different religious

33. It is important to note that Herder was writing before Voß's Homer had
brought the hexameter to German (1781–83). Voß was doing exactly what Herder
had been calling for, namely extending the range of German poetry; although,
ironically, Herder argued that 'so wenig ist der Hexameter [...] unsrer Sprache
natürlich' ('just as little is the hexameter [...] natural to our own language') (*DL*, I,
p. 175).

34. 'In the final analysis, a translation which endeavours to identify with the
original comes near to the interlinear version and greatly facilitates the understanding of the original, by which means we are led, even driven to the original text; and
thus is completed the whole circle in which is set in motion the rapprochement
between the foreign and the indigenous, the familiar and the unfamiliar.' 'Übersetzungen', in *Noten und Abhandlungen zu besserem Verständniß des West-*
östlichen Divans, *WW*, VII, p. 239.

35. Bassnett-McGuire and Lefevere (eds.), *Translation, History and Culture*,
p. 7.

persuasions within his national culture to listen to his plea for the improvement of German literature.

In Lefevere's view, *translatio* may be used for a translation exhibiting an exchange of words without much regard for connotations, cultural or otherwise. He uses the term *traductio* for a translation which lends equal weight to the linguistic, cultural and ideological components of the translation process.[36] The latter term would thus represent Herder's attempts to translate and comment on the Song of Songs. Indeed, Lefevere claims that translations since 1800 have been in this mould. One problem is the translation of cultural elements which are not immediately obvious, or which would seem out of place in the target language and culture. It will become clear that Herder essentially attempted to convey such images in German, but saved himself from the accusation of producing an opaque translation by his detailed commentaries in which he attempted to explain such imagery in terms of its cultural context. Without the commentaries he might have been forced to find in his translations images which were more in keeping with his own culture.

In assessing the detail of the commentaries and translations below, we must examine how far Herder succeeded in keeping the Song of Songs within its original *Sitz im Leben*, and the extent to which his own culture impinged, inevitably, on his reading of the text. It is clear that Herder had to translate into terms that his German readers would understand, therefore he must have been influenced at some point by his imagined readership, and thus by his own culture.[37]

Herder's Theories of Language

One of the major concerns of Herder's *Fragmente* was to show that a national language was the natural utterance of a people, and the expression of its inner genius. In his *Abhandlung über den Ursprung der Sprache*, Herder applied and developed the concept of organic growth and the principle of continuity in speech. In his advocacy of an 'organic' semantic model, namely one which allowed no real distinction

---

36. Bassnett-McGuire and Lefevere (eds.), *Translation, History and Culture*, p. 17.

37. On the existence and non-existence of referents in the receptor language, see Nida's section 'Relationship of Linguistic Form to Semantic Function' in 'Principles of Translation', pp. 29-31.

between the word and the idea it denoted, Herder developed the notion that language grew and enlarged its range by means of metaphors. Different languages generated their own metaphorical systems and were therefore not intertranslatable. This was Herder's linguistic relativism, and it is relevant to his views on translation. The traditional notion of translation presupposes a dualistic semantic model, a 'meaning' or 'content' which may or may not be the same in different languages. Herder's organic definition of language, however, imposed a semantic monism in which form and content were indistinguishable, and consequently the possibility of 'translation' in the usual or literary sense of the word was eliminated.[38]

Herder was the first to argue unreservedly that metaphor was formally intrinsic to language and that metaphors were generated within individual languages by principles not governing the formulation of all languages. Any linguistic form was not only functional in meaning, but was also peculiar to the language in which it occurred. While Etienne Bonnot de Condillac and Adam Smith, for example, had assumed that all languages followed the same formal growth patterns, Herder opened the way to an examination of languages in terms of their own individual cultures. He stated that a more primordial language would be less analytical and abstract in its terms. The oldest language was therefore no more than a dictionary of nature (*US*, V, p. 83). It was in his desire to return to the most primitive, natural and therefore divinely inspired poetry known to man, that Herder turned to the poetry of the Hebrews

---

38.   Stephen K. Land points out that the problem of translation had already been discussed in terms of linguistic relativism by John Locke, James Harris, David Hartley and Joseph Priestley. See Land's *From Signs to Propositions: The Concept of Form in Eighteenth-Century Semantic Theory* (Longman Linguistics Library, 16; London: Longman, 1974), pp. 69-70, and 'Universalism and Relativism: A Philosophical Problem of Translation in the Eighteenth Century', *JHI* 35 (1974), pp. 597-610. See also Locke's *An Essay Concerning Human Understanding* (London: Holt, 1689), and *Some Thoughts Concerning Education* (London: A. and J. Churchill, 1693); Harris's *Three Treatises: The First Concerning Art, the Second Concerning Music, Painting, and Poetry, the Third Concerning Happiness* (London: Nourse and Vaillant, 1774); Hartley's *Observations on Man, his Frame, his Duty, and his Expectations* (London and Bath: Leake and Frederick, 1749); and Priestley's *Essay on a Course of Liberal Education* (London: J. Johnson and Davenport, 1765), where he drew attention to the main historical sources, and *Lectures on History and General Policy* (London: J. Johnson, 1788), where he emphasized history rather than the classics.

as recorded in the Bible in general and the Song of Songs in particular. He argued for a return to nature in his desire to promote a German national literature, and he aimed to use the Song of Songs as a prime example of good (relative) literature.

Herder thought of grammar as something which, with increasing civilization, was brought to bear on language from without. He tried to counter the contemporary claim—posited by Lowth, for example—that only divine intervention could account for the complex grammatical structure of even the most primitive languages, such as Hebrew. To argue the natural origin of all language, Herder minimized the grammatical component of early speech, holding the figurative language of popular tradition to be superior to clear and abstract prose. Rhetorically enquiring 'in welchem genauen Bande steht Sprache und Denkungsart?' ('how closely are language and thought processes bound together?') (*FS*, I, p. 6), he claimed that 'jede Nation spricht also, nach dem sie denkt, und denkt, nach dem sie spricht' ('every nation speaks according to how it thinks, and thinks according to how it speaks') (*DL*, II, p. 18), for 'wir haben durch die Sprache denken gelernt: sie ist also ein Schatz von Begriffen, die sinnlich klar an den Worten kleben, und vom gemeinen Verstande nie getrennet werden' (*DL*, I, p. 417).[39]

As far as Herder was concerned, the language, the way of thinking and hence the literature of a people, were almost inextricably linked. He argued the impossibility of surveying a literature adequately without taking into account the original language in which it was written, for 'der Genius der Sprache ist also auch der Genius von der Litteratur einer Nation' ('the genius of the language is also the genius of a nation's literature') (*DL*, I, p. 148).

Herder's Theories of Translation

Herder's theorizing about translation highlights the paradox of the activity. On the one hand, throughout his *Fragmente* Herder argued the fundamental *a priori* organic unity of form, content, thought and word in poetry. Indeed, the title of the sixth part of the third collection of *Fragmente* is 'In der Dichtkunst ist Gedanke und Ausdruck wie Seele und Leib, und nie zu trennen' ('In poetry, thought and expression are

---

39. 'Through language we learned to think; thus it is a wealth of ideas which clearly adhere sensuously to the words and which are never separated from the general meaning.'

like body and soul—and they cannot be separated'). Here, too, Herder argued: 'So wenig ist in der wahren Dichtkunst Gedanke und Ausdruck von einander zu trennen: und es ist beinahe immer ein Kennzeichen einer mittelmäßigen Poesie, wenn sie gar zu leicht zu übersezzen ist' (*DL*, I, pp. 399-400).[40] He particularly used the verb 'kleben' ('cling/ adhere') to underpin his view of an inseparable whole, claiming that 'in der Dichtkunst, wo der sinnlich lebhafte Ausdruck alles ist: klebt also der Gedanke sehr am Worte' ('in poetry, where the sensuously active expression is everything, the thought adheres very much to the word') (*DL*, I, p. 414), and stressing that 'Gedanke klebt am Ausdruck' ('thought adheres to expression') (*DL*, I, p. 416, and II, p. 16), Thus, as a consequence of his organic position, Herder claimed that the unique beauties of poetry were virtually impossible to translate: 'Poesie ist beinahe in ihren Schönheiten unübersezzbar, weil hier der Wohlklang, der Reim, einzelne Theile der Rede, Zusammensezzung der Worte, Bildung der Redarten, alles Schönheit giebt' (*DL*, I, p. 240).[41] Indeed, he drew attention to parts of Homer's poetry which, in his view, remained untranslatable (*DL*, I, p. 291).

On the other hand, Herder's aim was to preserve the character of the original; the content could be conveyed elsewhere, presumably in a commentary such as that which accompanied his translations of the Song of Songs. In his view, translation was more than the mere transference of material from one language to another. It was to represent a complete reproduction of the original work, including the peculiarities of language, metre and feeling, in a form best suited to the target language. There is an inevitable paradox here, for this contradicts the 'impossible' organicist position outlined above. Kelletat points out that the authentically reproduced tone was more important to Herder than the concrete rendering of the content.[42] Purdie holds that with Herder a

40. 'In true poetry, thought and expression cannot be separated from each other, and it is almost always a characteristic of mediocre poetry if it is just too easy to translate.' In this regard, Edwin Muir's and Willa Muir's essay on translating Kafka into English is significant ('Translating from the German', in Brower [ed.], *On Translation*, pp. 93-96).

41. 'In its beauties, poetry is virtually untranslatable, since here everything provides beauty—the melodious sound, the rhyme, individual parts of the language, the juxtaposition of the words, the formation of the expressions.'

42. *Herder und die Weltliteratur*, pp. 52-53.

turning-point was reached in relation to the problem of fidelity to form,[43] one which Kelletat locates in his *Lieder der Liebe*, a translation preserving form and tone.

A mechanical, word-for-word translation was inadmissible for Herder, just as a free translation which ignored style, metre and linguistic peculiarities was likewise imperfect: 'Das Sylbenmaaß, dünkt mich, müsse sich der Sprache selbst einsingen' ('It seems to me that the metre should be appropriate to the language itself') (*TS*, XXVII, p. 277).[44] An ideal translation was one which allowed for a synthesis of both methods, although in fact the technical difficulties of language, such as syntax, word length and untranslatable idioms or 'Patronymische Schönheiten' ('patronymic beauties') (*DL*, I, p. 162), made this impossible. The translator therefore was striving after the unobtainable.

Herder argued that the translator either should alter the original to conform with the different means of thought and expression in the target language, or should treat the target language creatively to enable the original to be adequately expressed in it. In other words, the translator had to decide either to move the original text towards the linguistic peculiarities of the language into which it was being translated, or to bring the latter closer to the original language: 'Alles Schwanken [...] zwischen zwo Sprachen und Singarten, des Verfassers und Uebersetzers, ist unausstehlich' ('Any vacillation [...] between two languages and styles, namely those of the writer and translator, is intolerable') (*VL*, XXV, p. 333). For Herder, the decisive factor in this choice was the type of literature to be translated. Prose and poetry should be treated differently, and even the various genres of poetry should be taken into account: 'Die lyrische Poesie und das Epigramm sind vielleicht die eigensinnigsten unter allen; da sie nicht übersetzt seyn wollen, so muß man sie mit der gewissenhaftesten Treue täuschen, als ob sie nicht übersetzt würden' (*TS*, XXVII, p. 275).[45]

43. 'Some Problems of Translation in the Eighteenth Century in Germany', p. 200.

44. Herder used Luther's *Ein Sendbrief von Dolmetschen* as an example of his own views on translation, for Luther also held a mechanical word-for-word translation to be the least skilful (see *TS*, XXVII, p. 276).

45. 'Lyric poetry and the epigramme are perhaps the most obstinate of all; as they do not want to be translated, they must be duped by means of the most scrupulous accuracy, as if they were not being translated at all.'

Since lyrical poetry is highly subjective, Herder regarded it as virtually untranslatable, and thus he preferred the first method, offering the
translator more opportunity to reproduce the subjective thoughts of the
poet with less bondage of language. On the other hand, when translating folk-poetry he chose the second method in an attempt to preserve
the 'Ton und Weise' ('tone and melody') which he considered so essential to a good translation. And yet he claimed that the greatest problem
he had in his own translations of folk-poetry was 'den Ton und die
Weise jedes Gesanges und Liedes zu fassen' ('to express the tone and
melody of each poem and song') (*VL*, XXV, p. 333). For Herder, the
many variations in metre were all part of the patina of a poem, and if
the 'Ton und Weise' were to be preserved, the metre could not be
altered, for the metre and subject matter were inseparable. However,
one of Herder's greatest achievements was the recognition and copying
of the intricate 'Sprünge und Würfe' ('leaps and bounds') of a poem
into his own translations, for he had the ability to recreate in his own
language those peculiar gaps in logical thought which are characteristic
of the folk-song.

Continuing his relativistic theories into the realms of translation,
Herder demanded that the translator should submerge himself in the
spirit and times of the original and not impose his own prejudices on it.
The best translator should also be the best expositor of a text and should
enter as fully as possible into the *Sitz im Leben* of the work which he
was translating so that he could understand the national character,
thought and taste. This is what Herder sought to do in his translations of
and commentaries on the Song of Songs, although we shall judge below
how successful he was. Herder argued that the translator must understand the individuality and uniqueness of a poetic creation. He must
have the same thoughts and feelings as the original poet, attempting to
produce the same effect as if the author were reproducing his own
work. The result would be a new creation, or 'Nachdichtung' ('free version'), rather than a mere translation, and should be regarded as highly
as an original text (see *DL*, I, pp. 144 and 274, and II, p. 142). In other
words, the translator's work should raise him to the rank of an original
author. Thus the translator must be a creative genius 'wenn er hier
seinem Original und seiner Sprache ein Gnüge thun will' ('if here he is
to do justice to his original as well as to his own language') (*DL*, I,
p. 178). In his own translations of Ossian, for example—whom, of
course, he took in good faith—Herder showed considerable fidelity to

the English text. According to the Gaelic pattern, he used lines of unequal length and divided the whole into short sections. His was not a copy, but rather a re-creation of the original rhythm. He reproduced the simplicity of the original text and he maintained the national and individual characteristics. Seeing the affinity between Ossian and the style of the Bible which he so admired—a point made in Chapter 2 above—Herder was able to use the shortness, inversion and parallelism with which he was acquainted, and which he used in his translations of the Song of Songs. We have seen his plea that the translator of Ossian (in this case, Denis) ought to have become a Celt in spirit (*VL*, XXV, p. 325), forgetting all convention, seeing nothing but nature, and listening to and feeling nothing but the sound of the harp: 'Und sodann welch ein andrer Oßian! Wenn Hr. D. die Gallische Sprache studirt, auch nur im fernen Nachhall vernommen hätte? welch ein andrer Oßian!' (*DR*, V, p. 325).[46] A translator should be 'mit den Ebräern ein Ebräer, mit den Arabern ein Araber, mit den Skalden ein Skalde, [...] um Moses und Hiob, und Oßian in ihrer Zeit und Natur zu fühlen' (*KW*, III, p. 202).[47]

Similarly, Herder considered the Greeks worthy of imitation, yet he argued that the translator should know them first (*DL*, I, p. 286). Critical of the poetry of his own age, he claimed that the translator of Greek poetry must be able first of all to think and write like a Greek, 'mit starkem und innigem Gefühl des Schönen, nicht in dem süßen Geschmack unsrer Zeit' (*DL*, II, p. 142).[48] Herder wanted to be able to translate ancient literature into German in such a way that it would remain what it had been in the original language: 'O wäre mirs gelungen, von diesen goldnen Gaben und Gerüchten der Vorzeit, als den edelsten Volksgesängen etwas in unsre Sprache zu übertragen, daß sie noch einigermaassen, was sie sind, blieben!' (*VL*, XXV, p. 316).[49] Speaking of Homer, Hesiod and Orpheus, Herder bemoaned his inabil-

---

46. 'And then what a different Ossian! If only Herr Denis had studied the Gaelic language and understood it even if only as a distant echo—what a different Ossian!'

47. 'A Hebrew with the Hebrews, an Arab with the Arabs, and a Skald with the Skalds [...] in order to experience Moses and Job and Ossian in their own time and nature.'

48. 'With intense, inner feeling for the beautiful, not in the sugared taste of our own age.'

49. 'Oh, if only I had succeeded in transferring into our language something of these golden offerings and stories of ancient times as the noblest of folksongs, so that to some extent they might remain what they are.'

ity to convey their poetry into German satisfactorily: 'Mir fehlt das Schiff von euch in mein Land und meine Sprache' ('I lack the vessel to bring me from you to my own land and language') (*VL*, XXV, p. 316). He pleaded that Homer be judged not 'aus Uebersetzung und Wörter-buche, sondern aus dem lebendigen Gebrauche seiner Zeit' ('by trans-lation and dictionary, but rather by the living customs of his own age') (*KW*, III, p. 199). A translation might be admirable in many ways, and yet incomplete or incorrect if the temper of the original had been mis-understood. Herder cited Alexander Pope's translations of Homer by way of example: 'Hat der Übersetzer, oder Nachbilder die Manier seines Originals nicht recht studirt, nicht recht gefaßt, oder [...] nicht recht gesehen; schiebt er seiner Urkunde also eine andre Manier, ein andres Ideal unter—als Übersetzung, als Nachbildung betrachtet, wirds immer ein schiefes Werk seyn und bleiben' (*DR*, V, p. 323).[50]

For the translator of biblical literature in particular, Herder recom-mended a study of the Arabs, whose language and customs were similar to those of the Hebrews. Travel literature—so prevalent in Herder's day—was also vital for him in his search for an understanding of the cultural background within which a work of literature was produced, and particularly Chapter 5 of the present study will show how much use Herder made of such travel writing in his work on the Song of Songs:

> Nun sage man, wie einer unsrer Dichter, der Aegypten oft nicht einmal aus Reisebeschreibungen kennt, vom Leviathan und Behemoth singen darf? [...] Und wenn wir diese Bilder auch endlich verstehen—erklären, und aus den lebhaftesten Historischen und Geographischen Beschreib-ungen ihre Schönheiten ganz fühlen lernen; nie haben diese Historische Beschreibungen, Auslegungen, Erklärungen so viel Eindruck in uns, als die sinnliche Gegenwart dieser Oerter; nie das Leben der Anschauung, als wenn wir sie selbst sähen (*DL*, I, p. 259. See also I, p. 263).[51]

---

50. 'If the translator or imitator has not properly studied, comprehended or [...] seen the style of his original, then he foists upon his document a different style, a different model—and, viewed as a translation or imitation, it will be always a dis-torted work and will remain so.'

51. 'Now tell me how one of our poets can sing of Leviathan and Behemoth if he does not know anything about Egypt even from travel literature. [...] And even when we finally understand these images—how can we explain and come to feel fully their beauties even from the most vivid historical and geographical descrip-tions? These historical descriptions, interpretations and explanations never make such an impact upon us as does the sensual presence of these places; never is con-templation as impressive as if we were seeing these places for ourselves.'

Herder considered that there were literary works which could not be translated adequately, and it was his ideal to render superfluous any translation from the main European languages into German (*DL*, II, p. 8). Although it might be quicker and easier to read a translation rather than study a text in its original language, he claimed that this was inadequate (*FS*, I, p. 4). For example, in his view, those reading even the best translation of Homer in fact no longer read Homer, but something that merely approximated what he had said in his own poetic language—a language which could not be imitated (*DL*, I, p. 177). Herder argued that the reader should learn the original language, for the best translation was that which the reader undertook from the original text: 'Die beste Uebersetzung bleibt doch immer die in unsrer Seele' ('Yet the best translation always remains the one within our own soul') (*AD*, XXIV, p. 218). He urged his compatriots to read literature in its original language and thus to benefit more fully from what each literature had to offer. A mental translation of a poem was always the best (*AV*, XXV, p. 33). For Herder, translation was always an aid and could never be a substitute for the original, although he was happy to have a translation nearby for comparison. By comparing the German version with the foreign version the reader could treasure the beauties and national characteristics of the language of the original.

There are contradictions here, for while with one voice Herder spoke of the translator's creativity, here he argued for translation as a mere aid, yet elsewhere he considered the translator as critic–interpreter. Herder could assume acquaintance with Luther, so in a sense he was offering a variant in his translations of the Song of Songs. Clearly, however, he assumed different categories of imagined readership, for surely most of his readers would not know the original, nor would all require a critical interpretation.

As far as Herder was concerned, each language contained individual and peculiar beauties whose charms were intensified by the veil of language itself. As soon as that veil was removed, they disintegrated, as might also part of the character of the whole work (see *FS*, I, p. 4, and *Über Thomas Abbts Schriften*, II, p. 360). There were beauties and rareties in a language 'die [...] kein Nachbar durch eine Übersezzung entwenden kann, und die der Schuzgöttin der Sprache heilig sind: Schönheiten in das Genie der Sprache eingewebt, die man zerstört, wenn man sie austrennet' (*DL*, I, p. 162).[52] Thus each individual poetic spirit must be permitted to speak in its own language (*FS*, I, p. 5).

Herder maintained that the Hebrew poets used natural imagery, writing, for example, of the snows of Mount Lebanon, the beauties of Mount Carmel, and the thaws of Mount Hermon—images found frequently, of course, in the Song of Songs. A foreign poet using such imagery was not using imagery natural to his own geographical situation, but was borrowing figures of speech which were difficult for his readers to understand (*DL*, I, pp. 258-59). Significantly, Herder kept the original imagery of the Song of Songs in his translations, using his commentaries to provide explanatory notes.

For Herder, then, the aim of translation should be to convey the spirit of the foreign literature into one's own soul, an aim which could best be realized by means of the folk-song: 'Nur sie müssen es geben, wie es ist, in der Ursprache und mit gnugsamer Erklärung, ungeschimpft und unverspottet, so wie unverschönt und unveredelt' (*VÄ*, IX, p. 533).[53] Yet the goal of the true translator was higher than simply helping the reader to understand the original. For example, Herder saw in translation a way of showing how inadequate German literature was, and how it was imitating slavishly the wrong things: 'In dem Barbarischen unsrer Sprache, in den Inversionen, in den Sylbenmaaßen haben wir nichts von den Franzosen zu lernen' (*DL*, I, p. 211).[54] Yet German had much to learn from other languages such as English, French, Italian, Greek and Latin (see *FS*, I, p. 5, and *DL*, I, p. 240). From his interest in biblical literature it is likewise clear that Herder admired the language and culture of the Hebrews, and speaking almost prophetically in 1767 of his later work on the Song of Songs, he claimed that 'ein Theil unsrer besten Gedichte ist halb Morgenländisch: ihr Muster ist die schöne Natur des Orients: sie borgen den Morgenländern Sitten und Geschmack ab—und so werden sie Originale' (*DL*, I, p. 258).[55]

---

52. 'Which [...] no neighbour can misappropriate by means of a translation, and which are sacred to the goddess of language; beauties woven into the genius of the language, which are destroyed if they are separated.'

53. 'Just that they must render it as it stands in the original language and with sufficient explanation, unreviled and underided, as well as unembellished and unrefined.'

54. 'In the barbaric nature of our language, in the inversions, in the metres, we have nothing to learn from the French.'

55. 'Some of our best poems are half Oriental; their pattern is the beautiful

Herder demanded a sympathetic penetration into the spirit and background of the original. In this way the peculiar beauties of the foreign literature would be brought out so forcibly that they would be a constant source of instruction, more valuable than any number of philological notes and explanations. This would help the reader to understand the original nature of the foreign language, and would point the way to originality in the native language: 'Raube ihnen nicht das Erfundne, sondern die Kunst zu erfinden, zu erdichten, und einzukleiden!' (*DL*, I, p. 274).[56] Herder preferred translations from recognized originals and from writings in which 'zwar mindere Kunst, aber vielleicht eine schöne nachläßige Natur in der Schreibart hervorblickt: diese werden, ja sie müssen uns schätzbar bleiben, nicht blos als Werke aus der Morgenröthe des Geschmacks, sondern vielleicht als Mittel zu demselben zurück zu kehren' (IV, p. 272).[57] The translator's task would be to reveal and reproduce the sources and processes of poetic creation in other nations, and thus his work would resemble that of the critic.

It should not surprise us, therefore, that in Herder's work as a critic, the translations of others (such as Denis) should have come in for the heaviest criticism. It was here that Herder was so exacting. A good example is Herder's recension of Denis's translation of Ossian, in which he criticized the translator for replacing the original metre with German hexameters.[58] Herder picked up what he regarded as a fundamental error in Denis's work, namely that by using hexameters in his translation, he had shown clearly that he had failed to understand the spirit and essence of bardic poetry.[59] This was of utmost importance to

nature of the Orient, they borrow taste and customs from the Orientals—and thus they become originals.'

56. 'Do not take from them what has been discovered already, but rather borrow from them the art of discovery, of inventing, and of couching ideas in imagery.'

57. 'Maybe less art shows through in the style of writing, but rather, perhaps, a beautiful, casual character; these will, indeed they must, remain valuable for us, not merely as works from the dawn of good taste, but perhaps as a means of returning to such.' This is from Herder's recension of Carl Christian Gärtner (ed.), *Des Herrn Nicol. Dietrich Gieseke Poetische Werke*, published in Brunswick in 1767 (see *ADB*, VII/1, pp. 150-60, and *SWS*, IV, pp. 271-78).

58. The recension is in *SWS*, V, pp. 322-30. See also *AK*, V, p. 160-68; and *ADB*, X/1, p. 64, and *ADB*, XVII/2, p. 438.

59. In 'Michael Denis as a Translator of Ossian', *MLR* 60 (1965), pp. 547-52 (549), H.-C. Sasse compares Herder's translations of Ossian with those of Denis, arguing that Denis showed greater lyric sensitivity than Herder, as well as possess-

Herder, who argued that the translator should take into account the national speech characteristics when choosing a metre. The hexameter was unnatural in German and was indeed forbidden by 'Sprache und Ohr und Deklamation' ('language, ear and declamation') (*DL*, I, p. 175), for it produced artistic prose (*DL*, I, p. 178). Writing to Hamann about Denis's Ossian, Herder claimed: 'Ich kann ihn nicht ausstehen, er ist in Homerisch seyn sollende Hexameter hingeschwemmt—als wenn nicht ein großer Unterschied wäre, zwischen dem sanften süßen Geschwätze-ton des Griechen und der rauhen Kürze des Barden.'[60] Possibly alluding to Wieland's translations, Herder found Shakespeare to have been translated 'im ungleichsten, fast nie getroffenen Ton' ('in the most uneven tone, the like of which we almost never encounter') (*DL*, I, p. 217), and even Luther's translations of hymns he found 'ziemlich hart' ('rather rough') (*ZB*, XVI, p. 230).[61] We also note Herder's nega-tive comments about German attempts to translate from English: 'Wenn wird man aufhören, die besten Englischen Schriftsteller durch Ueber-sezzungen zu verunstalten, und Prior, Milton, Young in elende oder mittelmäßige Hexameter zu übersezzen: ein Sylbenmaas, an das sie nicht im Traume gedacht haben?' (*DL*, I, p. 217).[62]

At first Herder did not translate for publication, but rather because of its intrinsic attraction (*VL*, XXV, pp. 328-29). In this regard, he was fascinated by Percy's *Reliques*: 'Als vor zehn und mehr Jahren die *Reliques of Ancient Poetry* mir in die Hände fielen, freuten mich ein-zelne Stücke so sehr, daß ich sie zu übersetzen versuchte, und unsrer Muttersprache, die jener an Kadenzen und Lyrischem Ausdruck auf-fallend ähnlich ist, auch ähnlich gute Stücke wünschte' (*VL*, XXV,

ing a better knowledge of English. Nevertheless, this view does not touch Herder's theoretical position.

60. 'I cannot stand him, he is steeped in hexameters which are supposed to be Homeric in style—as if there were no great difference between the gentle, delicate chattering tone of the Greek, and the unpolished brevity of the bard.' Letter of the middle of March 1769 in Hoffmann (ed.), *Briefe an Hamann*, p. 55.

61. Herder did not specify which translations of Shakespeare, nor which of Luther's hymns he had in mind here. Cf. his views in his recension of Denis, noted above.

62. 'When will we stop disfiguring the best English writers through translations, and translating Prior, Milton and Young into pitiful or mediocre hexameters—a metre of which they never dreamed?'

pp. 328-29).[63] The same was true of the many songs which he translated from Shakespeare: 'Sie waren für mich gemacht' ('I did them for myself') (*VL*, XXV, p. 329). It is important to remember that it was only later that Herder saw in translation an instrument for propagating his own views on genuine poetry.

Writing of the ideal translator, Herder asked: 'Wo ist ein Uebersezzer, der zugleich Philosoph, Dichter und Philolog ist: er soll der Morgenstern einer neuen Epoche in unsrer Litteratur seyn!' (*DL*, I, p. 274).[64] With the benefit of hindsight, it could be argued that here Herder was prophesying his own work on the Song of Songs, as we noted above with his call in his Hase review for a 'Philolog *und* Poet' ('philologist *and* poet') to interpret the work. Considering the possible positive influence of translation on his own literature, Herder imagined the appearance of a book with the title '*Eine Poetische Übersetzung der Morgenländischen Gedichte; da diese aus dem Lande, der Geschichte, den Meinungen, der Religion, dem Zustande, den Sitten, und der Sprache ihrer Nation erklärt und in das Genie unsrer Zeit, Denkart und Sprache verpflanzt werden*' (*DL*, I, p. 274).[65] Such a work, he argued, would be an original work which could have more influence on the German literature of the time than many such original works (*DL*, I, p. 274). It was Herder's view that translations should be undertaken 'um unsrer noch gewiß unausgebildeten Sprache Reichthum, Fülle, Leichtigkeit zu verschaffen' (*Über Thomas Abbts Schriften*, II, p. 282).[66] Herder's translation theory and practice, then, provided a means for the renewal of German literature, liberating it from neo-classical norms,

---

63. 'When ten or more years ago the *Reliques of Ancient Poetry* came into my hands, I enjoyed certain poems so much that I attempted to translate them, and wished for similarly exquisite poems for our own language, which in its cadences and lyrical expression is remarkably similar to English.'

64. 'Where is there a translator who is a philosopher, poet and philologist all at the same time? He should be the morning star of a new era in our own literature!'

65. 'A poetic translation of Oriental poems, in which these are interpreted according to the landscape, the history, the opinions, the religion, the conditions, the customs and the language of their nation, and transplanted into the spirit of our own age, thinking and language.'

66. 'In order to offer opulence, wealth and agility to our own language, which is certainly still undeveloped.' See also *AV*, XXV, p. 33, and Hertha Isaacsen, *Der junge Herder und Shakespeare* (Germanische Studien, 93; Berlin: Ebering, 1930), p. 64, which refers to *SWS*, II, p. 282.

and his relativistic theory of culture provided an emerging German literature with greater self-confidence. His translations of the Song of Songs, like his *Volkslieder*, had a key function in both respects.

Herder's affirmation of the unique bonding of cultures and languages must present theoretical problems for translating. As I have endlessly pointed out, he did not share the universalist assumptions of eighteenth-century Euro-centred, indeed French-centred, polite poetic theory, so could not translate in the terms of current culture, as Wieland, for example, blithely did with Shakespeare. Instead, he proposed sympathetic identification with the foreign culture, an 'Empfindungspoetik, die letztlich alle Distanz ignorieren muß, um den "Ton" des Originals "hören" zu können' (a 'poetry of feeling which ultimately must ignore all distance if it is to be able to "hear" the "tone" of the original'), as Kelletat puts it.[67] His *Lieder der Liebe* demonstrates his desire to enter into the spirit and language of the time. As far as possible, Herder attempted to leave every line of the poems of the Song of Songs within its own *Sitz im Leben*, with—as we saw at the beginning of this chapter—'nichts verschönert, verneut, verschmäckelt' ('nothing embellished, nothing renewed, nothing distorted as far as taste is concerned') (*LL*, VIII, p. 533). We note the contradictoriness of Herder's position. Each culture is unique, but it may be possible to reach another culture by way of 'Einfühlung' ('empathy') and knowledge. Yet, as we shall see, Herder's own (mis)reading of the Song of Songs was heavily coloured by his own idealizing 'Empfindsamkeit' ('sentimentality').

The purpose of a careful comparison of Herder's translations with the original text of the Song of Songs—undertaken in Chapter 6 below—must be to discover how he achieved his effects as well as why he translated in the first place. Initially, however, we must consider Herder's reception of the Song of Songs, comparing and contrasting his views with differing interpretations of the work throughout history. This will enable us to ponder those strands of interpretation which Herder opposed or embraced, thus lending an adequate context for an appraisal of his very individual reading.

---

67. *Herder und die Weltliteratur*, p. 65.

Chapter 4

HERDER'S RECEPTION OF THE SONG OF SONGS: A COMPARISON
WITH OTHER INTERPRETATIVE APPROACHES

Introduction

I have pointed out the uniqueness of Herder's reading of the Song of
Songs, and in this chapter I examine in more detail his reception of the
work as one of naïve innocence. I consider Herder's attitude towards
the authorship and date of the Song of Songs, as well as towards its
place in the biblical canon. I draw comparisons with other views, particularly the two dominant modes of interpretation, namely allegorical
and literal, highlighting Herder's very individual approach to the Song
of Songs against the background of an outline of the most important
Jewish and Christian strands of interpretation throughout the centuries.[1]
I consider those who regarded the Song of Songs as a drama, and those
who interpreted it literally as a lewd poem and wished to exclude it
from the canon. I then examine Herder's reception of important interpretations published just before and at the same time as he was writing,
thus providing further contextualization for his views. The chapter
closes with a discussion of his attitude to other translations, with particular emphasis on the importance for him of Schöber's mediaeval
translation.

1.   There is an extensive bibliography of the works of interpreters of the Song
of Songs throughout the centuries at the end of Marvin Pope's translation, introduction and commentary in *The Song of Songs* (AB, 7C; Garden City, NY: Doubleday, 1977), especially pp. 233-88. In this chapter of the present study, theologians
may level the accusation that the words 'interpretation' and 'exegesis' are
employed too loosely. For most readers, the words will be interchangeable, but
strictly 'interpretation' implies what a particular text means for the reader today,
while 'exegesis' considers what the text or passage in question meant both to the
one who wrote it and to the readers within their own historical situation.

Marvin Pope claims that 'a thorough survey of the history of interpretation of the Canticle would require the lifelong labors of teams of
scholars',[2] and it is indeed probable that the Song of Songs has been
subjected to more interpretations than any other biblical book. The
various kinds of interpretation throughout the centuries have been
almost invariably allegorical in nature.[3] The Song of Songs has been
regarded as drama, as liturgy and as a cycle of wedding songs, although
with emphasis on its allegorical value, with a higher meaning for the
Jewish or Christian reader. Those who have regarded the Song of Songs
literally as nothing more than a collection of love songs have been few
and far between, and inevitably they have seen the work as secular,
erotic and without divine inspiration. Although much stress is placed on
Herder's literal reading, he belonged to neither camp. He severely
shook the allegorical and mystical tradition by failing to find in the
Song of Songs any meaning other than the obvious, literal one, and by
denouncing the allegorizers who, in his opinion, contravened established rules of linguistic and literary analysis. Exceptionally, however,
he was still able to justify the place of the Song of Songs in the Bible
through his unique interpretation of it as a divinely inspired work of
innocence, chastity and beauty.

Throughout his works, it is clear that Herder tended to ramble somewhat aimlessly at times, without ever drawing real conclusions. His
presentation was never tightly knit, and he was easily sidetracked. This
pertained also to his work on the Song of Songs, although in the main
his comments about the content, nature and purpose of the Song of
Songs in the Bible can be found in his essay of 1778, *Ueber den Inhalt,
die Art und den Zweck dieses Buchs in der Bibel* (VIII, pp. 529-58),
views which reflect—often almost verbatim—those throughout his
unpublished translation and commentary of MS(3) (1776) as given by
Redlich. This chapter draws material from his work of 1776 and 1778.

Emphasizing his call for a return to folk-song, Herder claimed that
Love was expressed in the shortest forms of poetry such as the sonnet
and ode, rather than in long, rambling lines where it lost its significance.
Doubtless Herder was jibing here against those who favoured the

---

2.   *The Song of Songs*, p. 89.

3.   Numerous allegorical and mystical interpretations have been documented,
for example, by Richard F. Littledale in his anthology *A Commentary on the Song
of Songs: From Ancient and Mediaeval Sources* (London: Masters; New York: Pott
and Amery, 1869).

classical hexameter, for example. He claimed that in the Song of Songs, Love was presented in all its aspects as simple, sweet, gentle and natural. He praised Love, claiming that when Christ brought his kingdom to earth, he knew Love as mankind's one duty and one reward. If a man failed to love his wife, he would not love others. If he were ashamed of the Song of Songs, he should also be ashamed of the woman who bore him. He should be ashamed too of his own child and thus, by extension, even of himself. Herder praised the natural, simple innocence of Solomonic love: 'In Einem Dichter der Natur und Liebe zeige man mir Eine Situation, die einfältig, wahr, rührend, menschlich sei: konnte sie zu dieser Zeit, unter diesem Himmel gedeihen; so will ich ihm gleich, als Blume oder Blüthe, eine beßre in diesem Buche zeigen' (VIII, p. 530. Cf. p. 632).[4]

We have in this essay an attempt by Herder to show a great work of poetry in its own cultural and natural context. Just as every aspect of Love and Nature was individually unique, so was each image and each song in this collection. We should not rob such poetry of 'dies Individuelle, diese einzelne Gegenwart' ('this peculiar character, this individual presence') (VIII, p. 592. Cf. p. 535) in order to form a personal hypothesis, nor take it out of its context by moving it to a *locus communis* (VIII, p. 531 and 594). Each individual song should be allowed to remain 'an Stelle und Ort, in seinem Duft, in seiner eignen Farbe' ('within its own local context, fragrance and hue') (VIII, p. 593). More importantly, if every song were 'eine einzelne lebendige Empfindung' ('an individual, living sensation'), then it must also be untranslatable (VIII, p. 594). Drawing several of his claims together, Herder pleaded: 'Ist überall nur der natürliche klare Sinn gezeigt, die Einzelheit jedes Stücks in seinem eignen Licht und Dufte bemerkt, sodenn der feine Faden verfolgt den der Sammler bei Reihung dieser kostbaren Perlen hatte; so bin ich zufrieden' (VIII, p. 628).[5]

4.   'In a poet of nature and love, let me be shown a situation which is simple, true, moving and human; could it flourish in our own time and beneath this very sky; then immediately I will show him, as flower or blossom, a better one in this book.'

5.   'If everywhere just the natural, obvious meaning is demonstrated, the individuality of each poem observed within its own light and fragrance, and then the delicate thread traced which the compiler used to arrange these precious pearls; then I am satisfied.'

Herder saw the Song of Songs as a collection of songs, and not as a single sprawling poem. Solomon wrote many songs and proverbs. If the proverbs may be regarded as separate pearls on a string (VIII, pp. 531 and 593), then why not the songs? Although Solomon wrote numerous individual songs, one interpreter after another saw the Song of Songs as a single unit.[6] Everything became one song, one drama, 'eine gefrorne Fensterscheibe' ('a frozen window pane') (VIII, p. 593. Cf. p. 531).[7] Yet if the individuality were removed, there would be complaints from 'jeder einzelne Baum, jede abgerißne, nun verwelkte Blüthe' ('each individual tree, and each blossom that had been snapped off and had subsequently withered') (VIII, p. 531). Mankind always wanted to build a whole from separate parts, and it was no different with poetry: 'Man reihete ihre einzelne Stücke auf, ordnete, deutete, flickte sie in Romane, Hypothesen, bis ein erträumtes Ganze da war' (VIII, p. 531. Cf. p. 593).[8] This happened to David and Solomon, as well as to Anacreon and Catullus, Horace and Petrarch (VIII, p. 531), and Homer, Dante and 'Voluspa' (VIII, p. 554): 'Je einfältiger, klärer und tiefnatürlicher ihre Worte sind, desto mehr wird man sie mit Auslegungen salben und [...] Sachen hineintragen, an die sie wahrlich nicht dachten' (VIII, p. 554).[9] Herder attempted once again to link in the minds of his readers the poetry of the Bible with the poetry of the Greeks and Romans. I have endlessly pointed out how the German mind of the eighteenth century revered and imitated, as purveyors of an absolute standard of literature, many ancient writers, whether of Oriental, Arabic, Greek or Latin origin, but rejected the poetry of the Hebrews as barbaric and primitive.[10]

---

6. In 1776, Herder in fact referred to Solomon's songs as numbering both a thousand and five (VIII, pp. 593 and 630) and three thousand and five (VIII, p. 629). According to 1 Kgs 4.32, the first figure is correct for his songs, and the second for his proverbs.

7. Presumably Herder was jibing here at Christian Ludwig Liscow's *Vitrea Fracta oder, des Ritters Robert Clifton Schreiben an einen gelehrten Samojeden betreffend die seltsamen und nachdencklichen figuren welche derselbe [...] auf einer gefrornen Fenster-Scheibe wahrgenommen* (Frankfurt and Leipzig: n.pub., 1732).

8. 'Their individual poems were arranged, they were classified, interpreted and patched into novels and hypotheses, until there existed an imagined whole.'

9. 'The simpler, clearer and more deeply natural their words are, the more they will be anointed with interpretations, and [...] the more will matters be introduced to them, about which in truth they did not think.'

10. For instance, Herder had no wish to defend Hebrew poetry against the 'neue

It was Herder's plea that all literatures were independent and should be viewed in their own cultural and geographical context, and we have noted how he discouraged copying foreign literatures which had little or nothing to do with the culture of Germany itself. Indeed, in the Song of Songs there was no imitation, for 'es ist die erste brechende Knospe, Einfalt, Natur, Wahrheit' ('it is the first opening bud, simplicity, nature, truth') (VIII, p. 637). Herder attempted to demonstrate that the Song of Songs, which he considered to be the epitome of Hebrew poetry, should be endowed with similar reverence and respect, and regarded even more highly than those other works. By way of example, he referred to a description in the writings of Lady Mary Wortley Montagu (1690–1752) of the Sultan's harem in Constantinople, pointing out that her ideas were almost entirely borrowed from Thomas Harmar, discussed in more detail below. In Herder's view, anyone reading Montagu must be reminded immediately of the Song of Songs, which was far more beautiful and more greatly to be treasured (VIII, pp. 529 and 591). Herder likewise referred to the work of Sir William Jones (1746–94), which contained fragments of Oriental poetry in general, and Persian poetry in particular.[11] Some of Hafiz's odes had already been translated in Jones's work, and would have been well known to Herder's readership. Thus Herder was able to draw a further comparison, challenging the readers of Hafiz to consider the 'lieblichere, einfältigere Salomo' ('the more charming, the more innocent Solomon') (VIII, p. 529). It was Herder's claim that the Song of Songs was like all 'Liebeslieder einfältiger, unverkünstelter Völker' ('love songs of innocent peoples unencumbered by artificial art forms') (VIII, p. 591. Cf. p. 529).

Despite Herder's theoretical argument for cultural uniqueness, Thomas Willi maintains that in Herder's actual translations from the Old Testament 'das Individuell-Jüdische [...] wird—allgemein Mensch-

---

Aufklärer' ('new enlightened thinkers') who only heard in it 'das Geklapper der alten Zimbeln und Pauken, kurz, die ganze Janitscharenmusik wilder Völker' ('the rattling of the ancient cymbals and drums, in brief, the janizary music of primitive peoples') (*EP*, XI, p. 224).

11. Herder was undoubtedly concerned primarily with Jones's *Poeseos asiaticae commentariorum libri sex, cum appendice* (London: Cadell, 1774). In 1777 Johann Gottfried Eichhorn produced a new edition, published in Leipzig by Weidemann and Reich as *Poeseos asiaticae commentariorum libri sex, cum appendice. Recudi curavit Io. Gottfried Eichhorn.* Presumably this was the edition to which Herder referred in 1778.

liches'.[12] Willi gives no textual examples, although, as I have stressed above, we will see in the examination of Herder's commentaries below a tendency to combine the particular and the universal. There is a potential contradiction here. As Kelletat has it:

> Er [Herder] stilisiert das *Hohelied* zu einer Urform allgemein-menschlicher Liebesdichtung. Historisches Denken gerät hier in den unausweichlichen Gegensatz zur Empfindungspoetik, die letztlich alle Distanz ignorieren muß, um den 'Ton' des Originals 'hören' zu können.[13]

Indeed, it is important to note that Herder appeared to be pleading the universalist cause despite his desire to maintain individuality:

> Es ist fast keine Situation [...], die nicht in diesem Liede, wenigstens als Knospe und Keim, vorkäme. Die Liebe des Mannes und Weibes, Jünglinges und Mädchens, vom ersten Kuß und Seufzer bis zur reifen ehelichen Treue—alles findet hier Ort und Stelle. Vom Schuh des Mädchens bis zu seinem Kopfputz, vom Turban des Jünglings bis zu seinem Fußschmucke, nackte Gestalt des Körpers und Kleidung, Pallast und Hütte, Garte und Feld, Gaßen der Stadt und Einöde, Armuth und Reichthum, Tanz und Kriegszug; alles ist erschöpft, alles gefühlt und genoßen (VIII, p. 530).[14]

Herder apparently espoused the view that the representation of specifics was so complete in the Song of Songs that it became universal.

We saw in Chapter 1 that Herder, upset by allegorical interpretations, took time off from more pressing work to write about the Song of Songs. Each new interpretation saddened him more as he considered 'das Buch ohn alle Hypothese in seiner Einfalt und nackten Unschuld so edler, anständiger und zugleich so unwidersprechlich klar' (VIII,

---

12. 'That which is particularly Jewish [...] becomes generally human.' *Herder's Beitrag zum Verstehen des Alten Testament* (Beiträge zur Geschichte der biblischen Hermeneutik, 8; Tübingen: J.C.B. Mohr, 1971), p. 51.

13. 'Herder stylizes the Song of Songs into a prototype of generally human love poetry. Historical thought passes here into the unavoidable antithesis of the poetry of feeling which ultimately must ignore all distance if it is to be able to "hear" the "tone" of the original.' *Herder und die Weltliteratur*, pp. 64-65.

14. 'There is almost no situation [...] which does not feature in this song, at least as a bud and shoot. The love of the man and the woman, the youth and the maiden, from the first kiss and sigh to mature, marital fidelity—everything has its place here. From the maiden's shoe to her head-dress, from the youth's turban to his footwear, the naked form of the body and its clothing, palace and hut, garden and field, alleyways in the town and desert, poverty and wealth, dance and military expedition; everything is treated in full measure, everything felt and relished.'

p. 533).[15] For him, the Song of Songs, the sister of all innocence, had become 'ein zertretner Garten' ('a garden trampled underfoot'), 'eine getrübte Quelle' ('a muddied spring'), and 'ein Myrthenhain der Liebe […] also entweiht' ('a myrtle grove of love […] thus desecrated') (VIII, p. 533).

Herder acknowledged his debt to Luther as far as his own system of biblical interpretation was concerned: 'Der Geist Luthers in Auslegung der Bibel ging vor mir, der mit seinem Feuerblicke immer so gerade in den ersten Sinn, den klaren Wortverstand drang' (VIII, p. 591).[16] Going straight to the primary text, he claimed that the best interpretation was the literal one, 'der von allen beleidigte klare Wortverstand' ('the plain, literal meaning which has been affronted by everyone') (VIII, p. 533). The wise could see what was really contained in the Song of Songs, but hypotheses were invented by 'das Hirn des Eitlen' ('the brain of the conceited') (VIII, p. 532). Yet it was in this latter way that the book had been treated more than all other Old Testament books. Herder accused his own age of being more guilty in this regard than any other: 'Da der Wortverstand des Textes so klar ist und dieser doch nicht in die Bibel der genannten Leute zu paßen schien; so quälte man sich, so ersann man' (VIII, p. 532).[17] Doubtless Herder was referring here to Michaelis, who chose to exclude the Song of Songs from his Bible translation. Unlike others, Herder claimed to have read the book 'ohne Vorurtheil und Hypothese' ('without prejudice and hypothesis') (VIII, p. 591) and to find no more in it than there was in the original text.

As Herder saw it, the main problem lay with the content of the Song of Songs, namely Oriental love of long ago. The Orientals had different views of modesty and innocence, as well as different tastes. It was not necessary to interpret love, and to interpret Oriental love was to make 'die Nacktheit noch nackter' ('nakedness even more naked') (VIII, p. 534). Herder referred to the Rabbi—clearly Akiba ben Joseph—who claimed of the Song of Songs: 'An dem Tage, da es der Welt erschien,

---

15. 'The book without any hypothesis, in all its simplicity and naked innocence so much more noble, decent and at the same time so irrefutably plain.'

16. 'In biblical interpretation I maintained before my very eyes the spirit of Luther, who with his intense gaze always penetrated so directly into the primary sense, the plain, literal meaning.'

17. 'Since the literal meaning of the text is so plain, and yet did not appear to fit into the Bible of those whom I have named, they tortured themselves and began to contrive.'

ist die Vollkommenheit der Dinge gebohren' ('On the day on which it appeared before the world, the perfection of all things was born') (VIII, p. 535. Cf. p. 592).

Herder, 'ein stiller Liebhaber dieses Rosenhayns' ('a silent lover of this rose grove') (VIII, p. 533), continued his invective against the critics of the Song of Songs. In all ages, hypocrites had been upset by love more than anything else. The Song of Songs, as well as other tender passages in the Bible, had been dubbed 'unerträgliche Hurensprache' ('intolerable language of fornication'), yet for Herder the innocence of the work was a 'heilige Gottesperle! Kann dich Heuchelei, Schminke, gefärbtes Glas, Trödelkram von Keuschheitpredigen und Affenmoralisiren ersetzen? [...] Man lese mit Schuldlosem Blick: was ist denn Arges im Hohenliede?' (VIII, p. 634. Cf. p. 546).[18] Any filth found in the work came from the reader rather than the author. The book contained 'Duft' ('sweet fragrance') rather than 'Koth' ('filth') (VIII, p. 634). Even the mention of polygamous relationships, so common at the time, was avoided. In Herder's view, this divine work shows us the way to happiness and fulfilment, and must be read without the 'Kopfschütteln, Ach! und Aber' (literally 'head-shaking, Alas! and But') (VIII, p. 635) of those who saw it as a rude, erotic poem. The innocent read the Bible, including the Song of Songs, and rejoiced, while philosophers became upset and closed it. Herder had nothing to do with such thinking.

Title, Authorship and Date

It is generally accepted that the text of the Song of Songs has been preserved accurately, particularly when compared with some other parts of biblical poetry. Theophile Meek suggests that the poem was carefully preserved to be in tune with the language of the common people, as folk-songs and similar compositions usually were, and was kept alive by continual recitation. The text has thus been well preserved with few emendations.[19]

In the Hebrew Bible, the Song of Songs is placed among the Writings which follow Job. It is the first of the Five Scrolls, or Megilloth, which

18. 'Sacred, divine pearl! Can you be replaced by hypocrisy, gloss, stained glass or a rag-bag of chaste preaching and scandalous moralizing? [...] Please read with an innocent eye: for what wickedness is there in the Song of Songs?'

19. Theophile J. Meek, Hugh T. Kerr and Hugh T. Kerr, Jr, *The Song of Songs*, *IB*, V, pp. 96 and 97.

consist of the Song of Songs, Ruth, Lamentations, Ecclesiastes and Esther. This order corresponds to the sequence of their use in the Jewish liturgy, although the Talmud[20] indicates that the older order was Ruth, Psalms, Job, Prophets, Ecclesiastes, Song of Songs, Lamentations, Daniel, Esther, Ezra and Chronicles.[21] Meek points out that historically the Song of Songs has been of liturgical importance within the Jewish tradition.[22] This is especially relevant in the light of Herder's views on the oral tradition of poetry. Indeed, M.H. Segal suggests that the poems continued to be recited and sung by the people long after they had been fixed in writing,[23] and we will note below that parts of the Song of Songs were sung in Akiba's time in a way which he found objectionable.

The Hebrew title of the book, שיר השירים, may be translated as 'Song of Songs' when rendered word for word into English. However, although an English-speaking reader unfamiliar with Semitic patterns of expression could understand this title as meaning 'the song made up of a number of songs', a Hebrew speaker would almost certainly understand the expression as meaning 'the greatest song/poetry ever composed'.[24] Thus the German title 'Das Hohelied' is possibly more accurate than the English 'Song of Songs', and clearly more correct than the frequent English title 'Song of Solomon'. It is just possible that Herder misunderstood the Hebrew title of the book, for he undoubtedly

---

20. The Talmud consists of the Mishnah, constituting the text, and the Gemara, which is the commentary. Originally the commentary on the Mishnah was known as Talmud rather than Gemara, the term Talmud not including the Mishnah itself. There are two Talmuds. One is Babylonian in origin, while the other has its source in Tiberius, but is called 'The Jerusalem, or Palestinian Talmud', where 'Jerusalem' stands for the land of Israel as a whole. These are based on the Palestinian Gemara, which was compiled at the end of the fourth century CE, and the Babylonian Gemara, which was compiled at the end of the fifth. The Babylonian Talmud is by far the longer, being about 6000 pages in length. It is also afforded greater authority. (See also Coggins and Houlden, *A Dictionary of Biblical Interpretation*, pp. 667-71.)

21. *B. Bat.* 14b, 15a (see Isidore Epstein [ed.], *The Babylonian Talmud* [Anniversary Edition in English] [London: Soncino Press, 1935], *Seder Nezikin*, II, pp. 70-71).

22. Meek, Kerr and Kerr, *The Song of Songs*, p. 91.

23. 'The Song of Songs', *VT* 12 (1962), pp. 470-90 (478).

24. In the Vulgate the title is translated literally as 'Canticum Canticorum', from which is derived the occasional English title 'Canticle(s)'.

interpreted the title as meaning 'one song formed from many', rather than the more likely 'greatest song of all'. On the other hand, it could be argued that Herder adopted both stances with his view of the work not only as a collection of poems, but also as the epitome of that poetry which he regarded as God's initial and purest revelation to the human race.

Much speculation has occurred over the centuries as to the authorship of the Song of Songs. The title given above is repeated at the beginning of the first line, and it is followed by אשר לשלמה ('which is by [?] Solomon'). Conventionally this has been taken as evidence of Solomonic authorship. However, the preposition ל has a variety of meanings, and the phrase could mean 'by/to/belonging to/for/concerning Solomon'. In other words, it by no means indicates authorship.

The traditional assumption that Solomon was the author of the Song of Songs is based on four main points which sum up the internal evidence in its favour. First, the author of the work displays considerable knowledge of plants and animals, and we read in 1 Kgs 4.33 (KJV) that Solomon 'spake of trees, from the cedar tree that is in Lebanon even unto the hyssop that springeth out of the wall: he spake also of beasts, and of fowl, and of creeping things, and of fishes'. Secondly, the author shows evidence of a wide acquaintance with foreign products of the kind that were imported in the time of Solomon. Thirdly, there is some similarity between the Song of Songs and certain parts of the book of Proverbs, a book also attributed to Solomon.[25] Finally, the language of the Song of Songs is such as might be expected from the time of Solomon. It belongs to the golden age of the Hebrew language, is highly poetical, vigorous and fresh, and bears no sign of the decay which set in once Israel and Judah had been divided. Indeed, Christian D. Ginsburg placed the date of the book 'in the most flourishing age of the Hebrew language, and about the time of Solomon'.[26] The purity of the language was an attraction for Herder, who deplored the fact that Hebrew later became mixed with foreign elements and declined as a

---

25. For example, compare the following sections: Song 4.5 and Prov. 5.19; Song 4.11 and Prov. 5.3; Song 4.14 and Prov. 7.17; Song 4.15 and Prov. 5.15; Song 5.6 and Prov. 1.28; Song 6.9 and Prov. 31.28; and Song 8.6, 7 and Prov. 6.34, 35.

26. Christian D. Ginsburg, *The Song of Songs: Translated from the Original Hebrew, with a Commentary, Historical and Critical* (London: Longman, Brown, Green, Longmans and Roberts, 1857); ed. and repr. by Sheldon H. Blank (New York: Ktav, 1970), p. 125.

language. It was, of course, a decline in the purity of the German language for similar reasons that equally concerned Herder in his work on the Song of Songs.

Although Herder frequently referred to the name 'Solomon', he apparently used it generically. He did not hold Solomon dogmatically as the author of the Song of Songs, but regarded the poems as linked by the name of Solomon. Whether Solomon actually wrote them or not, he was the instigator of the book which Herder viewed as 'ein Abdruck nemlich von dem Geschmack, von der Liebe, von der Ueppigkeit und Zier, wie sie zu Salomons Zeiten, und sonst nimmer im Hebräischen Volk, lebten' (VIII, p. 35).[27] With his view of the lyrical origins of all poetry, Herder stressed the disunity and the lyrical syncretism of the Song of Songs, but argued that the work was held together by the personality of Solomon and the atmosphere of his age. He did not find the disunity of the book in any way deplorable. The name of Solomon was a sufficient link. The important thing was that the songs all came from the Solomonic period and breathed the spirit of those times. In other words, they were a genuine document. Herder regarded the songs as being Solomonic in nature, then, but he was not interested in who the real author was. For him, it was sufficient that the songs all bore the imprint of the age of Solomon and his spirit, life and character (VIII, pp. 535 and 632): 'Auch als Friedenskönig und Fürst voll Herrlichkeit war er Meßias Vorbild—und siehe, in diese Zeit kam die Scene des Hohenliedes, der sichtbare Segen Jehovahs, die stille Auszeichnung des Gottgeliebten' (VIII, p. 46).[28]

Herder maintained that the Song of Songs could not stem from any other period of biblical poetry. In his refusal to question the age of the Song of Songs we find the same attitude which characterized his treatment of the book of Genesis (now regarded as much later in composition than Herder supposed) as the oldest document of the human race; an attitude which also promoted his original stubborn and adamant acceptance of the genuine antiquity of Macpherson's Ossian, whom he finally accepted in 1776 as 'glücklich nachgeahmt' ('fortuitously imitated') (VIII, p. 591).

27. 'An impression of the taste, love, lushness and ornamentation such as were found in the time of Solomon, and at no other time in the Hebrew nation.'

28. 'Even as a king of peace and as a prince full of glory, he was Messiah's prototype—and behold, into this age came the action of the Song of Songs, the visible blessing of Jehovah, the gentle honouring of the one loved of God.'

To underline his point, in 1778 Herder included a translation of Psalm 72, a psalm of Solomon. He claimed that this psalm sang of the ideals of Solomon's reign, and the flower of the Song of Songs could have bloomed only under such a regime of peace. Those who read the book would recognize its younger sister in Solomon's wisdom poetry of the book of Proverbs, and its older brother in the book of Ecclesiastes. Herder claimed that these works of Solomon formed a triangle of wisdom, and must be read together for mutual clarification and edification. The first two books warned against prostitution, adultery and seduction, and together with the Song of Songs formed 'die Summe Philosophischer Weisheit des Menschenlebens' ('the sum of the philosophical wisdom of human life') (VIII, p. 48). Indeed, the Song of Songs was the key to Solomon's other works: 'Unter den Büchern des alten Testaments ists eine Rosen- und Myrthenlaube im Thale des Frühlings rings umher voll schöner Aussicht auf alle Seiten der Menschheit' (VIII, p. 51. Cf. p. 591).[29] The same spirit of gentleness ran as a thread throughout the three books. Thus, for Herder, the seal of the spirit of Solomon was enough to convince him of the unity of the poetry in the Song of Songs, through which the editor or collector of the songs had woven as a thread the theme of love maturing from its beginnings right through to becoming ripe fruit: 'Kurz, [...] es ist das Lied der Lieder Salomo's, d.i. der Ausbund seiner Lieder der Liebe und Jugendfreude' (VIII, p. 43).[30]

Meek follows Herder with his claim that 'no serious scholar today believes that Solomon was the author, and there are few who believe that the book was the work of a single hand. It is too repetitious for that and too disorderly in its content'.[31] However, while commentators such as Paul Haupt[32] have denied that the Song of Songs—or Psalm 72, for that matter—were even the products of the time of Solomon, most modern scholars would agree with Herder that, although the Song of Songs was almost certainly not written by Solomon himself, it certainly was a product of his reign. Segal, for example, agrees with Herder by

29. 'Among the books of the Old Testament, it is a bower of rose and myrtle in the valley of spring, surrounded on every side by a glorious view of all aspects of humanity.'

30. 'In brief, [...] it is Solomon's Song of Songs, i.e. the embodiment of his songs of love and youthful pleasure.'

31. Meek, Kerr and Kerr, *The Song of Songs*, pp. 96-97.

32. *Biblische Liebeslieder*, pp. xiii and xli.

assigning the Song of Songs to the age of Solomon rather than to Solomon himself. It may not be the work of Solomon, but 'the whole contents of the Song breathe the particular atmosphere of the Solomonic age with its worldliness, its wealth and its luxury'.[33]

Canonicity

The early acceptance of the Song of Songs as part of the canon of the Old Testament is as well documented as for any other part of Jewish-Christian scripture. It has been regarded and transmitted as canonical by both Jews and Christians, being included both in the Babylonian Talmud's list of sacred books referred to above, and in the canon of Melito (Bishop of Sardis), who travelled to Palestine towards the end of the second century CE to find out what books were regarded as canonical there. Although there was some dissension about the book's canonicity at the Rabbinical Council of Yabneh (Jamnia) in the first century CE—a controversy in which Akiba took part—its esoteric significance saved it from exclusion from the biblical canon. It is generally believed that it initially secured its place in the canon because it was ascribed (perhaps wrongly) to Solomon, and it has remained there almost certainly because of the subsequent allegorical interpretations it has received.

We note Akiba's claim that 'all the ages are not worth the day on which the Song of Songs was given to Israel; for all the Writings are holy, but the Song of Songs is the Holy of Holies';[34] a claim echoed by Herder (see *HR*, I, pp. 90-91, and *LL*, VIII, pp. 535 and 592). Solomon Zeitlin accepted Akiba's statement that there had never been any dispute about the Song of Songs, and confirmed that it was universally agreed to be canonical.[35] There is little doubt, however, that what caused some to urge the work's exclusion from the canon was the sensuousness of its images and its apparent erotic character.

Herder remembered that 'schon Theodor von Mopsvest ward auf einem Concilium verdammt, weil er einen Wortverstand dieses Buches

---

33. 'The Song of Songs', p. 481.

34. *Yad.* 3.5 (*The Mishnah: Translated from the Hebrew with Introduction and Brief Explanatory Notes* [trans. Herbert Danby; London: Oxford University Press, 1933], Sixth Division [*TOHOROTH*], p. 782). The Mishnah is a code of Jewish law, arranged by topic in 63 tractates and compiled around 200 CE. (See also Coggins and Houlden, *A Dictionary of Biblical Interpretation*, pp. 667-71.)

35. *An Historical Study of the Canonization of the Hebrew Scriptures* (Philadelphia: Jewish Publication Society of America, 1933), pp. 10-11.

annahm' ('even Theodore of Mopsuestia was condemned by a council because he accepted a literal meaning for this book') (VIII, p. 32). The literal reading of Theodore, Bishop of Mopsuestia (360–429 CE), was rejected at the Council of Constantinople in 553 CE, but thereafter the canonicity of the work was not seriously questioned for hundreds of years. Allegory and mysticism replaced the literal meaning of the text in both the Jewish and Christian traditions, as I shall explore more fully below.

During all these years, the most powerful attack on the canonicity of the book was supplied by one of the early Reformers, Sébastien Castellion, whose literal reading was published in Geneva in 1547 in his *Notae in Canticum Canticorum in Biblia Latina*. He held it to be a lascivious and obscene poem, a dialogue between Solomon and a woman, in which Solomon described his love affairs. As it dealt merely with earthly affections, he deemed it unworthy of a place in the sacred canon and demanded its exclusion. This was a view which Calvin strongly condemned and which led to Castellion's departure from Geneva.[36] Similarly, when Luis de Léon rejected all allegories and explained the book literally in his *Tradducción literal y declaración del libro de los cantares de Salomón* (first published in 1768, but written two centuries earlier), he did not need to question its canonicity, for canonical status disappeared automatically with the allegory.[37] On the other hand,

---

36. See Harold Rowley, 'The Interpretation of the Song of Songs', in *idem*, *The Servant of the Lord and Other Essays on the Old Testament* (Oxford: Basil Blackwell, 2nd edn, 1965), p. 217 n. 1. See also Etienne Giran, *Sébastien Castellion et la réforme Calviniste: Les deux réformes* (Haarlem: Boissevain, 1913; repr. Geneva: Slatkine Reprints, 1970), pp. 65-68, and François Wendel, *Calvin: Sources et évolution de sa pensée religieuse* (Etudes d'Histoire et de Philosophie Religieuses, publiées par la Faculté de Théologie Protestante de l'Université de Strasbourg, 41; Paris: Presses Universitaires de France, 1950), pp. 55-56.

37. The discovery of the translation and commentary of Luis de Léon (1529–91) was responsible for putting a sudden end to the Spanish mystic's famous controversy with Léon de Castro, and precipitated his incarceration by the Holy Office from 1572 to 1576. See James Fitzmaurice Kelly, *A Short History of Spanish Literature*, in Edmund Gosse (ed.), *Short Histories of the Literatures of the World* (15 vols.; London: Heinemann, 1898), V, pp. 180-81; and Otis H. Green, *Spain and the Western Tradition: The Castilian Mind in Literature from 'El Cid' to Calderón* (3 vols.; Madison and Milwaukee: University of Wisconsin Press, 1963–65), III, p. 461.

Herder was able to reject an allegorical interpretation, and yet to regard the work as divinely inspired.

Thus, as far as canonicity is concerned, the abandonment of an allegorical interpretation usually leads, in the orthodox Christian view, to a literal interpretation implying that the book should be removed from the canon. By maintaining an allegorical interpretation, then, the Church was safe from having to take such steps. Indeed, by the eighteenth century, when the question of canonicity arose again, it had become commonplace for each interpreter to have a personal hypothesis. The rationalism of the age was strongly reflected by William Whiston, for example, who declared that the Song of Songs was written by Solomon 'when He was become Wicked and Foolish, and Lascivious, and Idolatrous'.[38] He found no allegorical or mystical meaning, and held that such an immoral book had no rightful place in the canon (p. 13).

After passionately asserting, in the face of contemporary criticism, that the Song of Songs was a loosely strung collection of Hebrew love lyrics of Solomonic antiquity, naïve and unallegorical in meaning, Herder located the book in the biblical canon on a non-theological but nevertheless metaphysical basis. He handled the question of inspiration—and thereby canonicity—in a way that could give comfort neither to orthodox commentators nor to those who had imbibed the spirit of the Enlightenment. He had no problem with the place of the Song of Songs in the Bible, attacking the view prevalent at the time that the work—like the Bible in general—should be 'nur eine Blumenlese kahler Moralen, und trockner Akroamen [...], um Wort Gottes seyn zu dörfen' ('merely an anthology of barren morals and dry acroamata [...] if it were to be the Word of God') (VIII, p. 28). With his demand for Nature rather than Art, he rejected such a view, pleading that 'in der Natur spricht Gott nicht vom Holzkatheder zu uns und so wollte er auch nicht in der Schrift zu uns sprechen; sondern durch Geschichte, durch Erfahrung, durch Führung Eines Volks, dem ganzen Menschengeschlecht zum Vorbilde' (VIII, p. 43. Cf. p. 628).[39]

---

38. *A Supplement to Mr. Whiston's Late Essay: Towards Restoring the True Text of the Old Testament, Proving that the Canticles is not a Sacred Book of the Old Testament* (London: Senex and Taylor, 1723), pp. 5-6.

39. 'In nature God does not speak to us from a professorial chair, and neither did he intend to speak thus in the scriptures; but rather as a model for the whole human race by means of history, experience and the leading of one nation.'

Solomon was in the Bible with his vices and virtues, and as the Song of Songs was the divinely inspired portrayal of his reign—or even his life and character—it was included among those holy books which contained other similar documents. Thus, all of Solomon's writings, including the Song of Songs, became historical and characteristic. If they were read in the context of his life and soul, they did not contradict each other, but rather explained each other: 'Zur Lehre [...] ist uns, was da ist, geschrieben, zur Beßerung und zum Unterrichte;[40] nicht zum dummen Anbeten und zum Verschlucken ohne Verdauung, wovon bei den besten sowohl als schädlichsten Kräutern auch das Vieh stirbt' (VIII, p. 45).[41] As far as the canonicity of the Song of Songs was concerned, Herder was unperturbed. The book was the production of an Oriental people and that was sufficient. He was able to read it literally, while accepting it as of divine inspiration, worthy of its place in the biblical canon.

Jewish and Christian Interpretations

Perhaps the best detailed appraisal of the extent of Herder's originality and the importance of his contribution to the history of interpretation of the Song of Songs is provided by comparing and contrasting his reading with a brief outline of the book's previous reception within the Jewish and Christian traditions. Such a survey will help to place Herder's work in context, and it will also serve to enlighten the non-specialist reader.

Both traditions had long held that any interpretation of the Song of Songs must of necessity be an allegorical one. The reasons are obvious. Critics such as Theodore, for example, thought that the Song of Songs was a rude poem, and thus the work's canonicity was immediately brought into question. Akiba, on the other hand, accepted the work as allegorical, realizing the dangers of a literal reading. Origen (185–254 CE) and Jerome (331–420 CE) similarly saw the Song of Songs in largely allegorical terms. Herder disagreed. Indeed, he was adamant that the Song of Songs was love poetry with no allegorical meaning, and in saying this he was going against the flow of almost two thousand

40. Cf. 2 Tim. 3.16.
41. 'What we find there was written for us [...] for instruction, improvement and education; not for foolish adoration, or to be swallowed without being digested, as a result of which even the cattle die from the best as well as from the most harmful plants.'

years of Christian and rabbinic tradition. Herder was not completely alone—we can think of Michaelis, for example—but he is marked out as an original and bold thinker by his insistence that the Song of Songs must be read literally and yet must be regarded simultaneously as a divinely inspired biblical document.

Jewish Interpretations

The Greek translation of the Old Testament, the Septuagint (conventionally designated by the Roman numerals LXX), is the starting point for the history of Jewish interpretation of Scripture. The Song of Songs was translated into Greek as literally as possible by Aquila between about 90 CE and 130 CE, and later by Symmachus and Theodotion before the end of the second century CE. Classical Jewish exegesis is represented in the Talmud, the Targum[42] and the Midrashim,[43] covering approximately the first five centuries of the Christian era. Three Midrashim on the Song of Songs have come down to us, namely the Midrash Rabba, Aggadat Shir Ha-Shirim and Midrash Shir Ha-Shirim. Allegorical, mystical, historical and eschatological interpretations are mixed together, and obviously the view that the poems are merely examples of erotic poetry was not accepted. For instance, the Rabbis pronounced a curse on all those who treated the book as a common ditty and sang passages from it at banquets: 'He who recites a

42. 'Targum' is an Aramaic word meaning 'translation'. It is used particularly of the various Aramaic versions of biblical books which were made in the early centuries of the Common Era. (See also Coggins and Houlden, *A Dictionary of Biblical Interpretation*, pp. 671-73.) For a modern edition of the Targum of the Song of Songs, with supralinear vocalization, see R.H. Melamed, 'The Targum to Canticles, According to Six Yemen MSS', in *Jewish Quarterly Review* 12 (1921–22), pp. 57-117. For a translation into English, see Hermann Gollancz, *The Targum to 'The Song of Songs'* (London: Luzac, 1908). Paul Vulliaud translated it into French in *Le Cantique des cantiques d'après la tradition juive* (Paris: Presses Universitaires de France, 1925), pp. 67-103, and Wilhelm Riedel into German in *Die Auslegung des Hohenliedes in der jüdischen Gemeinde und der griechischen Kirche* (Leipzig: Deichert, 1898), pp. 9-41.

43. The term 'Midrash' was used in early Hebrew literature for an interpretation of Scripture or a traditional commentary on the Torah. Through biblical studies the term entered modern academic vocabulary denoting early Jewish exegesis of the Bible. It may be applied to the whole range of Jewish biblical interpretation as found, for example, in the Septuagint, Philo, Josephus and the Targumim. (See also Coggins and Houlden, *A Dictionary of Biblical Interpretation*, pp. 452-59.)

verse of the Song of Songs and treats it as a [secular] air, and one who recites a verse at the banqueting table unseasonably, brings evil upon the world.'[44]

As we have seen, Akiba understood the Song of Songs allegorically, and Ulrich Simon points out that modern criticism is in danger of neglecting the revelatory and transcendent substance stressed by the Rabbi.[45] Akiba defended the book's inspiration, presumably against attacks now lost and against a distinction already being made between this and other canonical writings. In his opinion, the Song of Songs was a most sacred book for the Jews.[46] Jewish interpretations, then, have been essentially allegorical in approach. According to the Targum to the Song of Songs (believed to stem from the seventh or eighth century CE), the first half of the text was a symbolic picture of the history of Israel before the captivity, and the second half presented a prophetic view of the subsequent fortunes of the nation.[47]

After the Targum, there is a gap in information concerning Jewish exegesis of the Song of Songs until the time of Ben Joseph Saadia (892–942 CE). He was spiritual leader of the Jewish community in Babylon and he translated the Hebrew Scriptures into Arabic. He too continued the allegorical tradition by agreeing in essence with the interpretation of the Targum that in the Song of Songs Solomon related the history of the Jews, beginning with the Exodus and extending to the advent of the Messiah. A trace of this allegorical interpretation can be found in the Mishnah,[48] and the tradition was continued by Abraham

---

44. *B. Sanh.* 101a.

45. In Coggins and Houlden, *A Dictionary of Biblical Interpretation*, p. 643.

46. See Nathaniel Schmidt, *The Messages of the Poets: The Books of Job and Canticles* (London: J. Clarke, 1911), pp. 217-18.

47. The Targum to the Song of Songs is a version only in the sense that it is an indirect witness to the Hebrew text which it interprets, but it could hardly be called a translation. It is in Aramaic, and might be called 'an interpretative paraphrase' or indeed 'a midrash' to the Hebrew text. An authoritative edition of the Hebrew Scriptures, the Masoretic Text, was developed by Jewish scholars between about 500 CE and 950 CE. Vowel points were here introduced into the consonantal Hebrew text.

48. *M. Ta'an* 4.8 (Herbert Danby [trans.] *The Mishnah*, Second Division [*MOED*]). Here, Song 3.11 is given thus: 'Go forth ye daughters of Sion, and behold King Solomon with the crown wherewith his mother hath crowned him in the day of his espousals and in the day of the gladness of his heart.' The following comment is added: 'In the day of his espousals—this is the giving of the Law; and

ben Me'ir Ibn Ezra (1092–1167 CE).[49] Henry J. Mathews points us to Hirsch Graetz, who insisted that Ibn Ezra understood the Song of Songs in its literal meaning, but was not bold enough to proclaim his view, preferring to apply the work in an allegorical sense to the Synagogue for fear of being branded a rationalist.[50] Herder was brave to stand up to the Jewish tradition, although apparently he was also willing to compromise by accepting appropriate application ('Anwendung'), provided the primary literal meaning was not lost.

The commentary of Rabbi Solomon ben Isaac of Troyes, or Rashi (1040–1105 CE), translated into Latin in 1714 by Johann Friedrich Breithaupt as *R. Salomonis Jarchi [...] Commentarius Hebraicus in librr. Josuae [...] et Canticum Canticorum latine versus* (Gotha: Schall), is still held in high regard by the Jewish community. His view, as favoured also by the Midrash, was that the book represented successive events in the history of Israel. His grandson Rabbi Samuel ben Meir, or Rashbam, also produced a commentary along similar allegorical lines, and Samuel Ibn Tibbon (who died in 1230 CE) also insisted on an allegorical interpretation, disagreeing that the Song of Songs was merely a love poem.

Several allegorical Jewish commentaries were written over the next four centuries, although little of their content was novel. For example, in the late sixteenth century, Don Isaac Abravanel saw the protagonists of the Song of Songs as Solomon and Wisdom rather than God and Israel.[51] The Bride was seen as an allegorical figure, with Solomon speaking for himself as the Bridegroom and lover of Wisdom. This view was followed and developed by Abravanel's son, Leon Hebraeus

in the day of the gladness of his heart—this is the building of the Temple.'

49. Ibn Ezra's commentary, *Canticum Canticorum cum Commentariis* has come down to us in two recensions, one of which stands in the Rabbinical Bibles; the other was edited and translated by Henry J. Mathews in *Abraham Ibn Ezra's Commentary on the Canticles after the First Recension* (London: Trübner, 1874). Although frequently condemned by Christians, Ezra's work, suggesting a three-character dramatic scheme, undoubtedly reinforced Christian allegorical interpretation.

50. *Abraham Ibn Ezra's Commentary*, p. x. See Hirsch Graetz, *Schir Ha-Schirim [...] oder das Salomonische Hohelied übersetzt und kritisch erläutert* (1871), p. 119.

51. Abravanel was probably the first to advocate the view that the bride represented Wisdom. See Eduard Isidor Magnus, *Kritische Bearbeitung und Erklärung des Hohen Liedes Salomo's* (Halle: Lippert, 1842), p. 26.

(Judah).[52] Jewish interpretation continued to be allegorical until the middle of the eighteenth century when the Enlightenment initiated a new era in Jewish study of the Bible and Hebrew literature, especially through the work of Moses Mendelssohn.[53]

Given the moral dangers perceived in not following the allegorical tradition, Jewish law forbade adherents to read the Song of Songs before the age of 30, a point acknowledged by Herder who recognized the original intention, but demanded a more relaxed view (VIII, pp. 547 and 594). He argued that children should be taught that the Bible was the word of God, showing that love and marriage were a divine blessing. In such a context, the Song of Songs was not a shameful piece of writing, but was rather 'Kranz reiner Jugendjahre des Gottgeliebten' ('a garland of the pure, youthful years of one loved of God') (VIII, 547). For Herder, the Bible was 'lebendige Darstellung, [...] Geschichte Gottes über Völker und Zeiten' ('a living representation, [...] history of God through nations and ages') (VIII, p. 631). As we have seen, it was to be read as a human work, and not as 'Unsinn aus den Wolken' ('foolishness from the clouds') (VIII, p. 631). He abhorred the 'heuchlerische Kälte' ('hypocritical apathy'), 'ehrbares Busenlächeln' ('respectable smirking'), and 'ehrbare Erfrorenheit' ('respectable frigidity') of his own age (VIII, p. 547. Cf. p. 635). 'In unserm züchtigen Zeitalter! man entschleiert die Grazie des Hohenliedes zu einer Hure' ('In our own chaste age (!), the charm of the Song of Songs is being revealed as a harlot') (VIII, p. 594), causing people to blush and to regard it for the rest of their lives as unfit to read. Herder, however, saw the sweet innocence of the work as the cure for the ills of his time. With his literal but innocent reading, then, he pleaded for his readers to study the Song of Songs with their children.

Christian Interpretations

The first Christian known to have allegorized the Song of Songs was the Roman Hippolytus who lived around 200 CE, although only fragments of his commentary have survived.[54] Hippolytus doubtless influ-

---

52. See *Dialogi d'amore* (Rome: Blado d'Assola, 1535). An English translation by Jean H. Barnes and F. Friedeberg-Seeley appeared as *The Philosophy of Love* (London: Soncino Press, 1937).

53. Mendelssohn's translation of the Song of Songs, *Salomo's Hohes Lied*, was published in Berlin in 1788.

54. *In Canticum Canticorum*, *PG*, X, pp. 627-30. (Marvin Pope's reference

enced Origen, who wrote a ten-volume commentary in Greek on the Song of Songs, although most of this too has been lost.[55] He was convinced that the literal sense of the Song of Songs was something to be eliminated. There was nothing carnal in the book; rather, it was spiritual in meaning.

Despite the prevailing allegorical interpretations, however, there were those who regarded the Song of Songs as an ordinary song, and viewed it as nothing more than an erotic poem. For example, we have noted the literal view taken at the end of the fourth century CE by Theodore, who wrote a commentary on the Song of Songs in which he rejected any allegorical meaning. He read it as an erotic song in which Solomon boldly sang of his love when his subjects criticized his marriage to an Egyptian princess.[56] Unlike Theodore, though, Herder found room in the canon for a literal Song of Songs. Unfortunately Theodore's commentary has not survived apart from unimportant fragments, and it is known only from the attacks on it. Indeed, we have seen that Theodore was anathematized and his work condemned. The secular interpretation survived, however, and ultimately it was this interpretation which was developed by Herder and which received its unique interpretation from him.

At the same time as Theodore was causing disquiet in the Eastern church, the Roman monk Jovinian upset the Western church by taking the Song of Songs literally and invoking it in praise and sanctification of marital sex in his attack on asceticism. Generally speaking, however, the Church took from the Rabbis the allegorical method but reapplied it to Christianity, replacing God with Christ, and Israel with the Church. The Song of Songs thence became an allegory of the love of Christ for his Church (as in Origen's interpretation), or, on an individual basis, of the relationship between the Christian and Christ (as in Bonaventura's interpretation).

The allegorical interpretation of the Church, in its formulation by Origen, was made official—against Theodore's attacks—at the Council of Constantinople referred to above, and this view prevailed, as is evi-

---

[*The Song of Songs*, p. 236] is to *PG*, XXIII, p. 767, although this is incorrect.)

55. Four books were translated into Latin by Rufinus (see *Origenis in Canticum Canticorum Prologus. Interprete Rufino*, *PG*, XIII, pp. 61-216), and two of Origen's homilies were translated by Jerome (see *Origenis in Canticum Canticorum. Interprete Divo Hieronymo*, *PG*, XIII, pp. 37-58).

56. See *PG*, LXVI, pp. 699-700.

denced, for example, by the chapter headings of the Authorized Version of the English Bible of 1611. Indeed, since the condemnation of Theodore, there have been few direct attacks made by the Christian Church on the Song of Songs, although there have been some variations in the manner of explaining the allegory.

Origen's work was followed by other authorities of the Church, possibly including St Augustine who wrote in *De civitate Dei*: 'Iam uero Canticum canticorum spiritalis quaedam sanctarum est uoloptas mentium in coniugio illius regis et reginae ciuitatis quod est Christus et ecclesia. Sed haec uoluptas allegoricis tegminibus inuoluta est.'[57] Some of the early Christian fathers interpreted particular phrases in the Song of Songs in relation to the Virgin Mary. Late mediaeval commentators developed this Mariological line of interpretation, perhaps the prime example being Rupert von Deutz, who died in 1135 CE.[58] Naturally, such a view has been more prevalent in Roman Catholic circles than among Protestants.

The allegorical interpretation was introduced into the Western churches by Jerome. He embraced Origen's views almost entirely, regarding the Song of Songs as a nuptial and dramatic song celebrating the union of Christ with the Church and/or the human soul.[59] Towards the middle of the fifth century CE, Theodoret, Bishop of Cyrrhus in Syria, whose own commentary followed and elaborated on Origen's work, attacked those who did not accept the allegorical interpretation of the book.[60]

In the twelfth century there was a great renewal of interest in the Song of Songs, particularly on the part of the Mystics, among whom undoubtedly the most important was Bernard of Clairvaux. He too treated the book as an allegory, writing 86 sermons in which he

---

57. 'Now assuredly for those of innocent minds the Song of Songs is a certain spiritual delight in the marriage of that King and Queen of the city which are Christ and the Church. But this delight is enveloped in a cloak of allegory.' James E.C. Welldon (ed.), *S. Aurelii Augustini Episcopi Hipponensis De Civitate Dei Contra Paganos Libri XXII* (2 vols.; London: SPCK; New York and Toronto: Macmillan, 1924), II, p. 300. Please note that translations from Latin throughout this chapter are my own.

58. *In Cantica Canticorum de incarnatione Domini commentariorum, PL*, CLXVIII, pp. 837-962.

59. *Interpretatio Homiliarum duarum Origenis in Canticum Canticorum, PL*, XXIII, pp. 1117-44.

60. *Explanatio in Canticum Canticorum, PG*, LXXXI, pp. 27-214.

exhaustively treated every line up to Song 3.1.[61] It was his purpose to purge the Song of Songs of any suggestion of carnal lust. Herder claimed, however, that the point of the Bible was to humanize the divine, while the aim of the Mystics was to deify the human. He accused them of abusing all the books of the Bible and ruining their prime meaning, quite against the original intention of the Bible (VIII, p. 638). Solomon's wisdom was 'klarer Sinn in Anschauung der Dinge des Lebens' ('plain sense with regard to the things of life') (VIII, p. 552). It was Bernard who laid the foundation for a great deal of late mediaeval mysticism, and throughout the Middle Ages it would appear that no attacks were made by the Church on the canonicity of the Song of Songs. In this regard we note Herder's poignant use of a mediaeval translation to promote his view of the Song of Songs as a collection of folk-songs to be read literally rather than allegorically.

Fourteenth-century contributions included those of Nicolaus of Lyra, who continued an allegorical interpretation. Luther's reception of Nicolaus has been recognized and epitomized in the rhyme 'Si Lyra non lyrasset, Luther non saltasset' ('If Lyra had not played his lute, Luther would not have danced'). Among Protestant Christians, Luther, in the preface to his translation of the work, stands alone with his interpretation of the Song of Songs as a political allegory, a glorification of the ideal conditions of Solomon's reign when he ruled under the guidance of the Most High. Luther was unable to accept the allegorical interpretations handed down by the Fathers, but neither, unlike Herder, was he able completely to accept a literal, erotic sense. He thus propounded the theory that the Bride was the happy and peaceful State under Solomon's rule, and the Song of Songs was a hymn in which Solomon thanked God for the divine gift of obedience. Thus it was Luther who introduced the first historical-political interpretation of the book. The Swabian reformer John Brentius agreed with Luther's interpretation, but, despite this new allegory, the majority of Luther's followers retained the interpretation of Origen and Bernard.

It was not until 1547, then, that Castellion revived the view propounded by Theodore that the Song of Songs had no allegorical meaning. Yet, although Castellion (and Léon) interpreted the book literally,

---

61. *Sermones in Cantica Canticorum, PL*, CLXXXIII, pp. 786-1198 (Marvin Pope's reference [*The Song of Songs*, p. 240] is to pp. 799-1198, but this is incorrect). Bernard's disciple, Gilbert of Hoyland, or Gilbert Parretanus, carried on with his work and added 48 sermons, reaching halfway through the fourth chapter.

the prevailing allegorical view in both Catholic and Protestant circles remained generally orthodox. Later, Hugo Grotius adopted Castellion's view, maintaining that Solomon concealed all the intimacies of love under innocent terms: 'Nuptiarum arcana sub honestis verborum involucris hic latent: quae etiam causa est cur Hebraei veteres hunc librum legi noluerint.'[62] However, Grotius also gave the Song of Songs a mystical meaning, although apparently he did not attach much weight to this nor indeed devote so much trouble to the unfolding of the mystical meaning as to that of the erotic sense.

In England the traditional Christian view remained largely unchallenged, although in 1585 Thomas Wilcox, for example, affirmed in *An Exposition upon the Booke of the Canticles* (London: Man, 1585) that the book celebrated the marriage between Christ and his Church.[63] In the last years of the seventeenth century, Bishop Jacques Bénigne Bossuet developed a theory that the Song of Songs was epithalamic in form, divided into seven songs or cantos to accord with the seven days of Hebrew marriage celebrations, but he did not question the fact that the Song of Songs was generally accepted as allegory.[64] He held, like many who had preceded him from the time of Origen, that the occasion of the Song of Songs was the marriage of Solomon to Pharaoh's daughter. S.M. Lehrman has pointed out that Herder was the first to advance the view that the Song of Songs was simply a collection of love songs performed during the week of festivities after a wedding celebration, yet with no allegorical significance whatsoever.[65] Lehrman has put us on to an important point here; Herder was, it seems, highly original in his suggestion that the Song of Songs was simply a collection of love

62. 'The mysteries of marriage are concealed here beneath a respectable covering of words: and furthermore this is the reason why the ancient Hebrews were unwilling for this book to be read.' See 'Annotata ad Canticum Canticorum', p. 541.

63. See Ginsburg, *The Song of Songs*, pp. 69-70.

64. *Canticum canticorum Salomonis*, in Gabriel Louis Calabre-Pérau (ed.), *Oeuvres complètes* (12 vols.; Paris: Coignard and Boudet, 1748), I, pp. 463-500. Herder was doubtful about Bossuet's interpretation (VIII, p. 589).

65. 'The Song of Songs: Introduction and Commentary', in Abraham Cohen (ed.), *The Five Megilloth: Hebrew Text and English Translation* (Soncino Books of the Bible; London: Soncino Press, 13th impression, 1977), pp. i-xiii, 1-32 (xii). Lehrman confirms that J.G. Wetzstein supported this idea in 1873 by describing the *wasf* celebrations in Syria, where songs were sung describing the physical attributes of the bride and groom.

poetry to be read literally. Lehrman may have simplified the issue, for
we have seen how Theodore and Castellion, for example, also argued
that the work was of no allegorical significance. Nevertheless Herder
stands out as a major figure whose originality and boldness demanded a
literal interpretation without rejecting the canonicity which had
depended for so long upon divine inspiration and higher meaning.

Thus, despite a long tradition of Jewish and Christian allegorical
interpretations, Herder claimed that if he were led away from the literal
meaning, he was 'gleich einem groben blos' ('just like an uncouth
fellow') with his own allegorical interpretations,[66] and he scorned
Protestant allegory, as evidenced in this example:

> Dein Nabel wie ein runder Becher, ist der wiederhergestellte Kelch im
> Abendmahle, und dein Bauch wie ein Weizenhaufe, da die Irrthümer
> verworfen sind von Fegfeuer, Seelmessen und von Verdienst der Werke.
> Deine zwo Brüste, die Mittel der Seelennahrung, das evangelische Wort
> und die heiligen Sakramente—und so gehts zum Thor Bethrabbim, zum
> Elfenbeinern Thurm, d.i. zu der durch den Hals der Lehrer rein vorge-
> tragnen Lehre, zur Nase, dem *Emblemate* des Zorns über die Feinde der
> Kirche (VIII, pp. 553-54.).[67]

Herder personally found no allegorical interpretation whatsoever in
the Song of Songs: 'Ich lese das Buch und finde in ihm selbst nicht den
kleinsten Wink, nicht die mindeste Spur, daß ein andrer Sinn Zweck des
Buchs, erster Wortverstand Salomons gewesen wäre' (VIII, p. 552).[68]
He rejected any historical, mystical, metaphysical or political interpretations (VIII, p. 552), and sneered at the allegorizers (VIII, p. 638).
Solomon was not a mystic, nor was he interested in metaphysics or
church history. Yet every section of the Song of Songs had been

66. It is unclear to whom Herder was referring here. (See Redlich's note to
p. 553 in VIII, p. 676.)

67. 'Your navel like a round goblet—this is the chalice now restored to the
communion service; and your waist like a sheaf of wheat, since our errors have
been cast out by purgatory, masses for the dead, and works. Your two breasts, the
means by which the soul is nourished, are the word of the gospel and the holy
sacraments—and so we go to the gate of Bethrabbim, to the tower of ivory, i.e. to
those teachings which issue purely forth from the lips of the teachers, and then to
the nose, which represents anger upon the enemies of the Church.'

68. 'I read the book and find in it not the tiniest sign, not the least hint that any
other meaning was either the purpose of the book, or Solomon's initial understanding.'

allegorized and interpretations had been proposed which Solomon would never have contemplated.

Thus Herder was opposed to the allegorical view of both Jewish and Christian traditions, although he could accept the first Jewish interpretations such as the Zohar's explanation of the self-characterization of the beloved when she says: 'Schwarz, aber gar lieblich—das ist die israelitische Kirche, schwarz um ihrer Gefangenschaft, lieblich um des Gesetzes und ihrer Frömmigkeit willen' (VIII, p. 552).[69] Herder likewise had no objection to the allegorical application of the book by mystically minded persons. Such use was permissible metaphor, although he pleaded that this interpretation must be 'nur Anwendung, sollte und konnte nur Anwendung bleiben' ('just application, and must and should remain just application') (VIII, p. 556). To attempt such an interpretation—and he admitted that an allegorical reading could be possible—would end in the corruption of the clear, literal meaning of the text, with the result that finally 'ein dickhäutiges Schiffseil von Allegorik heraus [kommt], daß dem Leser die Nerven zittern' ('such a thick tissue of allegory emerges, that the reader's nerves jangle') (VIII, p. 552). In this Herder was a precursor of the views of Paul Haupt who noted that 'jede allegorische Erklärung des Hohenliedes ist, wie Herder mit Recht hervorhebt, *Anwendung*, nicht Wortsinn'.[70]

Likewise addressing the use the Christian Church had made of the Song of Songs over the centuries, Herder admitted that in the Old Testament Isaiah saw the Church as God's bride, and God as the bride's husband. In the New Testament, Christ was regarded as the groom in

---

69. 'Black, but very lovely—that is the Israelite church, black on account of her captivity, lovely on account of the law and her piety.' Arguably, Herder exhibited more apparent sympathy for Jewish rather than Christian interpretations. Indeed, Emil Adler argues thus: 'Obgleich Herder beide Allegorisierungsversuche des „Hohelieds", sowohl den jüdischen als auch den christlichen ablehnt, ist jedoch die freundlichere Beurtheilung der jüdischen Deutungsversuche auffallend' ('Although Herder rejects both allegorical readings of the Song of Songs, namely the Jewish and the Christian ones, nevertheless his more benevolent judgment of Jewish attempts at interpretation is evident'). 'Johann Gottfried Herder und das Judentum', in Kurt Mueller-Vollmer (ed.), *Herder Today: Contributions from the International Herder Conference, Nov. 5–8, 1987, Stanford, California* (Berlin: W. de Gruyter, 1990), pp. 382-401 (390-91). (In this article Adler actually refers only to the 1776 version in Redlich, but quotes from both versions without specifying.)

70. 'Every allegorical interpretation of the Song of Songs is, as Herder rightly emphasizes, *application*, rather than literal meaning.' *Biblische Liebeslieder*, p. xii.

the parables of Christ himself, in the writings of the Apostles and in the Revelation of John. Thus Herder agreed that it was natural for the Song of Songs to be so interpreted by the Church Fathers, who 'schütteten [...] auch in ihren Homilien, Glossen, Commentarien über dies Buch die Fülle ihres Herzens aus, jeder, wie er die Kirche sah und fühlte' (VIII, p. 555).[71] He encouraged such usage to enhance prayer, speech and love, although this did not remove the original, literal meaning. It rather served to augment it (VIII, pp. 554-55). Herder had no difficulty with individuals making use of those sections of the Song of Songs which were relevant to their needs, provided they did not contradict the word of God as a whole. For example, Church, State and Marriage were 'Ein Ding' ('one element'), along with the individual humanity inherent in all three. Without God, mankind was nothing. With God, mankind was the bride of Christ, a seal on his arm and on his heart.[72] Indeed, Herder noted Paul's use of the image of marriage in Eph. 5.22f., giving by way of support a translation from Proverbs 31 which, like the Song of Songs, praises the perfect wife.[73] However, he underlined that any use made of the Song of Songs must be merely 'Anwendung, nicht ursprüngliche Absicht' ('application, rather than original intention') (VIII, p. 557).

Thus, within Jewish and Christian culture, Herder could accept some examples of allegorical interpretation, many of which he regarded as moral, poetic or philosophical applications. However, such meanings were not 'Urgestalt und erste Lage; [...] nicht die klare Quelle des Ursprungs' ('primary form and initial position; [...] not the clear source of the origin') (VIII, p. 553). Nevertheless, Irmscher has drawn attention to MS(1) in particular, 'weil in ihrem Kommentar ein hermeneut-isches Grundproblem, das Verhältnis von "historischkritischer"[74] (V,

71. 'Poured out [...] upon this book, even in their homilies, criticisms and commentaries, the fullness of their hearts, each one according to how he saw and experienced the Church.'

72. See Song 8.6.

73. Cf. Herder's other translation of the same section in *EP*, XII, pp. 110-12.

74. Irmscher acknowledges here the use of the word 'historischkritisch' ('historical-critical') in Herder's recension of Johann Georg Sulzer's *Allgemeine Theorie der Schönen Künste, in einzeln, nach alphabetischer Ordnung der Kunst-wörter auf einander folgenden, Artikeln* (Leipzig: Weidemann and Reich, 1771), in *ADB* XXII/1 (1774), pp. 5-35. Speaking of the Ancients, the passage reads: 'Vielleicht sollten sie weniger entschuldigt oder gerechtfertigt, als historischkritisch behandelt werden' ('Perhaps they should be excused or justified rather less than

p. 391) Untersuchung und jeweiliger Auslegung (*applicatio, Anwendung*) deutlicher hervortritt als in den beiden gedruckten Niederschriften'.[75] Indeed, in MS(1), fols. 64[r], 74[v]-76[r] and 90[v]-95[v], Herder reinforced his view of the Bible as a human, historical document, yet opened the door for the response of the individual reader.[76] Stressing his view that 'ein Wortverstand ist und bleibt!' ('there is and there remains a literal meaning!'), he claimed that, as with any individual reading of Homer, for example, it was the reader's privilege 'alles zu eigen zu machen, was aus ihrem Geist in den Meinen übergehen kann und will' ('to make my own everything that can be transmitted easily from their thinking into my own'). After all, 'die Bibel hätte zu uns gar nicht überkommen müssen, wenn sie bei uns nichts thun soll' ('there was no need for the Bible to be transmitted to us at all, if it is not to serve any purpose for us'). As far as the Song of Songs was concerned, then, Herder pleaded that, although 'im Wortverstande sind oder sollen wir alle Eins seyn!' ('in the literal meaning we are all united, or at least we ought to be so'), individual application was vital if the work were to be more than an historical document. Again we find a hint of Herder's ability to regard the Song of Songs as a literal, human book, yet one also inspired by God. In other words, there could be no historical-critical examination of the text without admitting of a relevant application to a present situation. The Song of Songs must be treated as an historical document, but then as rather more than that, for 'solch ein Mannigfaltiges Eins, und Eins in tausendfacher Anwendung ist jedes lebendige Werk Gottes!' ('every living work of God is such a manifold unit, and a unit which has a thousand applications') (*ÄU*, VI, p. 319). In MS(2), fols. 49[v]-50[r], Herder argued that if a work of literature failed to penetrate 'in unsern Geist, in den Saft unsres Herzens [...]; was können wir werden als Motten oder Maulesel, Kritiker und Masorethen!'[77]

they should be treated in a historical-critical manner') (*SWS*, V, p. 391).

75. 'Because in its commentary, there emerges more clearly than in both published manuscripts a fundamental problem of hermeneutics, namely the relationship between 'historical-critical' investigation and actual interpretation (*application*).' 'Probleme der Herder-Forschung', p. 298. The two printed manuscripts are, of course, MSS(3) and (a).

76. See also 'Probleme der Herder-Forschung', pp. 298-301. The quotations below can be found on pp. 300 and 301.

77. 'Our spirit, the life-blood of our hearts [...], then what can we become other than moths or mules, critics and Masoretes.' 'Probleme der Herder-Forschung', p. 302.

Thus, while there is no hint of Herder's ever accepting an allegorical reading of the Song of Songs, it is clear from the tone of these two manuscripts that his argument in favour of a personal, relevant application of the Song of Songs had become less forceful by the time of publication.

The Song of Songs as Drama

Herder's strongly literary reading of the Song of Songs received some indirect support from interpretations of the book as drama, although his knowledge of Hebrew and Oriental custom did not allow him to accept such a view. Since drama began with the Greeks, it is fitting to look to them for the origins of a dramatic interpretation of the Song of Songs. As early as the third century CE, Origen regarded the Song of Songs as a nuptial poem written by Solomon in dramatic form: 'Epithalamium libellus hic, id est nuptiale carmen, dramatis in modum mihi videtur a Salomone conscriptus.'[78] Origen found four characters in the Song of Songs: the bridegroom (Christ); the bride (the Church); the friends of the bridegroom (angels, prophets or patriarchs); and the friends of the bride (the souls of believers). Origen was aware, however, that this was not an interpretation that would be obvious to all, and, as some of the Jewish Rabbis had done before him, he warned that because of any possible literal interpretation this was not a book to be put into the hands of everyone: 'I advise and counsel everyone who is not yet rid of the vexations of flesh and blood and has not ceased to feel the passion of his bodily nature, to refrain completely from reading this little book and the things that will be said about it.'[79] Indeed, it was in order to guard against such possible misunderstanding that Origen interpreted every detail allegorically.[80]

Other indications of a dramatic interpretation in Greece are to be found in the Codex Sinaiticus of the fourth century CE, and the Codex

---

78. 'This small book, a nuptial poem, a marriage song in the manner of a drama, seems to me to have been written by Solomon.' *PG*, XIII, p. 61.

79. Translated by R.P. Lawson in *Origen. The Song of Songs: Commentary and Homilies* (Ancient Christian Writers: The Works of the Fathers in Translation, 26; Westminster, MD: Newman, 1957), pp. 22f. and 313 n. 7, as quoted in Pope, *The Song of Songs*, p. 117.

80. See Remy Ceillier, *Histoire générale des auteurs sacrés et ecclésiastiques [...]*, II (Paris: Vivès, 2nd edn, 1859), pp. 158-59.

Alexandrinus of the fifth century, which supplied marginal notes to the text indicating the speakers and the persons addressed. It is not until after the Protestant reformation, however, that we find the dramatic interpretation fully developed. Following Origen, John Milton (1608–74) wrote in his introduction to *The Reason of Church-Government Urged Against Prelaty*, Book II, that 'the Scripture also affords us a divine pastoral drama in the Song of Solomon, consisting of two persons, and a double chorus, as Origen rightly judges'.[81]

Thomas Percy, Bishop of Dromore, whom I shall consider in more detail below, clearly followed Bossuet, but insisted on a dramatic structure rather than Bossuet's lyrical one. This thesis had already been propounded by several writers on the continent, although apparently without Percy's knowledge.[82] Johann Friedrich Jacobi revived the dramatic scheme of Ibn Ezra in *Das durch eine leichte und ungekünstelte Erklärung von seinen Vorwürfen gerettete Hohelied nebst einem Beweise, daß selbiges für die Zeiten Salomons und seiner Nachfolger sehr lehrreich und heilsam, und eines heiligen Dichters würdig gewesen*, published in Celle in 1771, showing that the importance of the Song of Songs was to celebrate fidelity.[83]

Many critics and commentators, then, have regarded the Song of Songs as a drama, although no other Semitic drama is known. Rowley, for example, notes that scholars of the highest repute accepted the dramatic view of the Song of Songs, and he emphasizes that this stance was adopted by Samuel R. Driver in *An Introduction to the Literature of the Old Testament* (Edinburgh: T. & T. Clark, 1892), which served as the standard English textbook for more than a generation.[84] Commenta-

81. Robert Fletcher (ed.), *The Prose Works of John Milton* (London: Westley and Davis, 1834), p. 43b.

82. The most notable was the Abbé Augustin Calmet (1672–1757) in his *Dissertations qui peuvent servir de prolégomènes de l'Ecriture Sainte* (Paris: Emery, 1720) and in his *Dictionnaire historique, critique, chronologique, géographique et littéral de la Bible* (Paris: Emery, 1722–28). Cf. *Dictionnaire de Théologie Catholique*, III (Paris: Lebuzey and Ané, 1903–50), 'Cantique de Cantiques'. Calmet had been preceded in this view by Gaspar Sanctius (Sanchez) in *Commentarium in Canticum Canticorum* (Lyons: Cardon, 1616) and by Laurentius Petraeus, whose metrical translation of 1640, *Canticum Canticorum Salomonis paraphrasi*, not only arranged the work in dramatic form, but also provided a musical setting. Cf. Schmidt, *The Messages of the Poets*, pp. 217-18.

83. It has proved impossible to locate a copy of Jacobi's work.

84. 'The Interpretation of the Song of Songs', p. 214.

tors such as Ginsburg have found three principal characters, namely Solomon, the Shulamite maid and her shepherd lover.[85] According to this plot, Solomon brought the Shulamite maid to his court in order to woo her, but was unsuccessful. The maid remained faithful to her lover and resisted Solomon's advances. Such an outline lends itself to a literal interpretation of the Song of Songs, but of course does not allow it to be regarded as an allegorical illustration of Christ's love for the Church.

As far as Herder was concerned, he too observed certain dramatic elements within the work. With its 'Absätze, Scenen, einerlei Anfänge und Schlußlieder' ('sections, scenes, similar beginnings and concluding songs') (VIII, p. 541) it could be viewed as a musical play, an opera, or a drama from the hand of Solomon. Herder denied this reading, however, and criticized the dramatic interpretation of Georg Wachter, in whose work he otherwise saw much good.[86] Herder maintained that the Orient had never known the drama as a literary form: 'Das Handeln und Gestikuliren auf dem Schauplatz ist einem Morgenländer verächtlich; auch im gemeinen Reden spricht er mit dem Munde, nicht mit den Händen' (VIII, p. 542).[87] Women were not put on display to act or dance for others, and Herder regarded it as most improbable that there should be anything theatrical in the Song of Songs. Solomon was not the kind of man to make a public spectacle out of his love. The work contained 'Auftritte der Natur und Liebe' ('scenes of nature and love') (VIII, p. 542) which, if brought to the theatre, would lose their charm and colour. Lest anyone should view the Song of Songs as a song about a marriage feast, or as a drama based on the seven days of a marriage celebration, Herder pointed out that nothing of this kind was known in the Orient. The bride was always silent and veiled. She was praised, but did not respond or dance in front of the guests.

Pastoral poetry and love poetry, Herder declared, enjoyed 'Abwechslung, [...] Gespräche, Wettgesänge, Amöbäische Lieder, wie wiederholte Küsse und Schwüre' ('variety, [...] conversations, song contests, Amoebaean verses, like repeated kisses and promises') (VIII, p. 543). Drawing on Thomas Shaw's account of his journeys to the Orient,

85. *The Song of Songs*, pp. 4-6.
86. *Das Hohe Lied des Salomo, [...] samt einer vorgesetzten Einleitung und Abtheilung desselben als eines geistlichen Singspiels [...]*, published in Memmingen in 1722.
87. 'It is despicable for an Oriental to act and gesticulate on a stage; even in general speech he speaks with his mouth rather than with his hands.'

Herder pointed out that song was so important there that people sang all night, often until morning.[88] Music and songs were prevalent at Oriental feasts, and for Herder the Song of Songs consisted of 'offenbare Abdrücke und Reste solcher Liebes- und Hochzeitfreuden' ('obvious copies and remnants of such joys of love and marriage') (VIII, p. 543). Thus Herder addressed the question of the Song of Songs as drama, but rejected such an interpretation on largely cultural grounds insofar as that culture was known to him. For him, the work was poetry rather than drama.

Literal Interpretations

We have observed that literal interpretations of the Song of Songs, whether Jewish or Christian, have immediately called the work's canonicity into question. Other literal interpreters such as the Deists, for example, claimed the Song of Songs as a human rather than a divine work, and were naturally unconcerned whether it was in the canon or not. Although Herder's reading was literal, it stressed the innocence of the work, unlike other such interpretations. Moreover, as I have pointed out, he regarded all poetry as a form of divine revelation, and the Hebrew poetry of the Bible as the original expression of God's revelation to the human race, the pinnacle of which poetry was that collection of songs of innocence known as the Song of Songs. Thus, despite writing as a Christian who read the Song of Songs literally, Herder was able to regard it as inspired and thereby rescue it by adopting the middle ground. Indeed, we have observed Herder's view of the Bible as at once human and divine, and it is essential to note that in his attempts to demonstrate the importance of the Song of Songs as a springboard for the renaissance of German poetry, Herder aimed to bring all groups onto his side. By adopting a unique stance, he sought to appeal to all his

88. Thomas Shaw was principal of St Edmund Hall, Oxford. His original work was *Travels, or Geographical, Physical and Miscellaneous Observations Relating to Several Parts of Barbary and the Levant* (Oxford: Theatre, 1738). The second edition was translated into German by Johann Heinrich Merck as *Herrn Thomas Shaws [...] Reisen, oder Anmerkungen, verschiedne Theile der Barbarey und der Levante betreffend. Nach der zweiten englischen Ausgabe ins Deutsche übersetzt* (Leipzig: Breitkopf, 1765). This is undoubtedly the edition read by Herder, and the one which I have used here. Cf. Herder's remarks in his recension of Shaw's *Reisen* on 7 October 1764 in the *Königsbergsche Gelehrte und Politische Zeitungen* (*SWS*, I, pp. 81-84). There is an extract from Shaw in *SWS*, I, pp. 84-87.

readers—whether allegorists, literalists, Deists, Catholics, Protestants or Jews. And yet his language was so strong—especially against the allegorists—that he ran the risk of offending those whom he attempted to woo. Rather than being conciliatory, his tone was very contentious.

Some non-religious literal and allegorical interpretations of the Song of Songs, however, have maintained various hypotheses without, of course, overtly raising the question of canonicity. In the seventeenth and eighteenth centuries interest began to shift from the question of canonicity to that of literary genre. In both Germany and England, advancing textual criticism, coupled with elements of Deism and Enlightenment freethinking, moved towards a literal interpretation of the work. Both Lowth and Percy, considered in more detail below, showed evidences of this trend by analysing the literal meaning which they regarded as fundamental to an understanding of any possible allegorical reading. It should be pointed out that neither ever questioned the divine inspiration of the book nor the authorship of Solomon, and anyway the age of the book justified its place in the canon regardless of whether the primary meaning was allegorical or not.

During the Enlightenment, theories based on the literary form of the Song of Songs were capable of being used for very secular purposes. A sufficiently established tradition of humanistic scholarship could, for instance, point out the close parallels between the Song of Songs and the idylls of Theocritus. At the beginning of the eighteenth century, philological comparisons convinced numerous writers that the book was much later than generally supposed, and these conclusions undoubtedly bolstered the case of those extreme rationalists who were seeking that Natural religion which in the last analysis resolved itself into pure Deism. On the other hand, scholars of the Pietistic movement were not at all averse to using theological weapons against the established orthodox churches.

Among the writers of this persuasion we may place Hermann von der Hardt (1660–1727), whose manuscript translation and interpretation of the Song of Songs were found by Gotthold Ephraim Lessing in the Wolfenbüttel library. Von der Hardt, a noted Orientalist of his day, had studied under the famous Talmudist Esra Edzard in Hamburg. He had embraced Pietism in 1683, and had cooperated with August Hermann Francke (1663–1727) in establishing the centre of Pietistic activities at Halle. In other words, he was a religious opponent of that German Protestant orthodoxy which was striving to maintain the absolute status quo in religion and state. Lessing's brother Johann Gottlieb (1732–1808) was working on the Song of Songs in 1774. On 8 December Gotthold Ephraim informed his brother that von der Hardt 'macht es zu einer blossen Allegorie, unter welcher *Vota reipublicae pro regno judaico per Hyrcanum instaurando* eingekleidet wären'.[89]

In his *Eclogae Regis Salomonis*, Johann Gottlieb Lessing was the first to declare the Song of Songs to be essentially disunified, an anthology of erotic lyrics comparable to those of Theocritus and Virgil.[90] He did not go so far as to contend—as some more recent critics do[91]—that the Song of Songs was postexilic, that the term 'Solomon' referred to the title given to any bridegroom in the week of nuptial festivities, that the relative pronoun was Aramaic and therefore much later than Solomon's time, and that the book was therefore possibly late enough to have been influenced by Theocritus rather than early enough to have influenced him. This would have been embarrassing for Herder with his position that the Greeks, for example, imitated earlier works of literature (such as the Song of Songs) just as the Germans had imitated the Greeks. In fact, the idyllic character of the Song of Songs caused commentators such as Anthony Blackwell (1674–1730) in *The Sacred Classics Defended and Illustrated* (1725), and Samuel Wesley (1662–1735) in *Dissertationes in Librum Jobi* (1735) to follow the thesis of Charles-Claude Genest (1639–1730), who pointed out that the book might have influenced the idylls of Theocritus. On this, Lessing was in agreement.

---

89. ('Makes it into a mere allegory in which were clothed *the pledges of the state to establish a Jewish kingdom throughout the land of Hyrcania*'), G.E. Lessing, *Sämtliche Schriften*, XVIII, p. 122.

90. On the title page of Lessing's work, published by Dyk in Leipzig in 1777, his names are given as 'Johann Theophilus'. Lessing followed the eight chapters of Luther's translation, producing a translation which consisted of eight eclogues. A Latin translation proceeds eclogue by eclogue as a drama between Salomo and Sulamitha, with notes at the end of every eclogue according to each verse of the relevant chapter. Herder referred to the work in his *Lieder der Liebe* (VIII, pp. 587 and 588), claiming that 'Leßings Eclogae sind der Uebersetzung und Noten wegen sehr zu empfehlen. In beiden herrscht viel kritischer Geschmack' ('on account of the translation and notes, Lessing's Eclogues are much to be recommended. In both we find much critical taste') (VIII, p. 588). Despite his praise, however, it should come as no surprise that Herder also held some reservations about the work.

91. See Clark, 'Herder, Percy, and the *Song of Songs*', p. 1091.

Three quarters of the way through the eighteenth century, the work of
Benjamin Kennicott (1718–83) and Thomas Harmar (or Harmer) in
England, and of Johann Salomo Semler (1725–91) in Germany, continued to add to the growing body of literal or unorthodox interpretations of the Song of Songs, while Herder's study and translation lay
unfinished. Harmar's *Outlines of a New Commentary on Solomon's
Song*, published in 1768, was known and condemned by Herder, as well
as by Percy, Semler and Michaelis.[92] Indeed, his lack of any conclusions whatever drew scathing condemnation from Herder (VIII, p. 529).
Harmar introduced a new theory. While agreeing with commentators
such as Grotius, Bossuet, Lowth and Percy that the Song of Songs celebrated the wedding of Solomon and Pharaoh's daughter, he added
another wife. The Shulamite was not the Egyptian wife, but the previous principal wife, a Jewish queen who was displeased at Solomon's
marrying a Gentile wife. The situation resembled the attitude of Christ
towards the Gentile and Jewish churches, but Harmar did not promote
any mystical interpretation beyond this point.

Semler was a theologian and higher critic greatly favoured by the
German 'Aufklärer'. His destructive exegesis and textual criticism,
which appeared in numerous *Dissertationes* beginning in 1750, was
historically relativistic in approach. Both before and after Michaelis, he
stated his disbelief in the inspiration of the Song of Songs—and of
numerous other parts of both Testaments—to the joy of the rationalists.

The textual-critical work of Kennicott began with *The State of the
Printed Hebrew Text of the Old Testament* (published between 1753
and 1759 and translated into German by the rationalist theologian A.W.
Teller in 1756), and moved into *Vetus Testamentum Hebraicum cum
variis lectionibus*, completed in 1780.[93] In the former work, Kennicott
too suggested that the Song of Songs was post-exilic. Herder knew

92. See Hans Hecht, *T. Percy, R. Wood und J.D. Michaelis* (Stuttgart: W. Kohlhammer, 1933), pp. 2 and 71. See also Harmar's *Observations on Divers Passages
of Scripture, Placing Many of Them in a Light Altogether New [...] Grounded on
Circumstances Incidentally Mentioned in Books of Voyages and Travels into the
East* (London: Field, 1764), translated into German (with notes by Johann Ernst
Faber) as *Beobachtungen über den Orient aus Reisebeschreibungen, zur Aufklärung der heiligen Schrift* (3 vols.; Hamburg: Bohn, 1772–79).

93. According to Würthwein (*Der Text des Alten Testaments*, p. 43), Kennicott
published the Masoretic text following the 1705 edition by E. van der Hooght, the
Dutch scholar, and the Samaritan text following Walton's London Polyglot of
1753–57.

Kennicott's work, but was clearly unaware in 1778 of what the final results would be. Actually, the latter work was to serve in Germany as a corrective to Semler's radicalism; but with regard to the Song of Songs he used linguistic evidence to maintain his surmise of 1753.

Contemporary Interpretations

Percy's *The Song of Solomon, Newly Translated from the Original Hebrew with a Commentary and Annotations* was edited by Robert Dodsley and published in London in 1764. It appeared anonymously one year before his *Reliques* which Herder so admired, although in none of Herder's works is there any reference to Percy's *The Song of Solomon*, nor is the book mentioned in any of his published letters. As Clark points out, 'when one considers Herder's usual scholarly habit of documentation and his willingness to acknowledge sources, one must conclude that he was ignorant of Percy's work'.[94] Whereas Herder interpreted the Song of Songs as a collection of folk-songs from the time of Solomon—in other words, a kind of Hebrew *Reliques*—Percy saw the book as a dialogue, divided into seven parts, on the occasion of King Solomon's marriage to a beautiful bride. Thus we cannot build a case for Percy having influenced Herder through his work on the Song of Songs per se, but we could arguably defend the view that Herder's reception of the *Reliques* was of prime importance in the shaping of his own unique views on the Song of Songs. In fact, Herder's conception of the Song of Songs was quite different from that reached by Percy himself, although strikingly similar to Percy's theory in one important point: a negative reaction towards the attitude of Michaelis vis-à-vis the Song of Songs.

Just as Percy was completing *The Song of Solomon*, in 1763 Michaelis published his *Roberti Lowth [...] de Sacra Poesi Hebraeorum Praelectiones [...] Notae et Epimetra*, a new edition of Lowth's work with notes by Michaelis, in which the latter denied the allegorical approach which had supported the canonicity of the Song of Songs for hundreds of years, declaring that the book had a literal meaning only.[95] Michaelis found nothing whatever in the book to suggest allegory, nor indeed anything to do with the marriage ceremony, since there was no mention of marriage rites anywhere in the work. He wrote (p. 605):

94. 'Herder, Percy, and the *Song of Songs*', p. 1087.
95. I have used the second edition (Göttingen: Dieterich, 1770) for this study.

'Restat, ut meam profitear sententiam, castos conjugum amores cani, non sponsi et sponsae.'[96] Indeed, we have noted that Michaelis went so far as to refuse to include the Song of Songs in his own translation of the Old Testament.

Faced with Michaelis's defection from Lowth, Percy took a stand on the allegorical interpretation. He had intended merely to investigate the literal meaning of the poem from a literary point of view, but now, seriously embarrassed by one of his authorities, he felt obliged to add a disclaimer to his own work and define his own position on the question of allegory. In a postscript, he noted that

> after the foregoing was committed to the press, appeared a new edition of the *Praelectiones*, accompanied with learned and ingenious Notes by Mr. Professor Michaelis. [...] Mr. Professor hath controverted the opinion, which is the basis of this whole work, viz. that the Song of Solomon is a nuptial poem, and describes the seven days of the marriage feast. [...] Mr. Michaelis seems to controvert the received opinion of this poem's being a sacred Allegory, and is inclined to look no farther than the literal meaning.[97]

Percy held that in order to understand the allegory—which he did not deny—it was necessary first to understand the literal sense. According to his preface, the sole purpose of his book was to elucidate this literal sense, yet Michaelis now denied also that the poem was an innocent marriage song, claiming (p. 606 n. 125): 'Hoc si ita est, mirum, primae noctis nulla cani gaudia, non pompam comitantium: nuspiam adclamationes, cantica, bona verba, audiri convivarum, ereptam virginitatem, cujus ad eos indicium deferri solet, more Orientali gratulantium. Omissum in carmine, quod primas in illo et praecipuas facere partes debuisset.'[98] Thus, despite the secular intentions of his preface, Percy was forced to admit his orthodoxy. This may explain why his work was not

---

96. 'It remains for me to declare my own opinion: that the chaste affection of married persons is described, rather than the passion of a bride and groom.'

97. *The Song of Solomon*, pp. 99-103.

98. 'If this is so, it is amazing that the delights of the wedding night are not sung, nor the procession of attendants. Nowhere are to be heard the shouts, songs, and witty remarks of the guests as they praise the loss of virginity, the signal of which is supposed to be given to them according to Oriental custom. That element of the song has been omitted which ought to have formed the first and foremost parts.' Herder quoted this passage—although somewhat differently each time—in 1776 (VIII, p. 589 n. a) and in 1778 (VIII, p. 532 n. t).

mentioned in the radical journals of Germany. In any event, by 1778 the German intellectual world was ready to dismiss the Song of Songs from the canon of the Scriptures as a secular work without divine inspiration. It was Herder who was to see it as secular and divine.

Despite his polemic against Michaelis, we note with some irony that Herder rejected the epithalamic theory himself, as did Michaelis. Referring to *Roberti Lowth [...] de Sacra Poesi Hebraeorum Praelectiones* (p. 593), Herder sarcastically accused Michaelis—'ein noch glücklicherer Ausleger' ('an even more auspicious interpreter')—of regarding the Song of Songs as a lewd marriage song full of Oriental passion: 'Er dichtete eine glücklichere Hypothese, von einem Eheliede voll Orientalischer Liebesränke, *intrigues d'amour*, Eifersucht, Brunst, Zank, Begier nach einer Nacht, wie sie zwar nicht bei uns, in unsern leider! einpaarigen Ehen, aber desto mehr in jenen Morgenländischen Harems statt finde' (VIII, p. 532. Cf. p. 589).[99] Speaking in a sarcastic vein against those who refused to accept the literal intention and meaning of the poetry—and clearly it was Michaelis whom he was attacking here—Herder imagined such a commentator addressing Solomon himself:

> Großer König, siehe, du sangest der Lieder viel, du gibst mir, selbst dem Namen nach, einen Ausbund, eine Blumenlese, ein Lied der Lieder; aber, König, ich habe eine glückliche Hypothese, mit der freilich alle einzelne Stücke, Personen und Situationen zerrißen und verschwemmt, deine viele Lieder aber alle nur Ein Lied werden. Ich nähe und flicke, deute und sticke, verunziere und lege Liebesränke, würdige Moralabsichten, Politik und Mystik hinein, daran du zwar, weiser König, nicht gedacht hast, ich aber denke und dein unwürdiges Buch seiner Biblischen Stelle würdige mache (VIII, p. 532).[100]

99. 'He invented an even more auspicious hypothesis of a marriage song full of Oriental intrigues of love, *intrigues d'amour*, jealousy, ardour, quarrelling and desire for a night such as would not occur in our country, in our unfortunately (!) monogamous marriages, but which would do so in those Oriental harems.'

100. 'Oh, great king, behold, you sang many songs, you give me, even by name, a paragon, an anthology, a song of songs; but, oh king, I have a propitious hypothesis in which admittedly every single item, person and situation is destroyed and washed away, but your many songs all become one song. I sew and patch, interpret and embroider, disfigure and impose upon them intrigues of love, respectable moral purposes, policies and mysticism, about which, oh wise king, you had not thought, but about which I think, and thus render your unworthy book worthy of its place in the Bible.'

As noted above, it was mainly the allegorical interpretations of his day which spurred Herder on to publish his translation of the Song of Songs, although it was also his intention to react against what he regarded as the clumsy, even frivolous, rationalistic literal interpretation of Michaelis, as well as 'das eckle Lob' ('the nauseous praise') of numerous contemporary theologians, which angered him greatly (VIII, p. 532 n. x). Herder was appalled that 'jede Meße kommen neue glückliche Hypothesen' ('at every fair we find new auspicious hypotheses'), each worse than the previous one (VIII, p. 533. Cf. p. 590). He deplored those theologians who protested against the book so much that they refused to translate it into German and who excluded it from their canon of scripture,[101] and he was deeply upset particularly by the fact that Michaelis did not deign to taint his translation of the Bible by including the Song of Songs.[102] We have noted Herder's contemptuous claim that Michaelis's omission of the Song of Songs from his Bible translation acted as a catalyst for his own work, and we read the words of a man who had taken the matter almost personally: 'Sie haben das Buch aus ihrem Kanon ruhig ausgeschloßen, verbitten es vornehmhöflich, daß der berühmteste Deutsche Uebersetzer es doch ja nicht Deutsch übersetze und seine Bibel damit verunziere. [...] So stehts also mit dir, schöner Garte, liebe unschuldige Perle!' (VIII, p. 533).[103]

It is no surprise that throughout his work on the Song of Songs Herder should attack the allegorists on the one hand and Michaelis the literalist on the other. His sense of the poetic and his respect for the Old Testament could not permit such interpretations to go unaddressed, and it was not until his *Theologische Briefe* that he was to restore to Michaelis some measure of the awe in which he had held him in earlier years.

---

101. Apart from Michaelis, Herder was probably referring here to Johann Salomo Semler's *Abhandlung von freyer Untersuchung des Canon* (Halle: Hemmerde, 1776). (Cf. Semler's *Kurze Vorstellung wider die dreyfache Paraphrasin über das hohe Lied* [Halle: Hemmerde, 1757].)

102. From Herder's comments both in 1776 (VIII, p. 590) and 1778 (VIII, p. 533), it is clear that he already knew that Michaelis was not planning to include the Song of Songs in his Bible translation. In the event, vol. VII was published in 1778 and contained only the book of Proverbs and the book of Ecclesiastes.

103. 'You simply excluded the book from your canon, and protest with an air of polite superiority that the most famous German translator should not translate it into German, and thereby disfigure his Bible. [...] Thus is the situation in which you find yourself, wondrous garden, dear innocent pearl.'

Lowth's *De sacra poesi Hebraeorum* (Oxford: Clarendon Press, 2nd edn, 1763) was a work known and used by Herder, Percy and Michaelis, and was of prime importance in the formation of the literary theories of all three.[104] The work's influence on Herder, and through him on Goethe, was clearly stated in *Dichtung und Wahrheit*:

> Die hebräische Dichtkunst, welche er [Herder] nach seinem Vorgänger Lowth geistreich behandelte, die Volkspoesie, deren Überlieferungen im Elsaß aufzusuchen er uns antrieb, die ältesten Urkunden als Poesie, gaben das Zeugniß, daß die Dichtkunst überhaupt eine Welt- und Völkergabe sei, nicht ein Privat-Erbtheil einiger feinen gebildeten Männer. [...] Er war mehr geneigt zu prüfen und anzuregen, als zu führen und zu leiten.[105]

In Germany, the importance of Lowth's book consisted largely in its aesthetic approach to the Old Testament and its author's application of the principles of literary criticism to the Bible, a book which was known to all literate Germans. Herder received the work with great acclaim, as did others such as Nicolai, Mendelssohn and Lessing, but it was Michaelis who, in his *Beurtheilung der Mittel, welche man anwendet, die ausgestorbene Hebräische Sprache zu verstehen* (Göttingen: Van den Hoek, 1757), brought Lowth's literary-critical method into agreement with the objectives of the Enlightenment. In dealing with the Song of Songs, Lowth followed the opinions of Bossuet. In Michaelis's interpretation, it seemed that Lowth was saying that the Old Testament was aesthetically beautiful, therefore need not be rejected as mere primitive superstition. This was important to Herder in his attempts to convince Germans that the Song of Songs was the epitome of primitive folk-poetry and that there was great value to be gained in returning to

---

104. Lowth's comments on the Song of Songs are in Lecture 30 ('The Song of Solomon not a Regular Drama') and Lecture 31 ('Of the Subject and Style of Solomon's Song') of his *Lectures on the Sacred Poetry of the Hebrews [...] to Which Are Added the Principal Notes of Professor Michaelis* (trans. G. Gregory; 2 vols.; Anglistica & Americana, 43; London: J. Johnson, 1787; repr. Hildesheim: Olms, 1969).

105. 'The Hebrew poetry, which he [Herder] treated ingeniously after the pattern of his predecessor Lowth; the folk poetry, the tradition of which he urged us to seek out in Alsace; the most ancient documents in the form of poetry; these bore testimony to the fact that the art of poetry is a universal and national gift, and not the private inheritance of a few refined, educated individuals. He was more given to examine and inspire than he was to guide and lead.' II, Book 10, *WW*, XXVII, p. 313-14. For details of Goethe's impressions of Herder, see pp. 302-23.

primitive German folk-poetry as a basis for a literary revival.

Lowth supported an allegorical reading: 'May we not therefore, with some shadow of reason, suspect, that under the allegory of Solomon chusing a wife from the Egyptians, might be darkly typified that other Prince of Peace, who was to espouse a church, chosen from among the Gentiles?'[106] However, he advised caution in carrying a figurative application too far.[107]

One remarkable reading of the Song of Songs was considered in Friedrich Esaias von Pufendorf's work of 1776, mentioned in the Introduction to this study. Referring in the course of his commentary of that year to Pufendorf's theory of the Song of Songs as a conversation in the realms of the dead, Herder sarcastically stated: 'Dieser Traum, der glücklichste von Allen, der auch nur unsrer Zeit aufbehalten seyn konnte, ist da! ist erschienen!' (VIII, p. 591).[108] According to Pufendorf, Solomon was acquainted with Egyptian mysteries and wrote the Song of Songs in hieroglyphics. Pufendorf's deciphering of these hieroglyphics showed that the Song of Songs treated of the sepulchre of the Saviour, his death and the communion of believers who longed for his advent. Both Pufendorf and Runge regarded Michaelis's interpretation as the clearest, most probable interpretation of what they considered to be an obscure book.[109]

Other Translations of the Song of Songs

Herder's reception of other translations he knew is given in the third part of his work of 1778, entitled *Von Uebersetzungen des Buches,*

106. *Lectures on the Sacred Poetry of the Hebrews*, II, pp. 329-30.

107. See *Lectures on the Sacred Poetry of the Hebrews*, II, pp. 322-24.

108. 'This dream, the most auspicious of all, which could be entertained only in our own age, is there, has arrived!' Cf. VIII, p. 529, where, undoubtedly referring to the same work, Herder stressed that the Song of Songs was about love, 'nicht blutige Eroberung, [...] noch Buße und Bekehrung. Es ist weder ein Dialog der Todten im Grabe, noch ein Compendium der Ketzergeschichte' ('not blood-stained conquest, [...] nor repentance and conversion. Neither is it a dialogue involving the dead in the grave, nor a compendium of the history of heretics').

109. In both 1776 and 1778 Herder quoted from the preface, although there are some slight differences in wording in the 1778 quotation. Runge also mentioned the theory of 'ein angesehener und feiner Gottesgelehrter' ('a fine, respected theologian') who was of the opinion that the woman had a second lover apart from Solomon. He was clearly referring to Johann Friedrich Jacobi's *Das durch eine leichte und ungekünstelte Erklärung von seinen Vorwürfen gerettete Hohe Lied.*

insonderheit Einer in alten Minneliedern (VIII, pp. 559-88). Rather than providing a short history of the most prominent expositions of the Song of Songs as he would have liked, he just mentioned several of the most noteworthy. Herder claimed that the German language was fortunate to have one of the oldest versions of the Song of Songs in the eleventh-century interpretation and Latin paraphrase of Willeram (Wollram, Abbot of Ebersperg in Bavaria), a work known to his readers from the *Schiltersche Sammlung Deutscher Alterthümer*. Although Willeram's paraphrase was a free prose translation from the Vulgate,[110] and did not follow the regular sequence of chapters, or even extend to the whole work, Herder recommended it, for 'dieser Reichthum unsrer Sprache soll meinem Mangel an Dichtkunst zu Hülfe kommen und mir die Muse Salomons unheiligen Augen verschleiern helfen' (VIII, p. 595).[111]

Arguably Herder's view of the Song of Songs as a collection of individual songs was dependent on the Minnelieder published by Schöber which he included in his published work of 1778, and on which I have commented above. Herder regarded this mediaeval poetic translation as 'völlig ohne Mystische Auslegung' ('totally lacking in mystical interpretation'), and 'ein Juwel unsrer Sprache' ('a jewel of our language') (VIII, p. 559), stemming from what he considered the golden age of the German language. Herder was convinced that the anonymous author had had the same premise as he himself had, namely that the Song of Songs was a cycle of sentimental love songs to be read literally. It may reasonably be argued that this medieval German lyrical treatment of the Song of Songs, along with Percy's *Reliques*, shared in the development of Herder's theory concerning the Song of Songs, and we have observed from the earlier manuscripts of *Lieder der Liebe* that these Minnelieder were of prime importance for him.

---

110. The Latin Vulgate *Canticum Canticorum* was produced in Bethlehem in 398 CE by Jerome, who translated from the Hebrew and the Greek Septuagint with the intention of conveying the sense rather than merely the words. Where he appeared to depart from the Hebrew and be influenced by the Greek, it must be remembered that he was working from an unpointed text which could be read in different ways. For 1000 years, Jerome's Bible translation was the standard Bible used in the Roman Catholic Church.

111. 'This richness of our language ought to come to the aid of my lack of poetic artistry, and help me to conceal the muse of Solomon from profane eyes.'

According to Herder, the Middle Ages had not been morally offended by the Song of Songs, and could accept it with or without allegory. Thus Herder's literal interpretation was based not merely on Theodore's views, but more particularly on the mediaeval reception of the work. Herder's inclusion in 1778 of an unspoilt Middle High German rendering of the Song of Songs may be viewed as an attack on contemporary allegorists, and particularly on Michaelis. At a time when most educated Germans regarded the Middle Ages and the Hebrew period alike as periods of unrelieved barbarism, his inclusion of the Schöber manuscript was of the greatest significance. In *Lieder der Liebe* Herder quoted extensively from Schöber, whose Old Testament manuscript dated probably from 1450 CE, or even some years earlier. The original manuscript probably dated from 1300 CE. Most of the Song of Songs was contained in verse form in the manuscript, which was a 'Historienbibel' of the Old Testament.[112] Schöber claimed (*SWS*, VIII, p. 561) that the German verse translations of the poems and their titles were made from the Vulgate. Redlich pointed out, however, that 'die Herkunft der Überschriften, die durch zahlreiche Fehler der Abschreiber entstellt sind, ist noch nicht völlig aufgeklärt. Die von Nr. 3, 8, 22, 32, 35 und 43 finden sich nicht in der Vulgata' (VIII, p. 677).[113] We may reasonably accept, then, that Schöber was wrong here.

Redlich included the poems, with notes and a glossary by Schöber, in VIII, pp. 561-86.[114] Herder held that these mediaeval poems were treasures for lovers of Minnesang in particular and the German language in general. The glossary was 'sinnreicher und dem Menschenverstande natürlicher, als zehn mystische Paraphrasen' (VIII, p. 586).[115] Indeed,

112. See Kenneth A. Strand, *German Bibles before Luther: The Story of Fourteen High-German Editions* (Grand Rapids: Eerdmans, 1966); and Timm (ed.), *Das Hohe Lied Salomos*, p. 12.

113. 'The origin of the titles, which have been distorted by numerous errors on the part of the copyists, has not yet been fully elucidated. The titles of numbers 3, 8, 22, 32, 35 and 43 do not appear in the Vulgate.'

114. They are numbered from 1 to 44, and are in a different order from the conventional order of the chapters of the Song of Songs in Luther's translation (see Appendix B). They follow the spirit rather than the letter of the biblical text and it is not always easy to establish exact correspondences.

115. 'More ingenious and more natural to common sense than ten mystical paraphrases.' Herder noted that Schöber also added a prose translation from the twelfth or thirteenth century (VIII, p. 587). In his view, this would interest only the lover of the old German language. Herder did not include it, but referred to it as *Das Hohe-*

Herder's unpublished translations were closer to these Minnelieder, but doubtless not wishing to be accused of heterodoxy, he adopted a more sober approach for his published translation. However, in essence Herder followed the spirit of his mediaeval text, for, as Timm points out, 'am Wohlklang der Wahrheit war dem Sänger das meiste gelegen. Auf die orthodoxe Richtigkeit hat er keine sonderliche Rücksicht genommen.'[116]

Herder referred to the translations of Hans Sachs, but did not comment on them except to point out that they were Meistergesänge, a form of poetry of which he was not fond. Indeed, he regarded Martin Opitz as the first modern German poet to translate the Song of Songs (VIII, p. 587). Opitz too translated the Song of Songs as a collection of shepherd songs rather than as drama or mystical allegory.[117] This was important for Herder's own reading, and he encouraged his readers to compare the beauties of Opitz 'mit denen nach Kapiteln veranstalteten, ungleichspielendern Uebersetzungen Caesii und andrer' (VIII, p. 587).[118]

Just before Herder's work, attempts were made to translate the Song of Songs poetically according to the metre of the original. As examples, Herder mentioned *Versuch über die biblischen Sylbenmaasse* by Christian Ludwig Leutwein (1730–99),[119] and the work of Anton, presum-

lied Salomonis aus zwoen alten deutschen Handschriften, published in Augsburg in 1752.

116. 'The poet cared most of all for the melodious sound of truth. He took no special notice of orthodox correctness.' Timm (ed.), *Das Hohe Lied Salomos*, p. 13.

117. See *Salomons des Hebreischen Königes Hohes Liedt; Vom Martin Opitz in deutsche Gesänge gebracht* (Breslau: D. Müller, 1627). Opitz's translation is also given as 'Die Romanze im gelobten Land' ('The ballad in the Holy Land') in Timm (ed.), *Das Hohe Lied Salomos*, pp. 85-113. It was written in rhyming verse, and it is divided into eight songs according to Luther's chapters (although Timm has omitted the title for the sixth song beginning on p. 106).

118. 'With the translations of Zesen and others which were arranged according to chapters, and which were more uneven in tone.' Clearly Herder was referring here to the work of Philipp von Zesen (1619–89), who wrote 'Das Hohe Lied des Weisen Königes Salomons: Nach Art einer Unterredung in unterschiedliche Lieder gebracht', in *Deutsches Helicons Erster und Ander Theil* (Wittenberg: Röhnern, 1641), Part 2, Book 3, pp. 110-42; reprinted as 'Salomons des Hebräischen Königs Geistliche Wollust, oder Hohes Lied. In Dactylische und Anapästische Verse gebracht', in Ulrich Maché and Volker Meid (eds.), *Sämmtliche Werke* (16 vols.; Berlin: W. de Gruyter, 1971), IX, pp. 355-88.

119. It would appear that Herder gave a wrong title here. The correct title should

ably Conrad Gottlob Anton, Oriental Professor in Wittenberg from 1780, whose Latin translation *Salomonis Carmen melicum quod Canticum Canticorum dicitur* appeared in Leipzig in 1772. Herder considered that both translations had been diligently prepared, although he had nothing to say concerning their success as literary works.

Herder drew attention to the translation of 'Marbod Evanx in Knittelversen und die Hexameter des Petrus de Riga in seiner Aurora' ('Marbod Evanx in "Knittelvers" and the hexameters of Petrus de Riga in his Aurora') (VIII, p. 587), although he did not claim acquaintance with them.[120] Herder saw nothing special or worthy of note in other translations and newer versifications such as that of Samuel Gloner[121] and 'die kirchliche des Beza' ('Bèze's ecclesiastical version') (VIII, p. 587).[122] He claimed knowledge of others, particularly in the Roman Catholic Church, although he did not name them. Herder referred favourably to Salomon Codomann's *Pervigilium Pacis*, published in Rothenburg ob der Tauber in 1628.[123]

As an example of an eighteenth-century version which he would have read very recently, Herder mentioned, with reservation, J.G. Lessing's *Eclogae Regis Salomonis* referred to above. We have also noted reservations in his recension of Hase's translation and commentary, used as a framework for Chapter 1 of this study.

Thus we find substantial allegorical and literal interest in the Song of Songs contemporary with Herder's own preoccupation with the work. This work in particular, with its doubtful canonical position and debat-

---

be *Versuch einer richtigen Theorie von der biblischen Verskunst* (Tübingen, 1777). If this is indeed the same work to which Herder referred, it is surprising that he should mistake the title, given that he would have read the work very recently indeed.

120. There would appear to be a misunderstanding and/or an error in spelling here. In MS(a), Evanx is given as Franx. Presumably Herder was referring to Marbodus, Bishop of Rennes, author of *Liber de gemmarum lapidumoß* in 1539. This work was attributed (apparently wrongly) to Evax, King of Arabia, although it was actually written by Marbod(us).

121. Presumably *Samuel Gloneri Prosodia* (Argentorati, 1639).

122. This would be Théodore de Bèze's *Canticum Canticorum Salomonis, latinis versibus expressum* (1584). See also his *Canticum Canticorum Salomonis, versibus et commentariis illustratum* (1585).

123. Codomann died on 18 July 1637. He also wrote *Salomonis Regis Hebraeorum, Canticum Canticorum Galliambo puro Latinè redditum* in 1611, although apparently Herder did not refer to this work.

able meaning, seemed to provide peculiarly suitable grist to the mill for the new critical theologians who were setting the terms for theological debate at the time. On the other hand, in a period self-consciously setting out to make a new German literature—although not *ab initio*, but rather seeking out an eclectic variety of models—the Song of Songs provided poets with a mode and a tradition of erotic poetry which had the considerable negative virtues of being neither French-rococo and neo-classical, nor pornographic. Both theological and poetic interests fed each other, and Herder, more than anyone else, combined them in his specific characterization of the work as folk-song.

Thus we have observed that Herder had little time for other translations and interpretations, with the exception of Schöber's mediaeval poems. After considering his unique reception of the Song of Songs within the framework of the wider historical context, we now turn our attention to a critical examination of the details of Herder's interpretation as given in the commentaries which accompanied the translations themselves.

Chapter 5

HERDER'S INTERPRETATION OF THE SONG OF SONGS

Introduction

Whereas in the previous chapter I dealt with Herder's general reception of the Song of Songs, in this chapter I consider his interpretation of the detail of the text by using as evidence selected examples from the commentaries of MS(3) (1776) and *Lieder der Liebe* (1778) as given by Redlich in *SWS*, VIII.

I pointed out in the Introduction to this study that Herder was perhaps unique in dividing his translations—albeit arbitrarily and differently in each case—to allow for comments to be interspersed, emphasizing his view that commentary (or interpretation) and translation are inextricably interdependent. Without the commentaries, much of the Oriental imagery maintained by Herder in his translations would have been meaningless to his readership, and so they must be regarded as an integral part of his translation process.

Although in this work I consider the commentaries first before moving on to an examination and comparison of the translations per se, this method by no means acknowledges that one is more important than the other; indeed, a certain overlap will be inevitable. Rather, I use it to facilitate presentation, especially given the highly detailed approach required for a comparison of the translations with each other, with the original Hebrew text, and with the traditionally accepted Lutheran text to which, whatever his claims to the contrary, Herder was providing an alternative.

We have seen how Herder's work was always in a state of flux, and never complete. Thus, although the two translations differ greatly, the published commentary repeats many of the ideas of MS(3) often almost verbatim, despite its less emotional tone. Although Herder's views did not change substantially, however, the commentary of 1776 was reduced considerably for publication. Indeed, including the Erste Zugabe, almost twice as much space was devoted to commentary per se in MS(3) as in the published work.[1]

Ideally this chapter would be based primarily on the published commentary, given that it should be regarded as superseding the earlier work. However, due to the remarkable similarity of the two commentaries, and the greater detail of the earlier one, I plan to consider Herder's views eclectically. Where relevant, I shall also expand on his views concerning other interpreters and commentators, both past and contemporary, accentuating those areas where his commentaries either subliminally or directly encouraged Germans to look to their own native roots for the production of their poetry. After all, this was a major consideration in Herder's whole undertaking.

This chapter is based, then, upon a parallel reading of the single unpublished section of 1776, to which Herder added an appendix containing further explanatory comments (VIII, pp. 589-658), and the first section of the published work, namely *Salomons Hohes Lied* (VIII, pp. 485-528). Herder supplemented his translations throughout with detailed comments on and explanations of the textual material, as well as with paraphrases of selected parts of the translations themselves. He thus compelled his readers to trust what they read. He gave them no opportunity to revert to traditional (allegorical) explanations when he reached those sections of the text whose meaning was not clear, for he commented not only on the peculiar tone of each song—indeed, of each line—but he also referred constantly to historical sources, drawing from relevant travel literature of the time those facts which would have been unknown to the average European reader. For this reason, I shall use as analytic tools his borrowings from contemporary travel writers. Herder wanted to share with others what he had found in the Bible, and specifically what he saw as the Oriental cast of mind.[2] He claimed that

---

1. In Redlich's printing, the 1776 version takes up approximately 475 column cm as opposed to only 275 in the 1778 version.

2. Hellmuth Robscheit has drawn attention to Herder's 'Einführung in die Schrift, damit der Leser mit der Sprache und dem Denken des morgenländischen Menschen vertraut wird' ('introduction to the Scriptures, so that the reader is acquainted with the language and the thought processes of the Orientals'). 'Herder als Ausleger des Alten Testamentes (dargestellt an seiner Schrift *Vom Geist der Ebräischen Poesie*)', in Eva Schmidt (ed.), *Herder im geistlichen Amt: Untersuchungen, Quellen, Dokumente* (Leipzig: Koehler & Amelang, 1956), pp. 26-38 (38).

his purpose was not to write a commentary in order to fight with his predecessors, although it will emerge that his commentaries demonstrated considerable disagreement with other interpretations, and contained rather more than the mere 'Winke, Züge aus Reisebeschreibungen, Erläuterung einiger Bilder' ('suggestions and ideas from travel writing, and explanation of a few images') (VIII, p. 642) which he purported to give.

Herder's was a re-reading of a text that had drawn a great deal of controversy and had received strong interpretations already. Although he was quite clearly aware of a possible sexual interpretation, he had harsh words for those who found anything suggestive in the Song of Songs. He rejected any interpretation of the book which suggested ambiguities in the text, maintaining that the Orientals, who thought and felt differently from Europeans, did not know such ambiguity: 'Man [...] hat Worte der Unschuld zu schändlichen Zweideutigkeiten machen wollen, die nach allen Zeugnissen, alt und neu, der Orient gar nicht kennet,[3] gar nicht leidet, sondern uns zweideutigen, gesitteten Euro-

---

3.   Herder's note at this point reads: 'S. d'Arvieux Th.2. S.163. 185. 264' ('See d'Arvieux part 2, pp. 163, 185 and 264') (VIII, p. 509 n. a). Although Herder gave the title of Laurent d'Arvieux's work simply as *Reisen* (VIII, p. 491 n. d), throughout his commentary he referred in fact to d'Arvieux's *Hinterlassene merkwürdige Nachrichten, worinnen er sowol seine Reise nach Constantinopel, in Asien, Syrien, dem gelobten Lande, Egypten, und der Barbarei, als auch die Beschaffenheit dieser Länder, die Religion, Sitten, Gebräuche, und Handlung dieser Völker, nebst der Regierungsart, der natürlichen Historie, und den besondern in diesen Gegenden vorgefallenen Begebenheiten, genau und richtig beschreibet, im Französischen herausgegeben von dem Herrn Labat, und ietzt ins Deutsche übersetzt* (6 vols.; Copenhagen and Leipzig: Ackermann, 1753–56), the German translation of *Mémoires du chevalier d'Arvieux [...] contenant ses voyages à Constantinople, dans l'Asie, la Syrie, la Palestine, l'Egypte, et la Barbarie, la description de ces païs, les religions, les moeurs, les coûtumes [...] recüeillis de ses mémoires originaux, et mis en ordre avec des réflections* (ed. Jean-Baptiste Labat; 6 vols.; Paris: Delespine, 1735). Herder's reference to d'Arvieux, II, pp. 163, 185 and 264 is wrong (see his published version of *Lieder der Liebe*, p. 50 n. a, and Redlich, *SWS*, VIII, p. 509 n. a, and VIII, p. 649). In fact, d'Arvieux's comments on the Orientals' lack of ambiguity are not in vol. II, but rather in vol. III, where, for example, we read: 'Ihr Umgang ist allezeit nach denen Regeln des strengsten Wolstandes eingerichtet' ('Their deportment at all times is regulated according to the rules of the strictest decency') (p. 163); and 'Obgleich die Araber in ihren Worten und Ausdrükungen sehr einfältig sind, indem sie ein iedes Ding bei seinem rechten Namen nennen, so unterlassen sie doch, wenn sie von etwas reden, dessen Vorstellung

päern als Schlamm und Schande ins Gesicht speiet' (VIII, pp. 509-10. Cf. p. 649).[4]

Throughout this chapter I shall consider in detail Herder's attempts to stress the innocent nature of the Song of Songs. It will become clear that his reading was heavily coloured by his own culture, and that he did exactly what he accused others of doing, namely using the text to suit their own theories and hypotheses. Although Herder was not a literary conservative, and although for him 'the Bible text grew out of historical conditions that were very different from the prudish eighteenth century', as Wulf Koepke has it,[5] his interpretation was surely that of a cautious eighteenth-century Lutheran pastor, and hence his apparent efforts to squeeze the Song of Songs at all costs into his own mould of innocence, modesty, chastity, naïveté, simplicity and beauty. He could also be accused of arguing for a thread of homogeneous continuity throughout the work, thereby creating his own hypothesis while berating those who did the same. This is a point which has been made by other commentators, although in rather general terms. For example, operating with an ideal of cultural 'faithfulness', Haym pointed out that Herder's interpretation was too innocent to be historically true, thus claiming that even he had failed to produce an unadulterated reading, and was therefore no more accurate than Michaelis, for example, whom Herder attacked vehemently.[6] Indeed, Meyer, subtler in his confrontation of two cultures, was surely right when he claimed that Herder's chaste refusal to find anything sensual in the Song of Songs

> stimmt viel besser zu dem höchst verfeinerten europäischen Kulturmenschen des ausgehenden achtzehnten Jahrhunderts, als zu dem alten

---

einige Unanständigkeit mit sich führet, niemals, diese Worte zu sagen' ('Although the Arabs are very innocent in their words and expressions, in that they call each thing by its right name, they still refrain from ever uttering these words when they speak of something the presentation of which might bring with it some degree of impropriety') (p. 185). This error of pagination is acknowledged by Gaier (*Lieder der Liebe*, p. 459 n. 24, and p. 1230), but it is missed by Otto (*Lieder der Liebe*, p. 40).

4. 'Attempts have been made [...] to make words of innocence into scurrilous ambiguities, with which, according to all testimonies, both old and new, the Orient is in no way acquainted, and which it in no way tolerates, but rather spits out as filth and shame into the faces of us smutty, well-bred Europeans.'

5. *Johann Gottfried Herder* (Twayne's World Authors Series, 786; Boston: Twayne, 1987), p. 53.

6. *Herder*, II, p. 85.

Morgenländer des neunten vor Christo. Aber ihm ist dies alles so selbst-
verständlich, daß er es gar nicht merkt, wie sehr er gelegentlich dem
Wortsinne Gewalt anthut, um ihn dieser Auffassung gefügig zu machen.[7]

Paul Haupt likewise asserted that 'von den Sitten (und Unsitten) des
Morgenlandes hatte Herder allerdings eine allzuhohe Meinung',[8] claim-
ing that he overestimated the innocence of the poems, and proposing
that 'der Mangel an Verständnis für orientalische Zweideutigkeiten kann
Herder nur ehren, ebenso wie es eine reine Frau ehrt, wenn sie eine
Zweideutigkeit nicht versteht'.[9]

Herder did not regard the Song of Songs as just an ordinary love
song, and he idealized it as the original pattern of all love poetry. He
imprinted his own ideal of a pure, untarnished humanity on the poetry
before him, and he truly believed that he was reading the simple meaning of the text according to the principles he had laid down. For him,
the Bible was not only a human book, a monument of ancient literature;
it also spoke with divine authority, and it was relevant for all time. No
longer was it the remnants of the national literature of a Semitic nation,
but rather it represented the plan of God in history, the divine education
of the human race. Thus its universal message must remain the same for
all peoples and all cultures, and yet Herder stands accused of reading
the text of the Song of Songs according to his own cultural background
and his understanding of the moral nobility of the Orientals. Here we
have an example of the dichotomy in Herder's work between the universal and the particular. This is an especially acute instance of the
paradox inherent in all of Herder's multicultural thinking.

Given Herder's view, however, that the Bible contained God's ideal
for the human race, it should not be surprising that he should seek to
find love between man and woman innocently idealized within its
pages. If the Bible were universal, it must include pure erotic love. We

7.   'Is far more in keeping with the extremely refined European individual of
culture of the end of the eighteenth century than the ancient Oriental of the ninth
century before Christ. But everything here is so self-evident to him, that he fails to
notice how much he occasionally violates the literal meaning in order to make it fit
this interpretation.' *Werke*, p. 15.

8.   'Herder certainly had far too high an opinion of the morals (and immoral
characteristics) of the Orient.' *Biblische Liebeslieder*, p. xi.

9.   'Herder's lack of understanding of Oriental ambiguities can simply honour
him, just as a pure woman is honoured when she fails to understand a double
entendre.' *Biblische Liebeslieder*, p. xi.

are reminded again of Herder's view that poetry was divine revelation and that Hebrew poetry, as the most original poetry known to mankind, was therefore God's first revelation to humanity. The thoughts expressed in the Song of Songs were the thoughts of Adam and Eve as expressed in their first song of love (VIII, p. 636). As the very first love poetry, the Song of Songs was *ipso facto* 'das Einzige und Schönste seiner Art' ('the only, and the most beautiful example, of its kind') (VIII, p. 637).

In his published translation Herder went through the Song of Songs section by section, both to demonstrate the thread of unity for which he pleaded, and to summarize the views expressed in his more detailed analysis of and commentary on the actual text (VIII, pp. 539-41). Although he rejected a dramatic interpretation, he followed Luther's chapter and verse divisions, dividing his own (dramatic?) reading into seven 'scenes', summarized below to serve as a useful frame of reference:

The first section of the work, Song 1.1-3, begins with a kiss, or a sigh, awakening the first signs of longing and pure love, with no knowledge of envy. Song 1.4-7 shows the woman more certain of her lover's feelings. Her poverty is contrasted with his wealth. She seeks comfort and solace as the initial signs of envy appear. The first germ of love almost dies, but it emerges all the stronger for the trials to which it has been subjected. Song 1.8-13 demonstrates love through tokens, symbols and gifts. In Song 1.14–2.7 we are introduced to the Bed of Nature, the Banner of Love and the image of the apple tree. The woman swoons and falls asleep. A lullaby closes the first scene.

The second scene is based on Song 2.8–3.5. It is a spring morning in a flower garden. Love awakens with spring and nature, and we hear a morning greeting, a song of spring. The woman does not reply, and we hear a song of the kind used to scare off the jackals, followed by a song of longing for the absent lover, who fails to materialize. The woman looks for him in her dreams. She searches high and low, finally finds him, and takes him to her mother's house. He is her prize, rather than she being his. The woman has her lover to herself, and we hear the lullaby again.

The third scene begins in Song 3.6 with the question 'Was steigt dort aus der Wüste?' ('What arises there from out of the desert?'), a question to be heard several more times in the whole work. The woman appears as a pillar of smoke in the twilight. The king's bed is described. Song of

Songs 4 contains songs of praise and love. The modest woman interrupts her lover in Song 5.1. He follows her and the scene ends in Song 5.2 with a feast among friends in the garden.[10]

Scene four, Song 5.2-16, introduces the ointment on the handle of the door. The woman delays and her lover disappears. She regrets her indifference and indolence, and sings her praises of him. From Song 5.17–6.2 her jealousy refuses to allow her friends to search for her lover with her. He is hers, and hers alone. She is rewarded with a song of praise in Song 6.3-8 (see VIII, pp. 540-41).

The fifth scene begins, similarly to the third, with 'Wer steigt dort aus der Wüsten empor?' ('Who arises up from out of the desert?') in Song 6.9. The bride is the goddess of beauty, love and desire, 'bis sie dem Liebhaber auf dem Gipfel seiner Trunkenheit sanft einfällt und als eine Blume der Unschuld auf dem Lande blühet' (VIII, p. 541. See Song 7.9–8.3).[11] Herder regarded this as the most splendid scene in the book. In his opinion, it was the 'Elysium des Buchs auch in seiner Wendung und Lehre, voll des tiefen Gefühls' ('Elysium of the book, also in its phraseology and instruction, full of deep feeling') (VIII, p. 541). The scene closes in Song 8.4 with the lullaby of innocence, sung for the third and last time.

The sixth scene begins, similarly to the third and fifth, with 'Wer steigt dort auf?' ('Who arises there?'). The woman, calm and still, is now in the autumn of her life, experiencing married love and fidelity, although reminded of the spring (Song 8.5-7). And so the Book of Love closes. Song 8.8-12 represents a scene of renewal, a conversation between brothers and their sister.

Thus, although Herder viewed the Song of Songs as a collection of songs, dividing his translations arbitrarily into independent sections rather than following the traditional chapter divisions, he used Luther's chapter divisions when presenting his summary. In the absence of any other clear division, then, it would seem appropriate to present and comment upon Herder's views as they pertain to the eight chapter divisions of the Lutheran text to which he constantly pointed his readers, and as reproduced in Appendix B of this study. I shall adopt this con-

---

10. In fact Song 5.1 in Herder is Song 4.17 in Luther, although, as Appendix B shows, Luther included the verse at the beginning of Song 5. Song 5.2 in Herder is thus Song 5.1 in Luther, although in each case both verses are essentially the same.

11. 'Until, at the peak of his intoxication, her lover tenderly remembers her, and she blossoms in the countryside as a flower of innocence.'

vention both in this chapter and the next in order to facilitate presentation and reading, although I recognize that such divisions of the text arguably contravene Herder's more fluid approach. For this reason, I shall use asterisks to subdivide the following commentary further, according to Herder's own division into the seven scenes outlined above. I shall give the 22 numbered and named songs of 1776 as points of reference within the Lutheran chapter divisions. (See Appendix A, in which I present the translations of 1776 and 1778 side by side for ease of comparison and contrast.)

Commentary

Luther: Chapter One

In Herder's first comments in 1778, he referred to the opening lines as 'dieser Seufzer' ('this sigh'), although the word does not appear in his translation. However, he actually named the first part of the 1776 translation 'Der Seufzer' ('The Sigh') (song I), based on Song 1.1-14, a passage which speaks of the first flush of love: 'Vielleicht ward dieser Seufzer mit einer schmachtenden Blume, mit einer duftenden Morgenrose übersandt; das sehnende Mädchen duftet mit hinüber' (VIII, p. 489).[12] We shall see how dependent Herder was on the travel writers of his time, and comments such as this were based on his reading of their works. Probably the Oriental custom of sending presents of flowers was discovered by Herder in the works of writers such as Lady Mary Wortley Montagu[13] and Fredrik Hasselquist, Swedish author of *Iter palaestinum, eller Resa til Heliga Landet [...] 1749 til 1752* (Stockholm: Salvius, 1757), who confirmed that presents of flowers 'dienen ihnen zu ihrem Liebeswerke' ('are used to help them express love').[14] Lovers conversed with each other by sending flowers, each flower having its own meaning in the dictionary of love.

---

12. 'Perhaps this sigh was sent with a languishing flower, with a fragrant morning rose; likewise, the yearning girl exhales her sweet fragrance.'

13. Lady Mary Wortley Montagu published various editions of her *Letters of the Right Honourable Lady M --- y W --- M --- u: Written during her Travels in Europe, Asia and Africa between 1763 and 1800*. Herder clearly read a pre-1776 version, most probably the 1764 edition.

14. The edition of Hasselquist's work to which Herder referred was undoubtedly Theodor H. Gadebusch's translation *Reise nach Palästina 1749 bis 1752* (ed. Carl Linnäus; Rostock: Koppe, 1762). The quotation here is from p. 37.

Although Herder noted that Hasselquist, for example, described the state of women in the Orient in negative terms as unliberated (VIII, p. 490 n. b),[15] his own positive reading was coloured by his view of the Song of Songs as a chaste, naïve and innocent work in which the opposite was true. He presented an ideal eighteenth-century world in which there was no room for realism, using adjectives such as 'schwesterlich' ('sisterly'), 'frei' ('independent'), 'klug' ('intelligent'), 'ruhig' ('serene'), 'liebevoll' ('affectionate') and 'sehnend' ('yearning') to describe the woman in the Song of Songs (VIII, p. 642).

In the first part of the work, the lover is absent, although even the mention of his name perfumes the air. He is loved by all, not just by the woman, although she occupies prime position in his thoughts.[16] She returns to her circle of companions, all of whom love and rejoice as she does: 'Ein schüchternes Täubchen bringt den Brief, und buhlt um ihn, aber nur als ihrer Schwestern Bote' ('A timid little dove bears the letter and woos him, but only as the messenger of her sisters') (VIII, p. 490). Herder saw perfect harmony here. There was no envy, jealousy, rancour or infidelity. There is a difference at this point between Herder's earlier and later readings. Although in 1776 the woman, by contrast, 'kämpft […] mit ihren Nebenbulerinnen' ('quarrels […] with her rivals') (VIII, p. 596), in Herder's view in 1778 a quite different woman speaks as the first voice grows silent.

As we have noted, Herder was adamant that the songs are a collection of individual, unrelated poems, and his anxiety to find an (unintended) common thread may appear inconsistent. He referred to the 'Faden der Liebe' ('thread of love') (VIII, p. 597), and, as we have seen, 'der feine Faden […] den der Sammler bei Reihung dieser kostbaren Perlen hatte' ('the delicate thread […] which the compiler used to arrange these precious pearls') (VIII, p. 628). He presented the thread running through the poems according to their content, yet argued that the individuality

---

15. Hasselquist wrote of the joys of Oriental women when allowed a little freedom on Mohammed's birthday, although, actually writing of Cairo, he claimed (*Reise nach Palästina*, p. 126) that 'es ist für das Geschlecht ein Unglück, daß es nicht alle die Freyheit an den Festtagen genießen kann, die es sich wünscht' ('for their sex, it is unfortunate that on feast days they are not able to enjoy all the freedom which they would like').

16. Herder regarded the word מישרים, meaning 'the straight, upright ones' who love the king, as referring to the woman herself, to 'ihr Innerstes, Herz und Seele' ('her innermost being, heart and soul') (VIII, p. 642).

of the various songs must be preserved: 'Die einzelnen Stücke [...] als einzeln zu fühlen, bleibt Hauptaugenmerk' ('The chief purpose remains to experience [...] the individual songs as such') (VIII, p. 628). He also spoke of the different 'Situationen' ('situations') and 'Stücke' ('songs') which changed in tone and content, underscoring his view of the Song of Songs as a collection of different poems (VIII, p. 634). Love was the only thread he found in the first two sections of 1776, although in his attempts to emphasize this thread, he expanded the concept of love to include 'Sehnen, Suchen, Irren, Verirrtseyn aus lauter Bescheidenheit und Blöde' ('yearning, searching, erring and going astray as a result of pure modesty and shyness') (VIII, p. 598). The theme was 'das nur Zusammenseynwollen, in Einer Gegend, an Einem Ort' ('simply desiring to be together, in one place, in one neighbourhood') (VIII, p. 598).

In the second section, entitled 'Liebe in Armuth' ('Love in Poverty') (song II) in 1776, and based on Song 1.5-8, the woman is a country girl whose lover, King Solomon, is a shepherd of other flocks (VIII, p. 598). She compares herself with the dark tents common at the time, asking of her lover: 'Liebt er nicht auch schwarze Gezelte? [...] Warum sollte er mich nicht lieben?' ('Does he not also love black tents? [...] Why should he not love me?') (VIII, p. 597). To the Western reader, this is a strange simile, but whereas translators may change such imagery to suit the cultural background of their readership, Herder felt able to keep it by explaining it in his commentary. He noted that the tents in the Orient had black canopies of camel hair so that they could be distinguished easily at a distance. The woman is presumably so beautiful that she is immediately noticeable, although it was Herder's contention that she was too modest to be referring to her beauty as such, for that had been lost in the sun. In fact, in Chapter 6 below I shall note in more detail that Herder translated with 'schwarz und doch ihm angenehm' ('black, and yet pleasing to him') and 'schwarz bin ich und doch lieblich' ('I am black, and yet lovely') in 1776 and 1778 respectively, suggesting beauty despite, rather than because of, a dark complexion.

Striving to demonstrate that this tent imagery was natural, Herder looked for support from d'Arvieux, referring (VIII, p. 491 n. d) simply to d'Arvieux, III, pp. 214-15. Here we read that the tents of the Arabs 'sind ganz aus schwarzen Ziegenhaaren gemacht' ('are made completely from black goat's hair'),[17] and that the Arabs 'lagern sich auf

---

17. *Hinterlassene merkwürdige Nachrichten*, III, p. 214.

Hügeln, welche sie *Rouhha* nennen, das ist, *schöne Luft*, und ziehen dieienigen Oerter vor, wo keine Bäume stehen, die ihnen hinderlich seyn könten, die Kommenden und Fortgehenden von weiten zu entdeken'.[18] Herder also drew on Thomas Shaw, who claimed that 'nichts kann einen anmuthigern Anblick verschaffen, als eine weitläufige Ebene [...] und diese beweglichen Wohnplätze in Kreisen auf derselben gestellt zu sehen'.[19] In the same way as the tents were coarse and rough, so Solomon loved this 'schwarzes niedriges Mädchen' ('black, humble girl'), a shy, unknown country girl (VIII, p. 643). Herder suggested that the Hebrew description of the woman as כעטיה ('veiled') portrayed well this 'Schmachten in Mittagssonne' ('languishing in the midday sun') (VIII, p. 643).[20]

In Herder's view the atmosphere of the whole work was one of simple, blameless naïveté, of freedom, nature, humility, innocence, modesty, simplicity and repose. Here too 'das ganze Stück athmet freies Feld, Mittagsruhe, Hirten—und Landeinfalt' ('the whole poem breathes open countryside, midday, repose, and pastoral and rustic innocence') (VIII, p. 491). His reading was an attempt to cleanse, purify and romanticize. It was his intention, of course, to underline the importance of creating literature from within its own *Sitz im Leben*, and in his comments on obscure images in the Song of Songs, such as that of the tents, he attempted to show that they were a natural product of the environment in which the poems were written. The richness of image in the Song of Songs was a result of 'die Sprache, die Gegenden und Sitten' ('the language, locality and customs') of the country of its origin (VIII,

18. 'Encamp on hills which they call *Rouhha*, i.e. *glorious air*, and prefer those places where there are no trees which might hinder them from detecting from afar those coming and going.' *Hinterlassene merkwürdige Nachrichten*, III, p. 215. Herder paraphrased this passage in his commentary, although the published version of 1778 (p. 12), Redlich (*SWS*, VIII, p. 491) and Otto (*Lieder der Liebe*, p. 12) in fact have '*Roubha*'. Gaier (*Lieder der Liebe*, p. 437) correctly uses d'Arvieux's '*Rouhha*'.

19. 'Nothing is able to offer a more charming aspect than seeing a distant plain [...] with these portable dwellings erected in circles thereon.' *Reisen*, p. 193. Herder (VIII, p. 491) in fact paraphrased Shaw, as he did (differently) in VIII, p. 642, with 'nichts ist anmuthiger [...] als eine weitläuftige Ebne voll dieser schwarzen Zelte' ('nothing is more graceful [...] than a distant plain full of these black tents') (VIII, p. 491).

20. Herder referred his readers to Albert Schultens, who similarly saw the scene as one of languishing and yearning (VIII, pp. 492 and 643).

p. 522). Herder regarded the vineyard lost while the woman was caring for her brothers' vineyard as representative of the woman's only possession, namely her lost beauty, for 'meinen Weinberg hütet' ich nicht' ('I did not take care of my own vineyard') (VIII, p. 490). He believed that his interpretation was too subtle for other interpreters. In the Orient, vineyards represented wealth, and similarly the woman's wealth was her beauty. Attempting to show that metaphors and similes which might seem strange to another culture were perfectly natural products of the culture within which they were created, Herder pointed his German readers in the direction of similar examples of their own sayings and proverbs where the same intention pertained. Thus Germans were encouraged to imitate rather than copy, and to use imagery from within their own culture, as occurred in the Song of Songs.

In the next section, entitled 'Brautgeschenke' ('Bridal Gifts') (song III) in 1776, and based on Song 1.9-14, the previous scene of shy poverty has become one of splendour and pride. Despite criticizing those who regarded the Song of Songs as drama, Herder called this 'ein Auftritt ganz anderer Art' ('a scene of a quite different nature') (VIII, p. 598). He acknowledged that the images of the horse and the palm tree were foreign to his readership, yet he argued for their beauty. Concerning the image of the horse, Herder called upon Shaw for support that 'das Pferd ist das Eigenthum und der Stolz Numidiens: heut zu Tage steht Aegypten allein im Ruf der besten Pferde' (VIII, p. 493 n. f, and VIII, p. 643).[21] From 2 Chron. 1.16 he demonstrated that the same was true of Solomon's era. The imagery was thus again unsurpassed 'im Sinne der Gegend und der Zeit' ('in the context of its locality and age') (VIII, p. 643). Just as the horse was the 'Prachtgeschöpf Orients' ('most magnificent creature in the Orient') (VIII, p. 493), so does the woman stand before the king, rewarded for her earlier shyness and modesty (VIII, pp. 493 and 599). Her only gifts to him are 'Natur, Einfalt, Lebensfülle' ('nature, innocence, vitality') (VIII, p. 599). Her lover is all she needs.

---

21. 'The horse is the property and pride of Numidia: nowadays Egypt alone has a reputation for the best horses.' Herder's quotation was a paraphrase, although his reference was correct. Shaw (*Reisen*, p. 147) actually wrote of 'das Pferd, der Stolz und das unterscheidende Kennzeichen Numidiens. [...] Heute zu Tage stehen daher die Aegyptier [...] mit Rechte allein in dem Rufe, daß sie die besten Pferde ziehen' ('the horse, the pride and the distinguishing mark of Numidia. [...] Nowadays, therefore, the Egyptians [...] are alone reputed to breed the best horses').

The woman uses imagery of flowers and plants peculiar to the Orient. Her lover is for her 'die junge Blüthentraube aus dem Palmenhayne zu Engeddi' ('the young grape from the palm grove of Engeddi') (VIII, p. 493). Herder regarded this as a most beautiful image, and he drew attention to passages in Hasselquist, who found both sexes portrayed and represented in the palm. Undoubtedly Herder had in mind the passage in Hasselquist (*Reise nach Palästina*, p. 223) which reads: 'Der Gärtner [...] wollte mir das Männchen und Weibchen der Palmen oder des Dattelbaums, als eine ganz bewundernswürdige Sache zeigen.'[22] The palm tree, then, was an important image in the culture in which the Song of Songs was written. Aware that some might find such imagery distasteful, Herder demanded 'daß man das zarte reine Bild nicht wieder mit einem Säurüssel behandle' (literally 'that the delicate, pure image should not be treated yet again with a pig's snout') (VIII, p. 644). The female palm tree is restored to life by means of the male flowers,

> oder man nimmt die männliche Blüthensproße, ehe sie ausbricht, und verhüllet sie in die kleinen Zweige der weiblichen Blume. In diesem Zustande heißt die Palmenblüthe Kopher, d.i. verhüllet: [...] In der weiblichen Blume verhüllet, haucht er sie an mit Duft und Leben' (VIII, p. 493-94).[23]

Herder admired this beautiful imagery. He saw purity and innocence throughout, comparing the image with the relationship between the woman and her lover. Without him she is lifeless. He breathes life into her, giving her new strength and feeling. He has made of her a new creation. In Herder's view, the different sexes thus give life to each other, and for him this was portrayed perfectly by the palm tree, 'das blühendste Bild der Schöne, Fruchtbarkeit, Süßigkeit, Rege und des Verhalts der Geschlechter gegen einander' (VIII, p. 599).[24]

*   *   *

The next section, entitled 'Träume der Zukunft' ('Dreams of the Future') (song IV) in 1776, is based on Song 1.15-17 and Song 2.1-6.

---

22. 'The gardener [...] wanted to show me the male and female of the palm trees, or of the date tree, as a thing quite to be admired.'

23. 'Or the male shoot is taken before it buds, and it is wrapped in the little twigs of the female plant. In this condition the palm blossom is known as Copher, i.e. veiled: [...] Covered thus by the female flower, it breathes fragrance and life into her.'

24. 'The most flourishing image of beauty, fecundity, sweetness, excitement and of the behaviour of the sexes towards each other.'

Luther: Chapter Two

Herder held that the first verse of Song of Songs 2 belonged to the end
of Song of Songs 1 rather than the beginning of Song of Songs 2 as in
the traditional divisions of the Bible (VIII, p. 645).[25] The man praises
the woman's beauty, particularly describing her eyes which he likens to
shy doves. In the Orient, the praise of beauty begins with the eyes, and
Herder noted (VIII, p. 495 n. k) the importance to the Orientals of the
eyes, pointing for support to d'Arvieux (III, pp. 249-50), which reads:

> Die gröste Schönheit des vornehmen *arabischen* und alles *morgen-*
> *ländischen* Frauenzimmers bestehet in grossen schwarzen wolgespal-
> teten und hervorragenden Augen. [...] Alle ihre Gesänge laufen nur auf
> die schönen Augen hinaus, welche sie allezeit mit denen Augen einer
> Gems vergleichen. Dieses Thier hat auch gewis schöne, schwarze, grosse
> und wolgespaltene Augen; man kan noch hinzusetzen, daß die Augen
> derer Gemse ungemein sitsam aussehen, wie einem Frauenzimmer und
> insonderheit einer manbaren Jungfrau anständig ist.[26]

Herder thus again highlighted the innocence, modesty and shyness of
the work in general and of the woman in particular.

In Herder's view, the woman quickly interrupts the man in order to
praise him too, and to decry her own beauty. Herder contrived to
explain this by suggesting that the woman is too modest to hear such
praise from her beloved's lips. She, 'die Tochter der Unschuld' ('the
daughter of innocence') (VIII, p. 495), is a mere flower, the forest's
'Schattenblume' ('lily') (VIII, p. 601), compared with the large cedars
and cypresses, which Hasselquist described as a pyramid rising to the
heavens, 'der größte Schmuck, welchen die Natur diesen Gegenden
geschenkt hat'.[27] Her lover takes her chaste words and turns them into a
compliment. Her modesty and humility are thus usurped by his praise, a
point which Herder believed had been overlooked (VIII, p. 645). He

---

25. See n. 10 above concerning Song 4.17 and Song 5.1.

26. 'The greatest beauty of the noble Arabic and totally Oriental woman is in
her large, dark, wide and prominent eyes. [...] All their songs refer only to the eyes,
which they always compare with the eyes of a chamois. This animal certainly also
has beautiful, large, dark, wide eyes; one might also add that the eyes of their
chamois look extraordinarily modest, as is proper for a woman and especially for a
desirable virgin.'

27. 'The most magnificent decoration which nature has given to these parts.'
Reise nach Palästina, p. 32 (see also p. 36). Herder quoted this reference wrongly,
using 'den Gegenden' ('the parts') instead (VIII, p. 496).

criticized those who regarded the flower here as the most splendid of flowers, claiming that this simple plant was the equivalent of what Germans would know as 'Veilchen' ('violet'), 'Mayblume' ('mayflower') or 'Thallilie' ('lily of the valley') (VIII, pp. 496 and 645), and observing the image as one of 'schöne Niedrigkeit' ('wondrous humility') and 'liebliche Demuth' ('delightful meekness') (VIII, p. 496). He supported his view with reference to Mt. 6.28, where Christ implies the flower's lack of beauty. Thus the woman's insistence that she is a flower must not be taken as self-praise, but rather as self-deprecation.

For supporting information about wild flowers in the Orient, Herder referred again to Hasselquist, where we read: 'Anemonen und Tulipanen zierten das Feld, und wuchsen in den Thälern und an den Füßen der Berge überall wild. Jene waren schön, von verschiedenen Farben, purpur, hochroth, Coccinelfarb mit einem weißen Kreise am Boden der Blätter.'[28] The fact that in this passage Hasselquist was actually writing about a journey to Smyrna and Magnesia either suggests a misreading on Herder's part or emphasizes his global, undifferentiated view of the Orient. For additional evidence, Herder called upon Richard Pococke who wrote: 'Ich sahe [...] viele Tulpen wild auf dem Felde wachsen, und wer die Schönheit dieser Blumen recht betrachtet, sollte denken, daß dieses die Lilien wären, von welchen es heisset, daß Salomo mit aller seiner Herrlichkeit damit nicht zu vergleichen wäre.'[29]

28. 'Anemones and tulips adorned the countryside and grew wild everywhere in the valleys and at the foot of the mountains. They were beautiful, and of various hues, purple, crimson and scarlet, with a white corolla on the bottom of the leaves.' *Reise nach Palästina*, p. 34.

29. 'I saw [...] many tulips growing wild in the countryside, and whoever observes properly the beauty of these flowers must think that these were the lilies with which we are told that Solomon in all his glory could not be compared.' Richard Pococke (1704–65) was successively Bishop of Ossory and of Meath, and his work was first translated from English into German by Christian Ernst von Windheim and the Chancellor of Mosheim, Johann Friedrich Breyer, as *Beschreibung des Morgenlandes und einiger andern Länder* (3 vols.; Erlangen: Breitkopf, 1754–55). I have used this edition. The work is in three parts: Part One deals with Egypt, whereas Part Two deals with Palestine, Syria, Mesopotamia and Cyprus. Herder quoted from Part Two throughout, although particularly from pp. 8-9 here. He also spelled Pococke's name as Pocock, Pokock, Pocok and Pokok. He sometimes referred to Pocock-Schreber. This was a second edition of Pococke's work by Johannes Christian Daniel Schreber (Erlangen, 1771–72), although the pagination is virtually identical to that of the first edition. Schreber was the editor of *Der Naturforscher*, published in Halle in 1774.

The woman interrupts once more, in Herder's view again for reasons of modesty. She likens her lover to an apple tree, and Herder pointed to Hasselquist as he attempted to demonstrate that all the images in the Song of Songs are indeed natural, stemming from the time and place of their conception. A glance at the words of Hasselquist to which Herder referred shows that of the many kinds of plant in the Orient 'keines ist so allgemein, als der Hagapfelbaum (*Arbutus Andrachne*). Dieses Gebüsch bedeckt die Berge überall.'[30]

In her imagination, the woman is no longer beneath a tree, but in a 'Haus des Weins' ('house of wine') (VIII, p. 496). Herder believed that Solomon understood the phrase to mean no more than 'Ort der Entzückung, der Freude' ('place of delight and joy') (VIII, p. 496 n. o). He maintained that no wine-cellar is intended here, and he complained that such beautiful imagery had been disfigured by commentators through the ages. Apparently he was unsure where to stop in his efforts to underline his reading of the work as one of naïve innocence and modesty. His interpretation was surely one of idealizing 'Empfindsamkeit' ('sentimentality'). The woman just wants to be cared for by her lover, to be supported and held. Herder insisted that she is not concerned with anything more overtly sexual. She is not saying 'bettet mich auf Weinflaschen, Aepfel und Arabische Kräuter' ('bed me on wine bottles, apples and Arabic plants') (VIII, p. 497 n. o). He was presumably alluding here to another translation he knew, and he warned against losing sight of the innocence of the whole image. He berated those who had painted a scene of debauchery in a wine cellar, portraying both as drunk and engaged in doing on a bed of apples and bottles 'was dort Virgils Aeneas und Dido weit züchtiger und sittsamer in ihrer Höle thaten' ('what Virgil's Aeneas and Dido did far more chastely and decently in their cave') (VIII, p. 646). He stressed the innocence of this 'unwißende, hoffende Braut der Unschuld' ('inexperienced, expectant bride of innocence') (VIII, p. 601). Arguably this is the most erotic of the poems, and thus Herder doubtlessly felt the need to overstate his case.

Although the banner had been interpreted by others as an inn-sign over the wine cellar, Herder maintained that it is the large tree above the bride, representing her lover (VIII, p. 646). He denied that the

---

30. 'None is as common as the bell heather shrub (*Arbutus andrachne*). This plant covers the mountains everywhere.' *Reise nach Palästina*, p. 44.

Hebrews enjoyed or even knew such debauched behaviour as other commentators had observed in this scene:

> O Sitten Morgenlandes! o Zucht! o Liebe! kannten die Morgenländer den fleischigten Amor? [...] und wird ein Lied der Liebe, wie das Unsrige, so etwas singen? Auch die schöne Erklärung: *oppugnat me (quasi pugnis) sub vexillo amoris* ist dem Texte ganz fremde. Das Panier der Liebe ist nichts, als das Bild des Baumes (VIII, pp. 496-97, n. o. Cf. p. 646).[31]

Herder's 1776 commentary on this section is poetic. The tree, the fruit and the lover merge into one, and 'sanft zerrinnen ihre Sinnen unter dem webenden Baum' ('tenderly their senses melt away beneath the rustling tree') (VIII, p. 602). The tree becomes the lover with his left hand supporting the woman's head, and she finds herself in the lap of 'Natur, Unschuld und Liebe' ('nature, innocence and love') (VIII, p. 497).

The text moves into the section which in 1776 Herder called the 'Schlummerlied' ('Lullaby') (song V), based on Song 2.7. Representative of all chaste brides, the woman slumbers innocently, while her lover sings a lullaby. Again, despite his rejection of the drama theory, Herder claimed that 'ein Auftritt des Buchs ist also geendet' ('thus another scene in the book draws to a close') (VIII, p. 602), and the woman awakes 'in ganz andrer Scene' ('in quite a different scene') (VIII, p. 603).

*   *   *

Herder did not try to link the next section of the work, entitled 'Morgenbesuch des Frühlings' (literally 'Morning Visit of Spring') (song VI) in 1776, and based on Song 2.8-14, with that of the preceding passage. However, in order to maintain the thread he claimed to find running through each of the poems in the work, he asserted that the male figure in the next section is the same person as before, coming now from afar. Perhaps Herder had almost abandoned his thematic thread of love for a distinct narrative thread.

---

31. 'Oh, morality of the Orient! Oh, propriety! Oh, love! Were the Orientals acquainted with fleshly love? [...] And would a song of love, such as the one we have here, sing of such a thing? Even the wonderful explanation 'he assaults me (as if with his fists) beneath the banner of love' is quite foreign to the text. The banner of love is nothing more than the image of the tree.' The Latin quotation is from Michaelis's *Roberti Lowth [...] de Sacra Poesi Hebraeorum Praelectiones*, p. 596 n. 127 (actually p. 608 in the second edition used for this study).

Winter and the rains are past. The woman is now awoken, although at a different time and in a different place, by the voice of her lover bringing the season of spring and joy. Herder realized he was fighting for credibility here, and again emphasized the individuality of each poem: 'So genau aber konnts bei ganz einzelnen Stücken nicht genommen werden: gnug, daß sie dort entschlief und hier erwachet' (VIII, p. 604).[32] He pleaded for different times and places, but endeavoured to keep the same thread. He argued that the truth and reality of the material could be borne out in view of the suddenness with which spring appears in the Orient, and for support he again called upon Hasselquist, who confirmed that 'die neuen Blätter brechen hervor, ehe die alten sämmtlich abgefallen sind',[33] certainly suggesting the rapidity of the onset of spring. Like a stag, the lover leaps over the hills of which Palestine is full, to join his beloved, likened to a dove who has spent the winter in the cleft of the rock. At pains to lead his readers away from accepting that which was 'künstlich' or artificial, Herder pointed out again that such imagery was natural, thus implying that in their own literature, Germans should be striving for that which was primitive, natural, visual and original.

Likewise, the following section, called 'Frühlingswerk' ('Act of Spring') (song VII) in 1776, and based on Song 2.15, is not joined to what has gone before, nor is it connected in any way with subsequent material. It is a single song, a 'Scheuchlied' (literally 'scaring song'), used for scaring away the jackals.[34] Herder linked these animals with the foxes in the story of Samson (VIII, p. 647), and in order to clarify to his readers their relevance within the text, he compared their nuisance value with that of sparrows in Germany (VIII, p. 605). In other words, in writing their own poetry Germans should use expressions and images with which they were familiar. They should not borrow obscurely from other literatures.

The foxes were harmful for the grapes, and Herder argued that the song is placed here because the previous song refers to the spring, the

32. 'And yet in the case of quite individual poems, we cannot be so precise: suffice it to say that there she fell asleep, and here she awakes.'

33. 'The new leaves burst forth before all the old ones have fallen off.' *Reise nach Palästina*, p. 261. Herder wrongly omitted the word 'sämmtlich' ('complete/ all/whole') in his quotation in VIII, p. 499 n. p.

34. Herder referred here to Shaw, *Reisen*, p. 155, where the whole section is entitled 'Der Dib oder Jackall' ('The Jackal').

time when the grapes first appear. Again he stressed that the whole book is a collection of different songs, yet he (artificially) continued his narrative thread. This particular (folk-)song was, he claimed, exactly the kind used by Germans while harvesting, spinning, hunting, fishing or even fighting, and thus Herder was insisting that just as the Orientals used such songs from within their own culture, so should Germans be looking to their own roots as the basis of their future literary development.

In Herder's opinion, the next poem also stands alone. He gave it the title 'Tagwerk des Geliebten' (literally 'The Lover's Daily Work') (song VIII) in 1776, based on Song 2.16-17. Not surprisingly, Herder viewed this song too as one of sweet innocence. The woman sings her loneliness away while her lover grazes his flocks among the flowers of the valleys and hillsides. Herder continued to underline the authenticity of the poet's descriptions and images: 'Auch das Weiden unter Blumen ist Wahrheit, und keine Dichtung der Zier halben' (VIII, p. 500 n. r).[35] Again he referred to Hasselquist's remarks (quoted above) concerning the many flowers to be found in the Orient, and he also drew on him to demonstrate that the region is indeed full of hills and valleys: 'Die Thäler zwischen den Bergen kamen mir nicht so merkwürdig vor, als die Berge selbst. [...] Reisende haben die garstigsten und unbequemsten Wege, weil sie beständig die höchsten Berge zwischen abgerissenen Steinen hinauf und hinabbreiten müssen.'[36] Writing specifically of Jerusalem, Hasselquist claimed that 'die ganze Gegend [...] besteht aus kleinen Hügeln, zwischen welchen die schönsten und ebensten Hügel sind',[37] and described the whole area of Judaea as 'ein Land voller Berge und Thäler'.[38]

Herder praised the repeated image of the lover as a stag, noting that it is an image which fits the landscape, but which would have been unreal on flat terrain, his inference being that the imagery in any work of lit-

35. 'Even the grazing among flowers is reality, not poetic licence for the sake of embellishment.'

36. 'The valleys between the mountains seemed to me just as remarkable as the mountains themselves. Travellers face the most unpleasant and uncomfortable paths, because constantly they have to ride up and down the highest mountains between rocks that have broken off.' *Reise nach Palästina*, p. 45.

37. 'The whole area [...] consists of small hills, between which there are the loveliest, flattest knolls.' *Reise nach Palästina*, p. 141.

38. 'A land full of mountains and valleys.' *Reise nach Palästina*, p. 148.

erature should be drawn from its own geography, climate and culture, and not borrowed from or transferred into a foreign setting.

Luther: Chapter Three

After the events of the day, the next song is a night song, given in 1776 as 'Nachtbegegniß' ('Nocturnal Meeting') (song IX), based on Song 3.1-4, and 'Schlaflied' ('Lullaby') (song X), based on Song 3.5. Again it is a song full of simplicity, standing alone. Once more the time and circumstances are different, although Herder maintained the thread throughout (VIII, p. 605). He regarded the whole scene as one of innocence, attempting to dispel the sexual innuendo seen in this lament by commentators such as 'ein neuer Ausleger' ('a new commentator'), certainly Michaelis.[39] Having found her lost lover, the woman takes him to her mother's house where he again sings the lullaby to her, bringing another scene to a close (VIII, p. 606). Herder's naïve reading maintained that 'es ist das Schlafgemach der Mutter, unter ihren Augen, eine Liebe wie im Paradiese' ('it is the bedroom of the mother, beneath her very eyes, a love as in paradise') (VIII, p. 606), and he pleaded the innocence of this scene which takes place 'vor den Augen der Schaam und Zucht' ('before the eyes of chastity and decorum') (VIII, p. 607).

In Herder's view, the lullaby does not fit in as well here as it did the first time. The collector of the various poems interposed it again at this point because it is night time, and he wanted to provide the woman with sweet repose after her nocturnal activities. Herder again emphasized the individuality of the song here, yet strove to show that it is linked to the overall thread within its own natural context: 'Stehet das Stück, so wenig es von außen zu den vorhergehenden paßt, so einzeln es ist, nicht treflich im Licht? an seiner Stelle, an diesem Orte?' (VIII, p. 607).[40]

*   *   *

There follows a series of further, equally independent night songs. In 1776 the first one is entitled 'Die süße Erscheinung' ('The Lovely Apparition') (song XI), based on Song 3.6. Herder regarded it as a fragment

---

39. In VIII, pp. 502-503 n. s, Herder took issue with Michaelis's interpretation of the deer, and, as we noted above, he also drew attention, for example, to Michaelis's (more realistic) interpretation of the wine cellar scene.

40. 'Does the song, little as externally it fits with the previous one, and unique as it is, not stand excellently in the light? In its locale? In this place?' Cf. VIII, p. 593, where Herder used the words 'Stelle' ('location') and 'Ort' ('place') to argue his case for a national literature rather than an imitative one.

which is later followed by two similar ones, both entitled 'Die Erscheinung' ('The Apparition'). The woman is described as a pillar of smoke—strange to the European mind, but Herder claimed that it was normal imagery in the Orient to describe in this way a woman in the dark: 'Nach Gefühlen des Morgenlandes konnte die lichte, schlanke, aufgehende Gestalt des Mädchens nicht lieber verglichen werden' (VIII, p. 607).[41] Indeed, he held that such a beginning was common for a new scene in Oriental literature, 'wie jede Nation und Sprache dergleichen hat' ('just as every nation and language has similar ones') (VIII, p. 502). Thus Herder again sought to ensure that the Song of Songs was understood in its own cultural and natural environment. He saw this as an independent literature, as he wished his own literature to be.

In the previous section, the poet modestly led the lovers to bed. In the section which follows, entitled 'Salomo's Bette' ('Solomon's Bed') (song XII) in 1776, and based on Song 3.7-11, the scene is continued and clarified. It consists of three stanzas, and is an introduction to the physical descriptions which follow. The previous nocturnal scenes have led to the inclusion here of this song which begins with night and fear. There is a link between the two beds of the first two stanzas of the song. The bed of the hero, itself adorned by heroes, leads us to the bed of matrimonial love. The marriage crown is adorned by the king's mother. 'Ward je eine Vermählung würdiger besungen?' ('Was ever a wedding celebrated in a more dignified way?'), asked Herder, attempting again to demonstrate the beauty and purity of the work (VIII, p. 504). The song moves from a beginning of fear, through splendour, to eternal love, although the bride herself does not appear here: 'Welch sonderbares Steigen vom Bett der Krieger, zum Bett der Liebe, zum Thron der Vermählung' ('What extraordinary intensification from the bed of the warriors, to the bed of love, to the throne of marriage') (VIII, p. 608). For Herder, proof of the veracity of these activities was found in 2 Chronicles.[42]

41. 'According to Oriental sentiment, the bright, slim form of the girl rising up could not be more felicitously compared.'

42. In VIII, p. 648 the text is given as 2 Chron. 1.2.8.9. Whether Herder meant 1.2 and 8.9, or 1.2, 8 and 9, or 1.1, 2, 8 and 9 is immaterial, for each verse is in fact relevant to the point he made.

Luther: Chapter Four

The next section is a song in praise of the bride's beauty, entitled 'Die Neuvermählte' ('The New Bride') (song XIII) in 1776, and based on Song 4.1-16 and Song 5.1. The poems and the imagery which follow become more daring now, as the man and woman are betrothed with the blessing of the mother. As before, Herder believed that the man's song of praise is interrupted by his chaste bride before he becomes too bold. He respects her modesty and continues in a different vein, only to be interrupted once more. Herder underlined the chaste restraint of the work in passages like this which others may have regarded as dubious. Almost foreshadowing reader-response criticism, Herder argued that the reader's attitude was important, for the Song of Songs could be approached with the 'Taubenauge der Unschuld' ('dove's eye of inno-cence') or with the 'Blick voll Unzucht und Schalkheit' ('look full of lasciviousness and wantonness') (VIII, p. 591). Herder also argued that the various interruptions form yet another thread running through the chain of individual poems, claiming: 'So hat der Sammler das ganze Buch geleitet und geordnet: vom ersten Seufzer bis zum letzten Nach-hall, wie an zwo Purpurfaden der Schaam und Wahrheit' (VIII, p. 634).[43]

This whole section was described by Herder as 'dies unvergleichliche Stickwerk von Zucht, Einfalt, Liebe und Schönheit' ('this incomparable embroidery of modesty, innocence, love and beauty') (VIII, p. 507). He attempted to explain it from what he understood as an Oriental perspec-tive rather than from a European point of view, defending his opinion of the work's conversational interruptions against those who might accuse both him and the compiler of the songs of veiling the true mean-ing: 'Ohne diese Zwischenrede und ihren Inhalt, verliert sie Sinn und Wesen' ('Without this interruption and its contents, it loses its meaning and character') (VIII, p. 609). He denied that he had tried to hide the real intention of the text, and challenged his readers to note the various responses in the poem. He urged them to appreciate the 'zartes Gefühl Morgenlandes' ('sensitive feeling of the Orient') (VIII, p. 611) and pointed out that the response which follows would be against the whole nature of the work if it contained the slightest ambiguity. He called the whole scene 'süßer Streit der Liebe und Unschuld, der männlichen Entzückung und weiblichen Schaamröthe!' ('sweet contest between

---

43. 'Thus did the compiler guide and arrange the whole book: from the first sigh to the final echo, as if on two purple threads of modesty and truth.'

love and innocence, masculine ecstasy and feminine blushing') (VIII, p. 509).

The man's portrayal of his beloved's form uses images which, in Herder's opinion, were perfectly natural to the Oriental mind. To Western thinking, most such images would seem unnatural and exaggerated, yet in the Orient they were common. As Herder pointed out, 'im Morgenlande müßen daher auch alle Bilder betrachtet werden: sodann thun sie Würkung' ('in the Orient all images must be observed thus: then they are effective') (VIII, p. 612).[44] This is why certain images appear repeatedly in the song. More than once the woman's eyes are described as timid doves behind her veil. Her hair is described as a herd of chamois, or goats, on Gilead. Herder again claimed that such imagery was natural (VIII, p. 648), and called for support from Hasselquist (p. 179)[45] and d'Arvieux (II, p. 238)[46] that herds of goats were a regular sight in the Orient. The woman's teeth are described as lambs, and Herder held that Oriental views concerning oral hygiene made this natural image quite felicitous. The Orientals attached more importance than Europeans to beautiful teeth, a clean mouth and fresh breath, for 'Duft der Gesundheit ist [...] der irrdische Geist Gottes' ('the fragrance of health is [...] the earthly spirit of God') (VIII, p. 648). Presumably attacking Michaelis again, Herder claimed that he failed to understand 'was die Dollmetschung eines neuen Auslegers sagen wolle, daß die

44. Significantly, a deletion in MS(3), fol. 24^r shows that Herder originally used 'gefühlt' ('felt') before rejecting it in favour of 'betrachtet' ('observed').

45. Hasselquist wrote: 'Nach einer zweystündigen Reise von Nazareth fiengen wir an den Tabor, von seinem lieblichen Thau abgekühlt, und von der Milch seiner Ziegenheerden erquickt, aufzusteigen' ('After a two-hour journey from Nazareth, we began to climb Tabor, cooled by its delightful dew and refreshed by the milk of its herds of goats').

46. This reference reads: 'Alle diese Gebürge ernähren eine unendliche Menge von Rindvieh, Schaafen, Ziegen, Haasen, Kaninchen, Rephühnern, Gemsen, und andere Thierarten. Die Gemsen sind eine Art Hinde; sie sind schön, lieblich, lassen sich leicht zähmen, und geben eine vortreffliche Nahrung. Die vierfüßigen Thiere sind alhier vortreflich, weil die wolriechenden Kräuter, so sie fressen, ihnen einen auserlesenen Geruch geben' ('All these mountains nourish an endless number of cattle, sheep, goats, hares, rabbits, partridges, chamois and other kinds of animal. The chamois are a kind of hind; they are pretty, charming, can easily be tamed, and provide excellent food. The four-legged animals here are all excellent, because the sweet-smelling herbs which they eat lend them an exquisite aroma').

Schaafe aus der Quelle kommen und *prohibitae potu* sind' (VIII, p. 507 n. t).[47]

The woman's lips are likened to a purple thread, and her blushing cheeks to a pomegranate which Herder described in both his translations as 'aufgeritzt' ('split open'), and in his comments of 1778 as 'aufgerissen' ('ripped open'), although I shall show in Chapter 6 that he may have misinterpreted the original Hebrew text here. The woman's neck is likened to David's Tower, a strange image which, not surprisingly, Herder found perfect, given that it portrays the neck as being 'vest und rund und schön und geziert' ('firm, round, beautiful and studied') (VIII, p. 507). Her breasts are regarded as 'Zwillingsrehchen' ('twin fawns of a doe'). In interpreting these animals as gazelles, Herder was influenced by Hasselquist (p. 564), who wrote:

> Die Araber und Türken bedienen sich verschiedener Gleichnisse, wenn sie eine Schönheit beschreiben wollen. [...] Eine der merkwürdigsten und gewöhnlichsten Vergleichungen ist, daß sie die Augen einer Schönen mit den Augen der Gazelle [...] vergleichen. [...] Salomo bedient sich in seinem Hohenliede eines Gleichnisses, das von diesem Thiere hergenommen ist, um seine feurigen Empfindungen für seine Schöne auszudrücken. Man kann nicht zweifeln, daß Salomo unter seinem Reh nicht dieses Thier sollte verstanden haben. Die Vielheit dieses Thieres in dem Lande, wo Salomo sein Buch schrieb, und der Gebrauch der Morgenländer, der itzt noch so ist, als zu Salomons Zeiten, bezeugen es.[48]

Herder enthused over such imagery: 'So lange Natur Natur ist, wird man aus der Schäferwelt und Gegend keine reizendere, lebendigere Bilder finden' (VIII, p. 508).[49] We have already noted Herder's comment that Oriental love poetry always had a reference to the gazelle. In

47. 'What the interpretation of a new commentator is trying to say, namely that the sheep come out of the spring and are prevented from drinking.'

48. 'The Arabs and Turks make use of different kinds of metaphors when they attempt to describe a beautiful woman. [...] One of the most remarkable and most common comparisons is when they [...] compare the eyes of a beautiful woman with the eyes of the gazelle. [...] In his Song of Songs, Solomon uses a metaphor which derives from this animal in order to express his ardent feelings for his sweetheart. There is no doubt that Solomon had this animal in mind when he spoke of his doe. The large numbers of this animal in the land where Solomon wrote his book, and the custom of the Orientals, which is still the same as it was in Solomon's time, bear witness to this fact.'

49. 'As long as nature is nature, it will not be possible to find from the world and domain of shepherds any images which are more charming or vivid.'

the Orient, the gazelle was symbolic of all that is gentle, shy and loving, a claim Herder supported from travel writing, although he gave no specific references.

In his additional notes in the 1776 commentary on Song 4.5 (verse 6 in Luther's text in Appendix B), Herder quoted 'zwo Reihen eines alten Englischen Liedes [...], das auch orientalisiret' ('two lines of an old English song [...] which also orientalizes'):

> hide o hide those hills of snow
>   which thy frozen bosom bears:
> on whose tops the pinks that grow
>   are of those that April wears:
> but first set my poor heart free
> bound in those icy chains by thee.[50]

For Herder, this was a crass example of literature which was 'gekünstelt', or artificial and imitative. He begged his readers to compare it with 'die ganze Natur, Freiheit und Einfalt des Hohenliedes' ('the whole nature, freedom and innocence of the Song of Songs') (VIII, p. 649).

Before the woman's modesty is transgressed by her lover's ardour, he praises her charm, her spotless nature and the sweetness of her love, rather than her beauty. He comments on the fragrance of her clothes, and claims that milk and honey are to be found under her tongue, while honey drips off her lips. The woman is described as a locked garden and a sealed fountain, traditional images of virginity. For Herder too, the fountain and the garden represented the modesty and chastity of the woman herself, who was not to be approached by any kind of impurity. Herder revelled in the imagery of the garden, of Eden, of paradise, of springs and rivers. He believed that the garden was sealed to prevent any impurity from entering it, and complained that 'gerade diese lebendige Quelle, das Heiligthum der Reinigkeit und Unschuld haben Säue von Auslegern am meisten verwüstet' (VIII, p. 612).[51] These were images of innocent, married love, and for those who sought to establish archaeological truth, Herder had nothing but sarcasm and scorn. In 1776, for example, he protested that 'd'Arvieux hat die versiegelte Wasserquelle Salomo's auch gesehen (Th.2, S.191) wie billig und recht

---

50. This is in fact from Percy's *Reliques*, I, p. 226. It is found in *SWS*, XXV, pp. 58, 204 and 669.

51. 'It is precisely this living spring, the shrine of purity and innocence, that distasteful interpreters have ravaged the most.'

ist: Schade, daß er nicht auch die zwei weidenden Rehchen und den Weizenhügel im Rosengebüsch sehen konnte!' (VIII, p. 650).[52]

Writing similarly in 1778, he complained:

> Den verschloßenen Garten Salomos hat Hasselquist, (S.167)[53] den versiegelten Brunnen Salomos Pocock, (Th.2, S.63)[54] und die versiegelte Wasserquelle d'Arvieux (Th.2, S.191) gesucht, und [...] auch würklich gefunden. Es wäre gut, wenn noch eine Gesandschaft ausgeschickt würde, die beiden Rehchen und den runden Becher und den Weizenhaufen Salomons zu suchen; sie würden es gleichfalls finden (VIII, p. 508 n. x).[55]

Herder maintained that everything in the Song of Songs was imagery. Nothing was meant to be real. Yet it must be remembered that these are

52. 'd'Arvieux also saw Solomon's sealed well (Part 2, p. 191), as is reasonable and right; what a pity that he was not also able to see the two fawns grazing, and the sheaf of wheat in the rose bush.' The page in d'Arvieux to which Herder referred reads: 'Eine Meile von diesem Closter sahen wir die versiegelte Wasserquelle, oder *fons signatus*, woraus Salomon das Wasser in den Tempel zu Jerusalem leiten lies, wohin es noch gegenwärtig durch einen sehr stark gebaueten steinernen Canal fliesset' ('A mile from this monastery [a Greek monastery visited by d'Arvieux], we saw a sealed well, or *fons signatus*, from which Solomon had the water piped into the temple in Jerusalem, to where even today it flows through a very strongly built channel made of stone').

53. Writing of two mountains, Hasselquist claimed here that 'beyde machten ein Thal, in dem Salomon einen Garten soll gehabt haben, und zwar, wie man vorgiebt, seinen verschlossenen Garten, von dem im Hohenliede IV, 2. geredet wird' ('both formed a valley in which Solomon is said to have had a garden, and allegedly his sealed garden, which is spoken of in Song 4.2').

54. The reference is on p. 64 of the edition used for this study. Here Pococke claimed: 'Es sollen hier auch Ueberbleibsel von zwei Wasserleitungen seyn, eine von dem versiegelten Brunnen Salomons, und eine andere von den Hügeln, die südwärts dieses Brunnens liegen. [...] Wir [...] reiseten [...] zu dem Flecken an der Seite des Hügels unter der Wasserleitung, welches das Flecken Salomons und des versiegelten Brunnens heißet' ('Here too are supposed to be the remains of two water conduits, one from the sealed well of Solomon, and another from the hills which lie to the south of this well. [...] We [...] journeyed [...] to the village on the side of the hill below the water conduit which is known as the village of Solomon and of the sealed well').

55. 'Hasselquist (p. 167) looked for Solomon's locked garden, Pocock (Part 2, pp. 63) for his sealed well, and d'Arvieux (Part 2, p. 191) for the sealed spring, and [...] they actually found them. It would be good if a further legation could be sent out to look for the two fawns, and the round goblet, and Solomon's sheaf of wheat. They would likewise find these things too.'

the words of a man who had maintained consistently that the Song of Songs must be read literally and in no way allegorically. Furthermore, Herder's claim that everything in the work is 'so bestimmt, so örtlich' ('so specific, so local') (VIII, p. 508) suggests an ability to accept real places. Indeed, for evidence that Gilead, for example, was 'noch bis auf den heutigen Tag der lachende Berg voll weidender Heerden aller Art' ('right up to the present day the laughing mountain full of grazing flocks') (VIII, p. 508), Herder drew on d'Arvieux,[56] and for a description of Mount Lebanon he referred not only to the same writer (see II, pp. 325-55, where the twenty-fourth chapter is entitled 'Algemeine Beschreibung des Berges Libanon' ['General Description of Mount Lebanon']), but also to Pococke (II, p. 152).[57] Thus arguably Herder showed inconsistency by arbitrarily selecting what he accepted as literal and what he regarded as figurative. In other words, although unwilling to endorse an allegorical interpretation of the Song of Songs, he was forced into an acceptance of that imagery which leads in the final analysis to allegory, for insistence on an entirely factual approach made little sense.

Herder believed that the whole section from 'Komm herab mit mir vom Libanon' ('come down with me from Lebanon') to 'Du hast mich beherzt gemacht' ('you have made me courageous') (VIII, p. 508) had been misunderstood and misrepresented in the past.[58] He rejected the interpretation of his time which held that the woman is standing up in the snows of Mount Lebanon surrounded by lions and leopards while the bridegroom is calling her from below, 'und doch ists auch noch von den neuesten geliebtesten und gelobtesten Erklärern, die ja allen Unsinn aus der Bibel wegerklären wollen, die geliebteste und gelobteste Mein-

---

56. Although Herder referred in his published work (p. 47 n. y) to d'Arvieux, II, p. 638, a study of the original text shows that this is a misprint and that it should be II, pp. 238, as quoted from in n. 46 above. This is acknowledged by Gaier (*Lieder der Liebe*, p. 458 n. 22, and p. 1229), but missed by Redlich (*SWS*, VIII, p. 508 n. y) and Otto (*Lieder der Liebe*, p. 38 n. 22).

57. For Herder, Mount Lebanon represented all that was superlative. It is part of a mountain chain that was the source of life for Judaea, and travel writers all praised the views from its slopes. Thus the lover here offers the woman the most beautiful journey possible. The perfume of her garments is like the fragrance of the whole Lebanon region, 'ein Bild aller Frische' ('an image full of freshness') (VIII, p. 649).

58. In his commentary here (VIII, p. 509), Herder paraphrased both his translations of 1776 and 1778.

ung' (VIII, p. 653).[59] Herder insisted that the woman is not on the mountain, but is with her beloved, standing at his side. She strengthens him and he leads her down through the haunts of lions and leopards to safety. He viewed this whole scene too as one of innocence, and he deplored those who had tried to destroy it. He stressed the differences between European and Oriental views of love, claiming that the latter view was one of freedom, simplicity and openness (VIII, p. 594). In his opinion, those who found ambiguity in Song 4.6 and 17 and Song 5.1, for example, 'sind keiner Zeile des Hohenliedes werth. Es ist sonderbar, daß das Feinste, Züchtigste, mißverstanden im Auge des Unsinns, auch immer das Gröbste und Erbärmlichste werden muste' (VIII, p. 649).[60]

*   *   *

Luther: Chapter Five

Another night scene follows, entitled 'Die Untreue' ('Infidelity') (song XIV) in 1776, and based on Song 5.2-17 and Song 6.1 and 2. It was Herder's wish for his readers 'daß sie das trefliche Stück ganz und allein und unvermengt mit vorigen Farben und Eindrücken fühlen!' (VIII, p. 510),[61] arguing that the compiler had placed several poems together here to form a whole. The woman returns to her shepherdess's songs and her flower songs, repeating her confession of love. The scene has changed greatly since the previous one. There she was a woman of influence and power, betrothed to a king. In this new scene we see a country woman again, asleep alone in her hut, although, not surprisingly, Herder regarded the story which follows as being 'im Faden des Vorigen' ('along the same lines as the previous material') (VIII, p. 614).

The man visits his beloved, whose hands drip with myrrh as she opens the door. Herder claimed that the ointment is clearly already on the handle before the woman opens the door, and not on her fingers already (VIII, p. 513 n. b), for he insisted that the lover smeared ointment on the handle when he arrived. He called upon the original text to

59. 'And yet even this is regarded as the most popular and most praised opinion by the most recent, most popular and most praised commentators, who, of course, want to explain away all absurdity from the Bible.'

60. 'Are not worth a single line of the Song of Songs. It is extraordinary that that which is purest and most chaste, if misunderstood in the eye of absurdity, always has to become the most obscene and detestable.'

61. 'That they should feel the excellent poem in its entirety, alone and without interference from previous nuances and impressions.'

support his claim here, as well as the fact that other translations had so understood and expressed it. He argued that the smearing of ointment or myrrh on a lover's door and adorning the door with flowers was an old custom in the Orient, as well as among the Greeks. For support he drew, for example, on Johann Gottlieb Lessing's *Eclogae Regis Salomonis*.[62] Thus again he sought to explain the poetry within the context of its own cultural background in order to clarify foreign customs and images to his readership.

Herder argued for the purity and poverty of the woman in this poem also. She opens the door too late, and her lover has gone. She pays for her delay when the city guards insult her, as was the custom of the time, by removing her veil, a garment representing honour and virginity. The women of Jerusalem ask her for a description of her lover, a literary device which serves as a natural cue for a paean of praise of the one whom she believes she has hurt and alienated. Herder complained that the mystics had purposely misunderstood this section: 'Auch hat die Mystik diesen Irrgarten der Liebe, dies Schweben von kleiner läßiger Untreu durch Suchen und Kampf, Unruh und Züchtigung zu größerer Treue sich treflich zu Nutz gemacht' (VIII, p. 616).[63] Mysticism, he argued, was the wisdom neither of Solomon, nor of the Orient (VIII, p. 630).

Herder's view that the woman speaks 'aus der Fülle eines liebesiechen, verwundeten, kranken Herzens' ('from the fullness of a sick, wounded heart, intoxicated with love') (VIII, p. 514) suggests a sentimental, Western reading. She describes her lover as 'ein wahres Prachtbild, Kolossus von männlicher Würde, Glanz und Schönheit' ('a true example of splendour, a colossus of masculine dignity, radiance and beauty') (VIII, p. 514). As a young woman looking upon the ideal male form, she innocently describes his looks, his clothes and his jewellery, although later on he is to describe her 'in Fülle ohne Hülle' ('in unveiled detail') (VIII, pp. 615-16). Undoubtedly Herder could be accused today of a chauvinistic reading, for this could be seen as an instance of the cultural construction of gender. His reading reflected the radical change in gender attitudes during the last quarter of the eighteenth century, with the ideal woman portraying soft wit and sensibility,

62. Herder referred to p. 90, but the reference is actually on pp. 91-92.

63. 'Even mysticism made excellent use of this labyrinth of love, this wavering from careless infidelity, through searching and quarrelling and correction, to greater fidelity.'

gentleness, emotion and, above all, submission to the male. Again we have an example of an ideologically loaded interpretation, for it is possible that Herder would have produced a rather different reading today, depending on his reception of current feminist theory.

Respect and propriety are mingled with love and desire. The woman's description differs greatly from her previous one, yet, in Herder's view, both have been linked by the compiler of the poems. Setting the description within its own culture, Herder pointed out that the Orientals loved veils and disguise, and regarded the body as a symbol of God. They would not forgive a bride who described her lover any differently from the description here, and thus the male figure is 'ein verhülletes Bild Gottes' ('a veiled image of God') (VIII, p. 616). Herder's attitude suggests that Meyer's 'verfeinerter europäischer Kulturmensch' ('refined European individual of culture') was in fact a male chauvinist.

The woman portrays her lover's head as fine gold, doubtless referring to his turban. For the Orientals, the turban was the symbol of masculinity, as well as a portrayal of class. She likens his hands to golden cylinders, presumably referring to the rings and jewellery on his fingers. Unlike some commentators, Herder did not believe that the fingers were thus regarded by the woman because they were dyed by henna. His head and feet are likewise golden, presumably bedecked with jewels and rings. Herder drew attention to the love of Oriental women for gold and metallic ornaments and pieces of bodily adornment, calling for support upon d'Arvieux[64] and Carsten Niebuhr.[65]

---

64. In the published version (p. 60 n. c), Herder referred to d'Arvieux, III, p. 241 and 163. A reading of the original shows that the latter reference is wrong and should be p. 253, which forms part of the eighteenth chapter, 'Von denen Kleidungen der Araber' ('On the Clothing of the Arabs'). This is followed by Gaier (*Lieder der Liebe*, p. 1231), but missed by Redlich (*SWS*, VIII, p. 514 n. c) and Otto (*Lieder der Liebe*, p. 47 n. 26).

65. Herder had in mind here Niebuhr's *Reisebeschreibung nach Arabien und andern umliegenden Ländern* (ed. J.N. Gloyer and J. Olshausen); published by Möller in Copenhagen and Hamburg in 1774, two years after the publication of his *Beschreibung von Arabien*. There are three volumes, and the section referred to is in I, pp. 156-67. Herder referred in VIII, p. 514 to the section in Niebuhr's work entitled 'Kleidertracht der Morgenländer' ('Costumes of the Orientals'), where much is made of the Orientals' use of gold and silver in their dress. One example (I, p. 164) reads: 'Sie hatte einen großen Ring von starken [*sic*] Silberdrath um den Hals, und sehr dicke Ringe, gleichfals von Silber, um die Füße' ('She had a large

The lover's belly is made of ivory,[66] while his belt and dagger are adorned with sapphires. His thighs are likened to pillars of marble on a golden pedestal. Herder insisted that 'Stärke und Vestigkeit wird mit Schmuck und Pracht nach Morgenländischer Weise Eins' ('in Oriental thinking, strength and ruggedness are one with jewellery and ostentation') (VIII, p. 514). The Orientals enjoyed a love of outward display which, to Western eyes, contradicted their desire for concealment. Thus Herder sought to underline again that such imagery was rooted in the customs of the people from whom the poetry originated.

Luther: Chapter Six
The woman's praise of her lover is countered with a further song of praise, entitled 'Die Einzige' ('The One and Only') (song XV) in 1776, and based on Song 6.3-8. It is followed by several similar songs, each bolder and more daring in imagery. Most of the characteristics of this song have already been mentioned above, although now the woman is compared to the royal Judean towns of Thirza and Jerusalem. Strangely, to Western readers, she is likened to dreadful armies of warriors. Her lover is unable to gaze upon her, and yet she is beautiful, a pure dove whom all must love and praise. 'Das Stück hatte schon prächtige, kriegerischkönigliche Züge' ('The poem already had splendid features which pertained to a warrior king') (VIII, p. 516), yet it is merely a prelude to the section in Song of Songs 7 which Herder regarded as the climax of the work.

*   *   *

Herder considered the song which he entitled 'Die Erscheinung' ('The Apparition') (song XVI) in 1776, based on Song 6.9-12, as the most obscure passage of the whole book, for the occasion to which it refers is unclear. The woman is no longer likened to the dawn, nor to a column of incense rising from the desert, but now she is compared to the moon, the sun and even a terrible army, as in the previous section. She appears in the splendour of love, first singing a shepherdess's song, almost as if to force a link with earlier parts of the work. She recalls her previous rustic simplicity, and her calm, quiet life within nature, although at the

---

ring of heavy silver wire around her neck, and very wide rings, likewise made of silver, around her feet').

66. In 1776 Herder used the adjective 'zart' ('tender') to describe it, almost as if striving to exclude anything harsh from this poem (VIII, p. 615).

time she had been unaware that she would become the 'Kriegeswagen meines edlen Volks' ('war chariot of my noble people') (VIII, p. 516). This expression is another which has sounded strange to Western interpreters, yet Herder claimed that it becomes clear from the story of Solomon within the context of the Hebrew language. He explained that 'Roß und Wagen Israels sind ein gewöhnlicher Ausdruck für Kriegsmacht, Schutz und Schirm, Heldenmäßige Bedeckung' (VIII, p. 520).[67] He referred to Ps. 20.8, although it is necessary to read v. 7 as well to establish the context. There the KJV has: 'Some trust in chariots, and some in horses: but we will remember the name of the Lord our God.'[68] Believing that the Song of Songs was at least Solomonic in character, Herder emphasized that Solomon did not make slaves of his subjects, but rather allowed them to be a free, noble people. He referred to 1 Kgs 9.22, which informs us that 'of the children of Israel did Solomon make no bondmen: but they were men of war, [...] and rulers of his chariots, and his horsemen' (KJV).[69]

In other words, it was natural for the king to describe his beloved in a way fitting to the concept of his society as portrayed here, and Herder claimed that it would be strange if the expression of Solomon's love were to be untouched by such imagery. He believed that the finest sections were often those which were most misunderstood, and regarded this as one of the most beautiful poetic passages in the book (VIII, p. 651). He saw in it 'Pracht, Schönheit, Anmuth, Heldenmuth, Landeinfalt, Hoheit, Demuth, Göttliches und Menschliches' ('splendour, beauty, elegance, heroism, rustic innocence, majesty, humility, divinity and humanity') (VIII, p. 651)—in fact, everything that he regarded as the hallmark of primitive poetry. He professed to be the first to have

---

67. 'Horse and chariot of Israel are a common expression for military forces, shield and shelter, protection of heroic proportions.'

68. Herder also referred to Isa. 31.1, which reads: 'Woe to them that go down to Egypt for help; and stay on horses, and trust in chariots, because they are many; and in horsemen, because they are very strong'; 2 Kgs 2.11 and 12, which reads: 'Behold, there appeared a chariot of fire, and horses of fire [...], the chariot of Israel, and the horsemen thereof'; and Deut. 20.1, which reads: 'When thou goest out to battle against thine enemies, and seest horses, and chariots, and a people more than thou, be not afraid of them' (KJV).

69. Herder also pointed to 2 Chron. 8.9, where the same sentiments are expressed. 1 Kgs 10.26 also states that 'Solomon gathered together chariots and horsemen: and he had a thousand and four hundred chariots, and twelve thousand horsemen' (KJV).

discovered the true meaning of this passage, as well as many others in the work, and again criticized the 'Mäuler und Krächzereien unsrer nachhinkenden Krähenkunstrichter' ('malicious tongues and the croakings of our squawking critics who hobble behind') (VIII, p. 651). Indeed, although Song 6.11 of the Lutheran text is the verse generally considered to be the most difficult to translate in the book,[70] Herder claimed that it was the easiest 'wenn man sie mit gesunden Augen ansieht' ('if regarded with a healthy eye') (VIII, p. 651). He insisted on the primary meaning of the text, asserting that no other aid was needed. After all, this is what he had argued for in the rest of the work. While other commentators had struggled with this verse, then, Herder disagreed that it was difficult: 'Mich dünkt, klärer, zusammenhangender und der Geschichte Salomos angemeßener kann nichts seyn' (VIII, p. 619).[71] Yet the questions posed particularly in his commentary of 1776 show how Herder struggled with the verse, and I shall discuss in Chapter 6 the extent to which his translations of it were accurate.

Luther: Chapter Seven
The scene changes to a dance of angels and heavenly hosts. Not unexpectedly, Herder claimed: 'Mir ist kein Lied bekannt, wo der Tanz so veredelt, so idealisirt wäre' ('I know of no song where dance is so ennobled and so idealized') (VIII, p. 520). Herder spared nothing to assure his readership that the Song of Songs was the epitome of primitive love poetry. A chorus (in 1776, a chorus of virgins) responds to the woman. Following Luther in his commentary of 1778, Herder used the expression 'Tanz der Mahanaim' ('dance of the Mahanaim') to describe the dance that the members of the chorus want the woman to perform (VIII, p. 520), whereas in both his translations he used the expression 'Tanz der Gottesheere' ('dance of the heavenly hosts'). He asserted that the detailed description of the dancing Salome or Sulamith is a song of joy, 'wo jeder Zug nur aus diesem Bilde Leben und Bewegung hernimmt, oder er stünde todt da' ('where every feature takes life and movement from this image alone, or otherwise it would lie there dead') (VIII, p. 520). It was Herder's wish, of course, that German literature

---

70. Even Marcia L. Falk chooses not to translate this verse at all in *Love Lyrics from the Bible: A Translation and Literary Study of the Song of Songs* (Bible and Literature Series, 4; Sheffield: Almond Press, 1982), p. 41.

71. 'It seems to me that nothing could be plainer, more coherent, and more fitted to the story of Solomon.'

should be creative and vital, rather than a dead copy, and this point is implied again here. Indeed, he claimed that there are no foreign women in the Song of Songs. The work is based entirely on Oriental customs, with a completely local flavour (VIII, p. 631). There is no hint of outside impurity, and similarly German literature was to be formed from its own native traditions rather than be diluted by foreign influences and borrowings.

Herder admitted that dance was something less than innocent to Western eyes, but he claimed that 'in den frühesten Zeiten der Unschuld' ('in the earliest times of innocence') (VIII, p. 521) the Orientals thought differently from eighteenth-century Europeans. To underline the innocence of dancing and rejoicing within Hebrew culture, Herder referred to Job 38.7 and Ps. 68.18 to demonstrate how the angels and the stars dance like a victorious army around the throne of the Most High.[72] For primitive man, dance was something holy, just like song (or folk-poetry). Aware that his contemporaries might find it distasteful for women to dance, Herder gave several biblical examples of women singing and dancing, citing particularly Miriam and Deborah.[73] Defending the innocent dance of the woman here against its possible critics, Herder claimed 'daß auch dieser Tanz nicht weich und wohllüstig sei, deshalb ist er so prächtig und kriegerisch eingeleitet worden' ('that even this dance was not gentle and voluptuous, which explains why it was introduced in such a splendid and warlike way') (VIII, p. 521). The description of the dancing woman is full of 'weiche, weibliche Natur' ('gentle, feminine nature') (VIII, p. 652). The Orientals wrote for themselves—as Germans also should—and not for other times and cultures. In 1776, the section describing the dance itself was entitled 'Der Palmbaum' ('The Palm Tree') (song XVII), based on Song 7.1-9. It is numbered XVI in Redlich's edition (VIII, p. 620), although clearly this is a printing error. Herder regarded this section as the climax of the work, in which the boldest imagery is used: 'Höher kann nun nichts steigen, seliger nichts gefühlt werden' ('Nothing can become more intense, or be experienced more blissfully') (VIII, p. 623). Yet this scene too, which could be misunderstood so easily, is interrupted suddenly 'mit der sittigsten Liebe der Landeinfalt und Unschuld' ('with the purest

72. Closer examination suggests that Herder had Ps. 68.17 in mind rather than v. 18.

73. As examples, he gave Exod. 15.20 and 21, Judg. 5.1, 1 Sam. 18.7 and 2 Sam. 6.5 and 14, pointing out that even David sang and danced.

love of rustic simplicity and innocence') (VIII, p. 623). Yet again Herder stressed his reading of rustic simplicity, of primitiveness, of innocence and naïveté, although Chapter 6 will demonstrate that Herder's pure interpretation of this section was almost certainly misguided.

Possibly in order to convince those who regarded Hebrew literature as barbaric and primitive, yet regarded Greek literature as an absolute for German literature to copy, Herder described the movements of the woman's hips as 'ein Theseischer Tanz, ein Gewebe der Ariadne' ('a Thesean dance, a thread of Ariadne') (VIII, p. 521). In other words, Hebrew poetry was just as beautiful as and no less 'absolute' than Greek poetry, or, for that matter, any poetry which—unlike Germany's—sprang from its own national roots.

Herder revelled in the beauty of the imagery demanded by the description of each part of the woman's body, although he admitted that much is lost when translating imagery based on the language, landscape and customs of the Orientals. For the Hebrews, the overflowing beaker of wine was an image of joy and happiness, in the same way as an empty cup was cause for sadness: 'Das *poco più* und *poco meno* kann kein lebenderes Bild [...] finden' (literally 'the *little more* and *little less* cannot [...] find a more vivid image') (VIII, p. 522). Herder again emphasized the life-like, vital, authentic nature of the imagery, although in Chapter 6 I shall question his pure reading here.

We have noted the importance to the Orientals of the eyes. Herder saw it as fitting that they should be regarded as pools, for the Orientals considered these to be the eyes of the earth, 'sprudelndes Leben, aufquillende Seele' ('bubbling life, a soul welling up') (VIII, p. 522). For them, a beautiful face without eyes was like a beautiful region without water.

The nose is compared with a tower on Mount Lebanon, with a view to Damascus and the sea beyond. From his Western standpoint, Herder objected to such an image, claiming that there was no such tower. Instead, it was a 'Lustgebäu' ('pleasure palace') (VIII, p. 521 n. k) to which Solomon invited his bride in order to see the view.[74] Herder

---

74. Herder referred here to 1 Kgs 9.19 and 1 Kgs 4.8, although the latter would appear to be the wrong text, given that it is part of a genealogy. 1 Kgs 9.24 would make more sense, where we read that Pharaoh's daughter (whom other commentators have suggested was Solomon's bride here) 'came up out of the city of David unto her house which Solomon had built for her' (KJV).

found this alternative description of the building, together with the beautiful view before it, far more valid. For support he drew attention to Pococke (II, p. 154), who stated that 'von der Spitze des Berges Libanon hat man eine schöne Aussicht auf die schönen Gegenden des untern Berges' ('from the peak of Mount Lebanon there is a beautiful view over the beautiful regions of the lower mountain'). As proof that the fortress image was based on fact, Herder claimed that Solomon's castle was still spoken of, even in his own day, referring (VIII, p. 521 n. k) to d'Arvieux (II, p. 355), although it is actually on p. 356 that we find: 'Das merkwürdigste darinnen [i.e. Baalbek] ist das Schlos. Einige meinen, es sey von Salomon erbauet worden.'[75] Although in Western cultures there was almost a fear of mentioning the nose, the Orientals often did so. In Herder's opinion, the image here had 'alle Reize der Neuheit und Phantasie des Königs' ('all the charms of the novelty and inventive faculties of the king') (VIII, p. 522).

Likewise, comparing the woman's head with Mount Carmel is not a flattering image unless it is seen as describing the joy, the sublimity and the striking impact of the head when seen from afar. Thus for the woman to carry her head like Mount Carmel is a strange image to Western readers, but to Herder's mind it was a perfectly authentic and beautiful one within the original context of the work. He described the mountain as 'das fröhlichste Gebürge Judäas und gleichsam das Haupt unter seinen Bergen' ('the most cheerful mountain area in Judaea and, as it were, the head of all its mountains') (VIII, p. 521), referring also to (but not quoting) Pococke, who wrote in March 1737 (II, p. 4) that 'das erste Land, das wir sahen, war der Berg Carmel' ('the first land which we saw was Mount Carmel'), and using him to demonstrate that the mountain is 'das schöne, Buschreiche Haupt des Jüdischen Landes' (literally 'the beautiful, bush-filled head of the land of Judaea') (VIII, p. 653). Clearly Mount Carmel was so striking that to compare the woman's head with it was an obvious image, portraying fertility and blessing.

The woman's hair is likened to a royal turban. We have already noted the importance of the turban in Oriental society. Here the woman's hair is possibly plaited or braided like a king's turban, denoting her class. It is 'das Diadem der ganzen edeln Gestalt, ihres Königlichen Wuchses

---

75. 'The most remarkable therein [i.e. Baalbek] is the castle. Some believe it was built by Solomon.' This error of pagination is not noted by Gaier (*Lieder der Liebe*, p. 473 n. 34, and p. 1234), nor by Otto (*Lieder der Liebe*, p. 57 n. 34).

und Schrittes die prangende Krone!' ('the diadem of her quite noble form, the glittering crown of her regal stature and gait') (VIII, pp. 521-22). Herder asked: 'Gibt der Königsturban nicht ein Bild, ohne daß man die Purpurschnecke aus Franziscus Michael Regenfuß dazu nehmen dürfe?' (VIII, p. 653).[76] Enjoying the imagery, Herder enquired: 'War also der Aufbund so prächtig als das Purpurdiadem des Königs: so wird ja weder die Farbe noch Schale des Purpurthiers Punkt der Vergleichung, sondern die Prachtgestalt des Haars auf dem frölichen Karmel' (VIII, p. 653).[77]

Again it is clear that Herder strove throughout to demonstrate how perfect the imagery of the poetry was within the culture and language that brought it forth. He challenged anybody to portray the dancing female figure more splendidly or decently—ironic indeed, given that this section, with its highly sexual content, would without doubt have caused grave concern to his contemporaries. Considering carefully the context within which the description of this dancing woman was created, Herder sought to show how beautiful the imagery actually is: 'Man setze die Bilder und Formen in die Bewegung, die ihr gebühren, und es wird eine tanzende Göttin' ('If the right and proper images and forms are used to describe the movement, then she becomes a dancing princess') (VIII, p. 522).

The image of the palm tree is introduced once more, and as the man becomes more ardent, so the woman modestly interrupts him yet again: 'Er […] wird so innig, daß die Braut selbst ihm auf die süße Weise der Unschuld die Wollusttrunkne Lippe versiegelt' ('He […] becomes so intimate that the woman herself charmingly seals his lips which are intoxicated with lust') (VIII, p. 522). Aware that others might find sexual euphemism in the image of the palm tree, Herder returned to its importance for married love within Oriental culture, as examined above: 'Es hiesse Licht in die Sonne tragen, wenn ich das Bild vom Palmbaum

---

76. 'Does the king's turban not offer an adequate image without our having to refer to Franziskus Michael Regenfuß's purple-fish?' According to Redlich (*SWS*, VIII, p. 680), Herder was referring here to Franz Michael Regenfuß's *Sammlung von Muscheln und Schnecken: 11 illumin. Blätter*, published in Leipzig in 1754. It is also possible that he was referring to Regenfuß's *Auserlesne Schnecken, Muscheln und andere Schaalthiere*, published in Copenhagen in 1758.

77. 'If then the hair decoration was as splendid as the king's purple diadem, then the point of comparison becomes neither the colour nor the shell of the purple-fish, but rather the magnificence of the hair upon cheerful Carmel.'

noch erläutern wollte. Er ist den Morgenländern an Wuchs, Blüthe, Fruchtbarkeit, Süßigkeit der Trauben, des Safts, der Früchte das liebste Sinnbild' (VIII, pp. 653-54).[78] Noting the value to the Orientals of palm honey, Herder drew upon Shaw (p. 128), who stated that 'unter Personen von einem gewissen Stande ist es bey einer Heurath, bey der Geburt oder Beschneidung eines Kindes, oder bey einem andern Festtage, gewöhnlich, ihre Gäste mit Honig [...] von dem Palmbaume [...] zu bewirthen'.[79] Herder reproved those who found anything repulsive or indecent about such imagery: 'Wer aber das Bild so wenig verstehet, den Palmbaum so zerreißet und verwüstet, daß er Säuereien dahinträgt—das Nord-Thier ist nicht für das Paradies der Palmen' (VIII, p. 623).[80] He rejected the slightest ambiguity in the imagery, imploring his readers to accept its innocent beauty, for 'jede Sprache hat Bilder und Ausdrücke der Art, die rein und züchtig sind, etymologisirt aber und mit Kupfern belegt, anstößig würden' (VIII, p. 654).[81] Thus Herder yet again highlighted the purity, innocence and simplicity of this collection of songs.

Herder's reading of the next section, entitled 'Die Unschuldliebe' ('Innocent Love') (song XVIII) in 1776, and based on Song 7.10-13 and Song 8.1-3, continued his thesis that the Song of Songs was a work of pure love. To prevent the innocent ear from hearing words of passion, the woman takes her lover away to the 'Wohnungen der Einfalt, wo noch die Natur rein und unverhüllet würkt' ('dwellings of innocence, where nature still operates in a pure and unveiled manner') (VIII, p. 523). Herder held the 'Blumen der Liebe' ('flowers of love') or 'Dudaim' (VIII, p. 518) to be the same plants as those discovered by Reuben in the wheat harvest (VIII, pp. 523 and 654). Presumably he had in mind Gen. 30.14, which reads: 'And Reuben went in the days of

78. 'It would be superfluous for me to comment further on the image of the palm tree. It is the Orientals' favourite symbol on account of its stature, its blossoms, its fecundity and the sweetness of its clusters, juice and fruit.'

79. 'Among those of a certain position, it is the custom at a wedding, at the birth or circumcision of a child, or at any other festival, [...] to treat one's guests with honey [...] from the palm tree.'

80. Literally 'yet whoever understands the image so little, and thus dismembers and lays waste the palm tree, and brings vulgarities to it—the animal of the north is not meant for the paradise of the palms'.

81. 'Every language has images and expressions of the kind which are pure and chaste, yet once they have become etymologized and overlaid with copper plates, they become offensive.'

wheat harvest, and found mandrakes in the field, and brought them unto his mother Leah' (KJV). It is clear from the context of the passage that mandrakes contain aphrodisiac qualities. Indeed, Herder followed the tradition that these plants were '*Alraun* (Mandragora)' (VIII, p. 654), yet dogmatically and predictably he was quick to beg the innocence of the text: 'Kann die Liebesblume je unschuldiger erscheinen, als hier?' ('Can the flower of love ever appear more innocent than here?' (VIII, p. 655). Lest anyone doubt the purity of the poetry, he emphasized that 'an *artes maritales* ist also hier kein Gedanke' ('thus here there is no thought of *artes maritales*') (VIII, p. 655). By comparing the image with the nightingale or lark as used in German literature to represent the innocence of nature calling a bride, Herder again reminded his readers that Germany had suitable imagery of its own without having to purloin that of other cultures. The door of the lovers' hut is adorned with fruit and flowers, and to demonstrate that this too was an Oriental custom, Herder again called for support from Hasselquist (p. 125), who stated that 'alle, welche diese heilige Reise gethan haben, lassen bey ihrer Zurückkunft das unterste Stockwerk ihres Hauses anmahlen, und hängen Aloe [...] über ihre Häuser, um durch dieses beständig lebendige Gewächse ihre Hoffnung auszudrücken'.[82] In fact, Hasselquist was actually describing a scene in Egypt during a journey to Mecca, and thus, as above, Herder may be accused yet again of taking him out of context. At best it demonstrates once more Herder's universal view of the Orient. Not surprisingly, he regarded this passage as another which portrays the sweet simplicity of rural life (VIII, p. 523).

Luther: Chapter Eight
At this point in his 1778 commentary, Herder quoted his 1776 translation with very few changes. This is the longest of the passages taken from the 1776 version and used in the 1778 commentary to elaborate upon the translation. According to Herder, the woman desires to chasten her love even more by turning it into a fraternal love: 'Wer ist der Sittenrichter, der die Liebe keuscher Vermählter je Paradiesischer gedacht hätte?' ('Who is the moral judge who might have thought of the love of a chaste married couple in a more delightful way?')

---

82. 'All those who have made this sacred journey have the bottom storey of their house painted on their return, and they hang aloe [...] over their houses in order to express their hope through this constantly living plant.'

(VIII, p. 524). The lullaby is sung again (song XIX, 'Schlummerlied' ['Lullaby'], based on Song 8.4).

*   *   *

The next poem is the third to be entitled 'Die Erscheinung' ('The Apparition') (song XX), based on Song 8.5-7. For the third time the woman appears in the desert, although no longer is she a column of incense, nor the dawn, the moon, the sun nor an army. She now walks on her lover's arm, and the scene is more peaceful and gentle than before. There follows what Herder described as 'ein Gespräch der ehelichen Treue' ('a conversation of marital fidelity') (VIII, p. 526), for maybe the woman has expressed concern about the permanence of the man's love towards her. They reach the tree where he first woke her, and the old covenant is renewed by the holy name of her mother, and the tree under which she gave birth to her daughter. This tree is to be their 'Altar, Familientempel, ewige Erinnerung unsrer ersten süßen Brautliebe' ('altar, family temple, eternal reminder of our first, sweet marital love') (VIII, p. 624). Herder regarded this scene too as chaste and pure, and used direct speech to paraphrase in prose the thoughts behind the poetry, thus suggesting the importance of the scene to his thinking. Love becomes maternal, mature and autumnal. The man and the woman are nourished by the fruits of spring and the memories of their first love. Herder thus connected the end of the book and its beginning. A seal is set on their relationship, and the seal of true, eternal love is placed upon the whole book: 'Tod und Hölle, Glut und Blitz, Ströme und Waßer, Haus und Gut kommt zusammen, die Stärke, die Ewigkeit der Liebe zu bewähren' (VIII, p. 526).[83]

It was Herder's view that the book closed essentially at this point. The rest was probably appended to the original collection, a witty, proud conversation between a sister and her brothers, entitled 'Das Mägdlein' ('The Maiden') (song XXI) in 1776, and based on Song 8.8-12. Although not in favour of a dramatic interpretation, Herder was forced to introduce three different characters. Advice is given to an adolescent sister by her brothers. If she is a wall—that is, if she holds fast to her honour—she should be rewarded. On the other hand, if she is a doorway, she must be closed in order to preserve her fidelity and chastity.

---

83. 'Death and hell, flame and lightning, rivers and waters, home and possessions, all join forces to confim the strength and eternity of love.'

Herder suggested that the story which follows at this point proves the meaning of what has preceded it. The girl cares for her vineyard herself, and does not need to pay for guardians to watch over it. Herder claimed that his (ironically allegorical?) explanation of this story was unique. In his view, 'dies ist sein klarer Sinn, und der Sinn ist schön' ('this is its obvious meaning, and the meaning is beautiful') (VIII, p. 528). In an attempt to disagree with his opponents, Herder challenged them thus: 'Wo ist nun das Unreine, das Kothige, das man auch hier fand?' ('Where, then, is the impurity, the filth which has been found even here?') (VIII, p. 626). Again he pleaded that literature must be studied in the context in which it was produced, within its own cultural setting.

Herder claimed that this poem contained for the Orientals 'würklich Klugheit und Moral' ('genuine wisdom and morality') (VIII, p. 626), and he reaffirmed that the work as a whole should be seen in its true, literal sense, and not as allegory. The Orientals loved riddles, images and examples, and he regarded this particular section of the Song of Songs as one of the best of its kind from Hebrew antiquity. The poem was probably added for this reason, and since Solomon's name and vineyard figure in it. Although Herder believed that the Song of Songs originally finished at the earlier point of the seal, there finally follows yet another fragment, a conversation entitled 'Besuch im Garten' ('Visit to the Garden') (song XXII) in 1776, and based on Song 8.13 and 14. As the whole work begins, so does it end with 'ein Seufzer, ein junger Hall der Liebe' ('a sigh, a youthful resonance of love') (VIII, p. 627. Cf. p. 541).

After this consideration of Herder's unique, innocent interpretation of the Song of Songs as borne out in his commentaries, we turn to a detailed study of the translations of 1776 and 1778. I shall show how they differ from each other, and I shall compare them with the Hebrew text; with Luther's translation of 1545 as a touchstone and classic rendering; and—where relevant—with Goethe's translation of 1775.

Chapter 6

HERDER'S TRANSLATIONS OF THE SONG OF SONGS

Introduction

After an assessment of Herder's commentaries as an essential and inseparable part of his whole interpretative approach to the Song of Songs, I now turn to Herder's translations of the biblical text per se. Robert Clark claims that, although Herder initially made a literal inter-linear translation of the Song of Songs from the Hebrew text, the 1778 publication shows that 'every change is in the direction of Luther'.[1] In other words, Clark argues that Herder finally rejected his own close reading of the original text in favour of a rendering which more closely followed Luther's (freer) translation. I have shown above that Clark's claims for a careful interlinear translation are exaggerated, although we have also noted that Herder encouraged his readers to consider Luther's translation as an inimitable absolute, and almost used Luther's text instead of his own (*TB*, X, pp. 132-33). However, in this chapter I seek to demonstrate that, far from distancing itself from the Hebrew text, Herder's translation of 1778 not only shows greater fidelity to it than do his earlier translations, but also exhibits considerable, although not total, independence of Luther, rather than the imitative accommodation suggested by Clark.

Given the undisputed importance of Luther's translation in Herder's thinking, I shall consider briefly Luther's work as a Bible translator. In view of the possible mutual influence, I shall then assess Goethe's prose translation of 1775 as an example of several translations contemporary

---

1. *Herder: His Life and Thought*, p. 257. See also Clark's 'Herder, Percy, and the *Song of Songs*', where he claims that 'Haym first called attention to these changes and showed that all are in the direction of Luther's Bible' (p. 1098). In fact, this is a misreading of Haym, who merely stated (*Herder*, II, p. 85) that Herder 'verweist schließlich von seiner auf die Luthersche Uebersetzung' ('ultimately refers [us] from his own translation to that of Luther').

with those of Herder. I shall then offer a short appraisal of Herder's translations, particularly as poetry, before providing a detailed analysis of the 1778 translation, comparing and contrasting it with Luther, Goethe, the Hebrew text and Herder's own earlier unpublished drafts, particularly that of MS(3) in 1776. Furthermore, apart from affording an opportunity to demonstrate thoroughly Herder's reception of the Lutheran and Hebrew texts, my commentary will show ways in which Herder's choices in his translations were influenced by his peculiarly 'innocent' reading of the Song of Songs. The concluding summary of all the emerging issues will attempt to suggest a possible reason for the considerable difference between Herder's rejected draft translations and the published version.

There is no evidence for Herder's use of a particular edition of Luther's translation. It is likely, of course, but by no means certain, that he used an eighteenth-century edition. However, as a new edition of Luther's Bible translation was published virtually every year between Herder's birth in 1744 and the publication of *Lieder der Liebe* in 1778, it has seemed safer to use Luther's text of 1545 as the definitive one for this study. In any case, the texts of the Nuremberg 'Weimar Bible' of 1768 and of the Halle 'Canstein Bible' of 1770 appear to be identical to that of 1545, except for additional adjectival inflections and some basic orthographical modernization.[2]

Luther's Translation

Although there had been Old High German and Middle High German Bible translations, the Latin Vulgate Bible was the basis for the first German printed Bible, published by Johannes Mentel in Strasbourg in 1466. The humanists, however, objected to this translation of a translation of a translation. With *ad fontes* as their watchword, they demanded a return to the original texts. Luther believed in the Bible as the sole basis of Christian doctrine, and he translated for theological rather than philological reasons. He knew the Vulgate well, but went to the original Greek and Hebrew texts which had recently become available in new printed editions. Ironically, given his hostility to the Vulgate, he was fluent in Latin, yet less assured in Greek, and he enjoyed only limited competence in Hebrew. However, he relied on Melanchthon and Auro-

2.   Even the British and Foreign Bible Society's Berlin edition of 1877 is the same, except for some orthographical changes.

gallus, an eminent Hebraist of the day, and worked closely with Erasmus's Greek text. He prepared his first version of the New Testament in 11 weeks, revised it in Wittenberg, and published it in September 1522 as the 'Septembertestament', with a reprinting in December of the same year. He published the Old Testament a part at a time, and then the complete Bible in 1534. He brought out the Song of Songs in 1524 and again in 1545.[3] By the time of his death in 1546, one in five German households had his translation of the Bible, either in whole or in part. Indeed, in most homes it was the only book, and thus the intense influence of its contents and language becomes clear. Luther continued to revise his work, and a comparative study of the differences between his own translations would make an interesting study of the development of the translator's art. His principles of translation are expressed throughout his works, but particularly in *Ein Sendbrief von Dolmetschen* and *Summarien über die Psalmen und Ursachen des Dolmetschens*.

The peculiarities of each individual language, so important to Herder, had been largely ignored by previous Bible translators. While the Mentelbibel, for example, followed the Latin syntax, Luther attempted to produce a work closer to German and further away from the original or Latin. For instance, for 1000 years the Vulgate's 'pater noster' (literally 'father our') had been translated literally as 'Vater unser'. Luther moved away from the Latin syntax, translating with 'unser Vater' ('our father'). In this regard, we have noted that Herder too was critical of those who slavishly followed foreign verse-forms or syntax.

Luther stressed the primacy of sense and meaning. In his opinion, a translator should not be an interpreter, yet, given his strong theological

---

3.   Luther's 1545 translation must be regarded as superseding that of 1524, although essentially they differ orthographically only. There are minor differences in Song 4.1 ('on was deyne zöpffe sind' in 1524, and 'zwisschen deinen Zöpffen' in 1545); Song 6.6 ('on was ynn deynen zöpffen ist' in 1524, and 'zwisschen deinen zöpffen' in 1545); Song 6.7 ('megde' in 1524, and 'Jungfrawen' in 1545); and Song 8.1 ('O wer gibt dich meyn bruder, der du meyner mutter brüste saugest, das ich dich draussen finde, und dich küssen müste, das dich auch niemant myr raubete' in 1524, and 'O das ich dich, mein Bruder, der du meiner Mutter brüste saugest draussen fünde, und dich küssen müste, das mich niemand hönete' in 1545). The difference in length (2402 words in 1524, and 2371 words in 1545) is largely due to the splitting of adverbs and compound nouns. Two examples from several are 'hynaus' (1524) and 'hin aus' (1545), and 'scheyde berge' (1524) and 'Scheideberge' (1545).

views, and the premise that all translation is in itself interpretation, it is not surprising that Luther's Bible translation was coloured by his own reading. The notorious example, of course, is his rendering of the Vulgate's 'arbitramur hominem iustificari ex fide absque operibus' ('we judge that a man is justified by faith, not by works') (Rom. 3.28) as 'so halten wir es nu das der Mensch gerecht werde on des Gesetzes werck alleine durch den Glauben' ('thus we believe that man is justified by faith alone, without the works of the law'). As the Latin does not contain the word 'sola' ('alone'), Luther's translation was influenced by his own theological views and his own sense-for-sense theory of translation. He defended his version vigorously in the *Sendbrief*, but arguably he exceeded the duties of the translator in this verse.

Luther held that the translator should respect the target language, rendering the sense and allowing a literal translation just occasionally. He stressed the immediacy of a translation. It should be a living, contemporary document, without the protective casing of an academic, elitist style which harked back to the original language. He demanded, for example, the avoidance of encapsulation and the use of the passive voice. The Bible was to be a conversation between the translator and the recipient of the translation. Thus we find already the germ of Herder's thinking in Luther, and we note the paving of the way for reception theory. In other words, the reader was to be the interpreter. This was in accordance with Protestant theology which taught that every soul needed its own access to God, the Great Author, without the mediation of a priest or a Book in a foreign tongue. However, Luther insisted that there was only one true reading, and he was by no means advocating the plurality of meanings envisaged by reception theory.

In practice, Luther tempered his theories of translation, for his translation of the Bible is poetic and carefully patterned. It is rhythmic, particularly in the Psalms, and is certainly not conversational. The language he used was not that of the lower classes. His style is intermediate and natural, yet never flippant or vulgar, even though he drew on everyday proverbs and usage. He respected the target language, the language of the people, and the sacred nature of the text itself.

Herder admitted that he himself was not a poet. He realized that Luther's language had become folk language and was therefore better adapted to the translation of Solomonic folk-poetry than a thoroughly new but possibly prosaic translation would be. Luther had become an established 'folk-poet', and, as noted above, Herder felt safe in pointing his readers to and anchoring his own work in Luther's translation.[4] It will emerge, however, that Herder was ultimately more faithful to the original Hebrew than to Luther, and thus he was arguably more successful in showing his readers the beauty of the Hebrew language. However, he did not attempt to improve upon Luther's translation, nor was he setting up his own work as a benchmark for subsequent translators to follow, for 'an meinen Versen darf niemand haften' ('nobody need adhere to my verses') (VIII, p. 594). In Herder's defence, we have noted endlessly his insistence on Luther as his touchstone, for poetic language 'quoll dem Gottesmann aus dem Herzen, uns fließt sie aus Kopf und Feder' ('sprang from the heart of the man of God, whereas in our case it flows from hand and pen') (VIII, p. 594). It will become apparent below, however, that Herder ultimately strove to produce a translation which was lexically more accurate than his earlier drafts had been.[5]

Goethe's Translation

We have noted that translations of the Song of Songs were attempted by a number of Herder's contemporaries, including Hamann, Gleim, Johann Gottlieb Lessing and Goethe. The most important translation for this study is undoubtedly that of Goethe, for it was almost certainly

---

4.   Whereas Herder firmly anchored MS(a) in Luther by using appropriate quotations fore and aft, as well as disclaimers within his commentary, he did not use the mottos in MSS(1), (2) or (3). However, the disclaimers within the text certainly appear in MSS(2) and (3) in very similar, although not identical, wording. This additional motto anchorage is very important for the published translation of 1778. Indeed, we have already seen in the Preface to this study that just as Herder encouraged his readers to turn to Luther should they find his own translation inadequate, this was a ploy also used by Luther regarding his own New Testament translation: 'Es ist niemand verboten, ein bessers zu machen. Wer's nicht lesen will, der laß es liegen' ('Nobody is forbidden from making a better one. Whoever does not wish to read it, let him leave it be' (quoted in Robinson, *The Translator's Turn*, p. 72).

5.   It is true that Paul Haupt (*Biblische Liebeslieder*, p. x.) maintained that Herder's 'Übertragung der biblischen Liebeslieder gibt ebensowenig einen rechten Begriff von dem Originale wie die Luthersche Übersetzung' ('translation of the biblical love songs results just as little in a true understanding of the original as does Luther's translation'), but this only suggests that Haupt did not fully understand Herder's purpose in translating the Song of Songs in the first place.

under Herder's influence that Goethe undertook his prose version of the Song of Songs which he published in 1775, three years before his mentor's published version.[6] It must be stressed that, with the possible exception of fragments, Goethe could not have seen Herder's *Lieder der Liebe* before his own version was published in 1775, since, as we have seen, the earliest manuscripts of any significant length date from 1776.

Goethe's translation could almost be called a version of Luther's translation. It consists of independent songs and fragments, not linked by any common thread. This fragmentary aspect is strengthened by the short, abrupt style, apparent on the page from the many exclamation marks. The work was never quite completed, as the last section is missing, as well as various verses throughout (its total length is only 1,666 words). There are 31 sections of seemingly arbitrary length, neither named nor numbered.[7]

According to Gustav von Loeper, Goethe's version of the Song of Songs was not from the Hebrew, but rather from the Vulgate with

---

6.   Goethe, *WW*, XXXVII, pp. 299-310. See also Benno Badt, 'Goethe als Übersetzer des Hohenliedes', *Neue Jahrbücher für Philologie und Pädagogik, oder kritische Bibliothek für das Schul- und Unterrichts-Wesen* 27 (1881), pp. 346-57.

7.   It would be helpful to compare how Goethe's divisions correspond to Luther's version of 1545 which is used to anchor the detailed commentary below. For ease of reference, Goethe's sections are numbered alongside the corresponding chapter and verse in Luther's translation.

(1)	1.1-4	(17)	5.2-7
(2)	1.5, 6	(18)	5.8-16
(3)	1.7, 8	(19)	5.17–6.2
(4)	1.9-11	(20)	6.3-4a (4b to 6 are omitted)
(5)	1.12	(21)	6.7, 8
(6)	1.13, 14	(22)	6.9
(7)	1.15-17	(23)	6.10 (11 is omitted)
(8)	2.1-7	(24)	6.12–7.9
(9)	2.8-15	(25)	7.10
(10)	2.16, 17	(26)	7.11, 12
(11)	3.1-4	(27)	7.13
(12)	3.6 (5 is omitted, as are 7-11)	(28)	8.1, 2 (3 and 4 are omitted)
(13)	4.1-7a (6 is omitted)	(29)	8.5a
(14)	4.7b, 8	(30)	8.5b
(15)	4.9-16	(31)	8.6, 7 (8-14 are omitted)
(16)	4.17–5.1		

Luther as an aid.[8] This is not surprising if we accept Timm's view that 'seine Hebräischkenntnisse waren nicht so gut, daß er auf die Mithilfe der Vulgata, Luthers und des Großen Englischen Bibelwerkes hätte verzichten können'.[9] In fact, my comments below on Goethe's translation will suggest that Luther was his main influence. Undoubtedly Herder convinced Goethe of the value of Luther's translation, and thus it should be no surprise that in his own rendering Goethe kept close to Luther rather than the Hebrew. Indeed, he argued that Luther's Bible translation 'hat die Religion mehr gefördert, als wenn er die Eigenthümlichkeiten des Originals im Einzelnen hätte nachbilden wollen'.[10] Arguably, then, Goethe's text is a combination of a translation and a version of Luther's text, although, as Timm has suggested, it is possible that he also used the English KJV, since occasionally he is closer to that than to the Latin or to Luther. Relevant examples will emerge from the detailed comments below.

Herder's importance for Goethe is well documented, but there is clearly a possibility that Goethe in turn had an influence on Herder's published work on the Song of Songs. Indeed, Claus Bock asserts that Herder's version of 1778 'shows a close approximation to Goethe's text—a fine tribute from mentor to pupil'.[11] This claim will be considered further below, although there would appear to be no real internal or external evidence for it.

Referring in his autobiography perhaps to his own (abridged) work, Goethe claimed that 'eine schlichte Übertragung bleibt immer die beste' ('an unpretentious translation is always the best'), arguing that others translating Job, the Psalms and 'andere Gesänge' ('other songs') (a reference to the Song of Songs?) had attempted unsuccessfully to present them in poetic form. It is just possible that this was a late indictment of Herder's work. If so, Goethe's plea that 'jene kritischen Übersetzungen, die mit dem Original wetteifern, dienen eigentlich nur zur

---

8.   *Briefe Goethes an Sophie von La Roche und Bettina Brentano mit dichterischen Beilagen*, p. 130.

9.   'His knowledge of Hebrew was not so good that he would have been able to dispense with the aid of the Vulgate, Luther's work and the great English Bible translation.' *Das Hohe Lied Salomos*, p. 117.

10.   'Has advanced religion more than if he had tried to reproduce in detail the specific peculiarities of the original.' *Dichtung und Wahrheit*, III, Book 11, *WW*, XXVIII, p. 74.

11.   'A Tower of Ivory?', p. 19.

Unterhaltung der Gelehrten unter einander'[12] is especially ironic, given that here was one reason why Herder undertook his own translation and commentary in the first place.

Herder's Translations

Herder's various attempts to translate the Song of Songs demonstrate an eclectic approach to his task, for his translations include lyrical poetry, represented by ode, elegy and song, as well as descriptive poetry, represented by pastoral, eclogue, idyll and description of scenes and places. His unpublished draft translations are far freer than the work of 1778. They are more of a poetic paraphrase, flowery and sentimental in style. The approach is much more in the mould of Klopstock than of Luther. His poetry is lush, baroque, exuberant, emotional and sentimental—a reading to which Haym also drew attention.[13] We note Herder's use of 'schwimmt' ('swims'), 'schwebt' ('hovers'), 'webt' ('floats'), 'schwind'' ('vanish') and 'sink' ('recede'), for example. His less chaste, more enthusiastic approach would possibly have been more acceptable to his open-minded contemporaries, for the 1778 version is less daring, and more modest and reserved. The language is more primitive than that used in the earlier manuscripts, and arguably closer to Goethe and folk-poetry. The sound was important to Herder, and the rhythm of the translation matches more the rhythm of the Hebrew.

Herder noted the vast differences between the poetry, language and love of the Orient, and those of his own German culture. By 1778 he felt unhappy with his earlier translations, considering that his attempts to place the poetry in a German setting and context had been a failure. He asserted that the caressing tone of the original was untranslatable, and he argued that he had produced German poetry and nothing more: 'Aller Gang des Originals [...] war damit verlohren. Es waren Deutsche Verse, nichts weiter' ('The whole character of the original [...] was thereby lost. They were nothing other than German verses' (VIII, p. 534). Indeed, Herder cast much of his unpublished versions in the language of Klopstock, to that extent re-casting the ancient poetry into the new terms available to his own time—a process quite contrary to

---

12. 'Those critical translations which vie with the original actually serve merely for the mutual amusement of scholars.' *WW*, XXVIII, p. 74.

13. *Herder*, II, p. 86. On Herder's translations from the Bible, see also Suphan's closing remarks to vols. X, XI and XII of his edition in *SWS*, XII, pp. 408-15.

what he criticized his contemporaries for doing, who imposed an old, alien, framework upon a new, native literature.

Herder realized the impossibility of translating Hebrew poetry into 'unsre schwere, kalte, nordische, ganz anders gebauete und geformte Sprache' ('our heavy, cold, northern language, which is constructed and shaped in a totally different way') (VIII, p. 534), claiming that it was equally impossible to transfer its metre into German. Herder accused 'Jemand' ('Somebody'), presumably Michaelis again, of wanting to translate Bible passages into German, using the same number of verses, syllables and sounds as the original. Dismissively he claimed that he would rather attempt to translate the cooing of a dove or the gurgling of his child into Cicero's oratorical style. However, it may not have been clear to Herder exactly what Hebrew metre was, for Hebrew poetry does not depend upon a verse scheme of regular rhyme and accent. Indeed, it has an irregular—though recurring—accent, and any rhyme appears accidental (as in Herder's 1778 translation). Unlike Paul Haupt, we should not be surprised that Herder's reproduction of the original metre is coincidental, for it was not Herder's intention to impose a foreign versification on German poetry. Yet Haupt argues that Herder 'bringt die poetische Form weit besser zur Anschauung als Goethe' ('brings out the poetic form much better than does Goethe'),[14] although this should be obvious too, given that Goethe's was a prose translation.

The characteristic feature of Hebrew poetry is parallelism, providing rhythm as well as balanced symmetry of form and sense. This is a poetic device which Herder sought to imitate in his translations, and examples will emerge in my commentary below.

The three primary forms of parallelism are synonymous, antithetical and synthetic. These main types were originally postulated by Lowth, and, although there is now some dispute about them, they are generally regarded as still valid. Examples for each type are given below from the Song of Songs (KJV):

a. Synonymous parallelism, in which the basic idea is reiterated in a different way in the next phrase or line. There are two examples in 'I held him, and would not let him go, until I had brought him into my mother's house, and into the chamber of her that conceived me' (Song 3.4). There are two further examples in 'Until the day break, and the shadows flee away, I will get me to the mountain of myrrh, and to the

---

14. *Biblische Liebeslieder*, p. xii.

hill of frankincense' (Song 4.6). The Song of Songs is replete with examples of this form of parallelism.

b. Antithetical or contrasted parallelism, in which the first thought is contrasted or reversed in the next phrase or line. For example, 'Love is strong as death; jealousy is cruel as the grave' (Song 8.6).

c. Synthetic or constructive parallelism, in which the second idea adds to the first by completing, enlarging or intensifying it. For example, 'I sought him, but I could not find him; I called him, but he gave me no answer' (Song 5.6).

Any opinion on Herder's biblical translations is likely to be divided, given both his multiple purposes and his dual identity as theologian *and* poetic mediator. It must necessarily focus on three aspects and the tensions between them: poetry, theological interpretation, and 'accuracy' towards the original text. Thomas Willi, for example, maintains that Herder was concerned 'immer mehr um eigene Nachschöpfung als um treue Widergabe' ('more and more about his own imitation than about faithful reproduction'),[15] that the 'Uebertragungen aus dem Hebräischen in erster Linie ein Exerzitium für die Bildsamkeit der deutschen Sprache (sind)' ('translations from the Hebrew [are] primarily an exercise for the flexibility of the German language') (p. 50), and that Herder offered poetry rather than theology—'schöpferische Nachbildung statt gehorsamer Auslegung' ('creative imitation rather than submissive exegesis') (p. 51). But to contrast thus 'Nachschöpfung' ('imitation') with 'treue Widergabe' ('faithful reproduction') is to ignore the very basis of Herder's view of translation: justice could be done to the original only by the method of creative reproduction. Herder attempted to explore the depths of the original by empathy with the foreign culture rather than analysis, and yet, as we have noted already, he produced a strongly interpreted translation of the Song of Songs which belonged to 'Empfindsamkeit' and 'Sturm und Drang', with elements of both folk-song and an idealizing, chaste, bourgeois view of love, based on partial information. This, despite his insistence on the difference and distinction of Oriental poetry.

Whereas Goethe and Luther both produced prose translations, Herder's versions were all in verse. He did not attempt to translate using a foreign verse form as so many others had done, and he accused Denis, for example, of imposing the hexametric form of his original

---

15. *Herders Beitrag*, p. 49.

upon the German language. Herder chose not to make the same mistake, translating rather into German folk-song forms, especially in the draft translations. He mainly used free verse, although the section on the foxes, for example, forms a song-stanza.

The line length in Herder's translations is erratic, tending—although not always—to be half the line length of the original Hebrew. In fact, a study of the Hebrew text of the Song of Songs demonstrates that the line length is very irregular, although—as is typical of Hebrew lyric poetry—each line is generally divided into two parts. Thus Herder was able to render the poetry in a verse form more familiar to his readership, although with the unpolished, unexpected metre and syntactical inversions of primitive poetry. Indeed, as we shall see, Herder inverted many normal clauses in the Hebrew to accord with his preconception of the frequency of inversion in primitive poetry. The original manuscripts show how often Herder translated with a normal clause before crossing out and changing words around in favour of inversion. Examples will be given below. And yet, on the other hand, although it is clear that Herder often inverted in keeping with his view of inversion as a hallmark of primitive poetry, there were occasions when he chose not to, even if Luther did so. This is an important point which contradicts Clark's assertion that 'numerous normal clauses of Luther's translation are inverted by Herder'.[16]

Herder seems to have made no obvious attempt to maintain a regular scansion pattern in any of his translations of the Song of Songs, a clear example being the couplet 'Seht mich nicht an, daß ich schwärzlich bin: / Mich brannte die Sonne' ('Do not look at me because I am swarthy: / The sun has burned me') (VIII, p. 490). However, a study of the scansion as a whole shows that the feet are predominantly iambic and trochaic, with the occasional anapaest and dactyl used to break up any monotonous regularity, thus lending a more primitive and authentic tone. The verse form is generally free verse. The opening lines of the 1778 translation exemplify Herder's varied approach, for he begins with a dimeter, a trimeter, a pentameter and a tetrameter. Indeed, these four line lengths are used throughout most of the translations, with just the occasional monometer. There are two iambic hexameters in 1776,[17] namely 'der Hals in Golde thront! und lieblicher wirds seyn' ('her neck

16. *Herder: His Life and Thought*, p. 257.
17. Unless otherwise stated, the date 1776 refers throughout this chapter to MS(3).

is enthroned in gold! And it will be even more lovely...'), and 'dem Reh, dem jungen Hirsch ist mein Geliebter gleich' ('my lover is like the roebuck, the young stag'), each with a caesura in the middle. There are two irregular pentameters in 1778, namely 'ein heiliger Garte bist du, meine Schwester-Braut' ('you are a sacred garden, my sister-bride'), and 'viel Wasser mögen nicht aus sie löschen, die Liebe' ('much water is unable to extinguish love'). These are the longest lines in either translation. Throughout the two translations in Appendix A, song VII ('Frühlingswerk') of 1776 shows the most regular scansion (principally iambuses and trochees), line-length (tetrameters) and rhyme (a a b b a a). Elsewhere, whenever the rhythm threatens to become regular, Herder inserts or omits a foot to disturb the flow of the poetry, thus producing the 'primitive' folk-poetry which he admired, rather than the polished art which he despised. Two examples illustrate the point, the first from 1776 and the second from 1778. Both are basically in iambic trimeters:

> (a) Dein Hals die Davidsveste
>   auf sichrer Brustwehr da
>   Umhangen rings mit tausend Siegesschilden
>   und Helden trugen sie.[18]

> (b) Ich kam in meinen Garten,
>   O meine Schwester Braut!
>   Und brach von meinen Myrrhen
>   Und meinen Würzen.[19]

The third and fourth lines respectively interrupt the rhythmic flow in each example.

Line length in 1778 is on the whole shorter than in the earlier drafts. For example, Herder translates with:

> Ich will aufstehn nun,
> Die Stadt umgehn,
> In den Strassen,
> In den Gassen,

18. 'Your neck is [like] David's fortress / standing on a secure parapet / Surrounded by a thousand shields of victory / and heroes bore them.'
19. 'I came into my garden, / Oh my sister-bride! / And plucked some of my myrrh / And my spices.' Each line of the published translation begins with an upper-case letter, and this is followed by Redlich. However, MS(a) shows some inconsistency in this regard.

> Und suchen ihn,
> Den meine Seele liebet.[20]

On the other hand, the corresponding passage in MS(3), with its longer, although more succinct lines, and its (incidental?) rhyme, reads:

> Aufstehen, sprach ich, suchen in den Gassen
> in Strassen groß und klein
> den Vielgeliebten mein.[21]

Here Herder adds material to the original which he has removed by 1778. Other examples of additional material in 1776 are 'bis die Schatten lang sich ziehn und verfliehn' ('till the shadows grow long and disappear') compared with 'und die Schatten fliehen' ('and the shadows flee') of 1778, and 'Das Bett der Liebe Salomo ist hold und froh' ('Solomon's bed of love is lovely and joyful') compared with 'Ein Prachtbett' machte der König Salomo sich' ('King Solomon made himself a bed of splendour'). Further examples will become clear from the detailed study below, as well as from an examination of the parallel presentation in Appendix A.

Admittedly, MS(3) also has short lines in places, particularly in song IV ('Träume der Zukunft') ('Dreams of the Future') where several lines consist of one or two words only. However, the general pattern is for lines of shorter length in 1778. In fact, the published translation is some 9 per cent shorter verbally than MS(3) (2206 words to 2411), but it is approximately 9 per cent longer in terms of lines—additional evidence that the average line length is shorter.

Paul Haupt complains that Herder's lines are too short, and he dislikes the way that a half line has been divided into two.[22] He gives the following examples:

> (a)   Er küsse mich
>   Mit seines Mundes Küssen.[23]

> (b)   So ist zerfliessender Balsam
>   Dein Name.[24]

---

20. 'I shall arise now, / Walk around the town, / In the streets, / In the alleyways, / And look for him / Whom my soul loves.'

21. 'Arise, I said, look in the alleyways / in streets large and small / for the one whom I love so much.'

22. *Biblische Liebeslieder*, p. xxxix n. 39.

23. Literally 'Let him kiss me / With his mouth's kisses.'

24. Literally 'Thus is flowing perfume / Your name.'

(c)   O sage mir,
      Den meine Seele liebt:
      Wo weidest du?
      Wo lagerst du
      Am Mittag?[25]

(d)   Seine Linke
      Mir unterm Haupt.
      Seine Rechte
      Umfaßt mich.[26]

(e)   Die Königinnen
      Und Bulerinnen
      Lobeten sie.[27]

Haupt clearly missed Herder's attempt to stress the folk-song element of the Song of Songs in his efforts to bring about a renewal of interest in Gemany's folk-poetry. It was for this reason that Herder reproduced Schöber's mediaeval translation of the work. Indeed, the effect of Herder's short lines is to remind the reader of the mediaeval version, as well as to draw attention to the practice of the early Goethe, for such short lines are not evident in the Hebrew text. Two obvious examples from Goethe will suffice:

O Mädchen, Mädchen,   Ich ging im Walde
Wie lieb' ich dich!   So für mich hin,
Wie blickt dein Auge!   Und nichts zu suchen
Wie liebst du mich![28]   Das war mein Sinn.

                                    Im Schatten sah ich
                                    Ein Blümchen stehn,
                                    Wie Sterne leuchtend,
                                    Wie Äuglein schön.[29]

25. 'Oh tell me, / Whom my soul loves: / Where do you graze? / Where do you rest / At noon?—'
26. 'His left hand / Beneath my head. / His right hand / Embraces me.'
27. 'The queens / And rivals / Praised her.'
28. 'Oh maiden, maiden, / How I love you! / How your eyes gaze at me! / How you love me!', *Mailied*, WW, I, p. 73.
29. 'I was walking in the woods / Just wherever I wanted to, / And I had no intention / Of looking for anything. / In the shadow I saw / A little flower growing, / Gleaming like stars, / Beautiful as little eyes', *Gefunden*, WW, I, p. 25.

The whole effect of Herder's translations of the Song of Songs is similar to Goethe's poetry here. Even the use of exclamation marks, particularly in MS(3), is reminiscent of Goethe.

Two examples from the medieval translation make the same point. The lines are taken from poems 2 and 3 respectively:

in dem garten.	Lieb mir kum.
wil ich warten.	zu deinen frum.
des vil zarten.	honig hat mein gum.[31]
gar mit allem fleizz.[30]	

Three skaldic examples from Herder's own *Volkslieder* underline the similarities with his (other?) folk-song translations:

Ich hört' in Norden	Zum Weingelage,	Der König hört
Ein Wetter aufstehn;	Zum Weibsgekose	Der Wählerinnen,
Hagel rasselt	Weck ich euch nicht;	Der schönen Jungfraun
Auf Helmen hart!	Zu harter Schlacht	Auf hohen Rossen,
Wolkensteine	Erwacht, erwacht![33]	Schicksalswort!
Stieben im Wetter		Nachsinnend standen
In der Streiter Augen		Im Helme sie da;
Vom scharfen Sturm.[32]		Sie standen gelehnt
		Auf Schwertes Schaft![34]

These examples abound with inversion and alliteration, poetic devices which Herder saw as fundamental to primitive poetry in general and Hebrew poetry in particular. Indeed, we note the heavy alliteration in the first line of the Song of Songs in Hebrew, namely שִׁיר לִשְׁלֹמֹה הַשִּׁירִים אֲשֶׁר. This alliteration is reproduced in Herder's own transliteration of this line as 'Schir haschirim, aschèr lischlomoh' (literally

---

30. 'In the garden / I will wait / for the one who charms me so / with all diligence', VIII, p. 562.

31. 'Come to me, oh love, for your own pleasure. My mouth has honey in it', VIII, p. 564.

32. 'In the north I heard / A tempest arising; / Hail clatters / Heavily onto helmets! / Stones from the clouds / Fly about like dust in the tempest / Fly from the furious storm / Into the eyes of the warriors', *Das Hagelwetter*, XXV, p. 262.

33. 'I do not wake you all/ To go to the wine store, / Or for the soft cooing of women. / Awake, awake / To fierce battle!', *Morgengesang im Kriege*, XXV, p. 223.

34. 'The king harkens / To the word of destiny / Of the electresses, / The beautiful virgins / On high steeds! / Deep in thought they stood there, / Helmeted; / They stood leaning / On the blades of their swords', *König Hako's Todesgesang*, XXV, p. 219.

'the song of songs which is to Solomon') in Kapsel VI 24 of the *Nachlaß*.

Herder tried to emulate abundantly such alliteration and assonance in his translations of the Song of Songs. The effect is frequently produced by repetition of words, especially in MS(3). Examples are:

1776   (a)   O welche Freuden da an dir! Wir denken
                 an deine Liebe mehr als Wein
           und alle Lust: sind froh an dir: die Treuen
                 sind dein! sind dein![35]

       (b)   denn o denn, denn seh ich ihn.[36]

1778   (a)   Er küsse mich
           Mit seines Mundes Küssen:
           Denn deine Lieb' ist lieblicher, denn Wein.
           Wie deiner süssen Salben Duft,
           So ist zerfliessender Balsam
           Dein Name:[37]

       (b)   Seht mich nicht an, daß ich schwärzlich bin:
           Mich brannte die Sonne.[38]

       (c)   Laß sehn mich deine Gestalt,
           Laß deine Stimme mich hören,
           Denn deine Stimme ist lieblich,
           Denn deine Gestalt ist schön.[39]

Examples in Herder's translations of the enjambment common to folk-song as he perceived it are 'Komm wie ein Reh / über Berg und Thal und Höh / zu Salome' ('Come like a stag / over mountain and valley and hill / to Salome'), and 'damit die Mutter ihn der Braut / am schönsten seiner Freudentage / nun anvertraut' (literally 'so that the mother him to the bride / on the most wondrous of his days of joy / now may entrust') (1776); and 'Bis daß ich ihn führe / Ins Haus meiner Mutter' ('Until I can lead him / Into the house of my mother'), and 'Mein

---

35. 'Oh, what joys there are in you! We think / of your love more than wine / and all pleasure: are joyful in you: the faithful ones / are yours! are yours!'

36. 'Then, oh then, then I see him.'

37. Literally 'Let him kiss me / With his mouth's kisses: / For your love is lovelier than wine. / Like your sweet ointment's fragrance / Is flowing perfume / Your name.'

38. 'Do not look at me because I am swarthy: / The sun has burned me.'

39. 'Let me see your form, / Let me hear your voice, / For your voice is lovely, / For your form is beautiful.'

Lieber streckte / Die Hand durchs Gitter' ('My lover stretched / His hand through the railing') (1778).

Onomatopoeia is exemplified by 'ergriff' ('seized'), 'duftet' ('smells sweetly'), 'hauchen' ('whisper softly'), 'quillt' ('flows'), and 'bis die Schatten lang sich ziehn ('until the shadows draw long') (1776); and 'flüchtig'('nimble'), 'jauchzen' ('shout with joy'), and 'aufgeritzt' ('split open') (1778).

The whole effect of the MS(3) translation—and indeed those of MSS(1) and (2), whose presentation and effect are similar—is fussier and more elaborate than that of the starker, less florid and more minimalist approach of 1778. Let us consider that section which, in the draft translations, certainly sounds more like a German hunting song than an Oriental poem. In 1778 we read:

> Faht uns die Füchse,
> Die kleinen Füchse,
> Die Weinbergverderber,
> Der Weinberg knospt.[40]

This is written in free verse, and is dependent on repetition for structuring. In MS(3), and in an almost identical fragment in the *Nachlaß* (Kapsel VI 59, attributed by Irmscher to 1777), where the song title is 'Scheuchlied der Morgenländer gegen die Yackalls' ('A Song used by the Orientals to Scare Off the Jackals'), we find the eminently freer and more folksy

> Laßt uns fahn! laßt uns fahn
> Die Füchslein dort auf grünem Plan
> Die den Weinberg uns verderben,
> Daß die schönsten Blüthen sterben,
> Junge Blüthen blühn uns an
> Laßt uns fahn! laßt uns fahn![41]

Of special note are the folk-song tone, the rhyme, the German-patterned metre and the archaic form of 'fangen' ('catch') in both versions, used to produce a primitive effect by following the mediaeval form 'vâhen'. Compared with the 1778 version, there is evidence in 1776 of

---

40. 'Catch for us the foxes, / The little foxes, / The spoilers of the vineyard, / The vineyard is in bud.'

41. 'Let us catch! Let us catch / The little foxes there on the verdant plain / Which spoil the vineyard for us, / So that the most beautiful blossoms die, / Young blossoms flower for us / Let us catch! Let us catch!'

a more drastic transformation of the original material, on account of the choice of versification. Other examples of the more elaborate tone of MS(3) are 'du führest / in deine Kammer—mich' (literally 'you lead / into your chamber—me'); 'Sonnenschein' ('sunshine') (as opposed to 'Sonne' in 1778); and the emotional

> Ich schwimm' an ihr
> in Düfte Wein
> in welch ein Meer der Lieb' hinein.
> Und Liebe über mir
> schwebt
> webt
> Panier!—[42]

While primitive folk-poetry does not always scan smoothly, and whereas there is an inconsistent rhythm, and variable line-length, the stanza-length tends to be constant. In his translations of the Song of Songs, Herder adopts varying stanza-lengths, yet his translations still bear the hallmark of primitive folk-song. The following is an example from the *Volkslieder* which is remarkably similar to the hunting song above in rhythm, line-length, stanza-length, inversion and general effect:

> Laßt uns tanzen, laßt uns springen!
> Denn der Wolken schneller Lauf
> Steht mit dunkelm Morgen auf:
> Ob sie gleich sind schwarz und trübe,
> Dennoch tanzen sie mit Liebe
> Nach der lauen Lüfte Singen.[43]

Herder's unpublished translations are altogether more dramatic than that of 1778, with greater use of orthographic devices such as exclamation marks and inverted commas for speech. Poetic and dramatic characteristics of MS(3) are repetition in phrases such as 'denn o denn, denn seh ich ihn' ('then, oh then, then I see him'), 'hört o höret meinen Schwur' ('hear, oh hear my oath'), and 'laßt uns fahn! laßt uns fahn!' ('let us catch! Let us catch!'); the use of the letters A, B and C to denote speakers; the indenting of lines for special dramatic effect; and the

---

42. Literally 'I swim next to her / in the fragrance of wine / into what a sea of love. / And love over me / hovers / floats / banner!—'

43. 'Let us dance, let us jump! / For the rapid path of the clouds / Arises with the dark morning: / Although they are black and gloomy, / They dance with love / In accordance with the singing of the mild breezes', *Tanzlied*, XXV, p. 347.

compulsion of the rhyme, that characteristic of German folk-song—for Herder made a clear attempt to produce occasional rhyme in his drafts, although the published translation suggests a rejection of it. There is no specific pattern as such, however, and in places there is absolutely no attempt at rhyme. Sometimes the rhyme is internal to a line, such as in 'o König mir, o mir dir nach' (MS(3)).

As Herder's rhyme varies inconsistently, yet appropriately, from poem to poem, it is probably more fitting to consider the rhyme scheme within each of the 22 sections of MS(3) rather than within each particular stanza. The corresponding chapter and verse in Luther's translation are given for ease of reference to parallel passages within Appendices A and B.

I   (1.2-4). Only the last four lines of this section demonstrate any kind of scheme, and even then it is not clear whether Herder is attempting to rhyme 'Treuen' ('faithful ones') with 'denken' ('think'). If so, then the rhyme scheme is a b a b.

II   (1.5-8). In this song and the next, there is an irregular, loose use of couplets. The rhyme scheme is a a b b c d e e d c c f c g h h g i i f j f b k k b k l l.

III   (1.9-14). The scheme here is a b a b a c c a a d d d d c c.

IV   (1.15–2.6). There is no rhyme scheme while speakers A and B are in conversation. The final section rhymes as follows: a a b c d e e f f e g g e h i h i h j j h k h, where the dominant sound is '…ich'.

V   (2.7). a a b b c c d c d.

VI   (2.8-14). a a b b c d d d d d, with the dominant sound 'ir' or 'ür'. The next section, the song, rhymes a a b b c c d d c c c d d d a a e e d d f f, where 'sehn' ('see') and 'schön' ('beautiful') rhyme.

VII   (2.15). This consists of three couplets, a a b b c c.

VIII   (2.16, 17). a a b b c c d e e e e, where 'Reh' ('doe') and 'Höh' ('height/hill') rhyme.

IX   (3.1-4). a b a b c b b b d e b b f f g h i.

X   (3.5). a a b b c c d c d. Apart from the initial inverted commas, the final exclamation mark and a difference in the placing of commas, this section is exactly the same as section V, whereas the parallel sections in 1778 differ somewhat from each other.

XI   (3.6). a b c c c.

XII   (3.7-11). a b a b c c d d e e e f f f g h h g i g.

XIII   (4.1–5.1). In this long section, Herder makes virtually no attempt to rhyme. The four lines in the second 'stanza' rhyme inasmuch as 'kühlt' ('cools') and 'spielt' ('plays') are juxtaposed, as do 'Myrrhenhöhn' ('hills of myrrh') and 'gehn' ('go/walk'). Otherwise there is no rhyme at all.

XIV (5.2–6.2). Again, it would appear that any rhyme in this section is coincidental. The semi-rhyming of 'Edelstein' ('diamond/precious stone') and 'Elfenbein' ('ivory'), and the hint of a rhyme in 'Fuß' ('foot') and 'Libanus' ('Mount Lebanon') are apparent on account of the lack of rhyme elsewhere.

  XV (6.3-8). The first four lines demonstrate the scheme a a b b, but thereafter any rhyme disappears.

 XVI (6.9-12). No rhyme.

XVII (7.1-9). No rhyme, although the visual aspect of the poetry is striking, since the second and fourth lines of each four-line stanza are indented.

XVIII (7.10–8.3). An irregular rhyme scheme re-emerges in this section after the first four-line 'stanza', namely: a a a a b b   c c d d. In the rest of this section, Herder relies more on alliteration than rhyme. Examples are 'bist' ('are'), 'Brust' ('breast') and 'geküßt' ('kissed') which end consecutive lines, as well as a sprinkling of 'ich' and 'ir' sounds throughout. Further alliteration is found in 'bringen mir in meiner Mutter Haus' (literally 'bring for me into my mother's house'), and 'seine Recht' umarmt mich hält mich' ('his right hand embraces me, holds me').

 XIX (8.4). The rhyme scheme is the same as in V and X, namely a a b b c c d c d.

 XX (8.5-7). No rhyme.

 XXI (8.8-12). The first part of this section is divided into speakers A, B and C. Only the middle stanza shows any rhyme scheme, namely a a b c c b, although 'thut' ('does') and 'wahren' ('care for') are each used twice. The final part, which is given a title as if it were a section on its own, demonstrates the rhyme scheme a a b c c b, where the preposition 'an' rhymes with 'Hütersmann' ('herdsman'), and d d e a d a, where 'Salomon' rhymes with 'Hüterlohn' ('herdsman's wages').

XXII (8.13, 14). There is no rhyme scheme here in the final five lines of the MS(3) translation.

Having thus flirted with rhyme in MS(3), it is clear that Herder abandoned it for the 1778 translation. While the repeating of rhymes in German folk-poetry is restricted and conventional, any end-rhyme here seems coincidental or intended for special effect. There are several instances of the same word being used to produce an a a or an a b a scheme, for example 'Duft' ('fragrance'), 'Füchse' ('foxes'), 'Mutter' ('mother'), 'mich' ('me') and 'Liebe' ('love'). 'Dich' ('you') and 'mich' ('me') are used in an a a scheme to stress a feeling of belonging and comfort. The same is true of the a b a scheme, traditional to German folk rhyme, produced with 'an dir' ('from you') and 'mit mir' ('with me'). The juxtaposition of 'mein' ('my') and 'sein' ('his')—conventional German folk-song rhymes—causes the same effect in 'mein Lieber ist mein / Und ich bin sein' ('my lover is mine / And I am his'), and 'mein Lieber, ich bin sein, / Mein Lieber, er ist mein' ('my lover, I am his, / My lover, he is mine'). The only other end-rhymes in this translation are 'aufstehn' ('arise') and 'gehn' ('go'); 'Königinnen' ('queens') and 'Bulerinnen' ('rivals'); 'Schwert' ('sword') and 'Kriegsgelehrt' ('warrior'); and 'Süßigkeiten' ('sweetness') and 'Lieblichkeiten' ('loveliness'). 'Strassen' ('streets') and 'Gassen' ('alleyways') are close to rhyming.

After this brief review of Herder's poetic devices and versification, I proceed to a detailed examination of his translations, mainly with an eye to linguistic problems. I shall concentrate primarily on Herder's published translation of 1778, drawing relevant comparisons with the unpublished translation of MS(3), used by Redlich, with the variants in MS(2), with other relevant fragments from Herder's *Nachlaß*, with Luther's translation of 1545 and with Goethe's translation of 1775, matching them with the original Hebrew text. With the exception of four sets of examples, quotations from the Hebrew are unpointed, as is the case in Herder's own commentaries. Where reference is made to 'both' translations, Herder's translation of 1778 and Luther's translation are intended. Unless otherwise stated, the 1776 translation referred to is that of MS(3). I have adopted Irmscher's system of numbering for the manuscript folders in Kapsel VI of the *Nachlaß*. I use square brackets to expand Herder's abbreviations where appropriate, and I use angled brackets to denote his deletions.

I shall divide my analysis according to Luther's chapter and verse divisions as given in Appendix B, and, as a point of reference throughout, I shall give the relevant passage from Luther's translation. It must be stressed that Herder did not recognize Luther's chapter and verse divisions within his own translations—indeed, his rearrangement of the poetic units is one of the most distinctive things about them—but such a verse-by-verse method will make reference easier. This is the theological model, but it is appropriate for a topic where there is inevitably some overlap between the theological, the linguistic and the literary. I recognize that the drawback of such an enumerative approach is that the points raised by each verse are unevenly distributed and accidental to what each happens to offer. It may also imply—misleadingly—that the unit of translation for Herder was the verse, whereas his metrical stanzas override the single verse as unit; indeed, his unit may sometimes be a group of verses. Arguably, however, the thoroughness of a verse-by-verse approach, together with the strong theological tradition behind it, as well as the convenience of reference, together form a compelling justification for this procedure.

As it is clearly undesirable, if not impossible, to comment on every detail of the translations, this chapter must be necessarily selective. A positivistic–tabular approach is intertwined throughout with the discursive–judgmental material and the overall line of exposition and lengthier argument. The verse-by-verse comments will be followed by a summary of the main points which have emerged.

Commentary

Luther: Chapter One
Das Hohelied Salomo
The title in Luther is verse 1, as the first chapter proper begins with verse 2. As Herder divides the 1776 work into sections, each with its own title, he dispenses with a main title. In 1778 he uses 'Salomons Hohes Lied' (literally 'Solomon's High Song'). Neither translator provides a formal-correspondence or word-for-word translation of the Hebrew here (as we have seen, שיר השירים means 'the song of songs' or 'the greatest of songs'), although clearly both provide an acceptable dynamic-equivalence of the opening line.

[2]Er küsse mich mit dem Kusse seines Mundes, Denn deine Brüste sind lieblicher denn Wein.
Herder already had trouble in reaching a definitive translation of the first part of this verse, as the numerous fragments in the *Nachlaß* show. The majority of the extant fragments in Kapsel VI of the *Nachlaß* show repeated attempts to translate in particular the material given in MS(3) as songs I, II and III. The following versions of this verse are extant:

> Ach küßte mich ein Kuß von Seinem Munde! (Kapsel VI 11)
> ('Oh, if only a kiss from his mouth were to kiss me!')

> Er küße mich
> Mit Küssen seines Mundes (12)
> ('Let him kiss me / With kisses of his mouth.')

> Er küße mich mit seines Mundes Küßen
> *and*
> Er küße mich mit Küssen seines Mundes (13)
> ('Let him kiss me with his mouth's kisses')

and
('Let him kiss me with kisses of his mouth.')

Ach er küße mich mit Küssen seines Mundes (14)
('Oh, let him kiss me with kisses of his mouth.')

Er küße mich
mit seines Mundes Küssen (15)
('Let him kiss me / with his mouth's kisses.')
(The split line is not reproduced by Irmscher.)

Ach küßte mich Ein Kuß von s[einem] Munde (16)
('Oh, if only a kiss from h[is] mouth were to kiss me.')

Er küße mich
mit Küßen seines Mundes (17)
('Let him kiss me / with kisses of his mouth.')
(Herder added the numbers 3, 1 and 2 above each of the last three words respectively, exemplifying an attempt to invert his original rendering.[44] This is acknowledged by Irmscher, although he does not split the line appropriately.)

Another inverted attempt reads:

O daß er mit Küssen seines Mundes
küßte mich (17)
(Literally 'Oh, that he with kisses of his mouth / were to kiss me.')
(Again, Irmscher does not split the line.)

Er küße mich (24)
('Let him kiss me.')
(This rendering stands alone.)

Er küße mich mit seines Mundes Kusse (61)
('Let him kiss me with his mouth's kiss.')

Er küße mich
mit seines Mundes Küssen (62)
('Let him kiss me / with his mouth's kisses.')
(These are two of the five lines in this fragment. They are given as one line only in Irmscher.)

---

44. For the result ('Seines Mundes Küßen'—literally 'His mouth's kisses'), cf. Goethe's *Gretchen am Spinnrade* in *Faust* (*WW*, XIV, p. 171), which has: 'Seines Mundes Lächeln' (literally 'His mouth's smile'), 'Seiner Augen Gewalt' (literally 'His eyes' power') and 'Seiner Rede Zauberfluß' (literally 'His speech's spellbinding fluency').

In the event, Herder finally decided on 'Ah küßte mich Ein Kuß von seinem Munde!' ('Oh, if only a kiss from his mouth were to kiss me') in 1776, and 'Er küsse mich / Mit seines Mundes Küssen' ('Let him kiss me / With his mouth's kisses') in 1778.

In this section, the present subjunctive mood appears both in Luther and in Herder's translation of 1778, although in 1776 Herder uses the imperfect subjunctive 'küßte' ('were to kiss'). The subject is 'er' ('he') in both, but it is the kiss itself which is the subject in 1776. Both translators use the genitive 'seines Mundes' ('his mouth's'), while in 1776 Herder uses the preposition with the dative case in 'von seinem Munde' ('from his mouth'). Unlike Luther, and in keeping with his views on primitive poetry noted above, Herder uses inversion in 'mit seines Mundes Küssen' ('with his mouth's kisses').[45] Luther's 'Kusse' ('kiss') is singular, whereas Herder's 'Küssen' ('kisses/kissing') could be plural, or a gerund. As the Hebrew is the plural מִנְּשִׁיקוֹת in the construct state ('with the kisses-of [...]'), it may be assumed that Herder has copied the original correctly. Herder's grammatical ambiguity, however, lends his reading a certain dynamism. Both translators use the comparative 'lieblicher denn Wein' ('lovelier than wine'), although Herder uses 'süßer' ('sweeter') in 1776 ('lieblicher' ['lovelier'] in MS(2), fol. 7ʳ), when the subject is still the kiss rather than love. Goethe uses 'trefflicher' ('more excellent').

While this is an issue of poetic rendering, the next issue is one of accurate interpretation of the original text. Already we find Herder rejecting Luther in favour of the Hebrew. Whereas Luther translates with 'Brüste' ('breasts'), Herder has 'Lieb'' ('love'). Presumably Luther has 'Brüste' on the basis of the Vulgate ('ubera') and the Septuagint ('μαστοί') (mis)reading of דֹדֶיךָ as דַּדֶּיךָ (i.e. דַּדִּים 'breasts' [dual

---

45. I use the term 'inversion' generically throughout. In fact, Herder used several devices to produce inversion. The example here is one where the archaic genitive results in inversion. Other types of inversion are typified as follows:

'Lieblich stehn in den Spangen deine Wangen' (literally 'charmingly stand between the bangles your cheeks') (Song 1.10), where the intrusion between verb and subject produces an inversion.

'Schön bist du' (literally 'beautiful are you') (Song 1.15), where the subject follows the verb after an emphatic at the beginning of the sentence. The emphatic may be the object, an adjective or an adverb.

'Er hat mich geführt in ein Haus des Weins!' (literally 'he has me led into a house of wine') (Song 2.4), where inversion is caused by irregular word order such as the unusual position of a past participle or other verb form.

of דַּד 'breast'] plus suffix), whereas Herder's 'Lieb' is on the basis of the Masoretic text's דֹּדֶיךָ (i.e. דֹּדִים 'love' [formally plural of דּוֹד 'lover'] plus suffix). Herder is apparently closer to the Hebrew, as is Goethe, thus asserting his independence of Luther and the other traditional texts. His rendering may be coloured by his chaste interpretation, but it also demonstrates a thorough awareness of the original text. Indeed, the mediaeval text used by Herder also shows the inaccurate 'Brüstlein' (MS(1), fol. 14ᵛ) and 'prüstlein' ('little breasts') (VIII, p. 561).

³*Das man deine gute Salbe rieche, Dein Name ist ein ausgeschütte Salbe, Darumb lieben dich die Megde.*
Following the Hebrew more closely, Herder uses the noun 'Duft' ('fragrance') while Luther uses a verb. Herder's plural form of 'Salbe' ('ointment') also follows the Hebrew שְׁמָנֶיךָ ('your ointments'). His genitive case produces inversion in 'wie deiner süssen Salben Duft' (literally 'as your sweet ointments' fragrance'). Goethe prefers to use 'Geruch' ('perfume'). As is normal in such constructions, there is no verb in the Hebrew, whereas Luther supplies one in the subjunctive mood. Luther uses 'gut' ('good'), while Herder uses 'süss' ('sweet'), as above. Luther is probably closer to the Hebrew טוֹבִים ('good', or 'pleasant'). Faithful to the original, Herder inverts with 'so ist zerfliessender Balsam dein Name' (literally 'so is flowing perfume your name'), having elected not to do so in 1776, when he uses the more elaborate clause 'wenn man Dich nennt' ('when one calls you') instead of 'dein Name' ('your name'). While Luther uses 'Salbe' ('ointment') twice, Herder uses 'Balsam' ('perfume'), then 'Salbe'. The Hebrew word שֶׁמֶן ('oil', 'ointment') is used both times, although it is plural in the first instance. Whereas Herder uses the present participle 'zerfliessend' ('flowing'), Luther uses the past participle 'ausgeschüttet' ('poured out'), followed by Goethe with 'ausgegossne' ('spilled/poured out'). At first sight it looks as if all three translators are close to the original, for Hebrew does not have a specifically *past* participle, but simply a participle, which may be rendered as past, present or future, as the context warrants. However, תּוּרַק is not the participle of רִיק in the Hophal (causative passive), but rather the second-person masculine singular imperfect ('you are/will be [caused to be] poured/emptied out'), or even the identically formed third-person feminine singular imperfect; the participle would be מוּרָק ('being [having been/yet to be] poured/emptied

out'), which may have been read or postulated by the Vulgate, the Septuagint, Luther and Goethe.

⁴Zeuch mich dir nach, so lauffen wir, Der König füret mich in seine Kamer, Wir frewen uns, und sind frölich uber dir. Wir gedencken an deine Brüste mehr, denn an den Wein, Die Fromen lieben dich.

Throughout his published translation Herder does not use the emotive exclamation mark as much as in 1776, but here he uses one in 'zeuch mich dir nach!' ('draw me after you'). In 1776 he uses the verb 'winken' ('beckon'), but in following Luther's 'zeuch' ('draw') in 1778 he becomes more physical, primitively archaic and direct. In 1776 he follows Luther with 'laufen' ('run'), adding 'Alle' ('all') as a subject. He opts for 'eilen' ('hurry') in 1778, ambiguously omitting 'alle'. He again inverts with 'mich führete der König' (literally 'me led the king'), following the inversion of the Hebrew. This literally reads 'he has brought me in, the king, (to) his chambers', with verb–subject–object being the customary Hebrew word order. In 1776 Herder uses the second-person singular in 'du führest in deine Kammer' ('you lead into your chamber'), while in 1778 he follows the original with 'führete der König in seine Kammer' ('the king led into his chamber'). The 1776 transposition, producing a more personal translation, is reminiscent of Herder's translation in the last stanza of *Weg der Liebe* in his *Volkslieder* (XXV, p. 360), where he transforms the third-person singular of the English to the first and second.[46] In fact, such a change from one grammatical person to another is a further peculiarity of Hebrew poetry (see Song 1.2, for example), and it is exploited by Herder here. He uses two verbs, 'jauchzen' ('shout with joy') and 'erfreun' ('rejoice'), while Luther uses a verb and then the adjective 'frölich' ('joyful'). In 1776 he uses the noun 'Freuden' ('joys') rather than a verb. While in 1776 his 'an dir' ('to you') is closer to Luther's 'über dir' ('over you'), he uses the poetic genitive 'dein' ('yours') in 1778. He omits the pronoun 'wir' ('we') and allows 'gedenken' ('remember') (as in Luther and MS(2), fol. 7ʳ, although he uses 'denken' ['think'] in MS(3)) to follow on from the previous sentence. He again uses 'Liebe' ('love') for the Hebrew plural, while Luther (wrongly) uses 'Brüste' ('breasts'), as noted above. He follows the original inversion with 'von Herzen lieben wir dich' (literally 'from our hearts love we you'), although incorrectly he uses

---

46. See Schumacher, 'Herder's Treatment of his English Sources in the Volkslieder', p. 133.

the first-person plural, since אהבוך is the masculine third-person plural with a suffix ('they love/have loved you'). The noun מישרים means 'uprightness', or 'the upright ones', but it is used adverbially by Herder to mean 'rightly'. In 1776 he uses the third person with 'die Treuen sind Dein! sind Dein!' ('the faithful ones are yours! are yours!'), using repetition for poetic effect. Goethe follows Luther's 'Kammer' ('chamber').

⁵*Ich bin schwartz, Aber gar lieblich, jr Töchter Jerusalem, wie die hütten Kedar, wie die teppiche Salomo.*
The *Nachlaß* shows how undecided Herder was here too. MS(1) has 'schwarz bin ich und doch angenehm / Ihr Töchter von Jerusalem!' ('I am black and yet pleasant / You daughters of Jerusalem'), while MS(2) has 'schwarz und doch ihm angenehm / Ihr Schönen von Jerusalem' ('black and yet pleasant to him / You beautiful women of Jerusalem'). As expected, this is identical to MS(3), except for an exclamation mark at the end. Additionally, Kapsel VI of the *Nachlaß* contains fragments with the following versions:

> Schwarz und doch ihm angenehm (as in MS(3)) (11)
> ('Black and yet pleasant to him.')
>
> Schwarz bin ich und doch lieblich (as in MS(a)) (12)
> ('I am black and yet lovely.')
>
> Bin schwarz und doch bin ich schön (14)
> ('Am black and yet I am beautiful.')
>
> Schwarz und doch ihm angenehm (16)
> ('Black and yet pleasant to him.')
>
> Schwarzbraunes Mädchen, die bin ich! (18)
> ('Dark brown girl, that I am!')
>
> Ein braunes Mädchen, die bin ich! (21)
> ('A brown girl, that I am!')
>
> Schwarz bin ich und doch bin ich schön (24)
> ('I am black and yet I am beautiful.')
>
> Schwarz bin ich und doch auch werth (61)
> ('I am black and yet also worthy.')
> (This variant was apparently missed by Irmscher.)

Herder's title for this section was 'Das braune Landmädchen' ('The Brown Country Girl') in MS(1), fol. 15ᵛ, and 'Das braune Mädchen' ('The Brown Girl') in MS(2), fol. 7ᵛ. Although ultimately rejected, these titles underscore his approach to the Song of Songs as folk-song, for they may be compared with the title *Das nußbraune Mädchen* ('The Nutbrown Girl') which he gave to his translation of a Scottish ballad (*VL*, XXV, pp. 415-20).[47] The fragment in (11) shows that the later title of this section in MS(3), namely 'Liebe in Armuth' ('Love in Poverty'), was originally 'Die braune Siegerin' ('The Brown Conqueress'), although the rest of the passage is identical to MS(3) as far as 'der Mein' ist hin' ('my [vineyard] has gone'). Herder's leap from victory to poverty is an acknowledgment of his reading of the work as one of innocent humility, and contrasts with Marcia Falk's view in 1982 that the passage here is 'a statement of self-affirmation and pride'.[48] In 1776 Herder does not invert, but follows the lack of a verb in the original by translating with 'schwarz und doch ihm angenehm' ('black and yet pleasant to him') (as in [16]). In 1778, he follows the Hebrew by inverting with 'schwarz bin ich und doch lieblich' ('I am black and yet lovely') (as in [12]). However, there is a problem presented by the Hebrew word ו, which can mean either 'and' or 'but', and so this phrase may carry a judgment suggesting beauty *because of* rather than *despite* dark skin. In every translation attempt except for those in (18) and (21), where the key 'doch' ('yet') is not present, Herder adopts the latter reading with 'und doch' ('and yet'), and in the context of the burning sun, Herder and Luther are arguably both correct in interpreting it as such. Indeed, most older translations follow this reading, although it is important to note Falk's claim that 'the woman's assertion of her blackness is affirmative, not apologetic'.[49] This conviction is supported by her own proudly affirmative translation: 'Yes, I am black! and radiant—'[50]

Yet Herder's ambivalent views on black races suggest that in his choice he may have been influenced by his own cultural background in his apparent belief that blackness and beauty were mutually exclusive. George Wells points out that in Herder's age the original whiteness of man was taken for granted,[51] and indeed Herder claimed that 'ein

---

47. 'Braun' ('brown') and 'nußbraun' ('nut-brown') indicate Herder's recognition of 'nut-brown' as a safe, conventional English/Scottish folk-song formula.

48. *Love Lyrics from the Bible*, p. 110. More recently, Jill M. Munro has taken issue with Falk's view in *Spikenard and Saffron: A Study in the Poetic Language of the Song of Songs* (JSOTSup, 203; Sheffield: Sheffield Academic Press, 1995), pp. 37-38.

49. *Love Lyrics from the Bible*, p. 110.

50. *Love Lyrics from the Bible*, p. 13.

51. See *Herder and After: A Study in the Development of Sociology* (Anglica

Negerkind wird weiß gebohren' ('a negro child is born white') (*IP*, XIII, p. 235. Cf. p. 277). He regarded the white races as better fitted for intellectual activity, while the black races were more sensually aware: 'Die feinere Geistigkeit, die dem Geschöpf unter dieser glühenden Sonne, in dieser von Leidenschaften kochenden Brust versagt werden muste, ward ihm durch einen Fibernbau, der an jene Gefühle nicht denken ließ, erstattet' (*IP*, XIII, p. 236).[52] And yet it is important to note that Herder's views were also enlightened and sympathetic, although condescending: 'Lasset uns also den Neger [...] bedauern, aber nicht verachten. [...] Was sollte ihm das quälende Gefühl höherer Freuden, für die er nicht gemacht war?' (*IP*, XIII, p. 236).[53]

The 'Weimar Bible' of 1768, referred to above, intersperses Luther's translation with allegorical explanation. As if to underline the racial bias inherent in the translation, the comment on this verse reads: '*Ich bin schwartz* (ungestalt und unansehnlich, dem äusserlichen Zustande nach, nemlich wegen der angeerbten Sünde und bösen Lust, Röm. 5 v.12, Galat. 5 v.17).'[54] In Herder's choice of 'und doch' ('and yet'), we have an example of what ideological freight can be carried by a prob-

Germanica: British Studies in Germanic Languages and Literatures, 1; 'S-Graven-hage: Mouton, 1959), p. 48.

52. 'The more refined intellectual strength which had to be denied this creature beneath this tropical sun, in this breast burning with passion, was replaced by a physiological make-up which did not permit him to think of such feelings.'

53. 'Thus let us [...] pity the negro, but not despise him. [...] What would be the point of the tormenting feeling of higher joys for which he was not made?' See also Ingeborg Solbrig, 'Herder and the "Harlem Renaissance" of Black Culture in America: The Case of the "Neger-Idyllen" ', in Kurt Mueller-Vollmer (ed.), *Herder Today: Contributions from the International Herder Conference, Nov. 5–8, 1987, Stanford, California* (Berlin: W. de Gruyter, 1990), pp. 402-14; and John Boening, 'Herder and the White Man's Burden: The *Ideen zur Philosophie der Geschichte der Menschheit* and the Shaping of British Colonial Policy', in Wulf Koepke (ed.), *Johann Gottfried Herder: Language, History, and the Enlightenment* (Studies in German Literature, Linguistics, and Culture, 52; Columbia, SC: Camden House, 1990), pp. 236-45.

54. '*I am black* (deformed and plain, as far as her external appearance goes, on account of inherited sin and wicked desire, Rom. 5.12, Gal. 5.17).' *The Red Letter Bible* (London: Collins, 1903) produces much of the Song of Songs (KJV) in red type, interpreting the work largely as an allegorical prophecy concerning Christ. Each section has a subheading, and the one for this verse still shows a similarly prejudiced view to that of a century and a half earlier: 'She [the Church] confesses her deformity.'

lem of philology. The translator's choice implies an ideological position, although clearly the black issue is closer to the surface and more politically acute today than it was in Herder's time.

Herder uses the genitive to create inversion in 'wie der Kedarenen Gezelte' ('like the tents of Kedar'). Goethe follows Luther's 'Hütten' ('huts'), while Herder uses 'Zelte' ('tents') in 1776 and 'Gezelte' ('pavilions') in 1778. The word translated by Herder as 'Decken' ('awnings') and by Luther as 'Teppiche' ('tapestries') is the Hebrew word for tent-curtains. Similarly, Goethe follows Luther with 'Teppiche', while Herder uses 'Decken' in both translations. In this verse, then, Herder is arguably closer to the original, and thus more exotic and Oriental, whereas Luther and Goethe are more Germanic.

[6]*Sehet mich nicht an, Das ich so schwartz bin, denn die Sonne hat mich so verbrand. Meiner mutter Kinder zürnen mit mir, Man hat mich zur Hüterin der Weinberge gesetzt, Aber meinen Weinberg den ich hatte, habe ich nicht behütet.*

Herder uses the imperative 'seht mich nicht an' ('do not look at me') in 1778, whereas in 1776 he uses twice the interrogative 'was schau(e)t ihr?' ('what are you looking at?'). Luther introduces the word 'so', presumably to temper the phrase, and he is followed by Herder in 1776, but not in 1778, where 'schwärzlich' ('swarthy') stands alone. Like Goethe, in 1776 Herder uses 'verbrannt' ('burned'), again closer to Luther in 1776 than 1778. Herder also omits any conjunction, in line with the original, when he translates with 'mich brannte die Sonne' ('the sun has burned me') (he uses the fussier 'Sonnenschein' ['sunshine'] in 1776, undoubtedly to ensure a rhyme with 'mein'). In both translations he uses the imperfect, while Luther uses the perfect. Both may be inferred from the original. Unlike Luther, but like the Hebrew, Herder avoids inversion in 1778 with 'Söhne meiner Mutter' ('sons of my mother'), being less accurate to the Hebrew, but also less sexist, with 'Brüder' ('brothers') and 'Schwestern' ('sisters') in 1776. Herder's use of the imperfect in 'zürneten' ('were angry with') is closer to the Hebrew than Luther's (historic?) present. Using an archaic form of the verb—presumably to connote primitivity—Herder inverts with 'sie satzten zur Weinberghüterin mich' ('they set me up as a guardian of the vineyard[s]'), using the imperfect tense, although he is closer to the original when he does not invert in 1776. Luther uses the perfect and does not invert. In 1776 Herder follows Luther with 'Hüterin der

Trauben' ('protector of the grapes'), but his compound 'Weinberg-hüterin ('guardian of the vineyard[s]') in 1778 is closer to the original construct chain נטרה את־הכרמים ('keeper of the vineyards').

In Hebrew, when two or more words are so closely connected that they represent a compound idea rather like a German compound noun, the dependent word is in the construct state, while the word in the absolute state upon which the construct depends is in the genitive. Given that the meaning demands that the words be inextricably linked as in a German compound, Herder's translation is closer to the original than any English translation could be.

The Hebrew stresses the possessive adjective by stating literally 'my vineyard, which is to me'. This is brought out in Luther by his use of the relative clause to stress possession, while in 1778 Herder repeats 'meinen' ('my') to produce the same effect. In 1776 he chooses not to use any stress. Herder again uses the imperfect in 'hütet'' ('protected'), while Luther uses the perfect. In 1776 Herder underlines the reason for the woman's neglect of her own vineyard in the line 'ihren Reichthum hütet' ich' ('I protected her wealth'). This is a further example of an addition to the sense of the original, and it is omitted in the truer translation of 1778.

[7]*Sage mir an du, den meine Seele liebet, Wo du weidest, wo du rugest im mittage? Das ich nicht hin und her gehen müsse, bey den Herden deiner Gesellen.*

Luther uses indirect speech in the first sentence here, albeit with a question mark at the end. Herder is closer to the original with his direct questions. His elliptical 'den meine Seele liebt' ('[the one] whom my soul loves') follows Luther, but also adopts the same construction as that used in the Hebrew. In 1776 Herder mistakes the subject in 'der meine Seel' entzückt' ('[the one] who delights my soul') ('der meine Seele liebt' ('[the one] who loves my soul') has been deleted in MS(3)). In 1776 Herder uses 'ruhen' ('rest') in line with Luther's 'rugen', although his use of 'lagern' ('lie down') in 1778 is closer to the original רבץ ('lie down' or 'recline'), and further from Luther. In 1778 Herder is more succinct in following the Hebrew with 'am Mittag'' ('at midday') than he is in 1776 with his more poetic clause 'wenn Mittag drückt' (literally 'when midday presses'). Once more the 1778 translation is more precise and concise than that of 1776. Luther omits any reference to the beloved being like a veiled woman, as does Herder in

1776 when he indulges in poetic licence with 'ich irr' auf allen Triften umher, und athme schwer, find' immer andre, nur nicht Dich den meine Seele liebt' ('I wander around in every pasture and breathe heavily, always finding others, but not you whom my soul loves'). In 1778 Herder follows the original כעטיה (feminine, 'as one veiled') with 'wie eine Verhüllete' (literally 'like a veiled woman'). Luther uses 'hin und her' ('here and there') which is not given in the Hebrew, but, more correctly than Herder's 'zu' ('to'), translates על with 'bey' ('beside/near/among'). Following the Hebrew, Herder avoids inversion with the genitive 'deiner Gespielen' ('of your playfellows'). Goethe follows Luther with 'an den Heerden deiner Gesellen' ('near the flocks of your companions').

[8]*Kennestu dich nicht, du schöneste unter den Weibern, So gehe hin aus auff die fusstapffen der Schafe, und weide deine Böcke bey den Hirten heusern.*

It is normal in Hebrew for the person to be denoted by the form of the verb rather like Latin or Greek, but here a pronoun is used for emphasis. Luther uses 'dich' ('you') as an emphatic pronoun rather than a reflexive pronoun, following the Hebrew construction. Herder omits such emphasis. Luther correctly uses the superlative 'schöneste' ('most beautiful'), copied by Herder in 1778 (where he also follows Luther's 'Weiber' ['women']), but missed in 1776 where he uses 'schönes' ('beautiful'). Where Luther has 'Schafe' ('sheep'), Herder uses 'Heerde' ('flock'). The Hebrew word צאן means either 'sheep' or 'flock (of sheep)', so both translations would appear to be equally accurate alternatives. Neither translator renders the emphatic pronoun לך, as done previously. Goethe is close to Luther with 'Tapfen' ('footsteps'). The Hebrew גדיתיך ('your kids') is rendered by Luther (and Goethe) as 'Böcke' ('rams'), and by Herder as 'Ziegen' ('goats'). Herder follows the Hebrew by using the genitive in 'bei den Zelten der Hirten' ('beside the tents of the shepherds'), avoiding inversion. Although not quite according to the original, his 'Zelte' ('tents') is certainly more Oriental than Goethe's Germanic (and wrongly singular) 'Wohnung' ('habitation/dwelling place'), or than Luther, who produces a dative with a split compound in 'bey den Hirten heusern' (literally 'beside the shepherds-houses'), which in essence is close to the construct chain in Hebrew ('the dwellings-of the shepherds'). Again we note Herder's freer translation of 1776.

⁹*Ich gleiche dich, meine Freundin, meinem reisigen Zeuge an den wagen Pharao.*

According to the *Nachlaß*, it is clear that Herder was undecided here too. Apart from the versions given in Appendix A, MS(1) has 'Aegyptus Roße gleich ich dich / am Wagen Pharao' ('I compare you to Egypt's steed / harnessed to Pharaoh's chariot'), and MS(2) has 'dem edlen Roße gleich' ich dich / in Pharaonenpracht' ('I compare you to the noble steed / in Pharaonic splendour'). Additionally, fragments in the *Nachlaß* show the following renderings:

Meinem Roß an Pharao's Wagen gleich ich dich (12)
('I compare you to my steed harnessed to Pharaoh's chariot.')

Meinem Roß am Wagen Pharao's gleich ich dich (14)
('I compare you to my steed harnessed to the chariot of Pharaoh.')
(Herder changed his inversion by adding the numbers 2 and 1 above 'Wagen' and 'Pharao's' respectively, and altering 'am' to 'an'.)

Dem edlen Roße gleich ich dich
        am Wagen Phar.[aoh] (16)
('I compare you to the noble steed / harnessed to the chariot of Phar[aoh].')

Aegyptus Roße gleich ich dich
        am Wagen Pharao! (22)
('I compare you to Egypt's steed / harnessed to the chariot of Pharaoh!')

Aegyptus Roße gleich ich dich (23)
('I compare you to Egypt's steed.')

In 1778 Herder inverts with 'meinem Roß an Pharao Wagen gleich' ich, o Freundin, dich' (literally 'to my steed harnessed to Pharaoh's chariot compare I, oh [female] friend, you'). The Hebrew specifies that the horse is a mare, a point which Herder misses, even though this seems to be the only place in the Old Testament where the feminine סוסה is used (albeit in its suffix form as סּתי, 'my mare') as opposed to the masculine סוס. Luther is even less direct in his translation, and Goethe follows him with 'reisig Zeug' ('horseman's harness'). Herder's translation of 'Wagen' ('chariot') could be singular, but presumably it is plural, as in Luther and the Hebrew. The 1776 translation is again freer: no mention is made of Pharaoh, although Herder has 'Roß Aegyptus' ('steed of Egypt'). From this verse until Song 2.6, the same translation demonstrates a dramatic reading, for Herder specifically designates the speakers as A and B.

¹⁰*Deine Backen stehen lieblich in den Spangen, und dein Hals in den Keten.*

In 1778 Herder inverts, as in the original, with 'lieblich stehn in den Spangen deine Wangen' (literally 'charmingly stand between the bangles your cheeks'). He is closer to Luther here than in 1776, adding 'schön' ('beautiful') to Luther's 'Hals in den Keten' (literally 'neck in the necklaces', which supplies no new adjective, but which relies on the initial 'lieblich' ('delightfully') to supply the meaning. No additional adjective is found in the Hebrew either. Goethe follows Luther with 'Backen' ('cheek'), 'Spangen' ('bangles'), 'Hals' ('neck') and 'Ketten' ('necklaces'). In 1776 Herder uses the singular 'Wange' ('cheek').

¹¹*Wir wollen dir güldene Spangen machen mit silbern Pöcklin.*

Herder follows the Hebrew construct chain תורי זהב ('ornaments/ borders-of gold') by using the compound 'Goldketten' ('golden necklaces'). Luther uses 'Spangen' ('bangles') both here and in the previous verse. The Hebrew uses the same word twice, while Herder decides to use a synonym, demonstrating a conflict between the principles of poetry and accuracy. Herder adds the past participle in 'mit Pünktchen Silber gesprengt' ('sprinkled with dashes of silver'). This is not in the Hebrew, nor does Luther use it. On the other hand, Luther uses the adjective 'silbern' ('silver-coloured'), while Herder makes use of the two juxtaposed nouns 'Pünktchen' ('dashes') and 'Silber' ('silver'), a reminder again of the Hebrew construct chain. Goethe follows Luther with 'Pöcklein' ('little dots'). Generally Herder's 1776 translation is poetically more ornate and indulgent than the 1778 version which is more faithful to the original, and this verse is no exception.

¹²*Da der König sich her wandte, gab mein Narde seinen ruch.*

Apart from the versions in the Appendix, fragments in Kapsel VI of the *Nachlaß* show the following attempts too:

> Sobald/als der König sich wandte (14)
> ('As soon as/when the king turned around.')
> (Herder added the numbers 2, 3 and 1 above
> each of the words 'der König sich' respec-
> tively, resulting in an inverted clause.)

> Der König wandte sich (16)
> ('The king turned.')

> Als er sich wandte! der König (18)
> (literally 'When he turned around! the king.')

In 1776 Herder chooses the phrase in (16), while in 1778 he prefers the different 'wohin der König sich wandte' ('where the king turned to'). Presumably Luther's 'da' has the meaning of 'as', 'while' or 'when', as suggested in the Hebrew. Herder's 'wohin' of 1778 would not appear to be correct, and he is closer in 1776 when he uses no conjunction. Luther's 'gab mein Narde seinen ruch' ('my spikenard gave off its scent') is closer to the Hebrew ריחו ('its fragrance') than is Herder's less specific 'gab meine Narde Duft' (literally 'my spikenard gave fragrance'). Goethe uses 'Ruch' rather than 'Duft', thus remaining close to Luther and consistent with his earlier use of 'Geruch' ('smell') instead of 'Duft' ('fragrance').

[13]*Mein Freund ist mir ein büschel Myrrhen, das zwisschen meinen Brüsten hanget.*
Luther is closer to the original in his use of the third person. Herder uses the second person 'du' ('you') in his correctly inverted 'ein Sträuschen Myrrhe sollt du, mein Lieber, mir zwischen den Brüsten ruhn!' (literally '[as] a bunch of myrrh should you, my love, rest between my breasts'). Here we have another example of his indecisiveness, for, in addition to the 1778 rendering, we find the compound 'Myrrhenstrauß' ('bunch of myrrh') in 1776, and again a diminutive ('Myrrhensträußchen', literally 'little bunch of myrrh') in a fragment in Kapsel VI 12. We note the diminutive form of the noun which replaces the regular compound 'Myrrhenstrauß' of 1776. Like Luther, Goethe uses 'Büschel Myrrhen' ('cluster of myrrh'). Herder's verb 'ruhn' ('rest') is closer to the original ילין ('lie') than is Luther's 'hanget' ('hang'), although, as the verb could also mean 'spend the night' or 'lodge', Goethe translates with 'übernachtet' ('stay overnight'), almost certainly following the KJV's 'he shall lie all night', or the Vulgate's deponent 'commorabitur' ('will dwell/sojourn/wait'). Luther follows the factual approach of the Hebrew, while Herder changes the mood to one of exhortation and wishing. Again we note Herder's use of exclamation marks, unusual for his work of 1778, although not of 1776.

Eric Blackall has drawn attention to Gottsched's objection to Luther's use of verb forms such as 'du sollt' ('you should'), 'du willt' ('you will') and 'ich sahe' ('I saw') throughout his Bible translation, as well as his use of inversions such as 'wie ein Bawm gepflantzet an den Wasserbechen' ('like a tree planted by the streams of water') in Ps. 1.3.[55]

---

55. *The Emergence of German as a Literary Language 1700–1775*, pp. 132-33.

Ironically, although such verb forms are not used by Luther in the Song of Songs either in 1524 or in 1545, in 1778 Herder imitates here a form used elsewhere in Luther's Bible which Gottsched already believed to be archaic and not worthy of imitation. This is important, for surely by doing so Herder was both refuting Gottsched and acknowledging that Luther had become a German 'folk-poet' worthy of emulation. Furthermore, it is also becoming clear that Herder inverted many of Luther's normal phrases, thus again going very much against Gottsched, whom he held to have violated the German language, bringing it from the age of poetry into the age of prose.

[14]*Mein Freund ist mir ein drauben Copher, in den Weingarten zu Engeddi.*
Herder wrongly persists with the second person here, while Luther correctly uses the third person. He continues to follow the inversion of the Hebrew, however, with 'ein Palmenknöspchen bist du, mein Lieber, mir aus dem Engeddi-Garten' (literally 'a little palm bud are you, my love, from the garden of En Gedi'). The Hebrew text reads אשכל הכפר, from which Luther has taken the word 'Copher' and used a separated compound which imitates the Hebrew construct chain. Goethe's 'Trauben Kopher' (literally 'grapes of Copher') suggests that he has adopted Luther's phrase deliberately, for the Hebrew refers to a cluster of henna flowers. Herder uses 'aus' ('from'), while Luther is closer with 'in'. The Hebrew בכרמי עין גדי is a construct chain meaning 'in the vineyards of Engedi'. Luther has a dative plural ('in den Weingarten', 'in the vineyards'), but Herder uses a singular both in 1776 ('Palmenhayn', 'palm grove') and in 1778 ('Garten', 'garden'). Although Herder's attempt to emulate the construct chain may be applauded, he has clearly missed the plural in the original text. Herder referred in his commentary on this section to 2 Chron. 20.2, which mentions that Engeddi is the same as Hazazon-Tamar (literally meaning 'pruning of the palm').

[15]*Sihe, meine Freundin, du bist schöne, schöne bistu, Deine augen sind wie Tauben augen.*
Herder omits Luther's 'sihe' ('behold'), but inserts the folksy 'O'. His 'Liebe'('love') is closer to the Hebrew than Luther's almost colloquial 'Freundin' ('[female] friend') (followed by Goethe's 'Freundinn'). Herder inverts with 'schön bist du' (literally 'beautiful are you'), and

Luther compromises by using regular and inverted forms. Herder's 'deine Augen Täubchen' (literally 'your eyes doves') follows the Hebrew text both verbally and (coincidentally?) in the ellipsis which is a hallmark of Hebrew poetry. The literal translation is almost certainly 'your eyes (are like the eyes of) doves', presumably hiding behind the veil. Luther's 'Tauben augen' ('doves' eyes') is either a split compound, as we have seen above, or an example of a preceding genitive. Either way, he does not follow the original. יונים ('doves') is the (masculine) plural form of the feminine singular יונה, one of a small class of Hebrew feminine nouns which form their plurals in what is usually the masculine plural form.

[16]*Sihe mein Freund, du bist schön und lieblich, Unser Bette grünet,*
The woman praises her lover, and Herder and Luther both use the word 'schön' ('beautiful') as above. The next adjective is translated by Herder as 'hold' ('fair'), but both translators have followed the Hebrew where the same adjective is used twice to describe the woman and once to describe the man, then followed by a different adjective. Goethe follows Luther with 'lieblich' ('lovely') and 'unser Bette grünt' ('our bed is verdant').

[17]*unser Heuser balcken sind Cedern, unser latten sind Cipressen.*
In line with the Hebrew text, Herder omits 'sind' ('are') both times, although the verb is supplied by Luther. With 'die Balken unsrer Häuser Cedern' (literally 'the beams of our houses cedars'), Herder avoids inversion, but uses the genitive, again in line with the original construct chain. He uses 'Wände' ('walls') for Luther's 'latten' ('laths'), but as the Hebrew רהיט means 'framework', 'panelling', 'rafters' or 'boards', both translators are essentially correct. In 1776 Herder uses the singular 'Wand' ('wall'). Goethe uses 'Zinnen' ('pinnacles'), and follows Luther exactly with 'unser Heuser balcken' ('our houses' beams').

Luther: Chapter Two
[1]*Ich bin ein Blumen zu Saron, und ein Rose im tal.*
As Herder does not divide his translations according to chapter divisions, 'und' ('and') serves as a link between those parts corresponding to Song of Songs 1 and 2 in Luther. The Hebrew חבצלת ('flower', 'daffodil', 'lily', 'crocus' or 'meadow-saffron') is translated by Herder

as 'Rose' ('rose') with the definite article, while Luther plays safe with 'Blumen' ('flowers'), correctly using the indefinite article. Although the Hebrew שָׁרוֹן ('Sharon') specifically represents the level coastal plain from Mount Carmel to Joppa, Herder renders this loosely with 'Feld' ('field') in 1778, although more closely than in 1776 with the inverted, yet more Germanic 'des Waldes Schattenblume' ('the forest's lily'). Where Luther uses 'Rose' ('rose') in the second part of the sentence, Herder translates the Hebrew construct שׁוֹשַׁנֶת הָעֲמָקִים ('the lily of the valleys') more correctly as 'Lilie im Thal' ('lily in the valley'), accurately using the definite article. Both Herder and Luther use the singular 'T(h)al' ('valley') for the Hebrew plural. Goethe uses the (culturally biased?) 'May Blümgen' ('mayflowers').

²*Wie eine Rose unter den Dörnen, So ist mein Freundin unter den Töchtern.*

Whereas Luther does not use quotation marks to denote a change of speaker here, Herder does so, hinting at a dramatization which he claimed to reject. The change of speaker is clear in the Hebrew from the inflection. Again we note that when Herder uses 'Rose' ('rose'), Luther uses 'Blumen' ('flowers'), and when he uses 'Lilie' ('lily'), Luther uses 'Rose'. Goethe follows Luther here. Herder follows Luther's 'Töchter' ('daughters'), having used 'Mädchen' ('maidens') in 1776. Goethe also has 'Mädgen'.

³*Wie ein Apffelbawm unter den wilden Bewmen, So ist mein Freund unter den Sönen. Ich sitze unter dem Schatten des ich begere, und seine Frucht ist meiner Kele süsse.*

Herder and Luther both miss the possibility of translating the Hebrew תַּפּוּחַ as 'apple' rather than 'apple-tree'. It is becoming apparent that Herder is often closer to the Hebrew than is Luther, and his 'im Walde' ('in the forest') follows the Hebrew יַעַר ('forest' or 'wood'). Given Luther's dependence upon the Vulgate, this is surprising, since the Latin reads 'inter ligna silvarum' ('among the trees of the woods'). Goethe is very close to Luther, again suggesting his dependence on him. Herder uses 'Lieber' ('[male] lover') rather than 'Freund' ('[male] friend'), although his 'unter den Söhnen' ('among the sons') in 1778 follows Luther. With his correctly inverted 'in seinem Schatten erquick' ich mich' (literally 'in his shadow refresh I myself'), Herder demonstrates a more chaste approach than Luther and Goethe, who follow the

Latin 'quem desideraveram' ('whom I had longed for'). Herder's 'sitze
nieder' ('sit down') accurately portrays the movement not implied by
Luther's simple 'sitze' ('sit'). The Hebrew חך signifies the palate, or
cavity/roof of the mouth, although Herder shows independence with
'Mund' ('mouth'), doubtless more readily understandable for his
readers.

⁴*Er füret mich in den Weinkeller, und die Liebe ist sein Panir uber mir.*
Luther uses the imperfect, and Herder uses the perfect tense, compared
with other occasions when their tense usage is reversed. Herder inverts
with 'er hat mich geführt in ein Haus des Weins!' ('he has led me into a
house of wine!'), although, unlike Luther, he misses the definite article
buried in the construct chain אל־בית היין ('to the house of wine'), where
the definiteness of the key word ('wine') makes the whole chain definite. He is closer to the original, however, than in his paraphrase of
1776, although we note his abundant use of exclamation marks throughout this section and those which follow.

⁵*Er erquicket mich mit Blumen, und labet mich mit Epffeln, Denn ich
bin kranck fur liebe.*
Herder's plural imperatives 'stärkt' ('strengthen') and 'labt' ('revive')
are more accurate than Luther's third-person singular, given that the
Hebrew סמכוני ('support = feed me') and רפדוני ('support = sustain
me') are Piel (intensive active) imperative second-person masculine
plural. His article in 'mit den Aepfeln' ('with the apples') is unneces-
sary. Both Luther and Herder are apparently wrong to use 'Blumen'
('flowers') (presumably from the Vulgate 'floribus') and 'Wein'
('wine') respectively, given that the Hebrew אשישות means '(raisin)
cakes' or 'pancakes', although Luther's line has become traditionally
definitive, wrong or not. Herder's 'Frucht' in 'Frucht von jenem
Baume' ('fruit from that tree') of 1776 is more accurate, although his
'Lindebaum' ('linden tree') in the rejected MS(2) shows a distinctly
Germanic reading. Herder follows Luther in 1778 with the archaic 'für'
('for [love]') rather than 'vor' ('with [love]'), thus attempting to underpin the primitivity of his original document. Goethe also follows
Luther, although he inverts with 'kranck bin ich für Liebe' (literally 'I
am sick for love').

[6]*Seine Lincke unter meinem Heubte, und seine Rechte hertzet mich.*
Goethe again follows Luther. Herder's 'wonniglich' ('blissfully') and
'süßiglich' ('sweetly') of MSS(2) and (3) respectively demonstrate a
choice of sentimental vocabulary which he rejects in 1778, when he follows the Hebrew by using no adverbs here at all.

[7]*Ich beschwere euch, jr töchter Jerusalem, bey den Rehen oder bey den
Hinden auff dem felde, Das jr meine Freundin nicht auffweckt noch
reget, bis das jr selbst gefellt.*
Herder and Luther interchange their use of 'Hinden' ('hinds') and
'Rehe' ('does'). Although both are plural in the original, Herder uses a
singular for the second phrase in 1778, and two singulars in 1776. The
Hebrew שׂדה infers a wider expanse of open, cultivated land than is
suggested by Herder's 'Flur' ('meadow') or Luther's 'Feld' ('field'). In
1776 Herder uses 'Solyme' rather than 'Jerusalem' in a section far
more detailed than that of 1778, which ends with three very short, pithy
lines. Herder uses a conditional in 1778, but fails to complete the
implied threat.

[8]*Da ist die stimme meins Freunds, Sihe, Er kompt und hüpffet auff den
Bergen, und springet auff den Hügeln.*
Herder's short, verbless 'Stimme meines Lieben' ('voice of my loved
one') (as in a fragment in Kapsel VI 24 of the *Nachlaß*) copies the
original construct chain קול דודי ('voice of my beloved'). In Kapsel VI
18 we find 'Ha! meines Lieblings Stimme!' ('Ha! my lover's voice'),
which is close to the 'Ha meines Lieben Stimme!' ('Ha! my loved one's
voice!') of MS(3). Whereas Luther uses 'hüpffet' ('leaps') and
'springet' ('bounds'), Herder transposes with 'springt' and 'hüpft'.

[9]*Mein Freund ist gleich einem Rehe oder jungen Hirss. Sihe, Er stehet
hinder unser Wand, und sihet durchs fenster, und gucket durchs gitter.*
Herder follows the Hebrew by inverting with 'Wie ein Reh ist mein
Lieber' (literally 'like a [male] doe is my lover'). In 1778 he asserts his
independence of Luther by using 'flüchtig' ('nimble') instead of 'jung'
('young'), having used 'jung' in 1776. While Luther uses 'Fenster'
('window'), Herder uses 'Geländer' ('balustrade'). Both use a singular,
although the Hebrew חלונות ('windows') is plural. Goethe follows
Luther with 'Wand' ('wall'), 'Fenster' ('window') and 'Gitter' ('railing').

[10]*Mein Freund antwortet, und spricht zu mir, Stehe auff meine Freundin, meine schöne, und kom her.*

The first clause in the original uses two different verbs, as does Luther. Herder uses 'spricht' ('speaks') for both in 1778, having used two verbs in 1776, namely the more poetic 'neigt sich' ('inclines himself') and 'singt' ('sings'). Whereas Luther uses 'stehe auff' ('arise') once only, Herder repeats his 'steh auf' for emphasis, ending with the more economical but effective 'komm!' ('come!'). In 1776 'schönstes Mädchen, komm' herauf!' ('most beautiful maiden, come up here!') replaces the earlier 'komm, mein Mädchen, komm' herauf' ('come, my maiden, come up here') of MS(2), fol. 13ᵛ.

[11]*Denn sihe, der Winter ist vergangen, der Regen ist weg und da hin,*

The Hebrew literally means 'the rain has passed and goes to itself'. Both Luther and Herder respect this double Hebrew verb with the adverbial phrases 'weg und da hin' ('away and gone') and 'über, vorüber' ('past, over') respectively. Herder is strongly rhythmical with 'denn siehe, der Winter ist über, der Regen ist über, vorüber!' ('for behold, the winter is past, the rain is past, is gone').

[12]*Die Blumen sind erfür komen im Lande, Der Lentz ist er bey komen, und die Dordeltaube lesst sich hören in unserm Lande.*

Herder's 'die Zeit des Gesanges' ('the season of song') of 1778 is more accurate than his peculiarly Germanic 'Lenz' ('spring-time') of 1776, used also by Luther (and hence Goethe). Herder and Luther avoid the passive in the Hebrew by using 'man hört' ('one hears') and the causative use of 'lassen' ('lets') respectively. Herder's 'Stimme' ('voice') is closer to the Hebrew. The 1776 translation is very poetic, but less true to the original with the economic, onomatopoeic 'Turteltäubchen girren schon' ('turtle doves already coo'). Luther translates ארץ as 'Land' ('land') both times here, although Herder uses 'Boden' ('earth') and 'Flur' ('meadow'). In 1778 Herder is truer to the original by omitting both words.

[13]*Der Feigenbawm hat knoten gewonnen, die Weinstöcke haben augen gewonnen, und geben jren Ruch, Stehe auff meine Freundin und kom, meine schöne kom her.*

The Hebrew in the first phrase means 'spices her unripe figs', so Herder is closer with 'hat seine Feigen mit Süße gewürzt' ('has seasoned its figs with sweetness'). In 1776 he is closer to Luther than to the Hebrew, with his diminutive 'Knöspchen' ('little buds') suggesting innocent affection. Goethe is very economical with 'knotet' ('produces nodules'). Luther makes no reference to grapes, but Herder does so with his culturally determined assumption that 'des Weinstocks junge Trauben duften' ('the vine's young grapes smell sweet'). In 1776 he is closer to Luther than in 1778 with 'unser Weinstock äugelt schon' ('our vine is already in bud'). The Hebrew makes no mention of grapes as such, but portrays the idea of fragrance from the blossom, suggesting that Luther's 'knoten' ('nodules') may be more accurate. Herder's acknowledgment of the verb as radical to Hebrew is denoted by his use of the onomatopoeic 'duften' ('smell sweet'), as opposed to Luther's stark noun 'Ruch' ('smell'). Herder again uses 'Liebe' ('love') for Luther's 'Freundin' ('[female] friend'). He uses 'steh auf' ('arise') twice and 'komm' ('come') once, while Luther uses 'stehe auff' once and 'kom' twice. Luther is closer to the Hebrew here, reflecting in his repetition the emphatic pronoun לך.

[14]*Meine Taube in den felslöchern, in den steinritzen, Zeige mir deine gestalt, Las mich hören deine stim, Denn deine stim ist süsse, und deine gestalt lieblich.*
Herder again uses an innocent, affectionate diminutive with 'Täubchen' ('little dove') in both translations. While Luther uses compound nouns, Herder uses the genitive 'in den Spalten des Felsen' ('in the clefts of the rock') and 'in den holen Klüften der Steige' ('in the hollow fissures of the footpaths'), perhaps surprisingly uninverted. The Hebrew suggests 'in the clefts of the rock', or 'in the secrecy of the steep place'—a singular not followed by either translator. Herder's 'laß sehn mich deine Gestalt, laß deine Stimme mich hören' ('let me see your form, let me hear your voice') shows an inversion not in the Hebrew, while his causative use of 'lassen' ('let') rejects Luther's harsher imperative 'zeige' ('show'). While Luther uses the inflected 'süsse' ('sweet') followed by 'lieblich' ('lovely'), Herder uses 'lieblich' first, then 'schön' ('beautiful'). The whole verse is paraphrased more poetically in 1776. Having followed Luther with 'Steinrizzen' ('crannies of the rock'), Goethe uses the more confining 'Antlitz' ('countenance') instead of the 'Gestalt' ('form') offered by Luther and Herder (1778). This suggests dependence here on the KJV ('thy countenance') or the Vulgate ('faciem tuam'). We note Goethe's rare independence of Luther, although as

the Hebrew מראה suggests 'appearance' or 'form', all three translators are essentially correct.

[15]*Fahet uns die Füchse, die kleinen Füchse, die die Weinberge verderben, Denn unsere Weinberge haben augen gewonnen.*
I have drawn attention above to Herder's more economical and interlinear approach to this verse in 1778 than in his more folksy version of 1776. Whereas the Hebrew uses a participle used adjectively, imitated by Luther's relative clause, Herder uses the compound noun 'Weinbergsverderber' (literally 'vineyard destroyers') in the published translation (actually 'Weinbergverderber' in MS(a)). He omits the Hebrew conjunction ו ('and' or 'but'), using the more succinct 'der Weinberg knospt' ('the vineyard is in bud'). Luther is more accurate with the possessive adjective and plural noun in 'unsere Weinberge' ('our vineyards'). In 1778 Herder again translates more closely to the Hebrew than in 1776, for the agent assumed in 'faht uns' ('catch for us') is more accurate than that in 'laßt uns fahn' ('let us catch').

[16]*Mein Freund ist mein, und ich bin sein, der unter den Rosen weydet,*
Herder again uses 'Lieber' ('lover') for Luther's 'Freund' ('friend'). Whereas earlier in this chapter he uses 'Lilie' ('lily'), here he translates the same word as 'Blumen' ('flowers'). Luther is consistent with his earlier 'Rose'.

[17]*Bis der tag küle werde, und der schatten weiche. Kere umb, werde wie ein Rehe mein Freund, oder wie ein junger Hirss auff den Scheidebergen.*
Herder's more poetic translation of 1776 is evidenced again here, where he shows more originality than in the more prosaic translation of 1778. Linked to the previous verse, we read:

> Er der unter Blumen weidet
> bis sich Tag und Kühle scheidet,
> bis die Schatten lang sich ziehn
> und verfliehn,
> denn o denn, denn seh ich ihn (VIII, p. 605).[56]

---

56. 'He who grazes among flowers / until day and coolness separate, / until the shadows draw long / and flee away, / then, oh then, then shall I see him.'

The effect of the rhyme and the essentially trochaic tetrameters in all but the penultimate line is to stress the length and disappearance of the shadows. In 1778 Herder uses the reflexive verb 'sich kühlt' (literally 'cools itself') rather than the noun 'Kühle' ('coolness') of 1776. The Hebrew פוח means 'blows', 'flows' or 'breathes', representing the final minutes of the heat of the day, and this is brought out accurately by Goethe's (independent) 'athmen' ('breathe'). Herder more accurately uses 'fliehen' ('flee'), whereas Luther's subjunctive 'weiche' ('retreat') is less aggressive than the Hebrew would suggest. Herder misses the inversion in the Hebrew with 'und die Schatten fliehen' ('and the shadows flee'), although he correctly uses the plural. Having followed Luther's 'mein Freund' ('my friend') in 1776, in 1778 he omits the possessive adjective in דודי, using the more folksy 'o Lieber' ('oh lover'). Both translators use imperatives in the last part of the verse, although Herder uses the imperative of 'sein' ('be') rather than 'werden' ('become') to convey the original sense of 'be like unto thyself'. In 1776 he is once more further away from the original with the looser 'Komm wie ein Reh' ('come like a [male] doe'). As above, Herder prefers 'flüchtig' ('nimble') to Luther's 'jung' ('young'). Luther's 'oder' ('or') is in the Hebrew, but Herder omits it. The original insists on three different animals, translatable as 'gazelle', 'young deer' and 'stag', although the latter is plural.

The final phrase is a difficult one. Close to the Vulgate ('super montes Bether') and the KJV ('upon the mountains of Bether'), Goethe departs from Luther with 'auf den Bergen Bether' ('on the mountains of Bether'). In 1778 Herder is closer to Luther's 'Scheideberge' (literally 'mountains of separation') with 'Berge, die jezt uns trennen' ('mountains which now separate us') (Redlich's 'uns jetzt' is inaccurate, both orthographically and in word order). As might be expected from a 'Druckmanuskript', MS(a) shows far more deletion than MSS(1), (2) and (3). One such deletion on p. 16[57] shows that Herder here originally used a noun in 'über die Berge, die Trennungs–' (literally 'over the mountains, the separation–'), ultimately opting for the action of the verb, radical in Hebrew and so typical of primitive folk-poetry. Herder is more poetic but less accurate in 1776, with 'über Berg und Thal und Höh zu Salome' ('over mountain and valley and hill to Salome'), with

---

57. Whereas only each folio is numbered in MSS(1), (2) and (3), resulting in the need to use [r](ecto) and [v](erso), the 'Druckmanuskript', MS(a), is numbered on each side, presumably for the printer's benefit.

Salome being the name of a woman, or possibly representing Jerusalem.

The Hebrew construct chain עַל־הָרֵי בָתֶר ('on the mountains of Bether') could represent no more than a place name, although Lehrman has suggested that 'Bether' could be the name of an aromatic plant, and translates accordingly with 'mountains of spices'.[58] Far more likely, however, is that some sexual euphemism is implied in the whole phrase, for not only can the word בתר mean 'divide' or 'cut into pieces' when pointed as בָּתַר (hence Luther's 'scheiden' ['divide'] and Herder's 'trennen' ['separate']), but, pointed differently as בֶּתֶר, it becomes a noun meaning 'cleft' or 'portion', with the possibility of a sexual implication. If this is so, Luther is arguably closer than Herder or Goethe with the (unintentional?) sexual pun in 'Scheideberge' (literally 'mountains of separation', although 'Scheide' can also mean 'vagina' or 'sheath'). Indeed, although Paul Haupt too translates with 'auf dem Berge (duftender) Myrrhe, auf dem Hügel (köstlichen) Weihrauchs!' ('on the mountain of [sweet-smelling] myrrh, on the hill of [delightful] incense'), he acknowledges the feasibility of 'auf den zerklüfteten Bergen' ('on the fissured mountains'). He further admits a possible sexual reading: 'Auch dies bezeichnet den Schoß der Geliebten (*Berg* = *mons Veneris*, und *Kluft* = *rima mulieris*)' ('this too designates the womb of the loved one [*mountain* = *mons Veneris*, and *cleft* = *rima mulieris*]', although he claims that Luther used 'Scheide' in the sense of 'separation' rather than 'vagina'.[59] It would be surprising if the scatological Luther had avoided a sexual interpretation, although undoubtedly Herder read the passage in all innocence. Thus Herder's choice of 'trennen' ('separate') arguably reinforces his chaste interpretation.

Luther: Chapter Three
[1]*Ich sucht des nachts in meinem Bette, den meine Seele liebet, Ich sucht, Aber ich fand jn nicht.*
Herder follows the inversion of the original with 'in meinem Bette suchte ich, die lange Nacht, den meine Seele liebet' ('in my bed I searched the long night through for the one whom my soul loves'). Goethe independently follows the theme of the previous chapter with the romantic 'Schlafstäte zwischen den Gebürgen' (literally 'sleeping place between the mountains'), omitting 'Bett' ('bed') and 'nachts' ('at night').

58. 'The Song of Songs', p. 9.
59. *Biblische Liebeslieder*, p. 78.

²*Ich wil auffstehen, und in der Stad umbgehen auff den gassen und strassen, und suchen, den meine Seele liebet, Ich sucht, Aber ich fand jn nicht.*

In 1778 Herder resorts to short lines in his poetry. Although the Vulgate 'circuibo civitatem' suggests otherwise, the Hebrew means 'go about inside the city' rather than 'go around the city'. Luther and Goethe are thus closer than Herder. The Germanic 'Gassen' ('alleyways') and 'Strassen' ('streets') in Luther are transposed by Herder. Goethe uses the equally Germanic 'Märckte' ('market places') and 'Strasen' ('streets').

³*Es funden mich die Wechter die in der Stad umbgehen, Habt jr nicht gesehen den meine Seele liebet?*

Herder avoids Luther's impersonal use of the verb, following the Hebrew inversion with 'mich fanden die Wächter' ('the watchmen found me'). The Vulgate has 'custodiunt civitatem', although the Hebrew uses the same verb as in the verse above. Herder again translates inaccurately with 'die die Stadt umgehn' (who walk around the city'), and inverts with 'den meine Seele liebet, sahet ihr ihn?' (literally 'the one whom my soul loves, have you seen him?'), keeping the relative clause and Luther's ellipsis, but using the imperfect rather than Luther's perfect.

⁴*Da ich ein wenig fur jnen uber kam, da fand ich den meine Seele liebet, Ich halt jn, und wil jn nicht lassen, Bis ich jn bringe in meiner Mutter haus, in meiner Mutter kamer.*

Herder's 'ein wenig weiter, ihnen vorüber' ('a little further on, past them') and his supplying of 'ihn' ('him') before the relative pronoun 'den' ('whom') are more modern. Herder does not follow Luther's inversion, although he maintains the genitive with 'ins Haus meiner Mutter' ('into the house of my mother'). However, he immediately inverts with 'in meiner Gebährerin Kammer' ('into the chamber of the one who gave birth to me'), moving away from Luther's second use of 'Mutter' ('mother') in his reflection of the Hebrew synonymous parallelism. He is supported here by the Hebrew הורתי ('she who conceived me'). In 1776 he opts for the effect of the verb in the relative clause 'die mich gebohren' ('who bore me'), rather than the more sober noun of 1778, and we note his chaste 'Brautgemach' ('bridal chamber'). Goethe's 'in meiner Mutter Haus, in meiner Mutter Kammer' ('into my mother's house, into my mother's chamber') yet again reflects Luther.

⁵Ich beschwere euch, jr töchter Jerusalem, bey den Rehen oder Hinden auff dem felde, Das jr meine Freundin nicht auffweckt, noch reget, Bis das jr selbs gefellet.

With minor orthographical changes, Herder and Luther are consistent with their translations of the parallel passage above, although Herder adds 'meine Liebe' ('my love') and 'selbst' ('herself').

⁶Wer ist die, die auff gehet aus der Wüsten, wie ein gerader Rauch, wie ein Gereuch von myrrhen, weyrauch und allerley puluer eins Apotekers?

The feminine verb is translated by Herder as 'steigt' ('comes up'), but he avoids Luther's inversion. He uses a genitive in 'wie Säulen Rauch' ('like pillars of smoke') to convey the Hebrew construct chain עשׁן בתימרות ('like pillars/columns of smoke'), and he is closer to the Hebrew plural than is Luther's paraphrase. Although Luther and Herder use the nouns 'Gereuch' ('smell') and 'Duft' ('fragrance'), the original suggests that an adjective would have been more accurate. Luther's (very Germanic) 'puluer eins Apotekers' ('powders of an apothecary')—not copied by Goethe—is closer to the Hebrew than is Herder's paraphrase 'und köstlicher Würze Duft' ('and the fragrance of exquisite spice'), as the original construct chain אבקת רוכל means 'powders of a merchant'.

⁷Sihe, umb das bette Salomo her, stehen sechzig starcken aus den starcken in Israel.

With 'Siehe das Bett', Salomo's Bett'!' ('behold the bed, Solomon's bed!'), Herder is closer to the original meaning of 'his bed, which is Solomon's'. He also follows the Hebrew with the genitive 'Israel', omitted in 1776.

⁸Sie halten alle Schwerter, und sind geschickt zu streiten. Ein jglicher hat sein Schwert an seiner hüfften, umb der furcht willen in der nacht.

As in 1776, Herder omits the verb in 'sie alle die Hand am Schwert' ('each of them with his hand on his sword'). His singular 'Schwert' is correct for חרב ('sword'). The capital letter in 'alle Kriegesgelehrt' ('all men seasoned in battle') suggests a plural noun rather than an adjective, and this would be closer to the original מלמדי מלחמה ('instructed in battle'). Herder's 'Hüfte' ('hip') is correctly singular, although the Hebrew ירך actually means 'thigh'. Herder's 'fürm Graun der Nacht' ('before the horror of the night') is more succinct than, but not as close as, Luther's translation. As above, Herder uses the archaic 'für', pre-sumably to stress the primitive and original nature of the poetry.

[9]*Der könig Salomo lies jm eine Senffte machen von holtz aus Libanon*, Herder follows the Hebrew with the inverted 'ein Prachtbett' machte der König Salomo sich' ('King Solomon made a bed of splendour for himself'). Luther's 'Senffte' ('sedan-chair') may be closer to the Heb-rew אפריון ('palanquin' or 'litter-bed'). Whereas Luther uses 'Holz' ('wood'), Herder uses 'Cedern' ('cedars') to follow the Hebrew plural. While the singular can mean 'wood' as a commodity, the plural should be rendered as 'trees'. This may represent a misreading on Luther's part.

[10]*Der selben Seulen waren silbern, die Decke gülden, der Sitz purpern, der Boden mitten inne war lieblich gepflastert, umb der Töchter willen zu Jerusalem.*
As in the Hebrew, Herder uses an active verb and a noun in 'die Säulen macht' er von Silber' ('he made the pillars from silver'). This may be compared with Luther's use of the phrase 'waren silbern' ('were [made of] silver'), and his own use of 'silber' ('silver') as an adjective in Song 1.11 in 1776. The original also suggests 'poles' rather than 'columns' or 'pillars', although Luther and Herder translate with 'Seulen'/'Säulen' ('pillars'). Herder uses 'Himmel von Gold' ('canopy of gold') while Luther uses 'die Decke gülden' (literally 'the cover golden'), and he uses 'Decke von Purpur' ('cover of purple') for Luther's 'Sitz purpern' (literally 'seat purple'). While Luther uses 'Decke' ('cover'), 'Sitz' ('seat') and 'Boden' ('floor'), Herder is independent with 'Himmel' ('canopy'), 'Decke' ('cover') and 'Mitte' ('middle'). As the Hebrew suggests 'back' or 'support', 'seat', and 'middle' respectively, neither translator is close with the first word, Luther is closer in the second, and Herder is closer in the third. Herder's 'gepolstert mit Liebe' ('uphol-stered with love') would appear closer than Luther's translation, although he supplies the preposition to render the ellipsis of the Hebrew which literally means 'was paved love'. Whereas Luther uses 'umb der Töchter willen' ('for the sake of the daughters'), and Herder has 'für die Töchter' ('for the daughters'), the original מבנות suggests that the daughters were the agents.

¹¹Gehet er aus und schawet an, jr töchter Zion, den könig Salomo, in der Krone, da mit jn seine Mutter gekrönet hat, am tage seiner Hochzeit, und am tage der freuden seines hertzens.

Luther's 1524 version uses the clearer 'gehet eraus' ('go out'). In 1778 Herder is generally close to Luther in this verse. While the Hebrew חתנתו means 'his nuptials', Herder uses 'Verlobung' ('betrothal'), perhaps influenced by his own courtship at the time of his interest in the Song of Songs. He correctly uses the singular 'Freude' ('joy') to render the Hebrew singular שמחה ('gladness'), here in the construct state שמחת.

Luther: Chapter Four

¹Sihe meine Freundin, du bist schön, Sihe, schön bistu. Deine Augen sind wie taubenaugen, zwischen deinen Zöpffen. Dein Har ist wie die Ziegen herd, die beschoren sind auff dem berge Gilead.

Herder again uses 'Liebe' ('love') for Luther's 'Freundin' ('[female] friend'). He inverts initially, with 'O schön bist du' ('Oh, you are beautiful'), substituting the 'O' for the fuller Hebrew הנך ('behold you'), as in Song 1.15. My comments under the same verse concerning Herder's use of 'deine Augen Täubchen' (literally 'your eyes doves') are valid here too. Whereas the Hebrew צמה means 'veil' or 'lock of hair', Luther, Goethe and Herder all accommodate their own culture with the particularly Germanic 'zwischen deinen Zöpffen' ('between your plaits'), 'zwischen deinen Locken' ('between your tresses') (the KJV has 'within thy locks'), and 'am Lockenhaar' ('in your curly hair') respectively. Although Herder is more (culturally) accurate in 1776 with 'dem Schleir herfür' ('from behind the veil'), he clearly held that 'Lockenhaar' ('curly hair') conveyed the right folk-song tone, for he also selected the word in his *Volkslieder* translation of *Fair Rosamond* (*Die schöne Rosemunde*), for example, which reads 'Ihr Lockenhaar— für feines Gold / hätts jedermann erkannt' (literally 'her curly hair—for fine gold would everyone have taken it') (XXV, p. 14. Cf. p. 135). Luther separates the compound noun 'Ziegenherd' ('flock of goats') (Goethe follows with 'Ziegenheerde'), while Herder uses 'Gemsen-heerde' ('flock of chamois'). Only the Latin, 'greges caprarum' ('herds of goats'), is plural. The Hebrew גלש ('lie down', 'recline', 'sit [up]' or even 'be white' or 'shine')[60] does not quite suggest the 'beschoren'

---

60. These last two possibilities are unusual, but they are suggested by Robert Young in his *Analytical Concordance to the Holy Bible* (London: Lutterworth Press, 8th edn, 1977), p. 45b.

('shorn') used by Luther, and Herder too paraphrases with 'klimmt' ('climbs') in 1776 and 'weidet' ('grazes') in 1778. Goethe is closest with 'blinckend' ('glistening'), describing the gleaming, shining flock possibly conveyed by the Hebrew. As he departs from Luther, the Vulgate ('ascenderunt') and the KJV ('appear'), this suggests a reliance at least here on the original.

[2]*Deine Zeene sind wie die herde mit beschnitten wolle, die aus der schwemme komen, die allzumal Zwilling tragen, und ist keine unter jnen unfruchtbar.*
Herder replaces 'Gemsenheerde' ('flock of chamois') with 'Lämmerheerde' ('flock of lambs'), although the Hebrew does not refer to any particular kind of animal, but rather to 'those (animals) having been shorn' (הקצובות). Herder uses the more romantic 'Quelle' ('spring') in both translations, while the Hebrew רחצה simply means 'washing-place'. Goethe follows Luther's 'Schwemme' ('watering place'). Luther's 'keine unter jnen ist unfruchtbar' ('none of them is infertile') is close to the Hebrew, which means 'barrenness is not among them', or 'none barren is among them'. Herder is further away with 'keins derselben fehlt' ('none of them is wanting'). In 1778 Herder rejects his compound noun 'Zwillinggebährerinnen' (literally 'bearers of twins') of 1776, again showing his preference for a verb in 'die alle Zwillinge tragen' ('who all carry twins').

[3]*Deine Lippen sind wie eine rosinfarbe schnur, und deine Rede lieblich. Deine Wangen sind wie der ritz am Granatapffel, zwischen deinen zöpffen.*
Herder uses 'süß' ('sweet') for Luther's 'lieblich' ('lovely'). As in the Hebrew, Herder inverts with 'wie ein Purpurfaden deine Lippen, und deine rede süß' (literally 'like a purple thread your lips, and your speech sweet'). His compound 'Purpurfaden' ('purple thread') imitates the original construct chain. Luther prefers the adjective 'rosinfarb' ('rose coloured'), copied by Goethe who also precisely follows his 'lieblich' ('lovely'), 'ritz am Granatapffel' ('split in the pomegranate') and the Germanic 'zwischen deinen zöpffen' ('between your plaits'). Herder inverts again with 'wie ein aufgeritzter Apfel deine Wangen' (literally 'like an apple split open your cheeks'). It is likely that both Herder and Luther have misinterpreted the Hebrew פלח, due to two possible ways of pointing the unpointed word. Rather than being the

verb פָּלַח ('split', 'cleave' or 'cut in pieces'), this is almost certainly the noun פֶּלַח, ('piece', 'slice' or 'half'). Indeed, a description of the cheeks as round and ruddy like a pomegranate half would be somewhat more flattering than that given by either translator. Herder's 'Apfel' ('apple') is a culturally biased translation, although a deletion in MS(a), p. 21 shows that he rejected his original exotically Oriental choice of 'Granat-apfel' ('pomegranate') in favour of the more mundane Western 'Apfel'. In 1776 he paraphrases with 'wie aufgeritzten Apfels Milch und Blut' (literally 'like the milk and blood of an apple split open'). As above, he uses 'Lockenhaar' ('curly hair').

[4]*Dein Hals ist wie der thurm David, mit brustwehr gebawet, daran tausent Schilde hangen, und allerley waffen der Starcken.*
Herder's mediaeval- and Germanic-sounding 'gebauet zur Waffenburg' (literally 'built for/as a castle of weaponry') is further from Luther but closer to the Hebrew which means 'built for/as an armoury'. Goethe is likewise closer than Luther, with 'gebauet zur Wehre' ('built for defence'), although he copies Luther's 'daran tausent Schilde hangen' ('on which a thousand shields hang'). In 1776 Herder is less accurate with 'auf sichrer Brustwehr da' ('there on a secure parapet'). Herder uses 'Schilde' ('shields') twice, whereas Luther uses both 'Schilde' and 'waffen' ('weapons'), following the Hebrew where two different words are used, namely מָגֵן and the construct state שִׁלְטֵי־ (from the absolute שֶׁלֶט). Where Herder used 'die Mächtigen' ('the powerful/mighty ones') above for Luther's 'die Starcken' ('the strong ones'), he uses 'Helden' ('heroes') here instead.

[5]*Deine zwo Brüste sind wie zwey junge Rehe zwillinge, die unter den rosen weiden,*
In 1778 Herder uses the poetic 'die zwo Brüste dein' (literally 'the two breasts yours'). While Luther again separates a compound noun, Herder uses the diminutive compound 'Zwillingsrehchen' ('twin little does'), producing an effect of innocence and affection, in line with his general reading of the work. MS(a), p. 22 shows that Herder originally used Luther's adjective 'jung' ('young') too, deleting it in favour of the diminutive alone. The Hebrew synthetic or constructive parallelism is brought out in the original amplification, the meaning of which is 'like two fawns, twins of a gazelle'. This is not emulated by either translator, despite Herder's obvious attempt to follow the original. Again we have

the word שׁוֹשַׁנִּים, translated by Herder as 'Lilien' ('lilies'), as above without the definite article.

⁶*bis der tag küle werde, und der schatten weiche. Ich wil zum Myrrhen-berge gehen und zum Weyrauch hügel.*
Herder here follows Luther's subjunctive mood, rejecting his own present indicative used above. Both translators again use 'der schatten weiche' ('the shadow retreats') and 'die Schatten fliehn' ('the shadows flee') respectively. Luther uses another separated compound in 'Wey-rauch hügel' ('hill of incense'). Herder wrongly uses the plural in 'zu den Weihrauchhügeln' ('to the hills of incense'), although basically he is closer to Luther here than in 1776.

⁷*Du bist aller ding schöne, meine Freundin, und ist kein flecken an dir. Kom meine Braut vom Libanon,*
Herder inverts with 'ganz bist du schön, o Liebe' ('you are quite beautiful, oh love'). He chooses 'Tadel' ('blemish') for Luther's 'flecken' ('spot') (followed by Goethe), although he uses 'Fleck und Tadel' ('spot and blemish') in 1776, perhaps mimicking Hebrew synonymous parallelism in his striving for primitive authenticity. He also inverts with 'mit mir vom Libanon, o Braut, vom Libanon wirst du kommen mit mir' (literally 'with me from Lebanon, oh bride, from Lebanon will you come with me'), reflecting—as does Goethe—the synthetic parallelism in the Hebrew which Luther avoids. Luther uses the imperative and the possessive adjective. Herder uses the softer (maybe more chaste?) future tense, and supplies the intimate 'mit mir' ('with me') which is absent in Luther but present in the original אִתִּי.

⁸*Kom vom Libanon, Gehe er ein, Trit her von der höhe Amana, von der höhe Senir und Hermon, von den wonungen der Lewen, von den bergen der Leoparden.*
As above, Luther uses 'er ein' instead of 'erein' (literally 'therein'), although this is absent in the original and in Herder. Herder persists with the future tense of 'sehen' ('see') (as in the Vulgate), and Goethe uses 'herschauen' ('look here'), while Luther perhaps wrongly translates with 'trit her' ('come here'), although the Hebrew word שׁוּר can mean 'go', 'wander' and 'travel', as well as 'look round' or 'view'. The Hebrew אֲמָנָה ('Amana') denotes the northern ridge of Antilibanus (Hermon was the southern ridge), and is retained as such by all three

translators. The Septuagint's rendering (Πίστεως, 'Truth') suggests an (allegorical) misreading (אמן = 'truth' or 'fidelity'), hinting that Herder was not influenced by the Greek.

⁹*Du hast mir das hertz genomen, meine Schwester liebe Braut, mit deiner augen einem, und mit deiner Halsketen eine.*

Herder uses the present tense in 'du beherzest mich' (cf. 'herzen', 'to hug', used previously), while Luther perhaps more accurately uses the perfect tense. Luther's rendering is more felicitous than Herder's 'Schwester-Braut' ('sister bride'), used in both translations. Herder's 'mit Einem deiner Blicke' ('with one of your glances') is not as accurate as Luther's translation. We note the two inversions made by Luther but surprisingly rejected by Herder. Luther does not inflect on the final article after the preposition 'mit' ('with').

¹⁰*Wie schön sind deine Brüste, meine Schwester, liebe Braut, deine Brüste sind lieblicher denn Wein, und der geruch deiner Salben ubertrifft alle Würtze.*

As in Song 1.2, Luther's 'Brüste' ('breasts') represents a misreading of the Hebrew. Herder's innocent 'Liebe' ('love') of 1778 is more accurate than his 'Küße' ('kisses') of 1776. He uses 'süß' ('sweet') and 'süßer' ('sweeter') for the Hebrew root word טוב ('beautiful', 'pleasant', 'lovely'), while Luther uses 'schön' ('beautiful') and 'lieblicher' ('more lovely'). Herder follows the original by not supplying a verb in 'der Duft von deinen Salben als aller Duft' (literally 'the fragrance of your ointments than the fragrance of all [ointments]'), making the whole phrase dependent upon the preceding 'süßer ist' ('sweeter is'). Goethe proceeds similarly, while Luther supplies the verb 'ubertrifft' ('surpasses'). Herder repeats 'Duft' ('fragrance') in 'Salben Duft' ('fragrance of ointments') in 1776, while Luther uses 'Würtze' ('spice'). As the Hebrew בשם means '(balsam) spices', Luther is apparently closer.

¹¹*Deine Lippen, meine Braut, sind wie trieffender honigseim, honig und milch ist unter deiner Zungen, und deiner Kleider geruch ist, wie der geruch Libanon.*

Herder inverts with 'Honig triefen deine Lippen' (literally '[with] honey drip your lips'), using an active verb while Luther uses a participle adjectivally. The Hebrew נפת ('honeycomb') is translated by Herder

as 'Honig' ('honey'), and by Luther as 'honigseim' ('liquid honey').
Herder prefers 'Duft' ('fragrance') to Luther's 'geruch' ('smell'), and
omits the conjunction as above, allowing the verb supplied earlier to
suffice for the second clause. Luther inverts, followed by Herder in
1776 with 'Duft des ganzen Libanus ist Dein Gewand' (literally 'fragrance of the whole of Lebanon is your apparel'), although Herder
rejects inversion in 1778.

[12]*Meine Schwester, liebe Braut, Du bist ein verschlossen Garten, Ein
verschlossen Quelle, ein versiegelter Born.*
Luther correctly renders the Hebrew passive participle in the phrase
נָעוּל גַן ('a garden locked up/barred/bolted'). Herder's innocent 'ein
heiliger Garte' ('a sacred garden') is not so accurate. He also has 'ein
heiliger Quell' ('a sacred spring'), which is likewise further away than
Luther. Goethe again follows Luther throughout. The adjective נָעוּל
('nailed', 'bolted') is used twice in the original, followed by חתום, also
the passive participle from חתם ('shut', 'close', 'seal', 'hide' or 'reveal
something as a secret'). The Hebrew גל means 'well', 'fountain' or
possibly even 'heap of stones/rocks'.

[13]*Dein Gewechs ist wie ein Lustgarte von Granatepffeln, mit edlen
Früchten, Cipern mit Narden,*
MS(a), p. 23 shows a deletion in Herder's translation, namely 'ein
<Paradies von> Aepfelparadies' (literally 'a[n] <paradise of> apple
paradise'). Herder's ultimate use of the succinct compound reflects the
original construct chain פַּרְדֵּס רִמּוֹנִים ('orchard of pomegranates') without orientalizing the fruit. He uses the singular noun in 'mit aller
köstlichen Frucht' ('with all kinds of delicious fruit'), while Luther
follows the Hebrew plural. Herder renders the henna and spikenard of
the original as 'Nardus und Krokus' ('spikenard and saffron').

While Herder and Goethe follow Luther's 'Gewechs' ('plants'), the
Vulgate uses the highly suggestive 'emissiones tuae', while the mediaeval text has 'mein auslatz' ('my emission') (VIII, p. 583, poem 40
['Emissiones']). The Hebrew noun שֶׁלַח can mean 'sprout' or 'shoot' if
pointed as שֶׁלַח, or, if pointed as שֶׁלֹחַ it could even refer to the Shiloah
aqueduct on the south-east of Jerusalem. The corresponding verb means
'send/shoot out'. Paul Haupt, very opposed to Herder's innocent
approach, uses 'Stollen' ('tunnel'), amplifying the sexual implications
and claiming: 'Ablaßstollen, Abzugstunnel, Wasserleitungstunnel; hier

die gekrümmte Röhre der *vagina*' ('drainage tunnel, sewer, water conduit; here the crooked passageway of the vagina').[61] Herder's 1776
version chastely avoids the issue altogether, although his more literal
reading of 1778 is no more explicit. Goethe follows Luther's suggestive
'Lustgarten' ('pleasure garden'), not followed by the innocent Herder.

[14]*Narden mit Saffran, Kalmus und Cynamen mit allerley bewmen des
Weyrauchs, Myrrhen und Aloes mit allen besten Würtzen,*
Following the original, Luther repeats his use of 'Narden' ('spikenard').
Herder, however, uses 'Cimmet' ('cinnamon') instead, rather than repeating 'Krokus' ('saffron'). Luther follows the Hebrew with 'mit allerley bewmen' ('with all kinds of trees'), as does Goethe. Herder omits
any reference to trees. Likewise, Herder is not quite close enough with
'mit allen treflichen Würzen' ('with all excellent spices'), although
even this is omitted in 1776. As the Hebrew suggests 'chief', 'main',
'most popular' or possibly 'best', Luther's 'best' and Goethe's 'treff-
lichst' ('most excellent') are closer.

[15]*Wie ein Gartenbrun, wie ein Born lebendiger Wasser, die von Libano
fliessen.*
Herder follows the Hebrew plural with 'Gärten' ('gardens'). He inverts
in the relative clause 'die rinnen von Libanon' ('which run from Lebanon'), using the more evocative verb 'strömen' ('stream') in 1776.
Luther uses 'Born' ('fountain'), while Herder uses 'Quell' ('spring').
Earlier we noted that Herder used 'Quell(e)' where Luther did so, and
'Brunn' ('well') where Luther used 'Born'. Goethe shadows Luther
closely with 'ein Garten Brunn, ein Born lebendiger Wasser' ('a garden
well, a fountain of living waters').

[16]*Stehe auff Nordwind und kom Sudwind, und webe durch meinen
Garten, das seine Würtze trieffen.*
The position of Herder's imperatives symmetrically supports the nouns
in 'erhebe dich, Nord! und Südwind, komm' (literally 'arise, north
wind! and south wind, come'). Herder uses the inseparable 'durchweh'
('blow through'), and he is perhaps more accurate with 'fließen'
('flow') than Luther's 'trieffen' ('trickle'), given that the Hebrew נזל
means 'flow'.

61. *Biblische Liebeslieder*, p. 90 n. 35.

Luther: Chapter Five
[17]*Mein Freund kome in seinen Garten, und esse seiner edlen Früchten.*
Luther designates this as v. 17, but includes it at the beginning of Song of Songs 5 in both his translations. Herder uses 'Geliebter' ('lover') for Luther's 'Freund' ('friend'), and he uses the accusative singular in 'esse seine köstliche Frucht' ('eat his delicious fruit'), while Luther uses the genitive plural.

[1]*Ich kom, meine Schwester, liebe Braut, in meinen Garten, Ich habe meine Myrrhen sampt meinen Würtzen abgebrochen, Ich hab meins Seims sampt meinem Honige gessen, Ich hab meins Weins sampt meiner Milch getruncken, Esset meine Lieben, und trinckt meine Freunde und werdet truncken.*
Luther uses the present tense 'kom' ('come'), while Herder and Goethe use the imperfect 'kam' ('came'). As the perfect in Hebrew may also express a definite future act, Luther is arguably closer. Herder's translation does not acknowledge Luther's 'sampt' ('together with'). Luther uses the perfect 'habe gessen' ('have eaten') and 'hab getruncken' ('have drunk'), whereas Herder uses the imperfect 'aß' ('ate') and 'trank' ('drank'). Luther favours the genitive, while Herder prefers 'von' ('of') with the dative. Herder uses 'meine Geliebten' ('my beloved ones') and 'ihr Lieben' ('you loved ones') for Luther's 'meine Lieben' ('my loved ones') and 'meine Freunde' ('my friends'). He inverts with 'trinkt, und werdet trunken, ihr Lieben' ('drink and become drunk, you loved ones'). He is closer to Luther here in 1778 than in his freer translation of 1776.

[2]*Ich schlaff, Aber mein hertz wacht, Da ist die stim, meins Freundes der anklopffet. Thu mir auff liebe Freundin meine schwester, meine Taube, meine frome, Denn mein heubt ist vol tawes, und meine locken vol nachtstropffen.*
Herder is succinct with 'Stimme meines Geliebten! Er klopft!' ('voice of my loved one! He knocks!'). Unlike 1776, he moves away from Luther in 1778 with the diminutive 'Täubchen' ('little dove'). Perhaps more accurately and, given his innocent approach, not unexpectedly, he uses 'Reine' ('pure woman') for Luther's 'frome' ('pious woman'), and repeats the inverted imperative 'Thu auf mir' ('open up for me') (as in 1776), presumably for poetic effect. In 1778 he omits the rest of this verse, although he includes it in 1776. It is just possible that he omitted

this section inadvertently, for he draws attention to it in his commentary (VIII, pp. 510 and 513). Goethe is very close to Luther throughout.

[3]*Ich habe meinen Rock ausgezogen, wie sol ich jn wider anziehen? Ich habe meine Füsse gewasschen, wie sol ich sie wider besuddeln?*
Herder's 'mein Kleid ist ausgezogen' ('my dress has been taken off') avoids Luther's active voice. In 1776 he is very economical, although assuming greater poetic licence, with the inverted 'Entkleidet . . soll ich an mich wieder kleiden? Gewaschen . . soll mein Fuß sich neu bestäuben?' (literally 'undressed . . must I dress again? Washed . . must my foot become dusty again?'). Goethe adopts Luther's 'besudeln' ('soil'), as does Herder (following Goethe?) in 1778.

[4]*Aber mein Freund steckt seine Hand durchs loch, Und mein Leyb erzittert da für.*
Herder uses the imperfect 'streckte' ('stretched') and 'bebte' ('trembled'), whereas in 1776 he uses the more poetic 'rauscht' (literally 'rustled') and 'zitterte' ('quivered'). The original חר ('hole') probably refers to the keyhole, thus Luther's 'Loch' ('hole') is closer than Goethe's 'Schalter' ('window') or Herder's (culturally determined?) 'Gitter' ('railing'). The Hebrew plural מעים means 'bowels', 'intestines', 'womb', 'belly', 'the inmost part' or 'the heart', so in this context Herder is closer than Luther with 'mein Innres' ('my innermost parts'). Goethe shows independence with 'mich überliefs' ('I was overcome').

[5]*Da stund ich auff, das ich meinem Freunde auffthet, Meine hende troffen mit Myrrhen, und Myrrhen lieffen uber meine Finger an dem rigel am schlos,*
Economically Herder uses an infinitive of purpose in 'zu thun ihm auf' ('to open up for him'), thus avoiding Luther's subjunctive. He uses the singular 'Hand' ('hand') in 1776, but the plural 'Hände' ('hands') in 1778. He avoids Luther's 'mit' ('with') in 1778 with the elliptical 'meine Hände troffen Myrrhen' (literally 'my hands dripped myrrh'), but he uses 'von' ('from') in 1776. Similarly he uses 'meine Finger troffen Myrrhen' ('my fingers dripped myrrh'), changing the subject from Luther's 'Myrrhen'. Whereas Luther uses one verb only in his final clause here, Herder uses a relative clause as well, and the verbs 'troffen' ('dripped') and 'liefen' ('ran'). While the Hebrew is plural, both translators use the singular 'Ri(e)gel' ('bolt').

⁶*Und da ich meim Freund auffgethan hatte, war er weg und hin gegangen. Da gieng meine Seele er aus nach seim wort, Ich sucht jn, Aber ich
fand jn nicht, Ich rieff, Aber er antwortet mir nicht.*
While Luther uses a pluperfect, Herder uses an imperfect. He inverts in
'auf that ich meinem Lieben' ('I opened [the door] for my love'), and
follows the original by repeating 'Lieber' ('lover'), while Luther uses a
pronoun. He uses the two past participles 'entwichen' ('fled') and 'ver-
schwunden' ('disappeared'), he more correctly uses a conjunction and
verb in 'da er zu mir sprach'('when he spoke to me'), and he rightly
insists on the direct object in 'ich rief ihn' ('I called him'). He translates
the first part of the second sentence in 1778, having omitted it in 1776,
perhaps demonstrating a move here in the direction of Luther.

⁷*Es funden mich die Hüter die in der Stad umbgehen, die schlugen mich
wund, Die Hüter auff der mauren namen mir meinen Schleier.*
While Luther uses the impersonal verb form, Herder inverts with 'mich
fanden die Hüter' ('the watchmen found me'). A deletion in MS(a),
p. 31 shows that although Herder originally intended to split this line in
the middle to form two lines, he changed his mind to increase the line-
length. As above, Herder's 'die Stadt umgehn' ('to walk around the
city') is debatable, compared with Luther's 'in der Stad umbgehen' ('to
walk around in the city'). Luther economically has 'schlugen mich
wund' (literally 'they beat me sore'), while Herder follows the original
parallelism of 'sie schlugen mich, sie verwundten mich' ('they beat me,
they hurt me'). Herder inverts with 'sie raubten mir den Schleier, die
Hüter der Mauern' (literally 'they stole my veil, the watchmen of the
walls'). Luther changes the meaning slightly by using the preposition
'auff' ('on') rather than the genitive. Luther's 'namen' ('took') (followed by Goethe) and Herder's 'raubten' ('stole') are too strong for the
original נשא, which means merely 'lift up'. Again in 1778 Herder is
further away from Luther than he is in 1776 when he too uses 'nahmen'
('took').

⁸*Ich beschwere euch jr Töchter Jerusalem, findet jr meinen Freund, so
saget jm, das ich fur Liebe kranck lige.*
Luther uses inversion to form the conditional. Herder retains the question in the original with 'was wollt ihr ihm sagen?' ('what do you want
to say to him?'), while Luther economically uses the imperative only.
Herder's 'bin' ('am') is more accurate than Luther's 'lige' ('lie'). In

1778 we note again Herder's use of 'für' rather than 'vor', following Luther as well as stressing the primitivity of his document.

[9]*Was ist dein Freund fur andern Freunden, O du schönst unter den Weibern? Was ist dein Freund fur andern Freunden, das du uns so beschworen hast?*
Herder uses 'dein Geliebter vor Geliebten' ('your lover before all others'), and he uses the imperfect 'beschwurst' ('conjured').

[10]*Mein Freund ist weis und rot, auserkoren unter viel tausent.*
Herder's 'ein Panier aus zehnmal Tausenden' (literally 'a banner from tens of thousands') appears to be a mistranslation. Apart from the specific number given in 1778, for which there is no evidence, the Hebrew דגול means 'set up a banner', or, as a passive participle, 'distinguished' or 'marked out'. It is the noun דגל which means 'banner' or 'flag'. Luther's 'auserkoren' ('chosen'), supported by the Vulgate's 'electus', is apparently more correct. Herder is actually more accurate in 1776 with the simple 'Einer aus Tausenden' ('one of thousands'). Goethe again follows Luther in all but orthography.

[11]*Sein Heubt ist das feinest Gold. Seine Locken sind kraus, schwartz wie ein Rabe.*
While Luther supplies the verb, Herder omits it, as in the Hebrew.

[12]*Seine Augen sind wie Taubenaugen an den wasserbechen, mit milch gewasschen, und stehen in der fülle.*
Herder's 'seine Augen wie die Täubchen' (literally 'his eyes like the little doves' or 'his eyes like those of little doves') could contain a definite article followed by a plural noun, but 'die' ('the/those of') is more likely to be a demonstrative pronoun, with 'Täubchen' ('little doves') a genitive plural. My remarks above on Luther's 'Taubenaugen' ('doves' eyes') are valid here too. Herder translates the final phrase with 'in Fülle schwimmend' (literally 'swimming in fullness'), failing, like Luther, to bring out fully the meaning and implication of the original. Depending on the pointing, the Hebrew מלאת can mean 'fullness/ abundance (of waters)', or it can refer to the eye within the eye-socket, or, as the construct form of מלאה, even to the setting of a gem. Goethe again follows Luther closely throughout.

[13]*Seine Backen sind wie die wachsende wurtzgertlin der Apoteker.*
Seine Lippen sind wie Rosen die mit fliessender Myrrhen trieffen.
Herder translates with the culturally biased 'Blumenbeete, wie Kästgen
Würze' ('flower beds, like caskets of spice'). The plural of 'Blumenbeete' ('flower beds') is undoubtedly a misreading on Herder's part,
because the feminine singular ערוגה ('garden-bed') is given in the
construct chain ערוגת הבשם ('a bed of balsam spices') where the singular in the construct state looks at first glance rather like the plural in the
absolute state ערוגות. Luther's 'Apoteker' ('apothecaries') suggests a
cultural bias. Goethe too has 'Würzgärtlein' ('little spice gardens').

[14]*Seine Hende sind wie güldene Ringe vol Türkissen. Sein Leib ist wie*
rein Elphenbein mit Saphiren geschmuckt.
As in verse 13, Herder follows Hebrew ellipsis by omitting Luther's
'wie' ('like'). His 'Bauch' ('belly') is inaccurately more specific than
Luther's 'Leib' ('body'). Having used 'Edelstein' ('precious stone') in
1776, his 'Tyrkiße' ('turquoise') of 1778 moves towards Luther.

[15]*Seine Beine sind wie Marmelseulen, gegründet auff gülden füssen.*
Seine gestallt ist wie Libanon, ausserwelt wie Cedern.
Herder prefers 'Schenkel' ('legs') here, again following the original by
not supplying a verb. His singular 'Fuß' ('foot') does not bear out the
plural in the Hebrew which is rendered by Luther. His 'Ansehn'
('countenance') differs from Luther's 'gestallt' ('form') (predictably
followed by Goethe), although the Hebrew מראה can mean either
'appearance' or 'form'. This again exemplifies the independence of
Herder's work where he felt it necessary. His 'erhaben wie ein Cederbaum' ('sublime as a cedar tree') is rather loose, with Luther (and
Goethe) closer with 'ausserwelt' ('chosen') and the plural noun.

[16]*Seine Kele ist süsse und gaantz lieblich, Ein solcher ist mein Freund,*
mein Freund ist ein solcher, jr töchter Jerusalem.
Herder inverts with 'und ganz Er Lieblichkeiten' ('and he [is] full of
charms'). Throughout, Herder omits any verb in this passage, as in the
original. Luther's 'lieblich' ('lovely') refers to 'Kele' ('throat'), while
Herder's 'Lieblichkeiten' ('charms'), used almost adjectivally, correctly
refers to the lover himself.

Luther: Chapter Six

¹⁷*Wo ist denn dein Freund hin gegangen, O du schönest unter den Weibern? Wo hat sich dein Freund hin gewand? So wöllen wir mit dir jn suchen.*

In the same way as at the beginning of Song of Songs 5, Luther assigns the number 17 to this verse, although he includes it at the beginning of Song of Songs 6 in both his translations. The division is not clear in either of Herder's translations. Herder begins this section with 'und', a conjunction not in the original Hebrew. He again uses 'Geliebter' ('lover') for Luther's 'Freund' ('friend'), and uses the imperfect for Luther's perfect tense. While Herder uses 'wo' ('where') in 1776, his 'wohin' ('whither') of 1778 reflects Luther's split interrogative. Luther's 'unter den Weibern' ('among the women') is closer to the prepositional בנשׁים ('among the women') than is Herder's genitive 'der Weiber' ('of the women'), which may follow Goethe. Like Luther, Herder inverts in the final sentence.

¹*Mein Freund ist hin ab gegangen in seinen Garten, zu den Wurtzgertlin, das er sich weide unter den Garten und Rosen breche.*
Herder again uses 'Lieber' ('lover'), and the imperfect 'ging' ('went'). As above, he uses 'Blumenbeete' ('flower beds') for Luther's 'Wurtzgertlin' ('little spice gardens'). He uses the infinitives 'zu weiden' ('to graze') and 'zu sammlen' ('to gather'), while Luther uses a purpose clause with the subjunctive, making 'weiden' ('graze') reflexive. Again we note the different words used for the flower. Herder uses the gentle and innocent 'sammlen' ('gather') ('sammeln' in 1776, used before rather than after 'weiden'), while Goethe and Luther use the more aggressive 'pflücken' ('pick') and 'brechen' ('pluck') respectively.

²*Mein Freund ist mein, und ich bin sein, der unter den Rosen sich weidet.*
Herder's 'mein Lieber, ich bin sein, mein Lieber, er ist mein' ('my lover, I am his, my lover, he is mine') follows the original reversal more accurately than Luther, to whom Herder is actually closer in 1776.

³*Du bist schön, meine Freundin, wie Thirza, lieblich wie Jerusalem, schrecklich wie Heerspitzen*
Herder inaccurately uses the singular 'Kriegsheer' ('army of warriors') for Luther's 'Heerspitzen' ('troops with banners'), which is emulated

by Goethe. My comments under Song 5.10 demonstrate that Herder's 'Kriegspanier' ('banner of war') of 1776 is more correct, although the Hebrew is plural. The full phrase, 'schrecklich, ein Kriegspanier' ('terrible, [as] a banner of war'), is proved to be an ellipsis, for in MS(3), fol. 29ʳ Herder has crossed out the 'wie' ('how') to which he returns in 1778.

[4](*Wende deine Augen von mir, Denn sie machen mich brünstig) Deine Har sind wie ein herd Ziegen, die auff dem berge Gilead geschoren sind.* [5]*Deine Zeene sind wie ein herd Schaf, die aus der schwemme komen, die allzu mal Zwilling tragen, und ist keine unfruchtbar unter jnen.* [6]*Deine Wangen sind wie ein Ritz am Granatapffel, zwisschen deinen zöpffen.*

Referring to the eyes, Herder translates with 'sie sind mächtiger, als ich' ('they are mightier than I'). In the Hiphil, the Hebrew רהב can mean 'enlarge', 'puff up', 'excite' or 'overcome', so both translators are essentially correct, although predictably Herder's reading is more chaste than Luther's, and certainly more innocent than might have been the case. Indeed, referring to the gaze of the eyes, his 1776 rendering is the rather weak 'ich ertrag' ihn nicht' ('I cannot bear it'). Goethe follows Luther in the first two clauses, but omits the rest of this section. The original Hebrew passage from 'deine har' ('your hair') to the end of verse 6 is identical to that in Song of Songs 4, except that 'mountain' is added, the comparison of the lips is omitted, and רחלים ('ewes', 'female lambs') replaces הקצובות, commented on above under Song 4.2. Like the Hebrew, the passage in Herder also is almost identical to the parallel passage above. Luther is very similar, although 'har' ('hair') is now plural, he omits 'mit beschnitten wolle' ('with shorn wool'), and he alters the word order. He keeps 'Ritz am Granatapffel' ('split in the pomegranate'), and Herder too adopts this rendering (as in 1776) instead of his 'aufgeritzter Apfel' ('apple split open') discussed above. Attention is drawn to my comments on פלח under Song 4.3. In 1778 Herder wrongly uses the singular 'Wange' ('cheek'), although he uses the plural in 1776. MS(3), fol. 29ʳ shows that Herder finally deleted 'kommend' in 'gebadet <kommend> aus der Quelle' (literally 'bathed <coming> from the spring'). Goethe economically omits this repeated section.

[7]*Sechzig ist der Königinnen, und achzig der Kebsweiber, und der Jung-frawen ist kein zal.*

Luther's 'Kebsweiber' ('concubines') is closer to the original פִּילַגְשִׁים ('concubines' or 'prostitutes') than is Herder's 'Bulerinnen' ('rivals'). Here is another example of Herder striving to maintain the purity of his reading, and we note his change from 'Lustgespielen' (literally 'com-panions of pleasure') in 1776. Like Luther, Goethe too uses 'König-innen' ('queens'), 'Kebsweiber' ('concubines') and 'Jungfrauen' ('vir-gins').

[8]*Aber eine ist meine Taube, mein Frome, eine ist jrer Mutter die liebste, und die ausserwelete jrer Mutter. Da sie die Töchter sahen, preiseten sie dieselbige selig, die Königinnen und Kebsweiber lobeten sie.*

Herder continues to stress purity with 'Reine' ('pure woman'), having used 'Treue' ('faithful woman') in 1776. Goethe has 'Fromme' ('pious woman'), following Luther. The next clause literally reads 'she is the only one of her mother', and Herder and Luther both attempt to convey the sense rather than the words. Herder uses the peculiarly German impersonal construction 'es sahen sie die Töchter' (literally 'it saw her the daughters', where 'daughters' is the subject), while Luther uses the conjunction 'da' ('as/when').

[9]*Wer ist die erfür bricht, wie die Morgenröte, schön wie der Mond, ausserwelet wie die Sonne, schrecklich wie die Heerspitzen.*

Although Herder follows Luther in 1776 with 'bricht hervor' ('sallies forth'), he asserts his independence in 1778 with 'aufglänzt' ('shim-mers'). Goethe's 'wer ist die hervorblickt wie die Morgenröthe?' ('who is this who looks out like the dawn?') is closest to the original. My comments on Luther's 'Heerspitzen' ('troops with banners') (now with the definite article) and Herder's 'Kriegsheer' ('army of warriors') under Song 6.3 pertain here too. Herder uses the softer 'lieblich' ('lovely') for Luther's 'schön' ('beautiful'), and the purer 'rein' ('unsul-lied') for 'ausserwelet' ('chosen'), although in 1776 he uses 'schön' ('beautiful') and 'hell' ('bright'). There is clearly some disagreement between the two translators here. Given that the Hebrew יָפֶה means 'beautiful', and בָּרָה means 'chosen' or 'selected', Luther is apparently closer. Herder follows Luther's 'schrecklich' ('terrible') in 1776, but distances himself in favour of 'furchtbar' ('dreadful') in 1778.

¹⁰*Ich bin hin ab in den Nussgarten gegangen, zu schawen die Streuchlin am Bach, zu schawen ob der Weinstock blühet, ob die Granatepffel grüneten.*

Herder inverts with 'zum Nußgarten war ich gangen' (literally 'to the nut orchard I had gone'), using a pluperfect rather than Luther's perfect. His archaic past participle is undoubtedly intended to underline the primitive nature of the original. His 'Früchte' ('fruits') is less accurate than Luther's 'Streuchlin' ('little shrubs'), given that the original (construct state plural) אבי means 'young shoots', 'buds' or 'sprouts'. He uses 'Sträuch'' ('shrubs') in 1776, but demonstrates his independence of Luther in 1778. His 'Thal' ('valley') differs from Luther's 'Bach' ('brook'), although the Hebrew נחל ('brook', 'stream', 'torrent', 'valley', 'gorge' or 'ravine') shows that both translations are possible. As Herder uses 'Bach' ('brook') in 1776, we have here yet another instance of his moving away from Luther in 1778. Goethe is again economical with 'das grünende Thal' ('the verdant valley'), a substantive which Herder may have copied. Luther's 'blühet' ('blossoms') is almost certainly a short form of the imperfect subjunctive, given the 'grüneten' ('becoming green') which follows. Herder uses the subjunctive 'knöspe' ('bud').

¹¹*Meine Seele wusts nicht, das er mich zum wagen Ami-Nadib gesetzt hette.*

Herder's inverted translation 'und wußte nicht, daß meine Seele mich gesetzt zum Kriegswagen meines edlen Volks' ('and knew not that my soul had placed me as the chariot of my noble people') is very different from Luther's. Firstly, the implied subject of 'wußte' ('knew') is the first person singular. Secondly, 'meine Seele' ('my soul') is the subject of 'setzen' ('place') in Herder, while it is 'er' ('he') in Luther. Although Herder is freer in 1776 with 'zu meines freien Volkes Schutz gesatzt [...]' ('placed as protection for my free people [...]'), he is still closer to his 1778 translation than to Luther.

The Hebrew עמי נדיב literally reads 'Ami-Nadib'. This is followed by the Vulgate ('Aminadab') and the Septuagint ('Αμιναδάβ'), and retained by Luther. Herder pointed out that the name did not appear in Solomonic history, nor was it a known heroic name, although one of the heroes who survived David was called Ammisabad (1 Chron. 27.6), and in 1 Kgs 4.14 we read of an Ahi-Nadab (see VIII, p. 618). Literally עמי means 'my people', and נדיב as a substantive means 'noble', 'prince' or 'tyrant', although as an adjective it signifies 'generous', 'liberal' or even 'princely'. Herder appears to be closer to the original in 1778, although he wrongly uses the singular 'Kriegswagen' ('chariot of war').

This section is omitted by Goethe, and, as noted in the previous chapter, other commentators such as Falk clearly prefer to avoid its obscurity. A study of various English translations shows how varied the interpretations have been, and explains why this passage is regarded as difficult. For example, the KJV has 'made me like the chariots of Amminadib', although the marginal reference reads 'or set me on the chariots of my willing people'; the Interlinear Version reads 'set me on the chariots of my princely people'; the RSV has 'in a chariot beside my prince'; the GNB translates with 'eager for love as a chariot driver is for battle'; and the NEB reads 'she made me feel more than a prince reigning over the myriads of his people'. According to Herder's statement, this song of interruption is sung by the woman, although all the above versions hold that the man is the speaker, except for the RSV, which is supported by the feminine past participle in the French rendering: 'Je me suis imprudemment laissée entraîner au milieu des chars d'un cortège de prince' ('I foolishly permitted myself to be carried into the midst of the chariots of a princely procession'). We noted in the previous chapter Herder's claim to have interpreted this verse correctly, an example of his very dogmatic approach.

[12]*Kere wider, kere wider, o Sulamith, kere wider, kere wider, das wir dich schawen, Was sehet jr an Sulamith, den Reigen zu Mahanaim?*
Herder uses 'kehr' um' ('turn round') here, although in 1776 he uses 'um' ('round') and 'wieder' ('back'). His 'daß wir dich schaun' ('that we may look at you') of 1776 is closer to Luther than in his 'wir wollen dich schaun' ('we want to look at you') of 1778, another example of his abandoning Luther. As above, Luther prefers a purpose clause. In 1778 Herder introduces the modal verb in 'was wollet ihr schaun?' ('what do you want to look at?'). As with 'Ami-Nadib', Luther chooses not to translate 'Mahanaim', possibly assuming it to be a place name. In fact the Hebrew מחנים suggests the dance of 'camps' or 'armies', and the Vulgate follows with 'choros castrorum'. Clearly Herder is closer with 'Gottesheere' ('divine armies') in both his translations, although there is no evidence in the original for the divine nature with which Herder endows his armies. Goethe is closer than Luther with ' [...] Tanz der Engel' (' [...] dance of the angels'), but further away than Herder.

Luther: Chapter Seven
¹*Wie schön ist dein gang in den Schuhen, du Fürsten tochter. Deine Lenden stehen gleich an einander, wie zwo Spangen, die des Meisters hand gemacht hat.*

Here we have another example of Herder's inability to reach a definitive translation. Apart from the versions given in Appendix A, MS(1) has 'schön' ist, o schön dein Tritt in seinem Schmuck / du Königskind' ('beautiful, oh beautiful [is] your footstep in its jewelled finery / you regal child'). MS(2) is identical to MS(3), apart from the exclamation marks at the end. Herder correctly uses the plural 'Tritte' ('footsteps'), although he uses the singular in 1776. Goethe's 'schön ist dein Gang in den Schuen, o Fürstentochter' (literally 'beautiful is your gait in its shoes, oh prince's daughter') further exemplifies reliance on Luther, who again splits a compound noun with 'Fürsten tochter' ('prince's daughter'). The Hebrew נדיב ('prince') is the same word 'nadib' commented on under Song 6.11. Luther's 'Lenden', copied by Goethe, is a little ambiguous, given that the word may mean 'hips', 'loins' or 'thighs'. The original construct chain חמוקי ירכיך suggests 'joints/curves of your thighs'. Herder's singular 'Hüft'' ('hips') of 1776 is arguably more chaste than his surprisingly erotic 'Schwingungen deiner Hüften' ('curves of your hips', or even 'swinging of your hips') of 1778. Goethe again follows Luther, as he does with 'Spangen' ('bangles'). Herder again shows his independence of Luther and his knowledge of the Hebrew, for in both translations he correctly renders חלאים ('jewels' or 'links of a chain') as 'Kettenwerk' ('chain work'). Rather than following Luther's relative clause, Herder is more economical with 'geschlungen von Meistershand' ('turned by a master's hand').

²*Dein Nabel ist wie ein runder Becher, dem nimer getrenck mangelt. Dein Bauch ist wie ein Weitzenhauffe umbsteckt mit Rosen.*
All three translators choose 'Nabel' ('navel') to translate the Hebrew root word שרר, although apart from 'navel' the Hebrew word may also mean 'vulva', and almost certainly does in this context. Herder's choice is in keeping with his chaste reading, and the often scatological Luther undoubtedly saw the need not to shock his readers. Goethe's rendering is surprisingly chaste, especially in the light of one of the (early) epigrams from his *Nachlaß*: 'Hättest du Mädchen wie deine Kanäle, Venedig, und F... / Wie die Gäßchen in dir, wärst du die herrlichste

Stadt.'[62] Although I shall comment in the next chapter on the work of nineteenth-century commentators such as Johann Christoph Döderlein, Wilhelm Friedrich Hufnagel, Friedrich Wilhelm Carl Umbreit and Georg August Heinrich Ewald, it is important to note that they translated here a little more closely with 'Schooß' or 'Schoos' ('womb/lap'). Umbreit acknowledged the difficulty of the verse: ' "שׁרר" eigentlich *Nabel* muß hier, wenn die Vergleichung einen Sinn haben soll, nothwendig für den ganzen Unterleib stehen [...]; wir können es durch *Schooß* geben.'[63] Ewald's 'Schooß rund und duftend' ('womb/lap, round and fragrant') also hints at a less innocent interpretation than that of Herder. He conceded that 'es ist wahr, daß dieser Vers etwas schwülstig ist' ('it is true that this verse is somewhat turgid in style').[64] Indeed, Falk accepts that the Hebrew probably refers to the vulva, although even she avoids the problem by using the innocuous 'hips' in her translation, pleading that the word—especially used in conjunction with 'bowl of nectar'—is at least more correctly erotic than 'navel'. Her need to circumlocute is based on her assertion that 'English has no word that is not either clinical or pornographic in tone',[65] although surely she is not right here.

Goethe economically has 'Becher der Fülle' ('goblet of fullness'), while Herder has 'dem's nimmer an Maas gebricht' ('which is never short of content') in 1778. Luther and Herder in 1776 ('nie gebricht ihm süßer Trank' ['it never lacks sweet drink']) are closer to the Hebrew, which refers to mixed or mingled wine. In Song 5.14, Herder translates with 'Bauch' ('belly'), and now does so again, following Luther, even though the Hebrew is different here. Both Herder and Luther use 'Rosen' ('roses'), although Herder adds 'umpflanzt' ('planted around

62. 'If you had girls like your canals, oh Venice, and c... like your alleyways, you would be the most splendid city.' Ernst Beutler (ed.), *Sämtliche Werke* (18 vols.; Zürich: Artemis Verlag, 1950; repr. Munich: Deutscher Taschenbuch Verlag, 1977), II, p. 182. It is interesting that David Luke provides an unexpurgated version of both the original and a translation in his *Johann Wolfgang von Goethe: Erotic Poems* (The World's Classics; Oxford: Oxford University Press, 1997), pp. 70 and 71.

63. 'If the comparison is to have any meaning, "שׁרר", actually *navel*, must of necessity stand here for the whole of the abdominal area [...]; we can render it as *womb/lap*.' *Lied der Liebe: Das älteste und schönste aus dem Morgenlande. Übersetzt und ästhetisch erklärt* (Heidelberg: Mohr, 2nd edn, 1828), p. 62 n. g.

64. *Das Hohelied Salomo's* (Göttingen: Deuerlich, 1826), p. 135.

65. *Love Lyrics from the Bible*, p. 127.

with'). MS(a), p. 41 shows a deletion in '<mit Rosen> umpflanzt mit Rosen' ('<with roses> planted around with roses'), demonstrating that Herder's inversion is deliberate. Goethe and Herder (in both translations) omit 'wie' ('like/as'), producing an ellipsis. Arguably this is an example of Herder's imitating Goethe. Indeed, Bock notes the 'sensuous realism' achieved by Goethe,[66] yet this ellipsis is present in the original Hebrew. As we have seen above, ellipsis is a characteristic of Hebrew poetry, and thus it is more likely that Herder was following the Hebrew rather than Goethe.

[3]*Deine zwo Brüste sind, wie zwey junge Rehe zwillinge.*
Luther again splits the compound noun, but he is more economical than Herder's more accurate 'Rehchen, die einer Mutter Zwillinge sind' ('young fawns, which are twins of one mother').

[4]*Dein Hals ist wie ein Elffenbeinen thurm. Deine Augen sind, wie die Teiche zu Hesbon, am thor Bathrabbim. Deine Nase ist wie der Thurm auff Libanon, der gegen Damascon sihet.*
Luther splits the compound noun in the first sentence. He again chooses not to translate an awkward word, leaving 'Bathrabbim'. In this he is followed by Goethe, by Herder in 1776, and indeed by most translators. However, the Hebrew construct chain בת־רבים means 'women/daughters of the mighty ones', and thus Herder's 'Fürstentöchter' ('prince's daughters') of 1778 suggests a careful reading of the original and is another example of where he is further away from Luther in 1778 than in 1776. The Hebrew word מגדל, used twice in this verse and translated on both occasions by Luther as 'Thurm' ('tower') (and Goethe as 'Turn'), could also mean 'raised bank of flowers', although this is unlikely here. Herder uses the imaginative and courtly 'Lustbau' ('pleasure palace') in 1776, and the Western 'Schloß' ('castle') in 1778. The considerable deletions in MS(3) show how Herder struggled with this word, rejecting 'Lustschloß' ('pleasure castle'), for example, which was doubtless too explicit for his chaste interpretation. Again Goethe and Herder produce an ellipsis, as in the Hebrew, by omitting Luther's 'wie' ('like/as').

66. 'A Tower of Ivory?', p. 19.

⁵Dein Heubt stehet auff dir, wie Carmelus. Das Har auff deinem heubt, ist wie die purpur des Königs in falten gebunden.

With 'dein Haupt wie Karmel' ('your head like Carmel') in 1776, Herder economically avoids the verb, preposition and pronoun used by Luther. In 1778 he follows closely the Hebrew עָלַיִךְ ('upon you') with 'dein Haupt auf dir' (literally 'your head upon you'). He uses the uninverted genitive in 'das Haar deines Hauptes' ('the hair of your head'), having opted for the more primitive 'deines Hauptes Haar' (literally 'your head's hair') in 1776. Due to the lack of punctuation in Hebrew, the following section is unclear. In 1778 Herder has 'wie Purpur, ein geflochtner Königsbund' ('like purple, a plaited royal head-dress'), while in 1776 he is more economical, although less literal, with 'ein Königsdiadem' ('a royal diadem'). Goethe is again almost identical to Luther, although the Hebrew could be read as 'the hair of your head is like purple; a king is held captive in [its] tresses'.

⁶Wie schön und wie lieblich bistu, du Liebe in wollüsten.

Goethe again follows Luther here, while the chaste Herder opts for a lower degree of desire with the relatively less erotic 'Lust' ('pleasure').

⁷Deine Leng ist gleich einem Palmbawm, und deine Brüste den Weindrauben.

Herder is more poetic in 1776 with 'ein Palmbaum blüht dein schlanker Wuchs empor' (literally '[like] a palm tree your slim figure blossoms upwards'), using 'Höhe' ('height') in 1778 for Luther's 'Leng' ('length'). Goethe opts for 'Gestalt' ('form'). The Hebrew תָּמָר means 'palm tree', but may also mean 'pillar'. Herder uses the simple word 'Trauben' ('grapes'), although the Hebrew suggests fuller 'clusters of the vine' rather than 'grapes' per se.

⁸Ich sprach, Ich mus auff den Palmbawm steigen, und seine zweige ergreiffen, Las deine Brüste sein wie Drauben am weinstock, und deiner Nasenruch wie Epffel,

Herder uses the elliptical 'deine Brüste sollen mir Trauben seyn' (literally 'your breasts shall be to me [as] grapes'), having used 'Busen' ('bosom') in 1776. While the Hebrew אַף can mean 'nose' or 'nostrils', Herder opts for 'deines Athems Duft' (literally 'your breath's fragrance'), using the inverted genitive. He omits any reference to apples in 1776, but adds 'wie Aepfelduft' ('like the fragrance of apples') in 1778. Goethe follows Luther closely throughout the verse.

[9]*und deine Kele wie guter Wein, der meinem Freunde glat eingehe, und rede von fernigem.*

In both translations, Herder correctly points out the change of speaker from male to female, beginning with the passage rendered by Luther above as 'der meinem Freunde'. Luther's 'Kele' ('throat') is a translation of the same Hebrew word חך ('palate' or 'cavity/roof of the mouth') as in Song 5.16, and Herder retains 'Gaume(n)' ('palate/roof of the mouth') in 1778, having used the more poetic 'Hauch' ('breath') and 'Mund' ('mouth') in 1776. Luther uses the subjunctives 'eingehe' ('go') and 'rede' ('speak'), while Herder uses the inverted 'der einschleicht meinem Lieben süß hinein' ('which steals sweetly upon my love') and the fussier 'und schlummert die Lipp' ihm säuselnd zu' (literally 'and whispering causes his lips to slumber'). The deletions in MS(a), p. 42 demonstrate the difficulty Herder had in translating the inverted clause definitively, for there we read 'der <sanft> <einschleicht> <mir> einschleicht meinem Lieben / <meinem> <Freund> <Lieben> / süß hinein'. Goethe's 'der die schlafenden geschwäzzig macht' ('which makes the sleepers loquacious') is closest to the Hebrew, which literally means 'gently moving the lips of those who are asleep'.

[10]*Mein Freund ist mein, und er helt sich auch zu mir.*

Herder's 'seine Lust zu mir' ('his desire [is] for me') is close to the Hebrew, which literally means 'his desire [is] towards me'. Here he may have considered Goethe's 'bin auch sein ganzes Begehren' (literally '[I] am also his whole desire'). Herder's 1776 translation, 'sein Herz ist ganz an mir' ('his heart is wholly with me') is arguably closer to Luther than is that of 1778.

[11]*Kom mein Freund, las uns auffs feld hin aus gehen, und auff den Dorffen bleiben.*

Herder again uses 'Geliebter' ('beloved'). Both translators use an exhortation, Herder using 'wir wollen [...]' ('let us [...]'). Herder uses 'Land' (countryside'), while Goethe follows Luther's 'Feld' ('field/plain'). The Hebrew שדה could be translated both ways. Herder's 'wohnen' ('live') is closer to the Hebrew לין ('lie', 'spend the night', 'lodge') than is Luther's 'bleiben' ('stay', 'remain'), as indeed is Goethe's 'schlafen' ('sleep') (see my comments under Song 1.13). Closer to Luther in 1778, Herder adds to the original in 1776 with

'komm' auf der Unschuld Flur' ('come into the meadow of inno-
cence'), stressing his chaste reading. He omits the definite article in 'auf
Dörfern' ('in villages') in 1778. Goethe is more Germanic with 'auf den
Landhäusern' ('in the country houses').

[12]*Das wir früe auffstehen zu den Weinbergen, Das wir sehen, ob der
Weinstock blühet und augen gewonnen habe, Ob die Granatepffelbewm
ausgeschlagen sind, Da wil ich dir meine Brüste geben.*
Luther again uses a purpose clause, while Herder uses a conjunction in
'und früh dann aufstehn' ('and then arise early'). Luther's 'zu den
Weinbergen' ('to the vineyards') is closer to the Hebrew than is
Herder's singular 'in den Weinberg' ('into the vineyard'). Herder uses
'sehn' ('see') as an infinitive of purpose, while Luther persists with a
subordinate clause. Herder uses the present subjunctives 'blühe'
('blossom') and 'aufthun' ('open'), while Luther uses imperfect and
perfect subjunctives. Herder uses 'Aepfel' ('apples'), while Luther
refers to the tree rather than the fruit. As the Hebrew רמון (see Song
4.13) means 'pomegranate' or 'pomegranate tree', both translators are
essentially correct, although Herder may again be accused of westerniz-
ing his translation. Goethe's 'Granatbäume' ('pomegranate trees') is
close to Luther. The original root word נוץ suggests 'send out buds' or
'be in flower', so both Herder and Luther are correct with 'blühn'
('blossom') and 'ausgeschlagen sind' ('are in leaf') respectively. As
noted above, Herder's 'Liebe' ('love') is more accurate than Luther's
'Brüste' ('breasts'), again exemplifying his careful reading of the original rather than of Luther. In MS(3) Herder inserted and then deleted the
line 'des Frühlings Aeugelein' ('the spring's little buds') between the
lines 'und wie der Obstbaum blüht so schön' ('and as the fruit tree blossoms so wondrously') and 'da Liebster will ich dein' (there, beloved, I
want you').

[13]*Die Lilien geben den ruch, und fur unser thür sind allerley edle
Früchte. Mein Freund ich hab dir beide heurige und fernige behalten.*
Goethe follows Luther again, although 'Lilien' ('lilies') is not as accu-
rate as Herder's 'Blumen der Liebe' ('flowers of love') (1778) and
'Liebes-Blumen' ('love flowers') (1776). The original דודאים suggests
'love apples' or 'mandrakes', but certainly not 'lilies'. We have noted
Herder's innocent reading of this in the previous chapter. MS(3), fol.
33[r] shows that he had difficulty in reaching a decision, originally trans-

lating with 'mir Blumen der Liebe' ('flowers of love for me') before deleting this in favour of 'die Liebes-Blumen mir!' ('the love flowers for me!'). Herder's 'jeder Art' ('of every kind') of 1776 was also changed in MS(3), fol. 33^r from 'aller Art' ('of all kinds'). In 1776 Herder expands with the more culturally biased 'Hütte Thür' ('hut door').

Luther: Chapter Eight
^{1}*O Das ich dich, mein Bruder, der du meiner Mutter brüste saugest draussen fünde, und dich küssen müste, das mich niemand hönete.*
The Hebrew literally means 'who can give you as brother to me?' and thus Herder is closer with 'wer gibt mir dich zum Bruder mir?' (literally 'who gives you to me as a brother to me?'). Luther is less accurate, referring to the lover as a brother in name. Luther uses a subordinate clause of purpose, while Herder uses a main clause with the imperfect subjunctive in 'und keiner verachtete mich' ('and nobody would despise me'). In 1776 he uses 'höhnte' ('would sneer at') in a far freer translation.

Having attempted to follow the Hebrew closely in 1778, Herder buried in his published commentary a freer reiteration of the first three verses of this chapter (VIII, pp. 523-24):

> Ach, daß du nicht mein Bruder bist!
> Und Einer Mutter Brust mit mir geküßt,
> Daß wo ich dich nur fände,
> Ich küßen könnte dich,
> Und niemand hönte mich,
> Und wähnet's Sünde.
> Umfaßen, umschlingen wollt ich dich,
> Und führen dich
> In meiner Mutter Haus.
> Du winktest mir,
> Ich brächte dir
> Den Trank, den ich bereitet,
> Den Most von meinem Baum.
>
> Und seine Linke
> Mir unterm Haupt:
> Und seine Rechte
> Umarmt mich.[67]

67. 'Alas, that you are not my brother! / And had kissed with me the breast of one mother, / That wherever I might find you, / I could kiss you, / And nobody

A comparison with the corresponding version in MS(3) will show its proximity to this additional translation of 1778, a point missed by Gaier in his edition.[68]

2Ich wolt dich füren und in meiner Mutter haus bringen, da du mich leren soltest, Da wolt ich dich trencken mit gemachtem Wein, und mit dem Most meiner Granatepffel.
Herder inverts twice with 'ich wollt dich bringen in meiner Mutter Haus' ('I would like to take you into my mother's house'). Luther's 'wolt' ('would like') is clearly an imperfect subjunctive expressing condition, while Herder uses a straightforward conditional tense. Herder uses a relative clause in the general 'Trank, den ich bereitet' ('draft which I had prepared'), although the Hebrew suggests a particularly 'spiced' wine. Herder chooses not to specify the tree, but his singular is closer to the original 'pomegranate tree' (see Song 4.13 and Song 7.12).

3Seine Lincke ligt unter meinem Heubt, und seine Rechte hertzet mich.
Luther is the same here as in Song of Songs 2, adding 'ligt' ('rests') and not inflecting 'Heubt' ('head'). Herder is the same as before, except for the added 'und'.

4Ich beschwere euch töchter Jerusalem, Das jr meine Liebe nicht auffweckt noch reget, bis das jr selbst gefellet.
Luther is the same as in Song of Songs 2, except for the phrase beginning 'bei den Rehen' ('by the does'), and his use of 'gefellet' ('pleases') for 'gefellt' and 'Liebe' ('love') for 'Freundin' ('[female] friend'). Herder is the same as above, with the same phrase omitted as in Luther, and with the addition of 'die Liebe' (literally 'the love'). MS(3), fol. 33[v] shows that 'reget nicht' ('do not rouse') was ultimately deleted in favour of 'störet nicht' ('do not disturb'), although in 1778 Herder here reverts to Luther.

---

would sneer at me / And believe it to be sinful. / I would like to embrace you and cling to you, / And lead you / Into my mother's house. / You would beckon to me, / I would bring you / The draft which I had prepared, / The wine from my tree. / And his left hand / [Is] beneath my head: / And his right hand / Embraces me.'

68. *Lieder der Liebe*, p. 1234, note to p. 475 line 22.

⁵Wer ist die, die er auff feret von der Wüsten, und lehnet sich auff jren Freund? Unter dem Apffelbawm weckt ich dich, da deine Mutter dich geboren hatte, da mit dir gelegen ist, die dich gezeuget hat.
Herder uses the past participle 'gelehnt' ('leaned') adjectivally, and 'Geliebte(n)' ('beloved') for Luther's 'Freund' ('[male] friend'). His 'da gebar dich deine Mutter, da gebar, die dich gebohren' (literally 'there your mother bore you, there bore the one who gave birth to you') follows Hebrew ellipsis more than Luther. The same verb is repeated in the synonymous parallelism of the original, which literally means 'she was in travail with you, there she was in travail and brought you forth'. As Luther uses three different verbs, Herder could again be deemed closer. Having used 'grüner Baum' ('verdant tree') in MS(1), fol. 58ᵛ, Herder follows Luther in 1776 and 1778.

⁶Setze mich wie ein Siegel auff dein Hertz, und wie ein siegel auff deinen Arm, Denn Liebe ist starck wie der Tod, und Eiuer ist fest wie die Helle, Ir glut ist fewrig, und eine flamme des HERRN,
I gave consideration in the Introduction to the state of the manuscripts and subsequent editions as far as the first clause of this verse is concerned. MS(2) is again identical to MS(3), except that the second indefinite article is omitted, and—as noted twice above—the final exclamation mark is not there. Herder's ellipsis rejects Luther's 'wie' ('like/as'), as on other occasions, although ironically this time the Hebrew also has the prefix כ ('as' or 'like') in the word כחותם ('like a seal/signet-ring'). Goethe follows Luther in the first clause. Herder inverts with 'denn stark, wie der Tod, ist Liebe' (literally 'for strong as death is love'). He introduces the possessive adjective in 'ihr Eifer hart' ('its [i.e. love's] jealousy [is] hard/ruthless'), adding a separate idea to the original, for Luther correctly has no possessive adjective. The Hebrew קשה means 'hard', 'severe', 'unfeeling' or 'cruel', so Herder's 'hart' is closer than Luther's 'fest' ('steadfast') or Goethe's 'gewaltig' ('mighty'). All translators render the Hebrew שאול as 'hell', although 'grave' would be more accurate. Once again Herder follows the original lack of verb with 'ihre Kohlen glühende Kohlen, Flamme des Herrn' ('its embers [are] red-hot embers, flame of the Lord'), the Hebrew literally meaning 'its sparks (flames) are sparks (flames) of fire, a flame of Jehovah'. Herder uses the plural 'Flammen' ('flames') in 1776. Goethe paraphrases with 'eine fressende Flamme' ('a consuming flame').

*⁷Das auch viel Wasser nicht mügen die Liebe auslesschen, noch die
ströme sie erseuffen, Wenn einer alles Gut in seinem hause umb die
Liebe geben wolt, so gülte es alles nichts.*
The deletion in MS(a), p. 58 in 'viel Wasser mögen <sie> nicht aus sie
löschen' (literally 'many waters are not able <it> to quench it') again
typifies Herder's efforts to invert. Luther uses a conditional clause
beginning with 'wenn' ('if'), while Herder uses the imperfect subjunctive in 'gäb' ein Mann auch Haus und Gut' ('were a man to give even
his house and possessions'). While Luther is succinct with 'so gülte es
alles nichts' ('it would all amount to nothing'), Herder is closer to the
Hebrew with the two verbs 'verschmähn' ('disdain') and 'verachten'
('scorn') in both his translations, although the Hebrew uses the same
verb twice. Goethe follows Luther with 'ersaüfen' ('drown'), closing
his translation with this verse.

*⁸Unser Schwester ist klein, und hat keine Brüste, Was sollen wir unser
Schwester thun, wenn man sie nu sol anreden?*
Despite rejecting a dramatic interpretation, Herder introduces a dramatic form here with the subheadings 'der Eine spricht' ('the one
speaks'), 'der Zweite' ('the second') and 'die Schwester' ('the sister'),
using 'A', 'B' and 'C' in 1776. This does not reflect the Hebrew, nor
Luther. Herder's 'noch knospet nur ihr Busen' ('her bosom is still just
budding') is not as close as Luther to the Hebrew, which literally reads
'breasts are not to her'.

There is a fragment in the *Nachlaß* (Kapsel VI 59) which reads:

> Wir haben ein Schwesterlein
> noch klein
> noch ohne Brüstlein
> was woll'n wir mit dem Mägdlein thun
> wenn Zeit kommt, sie zu werben [...].⁶⁹

This is more elaborate than the versions in Appendix A, which in turn
are still folksy in approach.

*⁹Ist sie eine Maure, so wöllen wir silbern Bollwerg drauff bawen. Ist sie
eyne Thür, so wöllen wir sie festigen mit Cedern bolen.*
Although in 1778 Herder is clearly still independent of Luther here, he
is certainly closer than in 1776. He inverts, and introduces an indefinite

69. 'We have a little sister / still small / still without little breasts. / What shall
we do with the maiden / when the time comes to offer her in marriage? [...]'

article and a compound noun in 'so wollen wir auf sie bauen einen Silberpallast' (literally 'thus we wish to build a silver palace upon her'), while Luther opts for an adjective and a noun. Both invert in the final sentence, with Luther using 'festigen' ('make fast'), while Herder, in keeping with his innocent approach, uses the far gentler 'verwahren' ('to have in safe keeping') for the Hebrew צור ('bind' or 'enclose'). He prefers the compound 'Cedernholz' ('cedar wood') to Luther's split and correctly plural compound 'Cedern bolen' ('cedar planks').

[10]*Ich bin eine Maur, und meine Brüste sind wie Thürne, Da bin ich worden fur seinen augen, als die Frieden findet.*
Herder inverts with 'eine Mauer bin ich' (literally 'a wall am I'). Although the original could more sensibly mean 'I was/used to be a wall', neither translator accepts this. In 1778 Herder is closer to Luther than in 1776.

[11]*Salomo hat einen Weinberg zu BaalHamon, Er gab den Weinberg den Hütern, das ein jglicher fur seine Früchte brechte tausent Silberlinge.*
Herder inverts with 'einen Weinberg hatte Salomon' (literally 'a vineyard had Solomon'), ignoring Luther's present tense. The deletions in MS(3), fol. 37[v] demonstrate Herder's indecision about how to translate Baal-Hamon.

[12]*Mein Weinberg ist fur mir. Dir Salomo gebüren tausent, Aber den Hütern zwey hundert sampt seinen Früchten.*
The Hebrew literally means 'my vineyard which [is] to me'. Herder is more expressive than Luther with 'mein Weinberg ist vor Augen mir' ('my vineyard is before my very eyes'). Again there is an ellipsis in Herder's 'die die Frucht ihm hüten' ('those who watch over the fruit for him'), where we note a preference for the verb, a reminder by Herder of the radical nature of the verb in his original primitive source.

[13]*Die du wonest in den Garten, Las mich deine stimme hören, Die Geselschafften mercken drauff.*
Ironically transposing their choices in the previous verse, Herder here chooses the noun 'Wohnerin' ('[female] dweller'), while Luther selects the verb 'wonest' ('dwellest'). Luther uses a preposition and dative plural, while Herder uses a genitive. The main clause in the Hebrew text reads 'the companions listen for your voice, cause me to hear it'.

Herder's inverted 'die Gespielen horchen auf deine Stimme / Laß mich sie hören' (literally 'the companions hearken to your voice. / Let me it hear') is thus closer to the original.

[14]*Fleuch mein Freund, und sey gleich eim Rehe oder jungen Hirssen auff den Würtzbergen.*

Herder denotes a change of speaker with inverted commas, having persisted here in 1776 with 'A' and 'B'. He follows Luther's 'Freund' ('friend') in 1776, but uses 'Geliebter' ('lover') in 1778. While Luther uses an indefinite article in 'gleich eim Rehe oder jungen Hirssen' ('like a doe or young stag'), Herder wrongly uses a definite article in both phrases with 'gleich dem Reh, dem jungen Hirsch'' ('like the doe, the young stag'). He matches Luther's correctly plural compound 'Würtz-berge' ('mountains of spices') with an adjective and a noun in the more poetic 'auf duftender Höh' ('on sweet-smelling height'). As the Hebrew construct הרי בשׂמים means 'mountains of (balsam) spices', Luther is more literal. It is almost as if Herder has opted deliberately to assert his independence, despite having to abandon a literal rendering. Although Herder uses 'fleuch' ('flee') three times altogether in 1776, this is the only instance in 1778. Given that his translation of the Song of Songs was to have formed part of the *Volkslieder*, it is important to note that he also used this archaic form in 'Fleuch zu mir!' ('flee to me!') in his folk-song translation *Alkanzor und Zaida* (XXV, p. 152), thus seeking to underline the primitivity of his original sources.

In this chapter I have considered closely Herder's translations of the Song of Songs, assessing them as poetry and comparing them in detail. With clear examples throughout, I have examined particularly the use and effect of the following: scansion and metre; rhyme and versification (including line-length and enjambment); stanza-size; alliteration, assonance and onomatopoeia; punctuation; alterations, deletions, additions, differences and elaborations (especially in 1776); inversion of different kinds; verbs (tenses, voices and moods); nouns (singular, plural, cases and compounds); articles; adjectives; and (universal) poetic effect vis-à-vis (local) literal accuracy. My comments have shown that Herder's use of these tools, especially in the unpublished drafts, resulted in translations which were closer to European folk-song, and thus more Germanic, than was the published version of 1778.

I have used strong examples to demonstrate ways in which Herder's choices of translation served to underline his peculiarly chaste reading of the work, and I have also shown how certain renderings—particularly prior to the 1778 publication—were determined by his own cultural bias. I have also touched on the debatable mutual influence between Herder and Goethe, and I have shown the extent of the latter's dependence upon Luther as he produced a version rather than a translation.

In this chapter I have assessed the extent of Herder's closeness to and accuracy in rendering the detail of the Hebrew text, and thus my commentary has also provided a basis for querying Clark's claim that Herder's translation of 1778 demonstrated a total move towards Luther. Although it cannot be disputed that Luther was a touchstone and anchorage for Herder, it is clear that the changes between the earlier drafts and the 1778 publication are not all in the direction of Luther. Admittedly, there is evidence in my comments above that in certain instances Herder is closer to Luther in his translation of 1778. However, there is greater evidence that the general pattern is for the changes to be in the direction of the Hebrew text and thus, if necessary, away from Luther. Indeed, I have shown that at times Herder is closer to Luther in 1776 than he is in 1778. The published translation is truer to the original than are the earlier, more creative draft paraphrases, and it represents a more prosaic, interlinear rendering.

Although the changes, then, are by no means all towards Luther, it is certainly beyond doubt that Herder's unrhyming, quasi-interlinear translation of 1778 is closer to the general effect of Luther's 'poetic' prose translation than are his earlier versions. However, as it was German *poetry* rather than prose that Herder was attempting to rescue, he could not produce a prose version like Luther and Goethe, but compromised with a sober verse translation which followed the original very closely. Had Herder used Luther's text instead of his own, it would have detracted from his efforts to show the importance of the Song of Songs as primitive poetry rather than prose.

We have seen that, for Herder, translation was ideally no more than an aid. In his view, no translation could adequately replace the original, although he gladly recommended the use of a translation for comparative purposes. Thus his ideal would have been for his readers to have the original Hebrew to hand, and perhaps also Luther's translation as a guide. It was never Herder's intention to translate for translation's sake. It was rather his initial aim to consider the purpose and spirit of the work (VIII, pp. 535 and 594, and *TB*, X, pp. 132-33). As with Shakespeare's songs, it may be that he translated originally for himself rather than for publication, and we have observed how he almost chose to use Luther's well-established translation rather than his own. The fact that he actually published his own version may be coincidental, for, whatever the end result, he was not making a deliberate attempt to provide an alternative to Luther, whom he respected highly, although his rejection of literary absolutes contradicts his apparent regard of Luther's translation as such. His own work—in every area—was always fluid, and this accounts for his various draft attempts at both commentary and translation. We have noted the many variations of the first line of his translation of the Song of Songs, and this serves as just one very strong example of his inability to produce a result which satisfied him. Indeed, it is surprising that he did not try again after 1778. Had translation per se been his goal, he surely would have done so, but for him it was the interpretation as a whole that was so important.

As with much of his work, then, Herder did not find it easy to produce a definitive version, for even the 1778 translation can hardly be regarded as definitive, given Herder's claim that Luther's was still a more pleasing translation. He admitted that if he had translated 'in einem Sylbenmaasse nach deutschen Mustern' ('in a metre according to German standards') (VIII, p. 529), his version may have been (Germanically?) more satisfying, and we have noted his dissatisfaction with his earlier attempts to place the poetry in a German setting. It was not Herder's desire, however, to lose anything from the original text as a result of 'Verschönerung' ('embellishment')—I have already drawn attention to the negative connotation of the prefix—and he attempted ultimately to reproduce as far as possible the primitive simplicity of the Hebrew (VIII, p. 529). His disclaimer 'so viel es anging' ('as far as it was appropriate to do so') is important, as is his 'soviel möglich' ('as far as possible') noted above.

Herder's comments are particularly significant when read in conjunction with his comments on literary imitation, particularly those in his review of Denis. He attempted to translate in a natural, poetic style without imposing the foreign metre and versification on German poetry, although, of course, it is the very word 'natural' which begs so many questions. Similarly, it was not his wish to impose German verse forms on the original, although at times, as we have noted, he could not avoid betraying his own poetic background, especially in his drafts. Despite the temptations to which he succumbed occasionally, his was an attempt to adopt a middle path by employing neither the Hebrew verse form nor the German.

Whereas MSS(1), (2) and (3) all show a predilection for more emotional paraphrase, the translation of 1778 is far more sober in approach. The draft translations tend to represent an original work in German poetic form rather than a re-creation (in German) of a primitive original. Herder was not attempting to produce original poetry, for his *Lieder der Liebe* was to be a catalyst to show others what German poetry could become. His purpose would have been ruined had his own translations detracted from the Hebrew poetry, and we may assume that it was for this reason that he chose ultimately to reject his earlier drafts and to keep close to the original, both lexically and in terms of simplicity. In attempting to show Hebrew parallelism, for example, he did not attempt to impose the device on German poetry, but demonstrated that it was an effective peculiarity of such primitive poetry. In the same way, Germans were encouraged to produce poetry peculiar to their own nation. Herder's translation of the Song of Songs, then, was for purposes of demonstration rather than to represent an original poetic creation.

The Reception of Lieder der Liebe

Chapter 1 of this study pointed out Herder's perception that his work on the Song of Songs had been poorly received by the journals. His reaction was wrong, in fact, although the reviews were neutral rather than effusive. Moreover, contemporaries of Herder such as Lavater, Gleim, Hamann and Goethe were greatly interested in his study of the Song of Songs.

Given the particular importance of Hamann for the development of Herder's thinking about poetry, his enthusiastic response to *Lieder der Liebe* was significant. In his reply to Herder's letter to him dated 29 December 1778 and 2 January 1779, in which Herder expressed discouragement about his work on the Song of Songs, Hamann wrote: 'Doch glückte es mir noch denselben Abend die *Lieder der Liebe* zu erhalten wornach die Lüsternheit unüberwindlich geworden war, daß ich mich angriff selbige zu stillen. Keins von allen Ihren Schriften hat mir einen so süßen Abend und Eindruck gemacht als dies.'[1]

Goethe's reception of Herder's work on the Song of Songs was of even greater significance, not so much for the impact on his own translation—for, as we have observed, this was published before Herder's *Lieder der Liebe*—but for its contribution to his views on poetry. In the world of creative literature, for example, Herder's *Lieder der Liebe* was a milestone on the way to Goethe's *West-östlicher Divan* of 1819, as can be seen from the latter's notes on this work. Speaking of Oriental poetry in general and the Bible in particular, Goethe acknowledged his debt to Herder and also to Herder's friend Eichhorn: 'Was solche Män-

---

1.   'Yet that same evening I managed to obtain *Lieder der Liebe* for which my desire had become so insurmountable that I had to do my utmost to quieten it. Of all your writings, none has provided me with such a delightful evening and made such an impression upon me as this.' Letter of 21 February 1779, in Walther Ziesemer and Arthur Henkel (eds.), *Johann Georg Hamann: Briefwechsel* (7 vols.; Wiesbaden: Insel-Verlag, 1955–79), IV, p. 51.

ner uns verliehen und hinterlassen, darf nur angedeutet werden, und man verzeiht uns die Eilfertigkeit, mit welcher wir an diesen Schätzen vorüber gehen.'[2] Indeed, one paragraph in particular shows how much Goethe (*WW*, VII, p. 8) had absorbed Herder's highly original interpretation of the Song of Songs:

> Wir verweilen sodann einen Augenblick bei dem hohen Lied, als dem Zartesten und Unnachahmlichsten, was uns von Ausdruck leidenschaftlicher, anmuthiger Liebe zugekommen. Wir beklagen freilich, daß uns die fragmentarisch durcheinander geworfenen, übereinander geschobenen Gedichte keinen vollen reinen Genuß gewähren, und doch sind wir entzückt uns in jene Zustände hinein zu ahnen, in welchen die Dichtenden gelebt. Durch und durch wehet eine milde Luft des lieblichsten Bezirks von Canaan; ländlich trauliche Verhältnisse, Wein-, Garten- und Gewürzbau, etwas von städtischer Beschränkung, sodann aber ein königlicher Hof, mit seinen Herrlichkeiten im Hintergrunde. Das Hauptthema jedoch bleibt glühende Neigung jugendlicher Herzen, die sich suchen, finden, abstoßen, anziehen, unter mancherlei höchst einfachen Zuständen.[3]

Speaking to Johann Peter Eckermann on 9 November 1824, Goethe acknowledged the debt owed by German literature to Herder and Klopstock, two men ahead of their time. However, he argued that by 1824 they had ceased to be so necessary and important, and warned that 'ein junger Mensch, der heutzutage seine Kultur aus Klopstock und Herder ziehen wollte, würde sehr zurückbleiben'.[4] Nevertheless, as Eduard

---

2. 'What such men imparted and bequeathed to us can only be hinted at, and may we be forgiven for the recklessness with which we pass over these treasures.' *Noten und Abhandlungen zu besserem Verständniß des West-östlichen Divans*, *WW*, VII, p. 7.

3. 'We linger, then, for a moment with the Song of Songs as the tenderest and most inimitable thing that has come to us from the expression of passionate, graceful love. Of course, we lament the fact that the poems, which have been mixed up as fragments and thrust one upon the other, do not afford us any full, unadulterated pleasure, and yet we are delighted to be able to imagine the circumstances in which the poets lived. Throughout, there blows a gentle breeze from the loveliest area of Canaan; rustic, intimate relationships, viticulture, horticulture and the growing of spices, something of urban limitation, but then a royal court with all its splendour in the background. Yet the main theme remains the ardent feelings of young hearts who look for, find, repel and attract each other under a host of highly innocent circumstances.'

4. 'A young person who, in this day and age, aimed to obtain his culture from Klopstock and Herder, would lag very much behind.' *Gespräche mit Goethe in den*

Castle pointed out, 'das Evangelium, welches er [Herder] verkündigte, haben andere erfüllt: Goethe und Schiller, die romantischen Dichter und Denker machten zur Tat, was er nur gewollt, machten zur Gewißheit, was er nur geahnt'.[5]

A number of writers followed Herder in their own work on the Song of Songs. For example, we have noted Emil Adler's suggestion that Herder showed some sympathy for Jewish interpretations of the Song of Songs, and he has reminded us that Moses Mendelssohn made particular use of Herder's work for his own translation of 1788: 'Im Brief an Herder vom 20. VI. 1780 heißt es von der Übersetzung: "das unschätzbare Büchlein die 'Lieder der Liebe'"'.[6] Furthermore, Johann Friedrich Kleuker elaborated on Herder's interpretation in 1780 in his *Sammlung der Gedichte Salomons, sonst das Hohelied oder Lied der Lieder genannt* (Hamm: Perrenon, 1780).

In the preface to his own translation of and commentary on the Song of Songs, Johann Christoph Döderlein followed Herder by ascribing the work to the genre of Oriental Minnelied, and he too rejected totally any allegorical interpretation. The following paragraph shows how far he had imbibed Herder's thinking:

> In einer Uebersetzung des Gesangs, den die Mystik *das hohe Lied* nennt, weil sie im Liebessang hohe Allegorie fand, kan ich weder neue Hypothesen über den Plan, Sinn und Absicht desselben versprechen, noch auch viele neue Erklärungen einzelner Stellen geben. *Mir* ist das Lied ein orientalisches Minnelied, gesungen von Einem Dichter, der Liebe fühlte und Liebe besang, innig, herzlich zart, nekend und unschuldig. Seitdem *Herder* in den *Liedern der Liebe* den deutschen Lesern die Unschuld, Anmuth, und Würde dieses Gesangs zu fühlen gab und in der Schule der Empfindung und der Natur den besten Commentar darüber fand und gab:

letzten Jahren seines Lebens, in Ernst Beutler (ed.), *Gedenkausgabe der Werke, Briefe und Gespräche* (24 vols.; Zürich: Artemis-Verlag, 1948), XXIV, pp. 122-23.

5. 'The gospel which he [Herder] proclaimed was fulfilled by others: Goethe and Schiller, the Romantic poets and thinkers, brought to fruition what he only wished, and turned into fact what he had only dreamed of.' 'Herder als Wiedererwecker des deutschen Volksliedes', in *In Goethes Geist: Vorträge und Aufsätze* (Vienna and Leipzig: Österreichischer Bundesverlag für Unterricht, Wissenschaft und Kunst, 1926), pp. 57-67 (57); repr. from *Zeitschrift für die österreichischen Gymnasien* 55 (1904), pp. 193-202.

6. 'In the letter to Herder dated 20/6/1780, we read of the translation: "The inestimable little book 'Lieder der Liebe'".' 'Johann Gottfried Herder und das Judentum', p. 391.

seitdem dürfte sich schwerlich eine andre Erklärungsart, welche Mystiker und Apokalyptiker einst um die Wette versucht haben, ihr Glück machen.[7]

Wilhelm Friedrich Hufnagel followed Herder's emotional outpouring of natural feeling in *Salomo's Hohes Lied, geprüft, übersetzt, erläutert* (Erlangen: Palm, 1784).[8] Indeed, Hufnagel even used the title 'Salomo's Lieder der Liebe' ('Solomon's Songs of Love') for his translation and commentary. Acknowledging in his preface (p. iii) the work of both Herder and Döderlein, he wrote:

> Keine Entschuldigung, daß ich dem Publikum nach Herder und Döder-. lein eine Uebersetzung des hohen Liedes vorzulegen wage. Wenn ich die Absicht hätte, mehr Licht über den wahren Gesichtspunkt und Gehalt dieser Gesänge zu verbreiten, so würd' ich mich entschuldigen, daß ich nun wieder und schlechter sage, was iene Männer von Gelehrsamkeit und Geschmack vor mir und treffender gesagt haben.[9]

Following closely the wording of Herder's title for the second part of *Lieder der Liebe*, he further acknowledged (p. vii) that 'Herder hat über den Inhalt des hohen Liedes, über die Art und den Zweck dieses Buches, weniger ängstlich geurteilt und mit einer Kunst die ihm eigen

---

7. 'In a translation of the song which mysticism calls the Song of Songs because it found much allegory in the love song, I can promise neither new theories about its intention, meaning or aim, nor give many new explanations about individual portions. As far as I am concerned, the song is an Oriental Minnelied, sung by a poet who experienced love and sang of love wholeheartedly and in an extremely tender, playful and innocent way. Since the time Herder helped German readers, by means of his *Lieder der Liebe*, to experience the innocence, grace and dignity of this song, and found and offered to us the best commentary on it in the school of feeling and nature; since then it has scarcely been possible for any other kind of interpretation to be successful, although at one time both mystics and experts in apocalyptic literature vied with one another in their efforts to produce one.' *Salomons Prediger und Hohes Lied* (Jena: Cuno, 1784), p. 167.

8. This work appears in a volume entitled *Salomons Schriften* which contains Döderlein's work too. It is actually anonymous, although the British Library catalogue (press-mark 3166.aa.57) claims that it is Hufnagel's work.

9. 'No apologies for daring to place before the public a translation of the Song of Songs after Herder and Döderlein. If I intended to shed more light on the true nature and value of these songs, I would apologize for saying again now, in an inferior way, what those men of erudition and taste said before me, and more pertinently.'

ist, seine Stelle in der Bibel fürs Volk gebilligt'.[10] Moreover, Hufnagel quoted from Montagu and Hasselquist, as Herder had done. He was aware of the importance of Herder's work, yet, despite his apologetic tone, he claimed (p. vii) that his own translation was 'doch nicht ganz überflüßig' ('nevertheless not entirely superfluous').

Still in the wake of Herder's work, Friedrich Wilhelm Carl Umbreit wrote his own translation and commentary, using the remarkably similar title *Lied der Liebe: Das älteste und schönste aus dem Morgenlande. Übersetzt und ästhetisch erklärt* ('Song of Love: the Most Ancient and Most Beautiful from the Orient. Translated and Aesthetically Interpreted').[11] Acknowledging the impact of Herder's work on German theological studies—particularly in the Lutheran tradition—in the decades since *Lieder der Liebe*, Umbreit (p. 2) wrote of the

> Uebergang von der mystisch-typischen Auslegung zur rein-ästhetischen, wie sie [...] Herder zuerst gewagt. Die *Lieder der Liebe* machen Epoche in der Geschichte der Erklärung des hohen Liedes. Was Hugo Grotius mit kluger Vorsicht und sichtbarer Aengstlichkeit nur angedeutet hatte, daß man bei demselben Auslegung und Anwendung genau unterscheiden müsse, sprach Herder's freimüthiger Geist mit Offenheit und Nachdruck aus. Mit seiner gewohnten Beredsamkeit suchte er zu zeigen, wie Unrecht man dem alten Testamente und der Natur des Menschen thue, wenn man die wörtliche Auslegung deshalb verwerfe, weil rein-menschliche Liebe kein Gegenstand eines biblischen Buches seyn könne. Sein die letzten Decennien des achtzehnten Jahrhunderts erleuchtender germanisch-orientalischer Genius siegte auch hier, und die ersten Theologen der evangelischen Kirche folgten seinem exegetischen Vorgange. Und so kann man bis in die neueste Zeit die wörtlich-natürliche Erklärung wenigstens in unserer Kirche als die vorherrschende betrachten. Jetzt

10. 'Herder has given his opinion less timidly on the content of the Song of Songs, and on the nature and aim of this book, and with a skill which is his own, he has sanctioned for the people its place in the Bible.'

11. The first edition was published in Göttingen by Vandenhoeck & Ruprecht in 1820. For this study I have used the second edition (Heidelberg: Mohr, 1828). Umbreit quoted Herder's title, acknowledging 'welcher Titel zu dem gegenwärtiger Bearbeitung des H.L. Veranlassung gegeben' ('which title gave rise to that of the present edition of the Song of Songs') (p. 2 n. d). (The title of Umbreit's *David und Jonathan: Lied der Freundschaft, das älteste und schönste aus dem Morgenlande* ['David and Jonathan: Song of Friendship, the Most Ancient and Most Beautiful from the Orient'] of 1844 also shows dependence on Herder.) Goethe wrote a brief appraisal of Umbreit's work on the Song of Songs (*WW*, XLII/2, pp. 40-41).

aber zeigt sich hie und da in auffallenden Erscheinungen ein neues Hinn-
eigen zur mystischen Auslegung.[12]

Despite Herder's influence on him, however, Umbreit disagreed that
the Song of Songs was a collection of different poems, claiming that the
work portrayed 'ein einziger Grundton' ('one single fundamental
tone'). This explains his modification to Herder's title, for 'ganz von
selbst verwandelten sich vor meinen Augen die *Lieder der Liebe* in ein
Lied der Liebe' (p. 12).[13] Significantly Franz Delitzsch wrote that at
Umbreit's death, the Church and Old Testament scholarship had lost a
man who had completed the work begun by Herder; a man who had
helped his readers to appreciate fully the human side of the Old Testament without overlooking its divine side.[14]

As we have seen, Herder's was a new and original approach to
Christianity. His was a humanizing and antidogmatic tendency that
reached its climax in the decade after the publication of *Lieder der
Liebe*. Of all the theories, Herder's is still the one from which modern

12. 'Transition from the mystically typical interpretation to the purely aesthetic,
as Herder was the first to dare to do. The *Lieder der Liebe* are of great importance
in the history of the interpretation of the Song of Songs. What Hugo Grotius, with
prudent caution and obvious timidity, only hinted at, namely that one should differ-
entiate precisely between interpretation and application in the Song of Songs,
Herder's candid nature articulated with frankness and vigour. With his customary
eloquence he attempted to demonstrate how one does an injustice both to the Old
Testament and to human nature when one rejects the literal interpretation simply
because purely human love cannot possibly be the theme of a book of the Bible.
Even here his Germanic–Oriental genius, which enlightened the final decades of the
eighteenth century, triumphed and the first theologians of the Protestant Church
followed his exegetical method. And thus, right up to the present day, the literal–
natural interpretation may be regarded as the prevailing one, at least in our Church.
Yet now we find here and there in outstanding publications a new tendency towards
the mystical interpretation.'

13. 'Quite independently the *Songs of Love* turned before my very eyes into a
Song of Love.' Umbreit drew attention to Ewald's translation and commentary *Das
Hohelied Salomo's*, a dramatic interpretation in three acts. In his remarks on other
interpretations, Ewald listed the works of writers such as Lessing, Jacobi, Hufnagel
and Umbreit. Herder's name is mentioned on pp. 42, 43 and 48, although Ewald
chose not to give any details of his work, thereby suggesting that he did not regard
it as highly as that of others.

14. See Karl Theodor Ullmann, 'Friedrich Wilhelm Carl Umbreit: Blätter der
Erinnerung', *Theologische Studien und Kritiken: Eine Zeitschrift für das gesammte
Gebiet der Theologie* (1862), pp. 437-79 (471).

scholarship about the Song of Songs proceeds, although often with minor variations, usually affecting in particular the date of the composition of the book. Haym, for example, wrote in 1885 that Herder's view of the Song of Songs 'ist im Wesentlichen die Ansicht der heutigen Wissenschaft'.[15]

Shortly afterwards, Meyer too pointed out that

> sein Gefühl für den individuellen Ton des Einzelnen ist so groß, daß es den Zusammenhang des Ganzen sprengt: nicht als ein Lied, sondern als eine Sammlung von Liedern und Liederfragmenten, die die stärksten Unterschiede in Situation und Darstellung zeigen, erscheint es ihm. Das Herausschälen und Abgrenzen der einzelnen Stücke und ihre ästhetische Charakterisierung gehört zu den größten Triumphen Herderscher Interpretationskunst und hat auch heute noch nichts an Wert verloren. Denn selbst die Vertreter der Einheit des Hohenliedes -und sie sind heutzutage in der Mehrzahl—stimmen in der Abteilung der einzelnen Scenen oder Abschnitte mit Herder überein, und wo sie abweichen, geschieht es meist nicht zu ihrem Vorteil.[16]

In 1946 Clark could still write that 'one can say that practically all non-allegorical theories now held are forms of Herder's main contention'.[17]

In his Latin translation of the Song of Songs in 1953, Cardinal Augustinus Bea acknowledged that 'ad explicationem *naturalisticam* maxime contulit J. G. von Herder, *Lieder der Liebe* (1778) qui, negata unitate, Canticum collectionem esse statuit carminum amoris plane profani. Quem secuti sunt Goethe (1819), Ed. Reuss (1893), P. Haupt (1902), G. Jacob (1902), W. Staerk (1911), M. Haller (1940)'.[18]

---

15. 'Is essentially the view of current scholarship.' *Herder*, II, p. 86.

16. 'His feel for the particular tone of the individual element is so great that it ruptures the coherence of the whole; it appears to him not as one song, but as a collection of songs and fragments of songs which demonstrate the widest differences in situation and presentation. The unravelling and defining of the individual songs and their aesthetic characterization belong to the greatest triumphs of Herder's interpretative art, and even today have lost nothing in terms of importance. For even those who plead for the unity of the Song of Songs—and nowadays they are in the majority—agree with Herder as far as the division of the separate scenes or sections is concerned, and where they differ, this occurs for the most part not to their advantage.' *Werke*, pp. 13-14.

17. 'Herder, Percy, and the *Song of Songs*', p. 1099 n. 29.

18. 'J.G. von Herder contributed very greatly to the naturalistic interpretation in his *Lieder der Liebe* of 1778 which rejected the unity of the poems and held the

Five years later Friedrich Ohly held that 'das Christentum der Zeit nach Goethe hat keine religiöse Begegnung mit dem Hohenlied mehr erlebt'.[19] Although 'dieses lyrischste Buch der Bibel' ('this most lyrical book of the Bible') (p. 5) had been repeatedly questioned by theologians since Herder as far as divine inspiration was concerned, it nevertheless became significant for its literary individuality as biblical poetry.

In 1982 Timm also acknowledged that in the 200 years since *Lieder der Liebe* 'die Skrupel über den allzu sinnlichen Charakter der alttestamentlichen Liebeslyrik sind verflogen. Sie bereiten keine religiösen Sorgen mehr [...]. Von seiner traditionellen Rahmung befreit, konnte das Hohe Lied eine zunehmend unbefangene Wertschätzung seines historisch-literarischen Ranges finden.'[20]

On the other hand, in 1984 Kelletat claimed that

> die wissenschaftliche Diskussion über die Entstehung, Struktur und Funktion des *Hohenlieds* ist nicht bei Herders neuer Interpretation, der Abkehr von allegorischen Deutungen stehengeblieben. Die grundlegende Frage 'Was ist das *Hohelied*?'[21] wird Ende des 19. Jahrhunderts noch einmal gestellt, mit interessanten Hinweisen auf palästinensische Hochzeitsbräuche. Seither ist zunehmend zweifelhaft geworden, ob die *Lieder der Liebe* tatsächlich als Empfindungspoesie, als Erlebnislyrik im Sinne der Sturm-und-Drang-bewegten siebziger Jahre des 18. Jahrhunderts verstanden werden dürfen.[22]

Song of Songs to be a collection of secular love songs. Goethe (1819), Ed. Reuss (1893), P. Haupt (1902), G. Jacob (1902), W. Staerk (1911), and M. Haller (1940) followed him.' *Canticum Canticorum: Novam Interpretationem Latinam cum Textu Masoretico et Notis Exegeticis* (Scripta Pontificii Instituti Biblici, 104; Rome: Pontificio Instituto Biblico, 1953), p. 21.

19. 'Christianity in the time since Goethe has not experienced any further religious encounter with the Song of Songs.' *Hohelied-Studien: Grundzüge einer Geschichte der Hohenliedauslegung des Abendlandes bis um 1200* (Schriften der wissenschaftlichen Gesellschaft der Johann Wolfgang Goethe-Universität Frankfurt am Main, Geisteswissenschaftliche Reihe, 1; Wiesbaden: Steiner, 1958), p. 5.

20. 'The scruples about the over-sensual nature of Old Testament love lyrics have vanished. No longer do they cause religious concern [...]. Liberated from its traditional setting, the Song of Songs has been able to find an increasingly unprejudiced appreciation of its historical-literary position.' *Das Hohe Lied Salomos*, p. 133.

21. Thus the title of a study by Karl Budde in *Preußische Jahrbücher* 78 (1894), pp. 92-117.

22. 'The scholarly debate about the origin, structure and function of the Song of

And yet, whatever the case, Herder's reading was clearly a watershed in the history of the interpretation of the Song of Songs. Indeed, arguably his influence has even extended to Robert Alter, whose view is that 'the Song of Songs is the only surviving instance of purely secular love poetry from ancient Israel'.[23]

Concluding Summary

In Germany some sort of foundation had to be laid for an autonomous, creative, non-dogmatic, non-rationalistic literature—the literature of the 'Sturm und Drang' on which Herder had such an influence. In this regard, whereas the importance of Herder's *Volkslieder* as a catalyst for the renewal of German literature has been widely acknowledged, the significance of *Lieder der Liebe*, which, as we have seen, essentially formed part of the *Volkslieder*, has too often been overlooked. This work has sought to fill that gap.

In order to bring his interpretation of the Song of Songs as a collection of the most beautiful and primitive Oriental '*Lieder der Liebe*' closer to his readership, Herder had to fight against prejudice which went even deeper than that which greeted the *Volkslieder* which were originally to have included his work on the Song of Songs. While Herder's contemporaries had only a vague notion of folk-song, they believed they were thoroughly familiar with the Old Testament and, of course, with the Song of Songs. Indeed, they thought that they understood the true significance of the Hebrew text, given centuries of allegorical interpretation. Thus, in order to free the primitive Hebrew love poetry of the Old Testament from its theological straitjacket, and to draw attention to its meaning within its own *Sitz im Leben*, Herder had to convince a readership whose thinking was already clouded by traditional allegorical readings, whether Jewish, Catholic or Protestant. As I have shown, Herder attacked such theological explanation of Old Tes-

---

Songs did not cease with Herder's new reading, namely the renunciation of allegorical interpretations. The fundamental question "What is the Song of Songs?" was asked again at the end of the nineteenth century, with interesting allusions to Palestinian wedding customs. Since that time it has become increasingly uncertain whether *Lieder der Liebe* should in fact be understood as sentimental poetry, as lyric poetry of experience in the sense of the seventies in the eighteenth century which were influenced by "Sturm und Drang".' *Herder und die Weltliteratur*, p. 62.

23. *The Art of Biblical Poetry* (New York: Basic Books, 1985), p. 185.

tament poetry with his translations and interpretation of the Song of Songs. Yet, as I have demonstrated also, he held his own strongly held views despite his claims to have attempted an undogmatic reading.

Philological-critical treatment of the Song of Songs was begun by Herder, whose concern was less with the place of the book in the Bible than with its intrinsic poetic values. Indeed, it was particularly here that he influenced Goethe and thus future German poetry, for it was through Goethe, and thence through writers such as Clemens Brentano and Ludwig Achim von Arnim, for example, that he pointed his native poetry back towards its sources. As Eduard Castle had it, 'wenn Arnim und Brentano ihr "Wunderhorn" ihm [Goethe] zu Füßen legten, so huldigten sie mittelbar auch dem Manne [Herder], der als erster der deutschen Dichtung wieder den Weg zum Urquell gewiesen hatte'.[24]

An orthodox allegorical or rationalistic interpretation of the Song of Songs would have contributed nothing to a renaissance of German poetry. Herder produced a theory whose extreme unorthodoxy made Michaelis's rationalizations appear pale and reactionary, but whose emphasis upon the work as Oriental love poetry broke through the bounds of theology and rationalism and contributed towards a most fruitful conception of the function and significance of poetry in society. In an age of reason, Herder sought to make the Bible live again. Herder was indeed a child of his time—we note his natural explanations of the miraculous, for example, as well as the influence of his own eighteenth-century background on his interpretation of the Song of Songs—yet, as Robscheit puts it, 'er hatte seine Aufgaben an den Menschen seiner Zeit' ('he had his mission to those of his own age'),[25] and should be judged accordingly. Herder helped the theology of his age out of mere reason towards fulfilling its real purpose, for although Herder was first and foremost a theologian, he was often regarded as a humanist who sympathized with the language and thought of other nations.

In this work I have assessed the importance for German literature of Herder's preoccupation with the Song of Songs, and the significance of the work for his own thinking. I have examined Herder's unique reading of the book within the context of other interpretative approaches. I

24. 'If Arnim and Brentano laid their "Wunderhorn" at his [Goethe's] feet, in so doing they also paid homage indirectly to the man [Herder] who was the first to show German poetry the way once again to the original source.' 'Herder als Wiedererwecker', p. 67.

25. 'Herder als Ausleger', p. 38.

have considered his work as a translator, comparing his translations of the Song of Songs as poetry. I have given close consideration to the details of the translations, comparing them with each other, and with those of Luther and Goethe. I have also demonstrated that the published translation of 1778 showed considerably more dependence upon the original Hebrew text than upon Luther's translation.

Two studies for the future spring readily to mind. First, we have noted the seemingly unparalleled interest in the Song of Songs among Herder's contemporaries, particularly between 1762 and 1784. A study of great interest and importance would be to undertake a close comparison of the interpretations and translations of others such as Hamann (1762), Hase (1765), Jacobi (1771), Goethe (1775), Pufendorf (1776), Johann Gottlieb Lessing (1777), Gleim (1779), Kleuker (1780), Döderlein (1780) and Hufnagel (1784), perhaps taking Herder's work of 1776–78 as a touchstone, and considering why there should be so much interest just at that time. Secondly, another significant study would be to trace in detail the subsequent historical development of the interpretation of the Song of Songs, thus providing a means of monitoring closely the extent to which Herder's interpretation had a part to play in future readings of the work, particularly as the nineteenth century progressed.

Apart from presenting new material per se and a novel, detailed analysis of Herder's commentaries and translations, this study of Herder's work on the Song of Songs has sought to combine the old and the new. For example, it is old in that it has found Herder's interpretation of the work confirming what is already known of his views on primitive poetry, on the tension between the especial quality of a national culture and its participation in a universal humanity, and on the direction ahead for a new German literature. This has formed an essential part of the basis of the argument. The study is new in that from a more distanced historical and theoretical vantage point, it has been able to point out that Herder's understanding of the eroticism of the text as pure and paradisal was a strong interpretation, historically, socially and perhaps personally determined. This does not invalidate it or discredit it, but it makes it partial, aspectival, ideological—and interesting, given that this came from a man who demanded a literal reading. Thus, in addition to material which is new in its own right, this work has brought new insights to old ground, yet has used that ground to support them thoroughly.

Finally, in Herder's *Lieder der Liebe* we have observed his attempts to struggle with the local and particular vis-à-vis the universal. Herder's views here are important for contemporary multicultural thinking as it grapples with the social and political problems of cultural encounter, especially in the United States, for example, which until recently had a policy of immigrant assimilation to European norms. There are implications too for the new Europe, where the breaching of frontiers has resulted in a flood of refugees and immigrants with a rise in right-wing nationalist activity as various cultural prejudices and expectations collide. Just under 200 years since Herder's death, his difficult combination of specific cultures within a wider human universality may perhaps have found its time.

Appendix A

HERDER'S TRANSLATIONS OF THE SONG OF SONGS

This Appendix reproduces the translations given in MS(3) of 1776 and the published *Lieder der Liebe* of 1778 (including Herder's idiosyncratic use of inverted commas). They differ very slightly from those given in *SWS*, VIII, principally in spacing, punctuation and orthography. Right-aligned text is a continuation of the line above, and should be read accordingly for a proper sense of Herder's scansion.

1776	*1778*
I. *Der Seufzer*	*Salomons Hohes Lied*

1776

Ah küßte mich Ein Kuß von seinem Munde!
 wie süßer mir als Wein!
Süß ist dein Duft! Es fleußt umher wie Balsam
 wenn man dich nennt.

Sie lieben alle dich die Mädchen. Winke
 o König mir, o mir dir nach.
Wir laufen Alle, König und du führest
 in deine Kammer–mich.

O welche Freuden da an dir! Wir denken
 an deine Liebe mehr als Wein
und alle Lust: sind froh an dir: die Treuen
 sind dein! sind dein!

1778

Er küsse mich
Mit seines Mundes Küssen:
Denn deine Lieb' ist lieblicher, denn Wein.
Wie deiner süssen Salben Duft,
So ist zerfliessender Balsam
Dein Name:
Darum lieben die Jungfrau'n dich.

Zeuch mich dir nach!–
Wir eilen; mich–
Führete der König in seine Kammer.
Wir jauchzen, wir erfreun uns dein!
Gedenken an deine Liebe,
Mehr als an Wein–
Von Herzen lieben wir dich.

II. *Liebe in Armuth*

Schwarz und doch ihm angenehm
Ihr Schönen von Jerusalem!
Liebt er nicht seine Zelte so?
Sind schwarz nicht auch die Decken Salomo?

Was schaut ihr mich, daß so verbrannt ich bin,
was schauet ihr?

Schwarz bin ich und doch lieblich,
Ihr Töchter Jerusalem!
Wie der Kedarenen Gezelte,
Wie die Decken Salomons.

Seht mich nicht an, daß ich schwärzlich bin:
Mich brannte die Sonne.

Mich brannte Sonnenschein!
Die Brüder mein, die Schwestern mein
zürnten mir.
Sie stiessen mich zur Hüterin
der Trauben hin:
Ach ihren Reichthum hütet' ich
der Mein' ist hin!- -

Sag' an mir du, der meine Seel' entzückt
wo weidest du?
wo ruhest du
wenn Mittag drückt?
Ich irr' auf allen Triften umher,
und athme schwer,
find' immer andre, nur nicht dich
den meine Seele liebt.

„Schönes Mädchen, suchst du mich
und weißt nicht wo?
Dort auf der Spur der Heerden,
da wird mein Ort dir werden,
da zeltet Salomo.
Da komm' zu meinen Heerden
mit deiner Böcklein Paar
und ruhe dar."

Die Söhne meiner Mutter zürneten mir:
Sie satzten zur Weinberghüterin mich,
Und meinen, meinen Weinberg
Hütet' ich nicht.

O sage mir,
Den meine Seele liebt:
Wo weidest du?
Wo lagerst du
Am Mittag?–
Daß ich nicht, wie eine Verhüllete, geh,
Zu Heerden deiner Gespielen.

„Und weissest du das nicht,
Schönste der Weiber;
So folge den Tritten der Heerde nach,
Und weide deine Ziegen
Bei den Zelten der Hirten."

III. *Brautgeschenke*

A. Dem Roß Aegyptus gleich' ich dich
   in Königs Wagenpracht.
   Wie lieblich
   aus dieser Goldschnur deine Wange lacht!
   Wie prächtig
   der Hals in Golde thront! und lieblicher
                                    wirds seyn,
   spielt Silber drein- -
B. Der König wandte sich:
   Ha, wie umduftet' mich
   die Narde! Mir
   ruht mein Freund am Herzen hier!
   ein Myrrhenstrauß da zwischen den
                                    Brüsten mir.
   Mein Freund, er ist mir
   junge Lebensblüthe mein–
   aus Engeddis Palmenhayn.

Meinem Roß an Pharao Wagen
Gleich' ich, o Freundin, dich.
Lieblich stehn in den Spangen deine Wangen:
Dein Hals in den Ketten schön.
Goldketten lass' ich dir machen,
Mit Pünktchen Silber gesprengt.

Wohin der König sich wandte,
Gab meine Narde Duft!
Ein Sträuschen Myrrhe sollt du, mein Lieber,
Mir zwischen den Brüsten ruhn!
Ein Palmenknöspchen bist du, mein Lieber,
Mir aus dem Engeddi-Garten.

IV. *Träume der Zukunft*

A. Schön bist du, meine Liebe. Du bist schön,
   ein Täubchen sanft im Blick.
B. Schön bist du, mein Geliebter. Du bist
                hold
    Schau, unser Bette grünt.

   Die Pfosten Zedern. Laub ist unser Dach
   Cypressen dichte Wand,
   und ich–des Waldes Schattenblume nur
    nur Lilie im Thal.

A. Die Lilie, die unter Dornen prangt
   bist du im Mädchenchor
B. Ein Apfelbaum im wilden Walde du
   vor allen Jünglingen.

   Wie lieb' ich mir den holden Baum
   und ruh in seinem Raum
   im Schatten
   des Lieben
   und lechze
   nach seiner Frucht.–Wie süße mir!–
   Ich schwimm' an ihr
   in Düfte Wein
   in welch ein Meer der Lieb' hinein.
   Und Liebe über mir
   schwebt
   webt
   Panier!–
   Wie wird mir? haltet mich,
   mit Frucht von jenem Baume- -
   mit seinem Balsam labt mich- -
   Ich schwind'! In seinem Traume
   sink ich- -
   Ruht mein Haupt
   sanft umlaubt
   auf seiner Linken. Süßiglich
   umschlingt mich seine Rechte
   hält mich- -

O schön bist du, meine Liebe,
O schön bist du!
Deine Augen Täubchen- -

„O schön bist du, mein Lieber,
Auch hold bist du,
Und unser Bette grünt.

Die Balken unsrer Häuser Cedern,
Die Wände Cypressen;
Und ich die Rose des Feldes,
Die Lilie im Thal."

„Wie die Lilie unter den Dornen,
Ist meine Freundin unter den Töchtern."
„Wie ein Apfelbaum unter den Bäumen
              im Walde,
So ist mein Lieber unter den Söhnen.
In seinem Schatten
Erquick' ich mich,
Und size nieder,
Und seine Frucht
Ist meinem Munde süß.

Er hat mich geführt
In ein Haus des Weins!
Und sein Panier,
Ueber mir droben,
Ist Liebe.

O stärkt mich mit dem Weine!
O labt mich mit den Aepfeln!
Denn ich bin krank für Liebe.

Seine Linke
Mir unterm Haupt.
Seine Rechte
Umfaßt mich."

V. *Schlummerlied*

Bei des Feldes leisem Reh,
horcht ihr Töchter Solyme.
Bei der Hindin auf der Flur
horcht dem Schwur!
Meiner Liebe naht euch nicht
weckt sie nicht, reget nicht
ihres Schlummers sanfte süße Nacht
bis aufgeht ihr Angesicht
sie erwacht!–

„Ich beschwör' euch, Töchter Jerusalem,
Bei den Hinden, bei dem Rehe der Flur.
Wenn ihr sie weckt!
Wenn ihr sie regt!–
Bis es ihr gefällt.

VI. *Morgenbesuch des Frühlings*

Ha meines Lieben Stimme! Ja
Er ists, er ist da!
Wie er über Hügel da fliegt,
jene Höh schon hinter ihm liegt!
Dem Reh, dem jungen Hirsch ist mein
        Geliebter gleich
Da steht er schon vor mir!
lauscht durch Gartens Thür,
blickt durchs Geländer herfür
neigt über sich mir,
singt mir:
  „Auf! Du liebstes Mädchen, auf!
  Schönstes Mädchen, komm' herauf!
  Sieh der Winter ist vorüber,
  Regengüsse, Stürm' hinüber,
  sind entflohn.
  Blümchen schon
  blühn her für.
  Lenz ist hier.
  Turteltäubchen girren schon
  Feigenbaum hat Knöspchen schon
  Unser Weinstock äugelt schon
  blickt nach dir
  duftet dir,
  Alles, Alles ist schon hier.–
  Nur du nicht, Liebchen, auf!
  Schönstes Mädchen komm herauf!
  Täubchen in den Felsenritzen,
  wo du Winters mustest sitzen,
  Fleuch herfür
  Zeig dich mir

Stimme meines Lieben!
Siehe, er kommt!!
Springt über die Berge,
Hüpft über die Hügel.
Wie ein Reh ist mein Lieber,
Wie ein flüchtiger Hirsch.

Siehe, da stehet er schon
Dahinter der Wand,
Schaut durchs Geländer,
Blinket durchs Gitter.
Er spricht mein Lieber,
Er spricht zu mir:

Steh auf, meine Liebe,
Steh auf, meine Schöne,
Komm!–

Denn siehe, der Winter ist über,
Der Regen ist über, vorüber!
Man sieht schon Blumen am Boden,
Die Zeit des Gesanges ist da.
Man hört die Stimme
Der Turteltaube
Auf unsrer Flur.

Der Feigenbaum hat seine Feigen
Mit Süsse gewürzt.
Des Weinstocks junge Trauben
Duften schon.
Steh auf, meine Liebe,
Steh auf, meine Schöne,
Komm!

Laß dich hören! laß dich sehn!
Singst so lieblich, bist so schön.- -

Mein Täubchen in den Spalten des Felsen,
In den hohlen Klüften der Steige,
Laß sehn mich deine Gestalt,
Laß deine Stimme mich hören,
Denn deine Stimme ist lieblich,
Denn deine Gestalt ist schön.

VII. *Frühlingswerk*

„Laßt uns fahn! laßt uns fahn
Die Füchslein dort auf grünem Plan
Die den Weinberg uns verderben,
Daß die schönsten Blüthen sterben,
Junge Blüthen blühn uns an
Laßt uns fahn! laßt uns fahn!–"

Faht uns die Füchse,
Die kleinen Füchse,
Die Weinbergsverderber,
Der Weinberg knospt.

VIII. *Tagwerk des Geliebten*

Mein Geliebter, Er ist mein
ich bin sein!
Er der unter Blumen weidet,
bis sich Tag und Kühle scheidet,
bis die Schatten lang sich ziehn
und verfliehn,
denn o denn, denn seh ich ihn.

Kehr um, mein Freund, daß ich dich seh!
Fleuch ein Hirsch! Komm wie ein Reh
über Berg und Thal und Höh
zu Salome.–

Mein Lieber ist mein,
Und ich bin sein.
Er weidet in Blumen,
Bis der Tag sich kühlt,
Und die Schatten fliehen.
Kehr um denn, o Lieber,
Sey wie ein Reh,
Wie ein flüchtiger Hirsch,
Ueber die Berge,
Die jezt uns trennen.- -

IX. *Nachtbegegniß*

Ich suchte Nachts in meinem Bette
den Vielgeliebten mein,
o daß ich ihn gefunden hätte,
fand ich ihn?–Nein!

Aufstehen, sprach ich, suchen in den Gassen
in Strassen groß und klein
den Vielgeliebten mein–
Ich fand ihn nirgend. Nein!

In meinem Bette suchte ich,
Die lange Nacht,
Den meine Seele liebet–
Ich suchte ihn und fand ihn nicht.

Ich will aufstehn nun,
Die Stadt umgehn,
In den Strassen,
In den Gassen,

Die Wächter kamen mir vorüber:
  „Saht Ihr nicht meinen Lieben?"
  Nein!
  Wir sahn ihn nicht den Vielgeliebten dein.

Ein wenig fürder und ich fand
den Lieben. Meine Hand
ergriff ihn. Mit mir ziehe
ich ihn in meiner Mutter Haus
ins Brautgemach zu der, die mich gebohren- -

Und suchen ihn,
Den meine Seele liebet;
Ich suchte ihn und fand ihn nicht.
Mich fanden die Wächter,
Die die Stadt umgehn:
  „Den meine Seele liebt,
  Sahet ihr ihn?"

Ein wenig weiter, ihnen vorüber,
Da fand ich ihn, den meine Seele liebt.

Ich hab' ihn und will ihn nicht lassen,
Bis daß ich ihn führe
Ins Haus meiner Mutter,
In meiner Gebährerin Kammer- -

X. *Schlaflied*

„Bei des Feldes leisem Reh
horcht ihr Töchter Solyme
Bei der Hindin auf der Flur
horcht dem Schwur!
Meiner Lieben naht euch nicht,
weckt sie nicht! reget nicht
Ihres Schlummers sanfte süße Nacht,
bis aufgeht ihr Angesicht
sie erwacht.- -

Ich beschwör' euch, Töchter Jerusalem,
Bei den Hinden, beim Rehe der Flur,
Wenn ihr sie weckt!
Wenn ihr sie regt!
Meine Liebe,
Bis ihr es selbst gefällt!-

XI. *Die süße Erscheinung*

Was steigt dort aus der Wüsten auf?
Schlank und licht, wie Säule Rauch!
Süßer Rauch, wie Myrrhenduft,
Balsam weit umher der Luft,
Weihrauchduft.

Wer ist, die dort
Aus der Wüsten steigt?
Wie Säulen Rauch,
Wie Duft von Myrrhen und Weihrauch,
Und köstlicher Würze Duft.

XII. *Salomo's Bette*

Des Königs Bette. Sechzig Krieger
  stehn rings umher.
Die Hand am Schwert ein jeder. Sieger
  sie all'. Ein Heldenheer.
Schwert an den Hüften, alle funkelnd Macht
  im Graun der Nacht.

Siehe das Bett', Salomo's Bett'!
Sechzig Mächtige stehn umher,
Aus den Mächtigen Israel.
Sie alle die Hand am Schwert,
Alle Kriegesgelehrt,
Jeder an der Hüfte sein Schwert,
Fürm Graun der Nacht.

Das Bett der *Liebe Salomo*
ist hold und froh.
Gebaut von Cedern Libanus,
Silber seiner Säulen Fuß
Der Himmel Goldesguß.
Die Decken Purpur. Angenehm
und lieblich und bequem
für Euch, ihr Mädchen von Jerusalem.

Hinaus ihr Töchter Zions, schaut
den König auf dem Throne,
in jener Krone
damit die Mutter ihn der Braut
am schönsten seiner Freudentage
nun anvertraut.

Ein Prachtbett machte der König Salomo
                 sich,
Aus Cedern vom Libanon.
Die Säulen macht' er von Silber,
Den Himmel von Gold,
Die Decke von Purpur,
Die Mitte gepolstert mit Liebe,
Für die Töchter Jerusalems.

Gehet hinaus und schauet ihn an,
Ihr Töchter Zions, den König
Salomo;
In der Krone, womit ihn seine Mutter
               gekrönt,
Am Tage seiner Verlobung,
Am Tage der Freude seines Herzens.

XIII. *Die Neuvermählte*

Schön bist du, meine Liebe, du bist schön!
Ein Täubchen blickt dein Auge
dem Schleir her für.
Dein Seidenhaar ist wie die zarte Heerde
die klimmt auf Gilead.
Dein Mund, wie Lämmer aus der Quelle
Zwillinggebährerinnen alle
und keine fehlt.

Die Lippen zarte Purpurfäden
und hauchen süß.

Die Wangen unterm Schleier
wie aufgeritzten Apfels Milch und Blut.

Dein Hals die Davidsveste
auf sichrer Brustwehr da
Umhangen rings mit tausend Siegesschilden
und Helden trugen sie.

Die Brüste, wie zwo Zwillingsrehchen
                 weidend
da unter Lilien–

„Bis bald der Tag sich kühlt
und mit den fliehnden Schatten spielt
will ich zu jenen Myrrhenhöhn
zum kühlen Dufthain gehn."

O schön bist du meine Liebe,
O du bist schön.

Deine Augen Täubchen,
Am Lockenhaar.

Dein Haar ist wie die Gemsenheerde,
Die weidet vom Gilead.

Die Zähne wie die Lämmerheerde
Die neugeschoren aus der Quelle steigt,
Die alle Zwillinge tragen
Und keins derselben fehlt.

Wie ein Purpurfaden deine Lippen,
Und deine Rede süß.

Wie ein aufgerizter Apfel deine Wangen
Am Lockenhaar.

Dein Hals, wie Davids Thurm,
Gebauet zur Waffenburg.
Tausend Schilde hangen an ihm,
Lauter Schilde der Helden.

Die zwo Brüste dein,
Wie zwo Zwillingsrehchen,
Die unter Lilien weiden.- -

Ganz bist du schön o meine Lieb'. An dir
    ist Fleck und Tadel nicht.
Und willst du wandeln, meine Liebe, komm
    komm ab vom Libanus.

Da blickst du von der Höh *Amana* weit
    von *Senir*, *Hermon* weit umher:
Ich führe dich durch der Löwinnen Reich
    der Pardel wilde Höhn.

Mein Herz entwendet hast du, Schwester-
                         Braut
    Ein Blick von deinen Blicken
    entwandt es mir!–
    Ein Wenden deiner Kette
    da war es dein!–

Und deine Küße–süßer, Schwester-Braut!
    sind sie als süßer Wein
Der Duft von deinen Salben lieblicher
    als aller Salben Duft.

Wie Honig fleußt es, träuft es, Schwester-
                         Braut
    von deinen Lippen dir,
Von Milch und Honig dir die Zunge. Duft
    des ganzen Libanus

Ist dein Gewand. Ein heilger Garte bist
    bist du mir, Schwester-Braut
Ein reiner heilger Quell versiegelt, bist
    mir ganz ein Paradies

Da duftet Duft, da blühen Blüthe! Da
    blüht Palm- und Apfelbaum
Und Nard' und Krokus, Weihrauch, Cinnamet
    und Myrrh' und Aloe.

Ein Quell lebendger Waßer quillet, strömt
    da ab vom Libanus.
Auf Nord und Süd! durch meinen Garten
                         weht
    regt seinen Duft! = =

    „So komm denn, Liebster, komm in
                       deinen Garten
    und brich dir edle Frucht!"

In meinem Garten war ich, Schwester-Braut
    und brach von meinen Myrrhen
    in ihrem Duft!

„Bis der Tag sich kühle,
Und die Schatten fliehn,
Will ich dort zum Myrrhenberge,
Zu den Weihrauchhügeln gehn."

Ganz bist du schön, o Liebe
Kein Tadel ist an dir.
Mit mir vom Libanon, o Braut,
Vom Libanon wirst du kommen mit mir,
Wirst von der Höh Amana sehn,
Von Senir, Hermon weit umher
Von den Wohnungen der Löwen,
Von den Bergen der Parden–

Du beherzest mich, o meine Schwester
                         Braut!
Du beherzest mich mit Einem deiner Blicke,
Mit Einer Ketten an deinem Halse.

Wie süß ist deine Liebe,
Du meine Schwester-Braut
Wie süsser ist deine Liebe denn Wein!
Der Duft von deinen Salben
Als aller Duft!

Honig triefen deine Lippen, o Braut!
Milch und Honig ist unter deiner Zunge,
Der Duft von deinen Kleidern,
Wie Libanons Duft.

Ein heiliger Garte bist du, meine Schwester-
                         Braut,
Ein heiliger Quell, ein versiegelter Brunn,
Deine Gewächs' ein Aepfelparadies
Mit aller köstlichen Frucht.

Nardus und Krokus,
Cimmet und Kanna,
Weihrauch allerley Art.
Aloe und Myrrhen
Mit allen treflichen Würzen.

Ein Brunn der Gärten,
Ein Quell lebendiger Wasser,
Die rinnen von Libanon–

Erhebe dich, Nord!
Und Südwind, komm,
Durchweh meinen Garten,
Daß seine Würze fliessen.- -

Und aß von meinem Honig'
und Honigseim,
und trank von meinem Weine
und meiner Milch.
Nun eßet ihr, Geliebte! trinket satt
und trinket frölich Euch ihr Freunde,
Der Gart' ist Euer nun!–

So komme, mein Geliebter,
In seinen Garten
Und esse seine köstliche Frucht.

Ich kam in meinen Garten,
O meine Schwester Braut!
Und brach von meinen Myrrhen
Und meinen Würzen,
Und aß von meinem Honig
Und Honigseim,
Und trank von meinem Weine
Und meiner Milch.
Nun esset, meine Geliebten,
Und trinkt, und werdet trunken, ihr Lieben- -

XIV. *Die Untreue*

Ich schlafe, aber nicht mein Herz. Das
                                    wacht! . .
Wer ist da? - - Ists nicht meines Lieben
                                    Stimme? . .
Er klopft, er ruffet: „Thu mir auf!
Geliebte, Schwester, meine treue Taube!
Thu auf! . .
Mein Haupt träuft Thau!
Mein Haar träuft kalte Nacht! . ."

Entkleidet . . soll ich an mich wieder
                                    kleiden?
Gewaschen . . soll mein Fuß sich neu
                                    bestäuben?–
Da rauscht' am Riegel meines Freundes
                                    Hand–
mein Innres zitterte!–
Aufstand ich meinem Lieben aufzuthun-
von Myrrhen trof die Hand mir–Myrrhen
                                    rannen
an Riegels Lauf . .
Aufthat ich und mein Freund war weg-
war still entwichen . . Ich ging schnell
ging seinem Ruf nach . . suchte . . fand ihn
                                    nicht . .
Ich rief und keine Stimme! . .

Es fanden mich die Hüter,
die Wächter auf den Strassen,

Ich schlafe und mein Herz wacht!

Stimme meines Geliebten!
Er klopft!

„Thu auf mir, meine Schwester, meine
                                    Freundin,
Mein Täubchen, meine Reine,
Thu auf mir."

„Mein Kleid ist ausgezogen;
Wie? soll ichs anziehn?
Meine Füsse sind gewaschen;
Soll ich sie neu besudeln?"–

    Mein Lieber streckte
Die Hand durchs Gitter,
Mein Innres bebte mir.

    Schnell stand ich auf,
Zu thun ihm auf, dem Lieben.

    Meine Hände troffen Myrrhen,
Meine Finger troffen Myrrhen,
Die über den Riegel liefen.

    Auf that ich meinem Lieben;
Mein Lieber war entwichen,
Verschwunden- -

Meine Seele war mir entgangen,
Da er zu mir sprach–

sie schlugen mich,
verwundten mich,
sie nahmen mir den Schleier
die Wächter auf der Mauer–
Hört o höret meinen Schwur
Töchter Solyme,
find't ihr ihn
saget ihm–
sagt ihm nur–
ich bin krank vor Liebe.

„Und was vor andern Jünglingen
Ist dein Geliebter, Mädchen,
Daß du uns so beschwurst?"

Mein Liebling, weiß und roth, ist Einer
aus Tausenden.
Sein Haupt geläutert Gold, die Locke
wie Raben schwarz.
Die Augen Täubchen über regen Quellen
sie schwimmen Milchweis, baden reine Fülle.
Die Wangen Blumenhügel
voll Blüthenduft.
Die Lippen Myrrhen strömend
wie Rosen zart.
Die Hände goldnes Rund, umfunkelt
mit Edelstein.
Der Leib, umgürtet mit Sapphieren
zart Elfenbein.
Die Beine Marmorsäulen
auf goldnem Fuß.
Sein Wuchs hoch wie die Zeder
wie Libanus.
Sein Hauch so süß! o lieblich–
und Alles an ihm angenehm.
Der ist mein Freund! der ist mein Freund!
Ihr Töchter von Jerusalem!–

„Wo ist denn, Schönste, dein Geliebter?
Wohin gewandt ist dein Geliebter?
daß wir ihn mit dir suchen!–"

In seinen Garten ging mein Lieber
auf seine Blumenflur.
Sich Lilien zu sammeln
zu weiden unter Duft.
Mein Lieber, er ist mein
Mein Lieber, ich bin sein
Er weidet unter Blumen- -

Ich sucht' ihn nun, und fand ihn nicht.
Ich rief ihn, aber Er
Antwortete mir nicht.

Mich fanden die Hüter,
Die die Stadt umgehn.
Sie schlugen mich,
Sie verwundten mich,
Sie raubten mir den Schleier,
Die Hüter der Mauern.

Ich beschwör' euch, Töchter Jerusalems!
Wenn ihr ihn findet,
Meinen Geliebten,
Was wollt ihr ihm sagen?–
Daß ich vor Liebe krank bin.

„Was ist denn dein Geliebter vor Geliebten,
Du Schönste der Weiber!
Was ist denn dein Geliebter vor Geliebten,
Daß du uns so beschwurst?"

Mein Lieber ist weiß und roth,
Ein Panier aus zehnmal Tausenden.

Sein Haupt das feinste Gold,
Seine Locken kraus,
Und schwarz, wie ein Rabe.

Seine Augen wie die Täubchen über
                                    Quellen,
In Milch gebadet,
In Fülle schwimmend.

Seine Wangen sind wie Blumenbeete,
Wie Kästgen Würze.

Seine Lippen Rosen,
Sie triefen strömende Myrrhe.

Seine Hände güldne Cylinder,
Voll Tyrkisse.

Sein Bauch ein lauteres Elfenbein,
Mit Sapphieren bedeckt.

Seine Schenkel Marmorsäulen,
Gegründet auf güldnem Fuß.

Sein Ansehn wie der Libanon,
Erhaben wie ein Cederbaum.

Sein Gaume Süßigkeiten,
Und ganz Er Lieblichkeiten.

Der ist mein Lieber, der ist mein Freund,
Ihr Töchter Jerusalems.

„Und wohin ging denn dein Geliebter?
Du Schönste der Weiber!
Und wohin wandte sich dein Geliebter?
Wir wollen ihn suchen mit dir.“

Mein Lieber ging in seinen Garten,
Zu seinen Blumenbeeten,
Zu weiden in den Gärten
Zu sammlen Rosen sich.

Mein Lieber, ich bin sein,
Mein Lieber, er ist mein,
Der unter den Rosen weidet.- -

XV. *Die Einzige*

Wie Thirza bist du, meine Liebe, schön
lieblich, wie Jerusalem
Schrecklich, ein Kriegspanier.

Wend’ ab den Blick mir
ich ertrag’ ihn nicht!–

Dein Haar ist wie die Heerde
die klimmt auf Gilead.–

Dein Mund voll weißer Lämmer
gebadet aus der Quelle
Zwillinggebährerinnen Alle,
und keine fehlt.

Die Wangen wie ein Ritz am Granatapfel
den Schleir herfür!

Sechzig der Königinnen
und achzig meiner Lustgespielen
und Mädchen sonder Zahl;

Doch Eine meine Taube, meine Treue
der Mutter liebstes Kind.
Die Mädchen sahn und preiseten sie selig
Die Königinnen all’ und Lustgespielen
frohlockten ihr.–

Schön bist du, meine Freundin,
Wie Thirza schön,
Lieblich wie Jerusalem,
Furchtbar wie ein Kriegsheer.

Wend’ ab die Augen,
Vor mir über,
Sie sind mächtiger, als ich.

Dein Haar ist wie die Gemsenheerde,
Die weidet vom Gilead.

Die Zähne wie die Lämmerheerde,
Die aufsteigt aus der Quelle,
Die alle Zwillinge tragen,
Und keins derselben fehlt.

Wie ein Riz am Granatapfel deine Wange,
Am Lockenhaar.

Sechzig sind Königinnen,
Und achtzig Buhlerinnen,
Und Jungfraun ohne Zahl;
Eine die ist meine Taube,
Meine Reine,
Sie, die Eine ihrer Mutter,
Sie, die Liebste ihrer Mutter.

Es sahen sie die Töchter,
Und preiseten sie selig;
Die Königinnen
Und Buhlerinnen
Lobeten sie.

XVI. *Die Erscheinung*

Wer bricht hervor dort, wie das Morgen-
roth,
Schön wie der Mond, hell wie die Sonn'
ein schrecklich Kriegesheer?–

„Ab zum Nußhain war ich gangen
   wollte schaun die Sträuch' am Bach,
schaun, ob schon der Wein uns knospe
schaun, ob schon der Apfel blüht

Und wußte nicht, und dachte nicht
   daß mich mein Muth
zu meines freien Volkes Schutz
   gesatzt zu Kriegesmacht.–"

   Kehr um o kehre wieder
   o Salome!
   Kehr um, o kehre wieder
   daß wir dich schaun!
   - „Was schauet ihr an Salome?"
Chor: Den Tanz der Gottesheere!–

Wer ist, die aufglänzt wie das Morgen-
roth?
Lieblich wie der Mond,
Rein wie die Sonne,
Furchtbar wie ein Kriegesheer?

„Zum Nußgarten war ich gangen,
Nach den Früchten im Thal zu sehn;
Zu sehn, ob schon der Weinstock knospe,
Ob schon die Aepfel blühn?

Und wußte nicht, daß meine Seele
Mich gesetzt zum Kriegeswagen
Meines edlen Volks."

Kehr um, kehr um o Sulamith!
Kehr um, kehr um,
Wir wollen dich schaun!

„Was wollet ihr schaun an Sulamith?"

Den Tanz der Gottesheere.

XVII. *Der Palmbaum*

Schön ist, o schön dein Tritt in seinem
Schmuck
   du Fürstenkind!
Sie wendet sich, die Hüft', ein Kettenwerk
   gefügt von Meisterhand.

Dein Nabel quillt, ein runder Becher. Nie
   gebricht ihm süßer Trank.
Dein Bauch ein Weizenhügel
   mit Rosenbusch umpflanzt.

Die Brüste, wie zwo Zwillingsrehchen jung.
   Der Hals von Elfenbein
ein Thurm. Die Augen schwimmen
   wie Hesbons Teiche vor Bethrabbims
Thor.

Die Nase, wie der Lustbau Libanus
   der nach Damaskus schaut:

Wie schön sind deine Tritte in den
Schuhn,
Du Tochter des Edlen!
Die Schwingungen deiner Hüften sind
Wie Kettenwerk, geschlungen von
Meistershand.

Dein Nabel ein runder Becher,
Dem's nimmer an Maas gebricht.

Dein Bauch ein Weizenhügel,
Umpflanzt mit Rosen.

Deine zwo Brüste wie zwo Rehchen,
Die Einer Mutter Zwillinge sind.

Dein Hals ein Thurm von Helfenbein.
Deine Augen Teiche zu Hesbon,
Am Thore der Fürstentöchter.

Dein Haupt wie Karmel. Deines Hauptes
　　　　　　　　　　　　　　Haar
ein Königsdiadem.

Schön bist du, lieblich meine Liebe! Du
　　ganz Lust und Liebe selbst.
Ein Palmbaum blüht dein schlanker Wuchs
　　　　　　　　　　　　　empor,
　　mit Trauben an der Brust.

Hinan den Palmbaum! sprach ich, seine
　　　　　　　　　　　　　Zweig
　　erfaß' ich, schlinge mich
ihm an. Dein Busen soll mir Traube seyn,
　　dein Athem süßer Duft.

Dein Mund mir Nektar–

„Süßer Nektar, der dem Lieben
　　sanft und schweigend
geht zum Herzen, dir die Lippe
　　säuselt ein,
und vom Schlummer dir sie wieder
　　säuselt auf!–"

Deine Nase wie das Schloß auf Libanon,
Das gen Damaskus schaut.

Dein Haupt auf dir, wie der Karmel.
Das Haar deines Haupts, wie Purpur,
Ein geflochtner Königsbund.

Wie schön bist du,
Und wie so lieblich bist du,
O Liebe in der Lust!

Deine Höhe
Ist gleich dem Palmenbaum,
Und deine Brüste den Trauben.

Ich sprach: „ich klimm' auf den Palmen-
　　　　　　　　　　　　　baum!
Ich erfasse seine Zweige.
Deine Brüste sollen mir Trauben seyn,
Und deines Athemsduft
Wie Aepfelduft,
Und koste deinen Gaumen
Wie guten Wein–"

„Der einschleicht meinem Lieben
Süß hinein,
Und schlummert die Lipp' ihm
Säuselnd zu.

XVIII. *Die Unschuldliebe*

Ja, Liebster, ich bin meines Lieben, ganz
　　sein Herz ist ganz an mir:
Nur mein Geliebter, komm' hinaus,
　　komm' auf der Unschuld Flur.

Da wollen früh wir aufstehn
und in den Weinberg gehn
und seine junge Knöspchen sehn
und wie der Obstbaum blüht so schön–
Da Liebster will ich dein
mit aller Liebe seyn!–

Schon duften die Liebes-Blumen mir!
Ueber unsrer Hütte Thür
blühn edle Früchte jeder Art
und was ich, alt und neu, dir immer auf-
　　　　　　　　　　　　　bewahrt!

Ja ich bin meines Lieben
Und seine Lust zu mir;
Komm mein Geliebter,
Wir wollen aufs Land,
Auf Dörfern wohnen,
Und früh dann aufstehn,
In den Weinberg gehn,
Sehn, ob der Weinstock blühe?
Ob seine Trauben sich aufthun?
Ob die Aepfel blühn?

Da will ich dir
All meine Liebe geben!

Die Blumen der Liebe duften schon,
Und über unsrer Thür
Ist allerley Schönes,

Ach, daß du nicht mein Bruder bist!
und Einer Mutter Brust
mit mir geküßt!
mein Liebster!–daß wo ich dich fände
ich küßen könnte dich
und niemand höhnte mich
und wähnets Sünde.

Umfaß'n, umschlingen wollt' ich dich
mit Herzenslust,
und führen dich
und bringen mir
in meiner Mutter Haus
Du winktest mir,
ich brächte dir
den Most von *meinen* Bäumen,
den Trank von meiner Hand.

Und seine Linke ruhet
mir unterm Haupt
und seine Recht' umarmt mich
hält mich–

Neues und Alt,
Mein Lieber, ich barg es dir.

Wer gibt mir dich
Zum Bruder mir?
Der meiner Mutter
Brüste gesogen.

Ich fände dich draussen
Und küßte dich,
Und keiner verachtete mich.

Ich wollt dich führen,
Ich wollt dich bringen
In meiner Mutter Haus.

Du solltest mich lehren,
Ich würde dich tränken
Mit Trank, den ich bereitet,
Mit Most von meinem Baum.

Seine Linke
Mir unterm Haupt,
Und seine Rechte
Umfaßt mich."

XIX. *Schlummerlied*

„Bei des Feldes leisem Reh
horcht ihr Töchter Solyme.
Bei der Hindin auf der Flur
hört den Schwur!
Meiner Lieben naht euch nicht
weckt sie nicht! störet nicht
ihres Schlummers sanfte süße Nacht,
bis aufgeht ihr Angesicht
Sie erwacht!"

„Ich beschwör' euch, Töchter Jerusalem,
Wenn ihr sie weckt!
Wenn ihr sie regt, die Liebe!
Bis es ihr gefällt!"

XX. *Die Erscheinung*

Wer kommt dort aus der Wüsten herauf?
　Gelehnt auf ihren Freund!–

　Unter dem Apfelbaum,
　wo deine Mutter dich empfing
　wo deine Mutter dich gebar
　da wars, da weckt' ich dich!–

Ein Siegel präg mich dir aufs Herz,
Siegel auf deinen Arm!–
Stark ist die Liebe, wie Tod,
Ihr Eifer hart wie die Höll'.
Glut ihre Kohlen
Flammen des Herrn!
Viel Waßer mögen nicht aus sie löschen,
　　　　　　　　　　　　die Liebe!
Ströme sie nicht ersäufen!
Und gäb' ein Mann auch Haus und Gut um
　　　　　　　　　　　　　Liebe,
sie verschmähn, sie verachten ihn!–

Wer ist, die dort aufsteigt
Aus der Wüsten her?
Gelehnt auf ihren Geliebten.

Unter dem Apfelbaume
Wecket' ich dich.
Da gebar dich deine Mutter,
Da gebar, die dich geboren.

„Ein Siegel präge mich auf dein Herz,
Ein Siegel auf deinen Arm!
Denn stark, wie der Tod, ist Liebe;
Ihr Eifer hart, wie die Höll.
Ihre Kohlen glühende Kohlen,
Flamme des Herrn.

Viel Wasser mögen nicht aus sie löschen,
　　　　　　　　　　　　die Liebe,
Und Ströme sie nicht ersäufen.
Und gäb' ein Mann auch Haus und Gut
　　　　　　　　　　　um Liebe;
Sie verschmähn, sie verachten ihn.

XXI. *Das Mägdlein*

A.　Noch ist unsre Schwester klein
　　　noch knospet nur ihr Busen:
　　wie werden wir dem Mägdlein thun,
　　　wenn man wird um sie buhlen?

Der Eine spricht:
Unsre Schwester ist noch klein,
Noch knospet nur ihr Busen;
Was wollen wir unsrer Schwester thun,
Wenn man wird um sie werben?

B.　Wie man der Mauer thut,
　　wie man den Pforten thut,
　　sie wahren!
　　Bester man auf Mauern baut,
　　Cederpforten man sich traut,
　　die wahren!–

Der Zweite:
Ist sie eine Mauer,
So wollen wir auf sie bauen
Einen Silberpallast.
Ist sie eine Pforte,
So wollen wir sie verwahren
Mit Cedernholz.

C.　Und bin ich eine Mauer denn
　　　mein Busen der trägt Vesten,
　　Kaum als er diese Vesten sah
　　　gab er der Stadt den Frieden.–

Die Schwester:
Ja eine Mauer bin ich,
Und meine Brüste Thürme.
Da war ich in seinen Augen,
Wie Eine, die Frieden fand.

Das Hüten und Wahren.

Zu Baal-Hamon
hatt' ein'n Weinberg Salomon:
Der that den Weinberg Hütern an,
daß tausend Silberlinge
ihm für den Weinberg bringe
Ein Hütersmann.
   Wohl mir! wohl mir!
Mein Weinberg, der blüht nah vor mir.
Sie bringen dir die tausend über,
O Salomon,
und jeder schafft sich noch wohl zweimal-
                     hundert drüber
- *Hüterlohn*.

Einen Weinberg hatte Salomon
Zu Baal-Hamon.
Er that den Weinberg Hütern aus,
Daß jeder ihm für seine Früchte
Tausend Silberlinge brächte.

Mein Weinberg ist
Vor Augen mir:
Die Tausend werden dem Salomo,
Und die die Frucht ihm hüten,
Haben zweihundert noch.

XXII. *Besuch im Garten*

A. Du Wohnerin der Gärten,
   Die Mitgespielen horchen deiner Stimme
   Laß hören sie mich!–
B. Fleuch, mein Freund, sei gleich dem
                     Reh
   Dem jungen Hirsch auf duftiger Höh - -

Du Wohnerin der Gärten,
Die Gespielen horchen auf deine Stimme,
Laß mich sie hören- -

„Fleuch, mein Geliebter, gleich dem Reh,
Dem jungen Hirsch auf duftender Höh- -

Appendix B

LUTHER'S TRANSLATION OF THE SONG OF SONGS

This Appendix reproduces the translation of 1545 given in *Die Deutsche Bibel 1522–1546* (*WKGB*, X/2, pp. 134-47).

Das Hohelied Salomo

I

[2]Er küsse mich mit dem Kusse seines Mundes, Denn deine Brüste sind lieblicher denn Wein. [3]Das man deine gute Salbe rieche, Dein Name ist ein ausgeschütte Salbe, Darumb lieben dich die Megde.

[4]Zeuch mich dir nach, so lauffen wir, Der König füret mich in seine Kamer, Wir frewen uns, und sind frölich uber dir. Wir gedencken an deine Brüste mehr, denn an den Wein, Die Fromen lieben dich.

[5]Ich bin schwartz, Aber gar lieblich, jr Töchter Jerusalem, wie die hütten Kedar, wie die teppiche Salomo. [6]Sehet mich nicht an, Das ich so schwartz bin, denn die Sonne hat mich so verbrand. Meiner mutter Kinder zürnen mit mir, Man hat mich zur Hüterin der Weinberge gesetzt, Aber meinen Weinberg den ich hatte, habe ich nicht behütet.

[7]Sage mir an du, den meine Seele liebet, Wo du weidest, wo du rugest im mittage? Das ich nicht hin und her gehen müsse, bey den Herden deiner Gesellen.

[8]Kennestu dich nicht, du schöneste unter den Weibern, So gehe hin aus auff die fusstapffen der Schafe, und weide deine Böcke bey den Hirten heusern.

[9]Ich gleiche dich, meine Freundin, meinem reisigen Zeuge an den wagen Pharao. [10]Deine Backen stehen lieblich in den Spangen, und dein Hals in den Keten. [11]Wir wollen dir güldene Spangen machen mit silbern Pöcklin.

[12]Da der König sich her wandte, gab mein Narde seinen ruch. [13]Mein Freund ist mir ein büschel Myrrhen, das zwisschen meinen Brüsten hanget. [14]Mein Freund ist mir ein drauben Copher, in den Weingarten zu Engeddi.

[15]Sihe, meine Freundin, du bist schöne, schöne bistu, Deine augen sind wie Tauben augen. [16]Sihe mein Freund, du bist schön und lieblich, Unser Bette grünet, [17]unser Heuser balcken sind Cedern, unser latten sind Cipressen.

II

[1]Ich bin ein Blumen zu Saron, und ein Rose im tal. [2]Wie eine Rose unter den Dörnen, So ist mein Freundin unter den Töchtern. [3]Wie ein Apffelbawm unter den wilden Bewmen, So ist mein Freund unter den Sönen. Ich sitze unter dem Schatten des ich begere, und seine Frucht ist meiner Kele süsse.

[4]Er füret mich in den Weinkeller, und die Liebe ist sein Panir uber mir. [5]Er erquicket mich mit Blumen, und labet mich mit Epffeln, Denn ich bin kranck fur liebe. [6]Seine Lincke unter meinem Heubte, und seine Rechte hertzet mich.

[7]Ich beschwere euch, jr töchter Jerusalem, bey den Rehen oder bey den Hinden auff dem felde, Das jr meine Freundin nicht auffweckt noch reget, bis das jr selbst gefellt.

[8]Da ist die stimme meins Freunds, Sihe, Er kompt und hüpffet auff den Bergen, und springet auff den Hügeln. [9]Mein Freund ist gleich einem Rehe oder jungen Hirss. Sihe, Er stehet hinder unser Wand, und sihet durchs fenster, und gucket durchs gitter.

[10]Mein Freund antwortet, und spricht zu mir, Stehe auff meine Freundin, meine schöne, und kom her. [11]Denn sihe, der Winter ist vergangen, der Regen ist weg und da hin, [12]Die Blumen sind erfür komen im Lande, Der Lentz ist er bey komen, und die Dordeltaube lesst sich hören in unserm Lande. [13]Der Feigenbawm hat knoten gewonnen, die Weinstöcke haben augen gewonnen, und geben jren Ruch, Stehe auff meine Freundin und kom, meine schöne kom her. [14]Meine Taube in den felslöchern, in den steinritzen, Zeige mir deine gestalt, Las mich hören deine stim, Denn deine stim ist süsse, und deine gestalt lieblich.

[15]Fahet uns die Füchse, die kleinen Füchse, die die Weinberge verderben, Denn unsere Weinberge haben augen gewonnen. [16]Mein Freund ist mein, und ich bin sein, der unter den Rosen weydet, [17]Bis der tag küle werde, und der schatten weiche. Kere umb, werde wie ein Rehe mein Freund, oder wie ein junger Hirss auff den Scheidebergen.

III

[1]Ich sucht des nachts in meinem Bette, den meine Seele liebet, Ich sucht, Aber ich fand jn nicht. [2]Ich wil auffstehen, und in der Stad umbgehen auff den gassen und strassen, und suchen, den meine Seele liebet, Ich sucht, Aber ich fand jn nicht. [3]Es funden mich die Wechter die in der Stad umbgehen, Habt jr nicht gesehen den meine Seele liebet? [4]Da ich ein wenig fur jnen uber kam, da fand ich den meine

Seele liebet, Ich halt jn, und wil jn nicht lassen, Bis ich jn bringe in meiner Mutter haus, in meiner Mutter kamer.

⁵Ich beschwere euch, jr töchter Jerusalem, bey den Rehen oder Hinden auff dem felde, Das jr meine Freundin nicht auffweckt, noch reget, Bis das jr selbs gefellet.

⁶Wer ist die, die auff gehet aus der Wüsten, wie ein gerader Rauch, wie ein Gereuch von myrrhen, weyrauch und allerley puluer eins Apotekers?

⁷Sihe, umb das bette Salomo her, stehen sechzig starcken aus den starcken in Israel. ⁸Sie halten alle Schwerter, und sind geschickt zu streitten. Ein jglicher hat sein Schwert an seiner hüfften, umb der furcht willen in der nacht.

⁹Der könig Salomo lies jm eine Senffte machen von holtz aus Libanon, ¹⁰Der selben Seulen waren silbern, die Decke gülden, der Sitz purpern, der Boden mitten inne war lieblich gepflastert, umb der Töchter willen zu Jerusalem.

¹¹Gehet er aus und schawet an, jr töchter Zion, den könig Salomo, in der Krone, da mit jn seine Mutter gekrönet hat, am tage seine Hochzeit, und am tage der freuden seines hertzens.

IIII

¹Sihe meine Freundin, du bist schön, Sihe, schön bistu. Deine Augen sind wie taubenaugen, zwischen deinen Zöpffen. Dein Har ist wie die Ziegen herd, die beschoren sind auff dem berge Gilead. ²Deine Zeene sind wie die herde mit beschnitten wolle, die aus der schwemme komen, die allzumal Zwilling tragen, und ist keine unter jnen unfruchtbar. ³Deine Lippen sind wie eine rosinfarbe schnur, und deine Rede lieblich. Deine Wangen sind wie der ritz am Granatapffel, zwischen deinen zöpffen. ⁴Dein Hals ist wie der thurm David, mit brustwehr gebawet, daran tausent Schilde hangen, und allerley waffen der Starcken. ⁵Deine zwo Brüste sind wie zwey junge Rehe zwillinge, die unter den rosen weiden, ⁶bis der tag küle werde, und der schatten weiche. Ich wil zum Myrrhenberge gehen und zum Weyrauch hügel.

⁷Du bist aller ding schöne, meine Freundin, und ist kein flecken an dir. Kom meine Braut vom Libanon, ⁸Kom vom Libanon, Gehe er ein, Trit her von der höhe Amana, von der höhe Senir und Hermon, von den wonungen der Lewen, von den bergen der Leoparden. ⁹Du hast mir das hertz genomen, meine Schwester liebe Braut, mit deiner augen einem, und mit deiner Halsketen eine.

¹⁰Wie schön sind deine Brüste, meine Schwester, liebe Braut, deine Brüste sind lieblicher denn Wein, und der geruch deiner Salben ubertrifft alle Würtze. ¹¹Deine Lippen, meine Braut, sind wie trieffender honigseim, honig und milch ist unter deiner Zungen, und deiner Kleider geruch ist, wie der geruch Libanon.

[12]Meine Schwester, liebe Braut, Du bist ein verschlossen Garten, Ein verschlossen Quelle, ein versiegelter Born. [13]Dein Gewechs ist wie ein Lustgarte von Granatepffeln, mit edlen Früchten, Cipern mit Narden, [14]Narden mit Saffran, Kalmus und Cynamen mit allerley bewmen des Weyrauchs, Myrrhen und Aloes mit allen besten Würtzen, [15]Wie ein Gartenbrun, wie ein Born lebendiger Wasser, die von Libano fliessen.

[16]Stehe auff Nordwind und kom Sudwind, und webe durch meinen Garten, das seine Würtze trieffen.

V

[17]Mein Freund kome in seinen Garten, und esse seiner edlen Früchten. [1]Ich kom, meine Schwester, liebe Braut, in meinen Garten, Ich habe meine Myrrhen sampt meinen Würtzen abgebrochen, Ich hab meins Seims sampt meinem Honige gessen, Ich hab meins Weins sampt meiner Milch getruncken, Esset meine Lieben, und trinckt meine Freunde und werdet truncken.

[2]Ich schlaff, Aber mein hertz wacht, Da ist die stim, meins Freundes der anklopffet. Thu mir auff liebe Freundin meine schwester, meine Taube, meine frome, Denn mein heubt ist vol tawes, und meine locken vol nachtstropffen. [3]Ich habe meinen Rock ausgezogen, wie sol ich jn wider anziehen? Ich habe meine Füsse gewasschen, wie sol ich sie wider besuddeln?

[4]Aber mein Freund steckt seine Hand durchs loch, Und mein Leyb erzittert da für. [5]Da stund ich auff, das ich meinem Freunde auffthet, Meine hende troffen mit Myrrhen, und Myrrhen lieffen uber meine Finger an dem rigel am schlos, [6]Und da ich meim Freund auffgethan hatte, war er weg und hin gegangen.

Da gieng meine Seele er aus nach seim wort, Ich sucht jn, Aber ich fand jn nicht, Ich rieff, Aber er antwortet mir nicht. [7]Es funden mich die Hüter die in der Stad umbgehen, die schlugen mich wund, Die Hüter auff der mauren namen mir meinen Schleier. [8]Ich beschwere euch jr Töchter Jerusalem, findet jr meinen Freund, so saget jm, das ich fur Liebe kranck lige.

[9]Was ist dein Freund fur andern Freunden, O du schönst unter den Weibern? Was ist dein Freund fur andern Freunden, das du uns so beschworen hast? [10]Mein Freund ist weis und rot, auserkoren unter viel tausent. [11]Sein Heubt ist das feinest Gold. Seine Locken sind kraus, schwartz wie ein Rabe. [12]Seine Augen sind wie Taubenaugen an den wasserbechen, mit milch gewasschen, und stehen in der fülle. [13]Seine Backen sind wie die wachsende wurtzgertlin der Apoteker. Seine Lippen sind wie Rosen die mit fliessender Myrrhen trieffen. [14]Seine Hende sind wie güldene Ringe vol Türkissen. Sein Leib ist wie rein Elphenbein mit Saphiren geschmuckt. [15]Seine Beine sind wie Marmelseulen, gegründet auff gülden füssen. Seine gestallt ist wie Libanon, ausserwelt wie Cedern. [16]Seine Kele ist süsse und

gaantz lieblich, Ein solcher ist mein Freund, mein Freund ist ein solcher, jr töchter Jerusalem.

VI

[17]Wo ist denn dein Freund hin gegangen, O du schönest unter den Weibern? Wo hat sich dein Freund hin gewand? So wöllen wir mit dir jn suchen. [1]Mein Freund ist hin ab gegangen in seinen Garten, zu den Wurtzgertlin, das er sich weide unter den Garten und Rosen breche. [2]Mein Freund ist mein, und ich bin sein, der unter den Rosen sich weidet.

[3]Du bist schön, meine Freundin, wie Thirza, lieblich wie Jerusalem, schrecklich wie Heerspitzen [4](Wende deine Augen von mir, Denn sie machen mich brünstig) Deine Har sind wie ein herd Ziegen, die auff dem berge Gilead geschoren sind. [5]Deine Zeene sind wie ein herd Schaf, die aus der schwemme komen, die allzu mal Zwilling tragen, und ist keine unfruchtbar unter jnen. [6]Deine Wangen sind wie ein Ritz am Granatapffel, zwisschen deinen zöpffen.

[7]Sechzig ist der Königinnen, und achzig der Kebsweiber, und der Jungfrawen ist kein zal. [8]Aber eine ist meine Taube, mein Frome, eine ist jrer Mutter die liebste, und die ausserwelete jrer Mutter. Da sie die Töchter sahen, preiseten sie dieselbige selig, die Königinnen und Kebsweiber lobeten sie. [9]Wer ist die erfür bricht, wie die Morgenröte, schön wie der Mond, ausserwelet wie die Sonne, schrecklich wie die Heerspitzen.

[10]Ich bin hin ab in den Nussgarten gegangen, zu schawen die Streuchlin am Bach, zu schawen ob der Weinstock blühet, ob die Granatepffel grüneten. [11]Meine Seele wusts nicht, das er mich zum wagen Ami-Nadib gesetzt hette.

[12]Kere wider, kere wider, o Sulamith, kere wider, kere wider, das wir dich schawen, Was sehet jr an Sulamith, den Reigen zu Mahanaim?

VII

[1]Wie schön ist dein gang in den Schuhen, du Fürsten tochter. Deine Lenden stehen gleich an einander, wie zwo Spangen, die des Meisters hand gemacht hat. [2]Dein Nabel ist wie ein runder Becher, dem nimer getrenck mangelt. Dein Bauch ist wie ein Weitzenhauffe umbsteckt mit Rosen. [3]Deine zwo Brüste sind, wie zwey junge Rehe zwillinge. [4]Dein Hals ist wie ein Elffenbeinen thurm. Deine Augen sind, wie die Teiche zu Hesbon, am thor Bathrabbim. Deine Nase ist wie der Thurm auff Libanon, der gegen Damascon sihet. [5]Dein Heubt stehet auff dir, wie Carmelus. Das Har auff deinem heubt, ist wie die purpur des Königs in falten gebunden. [6]Wie schön und wie lieblich bistu, du Liebe in wollüsten. [7]Deine Leng ist gleich einem Palmbawm, und deine Brüste den Weindrauben. [8]Ich sprach, Ich mus auff den Palmbawm steigen, und seine zweige ergreiffen, Las deine Brüste sein wie

Drauben am weinstock, und deiner Nasenruch wie Epffel, [9]und deine Kele wie guter Wein, der meinem Freunde glat eingehe, und rede von fernigem. [10]Mein Freund ist mein, und er helt sich auch zu mir.

[11]Kom mein Freund, las uns auffs feld hin aus gehen, und auff den Dorffen bleiben. [12]Das wir früe auffstehen zu den Weinbergen, Das wir sehen, ob der Weinstock blühet und augen gewonnen habe, Ob die Granatepffelbewm ausgeschlagen sind, Da wil ich dir meine Brüste geben. [13]Die Lilien geben den ruch, und fur unser thür sind allerley edle Früchte. Mein Freund ich hab dir beide heurige und fernige behalten.

VIII

[1]O Das ich dich, mein Bruder, der du meiner Mutter brüste saugest draussen fünde, und dich küssen müste, das mich niemand hönete. [2]Ich wolt dich füren und in meiner Mutter haus bringen, da du mich leren soltest, Da wolt ich dich trencken mit gemachtem Wein, und mit dem Most meiner Granatepffel. [3]Seine Lincke ligt unter meinem Heubt, und seine Rechte hertzet mich.

[4]Ich beschwere euch töchter Jerusalem, Das jr meine Liebe nicht auffweckt noch reget, bis das jr selbst gefellet. [5]Wer ist die, die er auff feret von der Wüsten, und lehnet sich auff jren Freund? Unter dem Apffelbawm weckt ich dich, da deine Mutter dich geboren hatte, da mit dir gelegen ist, die dich gezeuget hat.

[6]Setze mich wie ein Siegel auff dein Hertz, und wie ein siegel auff deinen Arm, Denn Liebe ist starck wie der Tod, und Eiuer ist fest wie die Helle, Ir glut ist fewrig, und eine flamme des HERRN, [7]Das auch viel Wasser nicht mügen die Liebe auslesschen, noch die ströme sie erseuffen, Wenn einer alles Gut in seinem hause umb die Liebe geben wolt, so gülte es alles nichts.

[8]Unser Schwester ist klein, und hat keine Brüste, Was sollen wir unser Schwester thun, wenn man sie nu sol anreden? [9]Ist sie eine Maure, so wöllen wir silbern Bollwerg drauff bawen. Ist sie eyne Thür, so wöllen wir sie festigen mit Cedern bolen. [10]Ich bin eine Maur, und meine Brüste sind wie Thürne, Da bin ich worden fur seinen augen, als die Frieden findet.

[11]Salomo hat einen Weinberg zu BaalHamon, Er gab den Weinberg den Hütern, das ein jglicher fur seine Früchte brechte tausent Silberlinge. [12]Mein Weinberg ist fur mir. Dir Salomo gebüren tausent, Aber den Hütern zwey hundert sampt seinen Früchten.

[13]Die du wonest in den Garten, Las mich deine stimme hören, Die Geselschafften mercken drauff. [14]Fleuch mein Freund, und sey gleich eim Rehe oder jungen Hirssen auff den Würtzbergen.

Appendix C

GOETHE'S TRANSLATION OF THE SONG OF SONGS

This Appendix reproduces the translation of 1775 given in *WW*, XXXVII, pp. 299-310.

Das Hohelied Salomons

Küss er mich den Kuss seines Mundes! Trefflicher ist deine Liebe denn Wein. Welch ein süser Geruch deine Salbe, ausgegossne Salb ist dein Nahme, drum lieben dich die Mädgen. Zeuch mich! Laufen wir doch schon nach dir! Führte mich der König in seine Kammer, wir sprängen und freuten uns in dir. Priesen deine Lieb über den Wein.

Lieben dich doch die Edlen all!

*

Schwarz bin ich, doch schön, Töchter Jerusalems! Wie Hütten Kedars, wie Teppiche Salomos.

Schaut mich nicht an dass ich braun bin, von der Sonne verbrannt. Meiner Mutter Söhne feinden mich an, sie stellten mich zur Weinberge Hüterinn. Den Weinberg der mein war hütet ich nicht.

*

Sage mir du den meine Seele liebt, wo du weidest? Wo du ruhest am Mittag? Warum soll ich umgehn an den Heerden deiner Gesellen.

Weist dus nicht, schönste der Weiber, folg nur den Tapfen der Heerde, weide deine Böcke um die Wohnung der Hirten.

*

Meinem reisigen Zeug unter Pharaos Wagen vergleich ich dich, mein liebgen. Schön sind deine Backen in den Spangen, dein Hals in den Ketten. Spangen von Gold sollst du haben mit silbernen Pöcklein.

*

So lang der König mich koset giebt meine Narde den Ruch.

*

Ein Büschel Myrrhen ist mein Freund, zwischen meinen Brüsten übernachtend. Ein Trauben Kopher ist mir mein Freund in den Wingerten Engedi.

*

Sieh du bist schön, meine Freundinn! Sieh du bist schön! Tauben Augen die deinen.

Sieh du bist schön, mein Freund. Auch lieblich! Unser Bette grünt, unsrer Hütte Balcken sind Cedren, unsre Zinnen Cypressen.

*

Ich bin die Rose im Thal! Bin ein May Blümgen! Wie die Rose unter den Dornen so ist mein Liebgen unter den Mädgen. Wie der Apfelbaum unter den Waldbäumen, ist mein liebster unter den Männern. Seines Schattens begehr ich, nieder sizz ich und süss ist meinem Gaum seine Frucht. Er führt mich in die Kelter, über mir weht seine Liebe. Stüzzet mich mit Flaschen, polstert mir mit Äpfeln denn Kranck bin ich für Liebe. Seine lincke trägt mein Haupt, seine rechte herzt mich. Ich beschwör euch, Töchter Jerusalems, bey den Rehen, bey den Hinden des Feldes, rühret sie nicht, reget sie nicht meine Freundinn biss sie mag.

*

Sie ists die Stimme meines Freundes. Er kommt! Springend über die Berge! Tanzend über die Hügel! Er gleicht mein Freund einer Hinde, er gleicht einem Rehbock. Er steht schon an der Wand, siehet durchs Fenster, gucket durchs Gitter! Da beginnt er und spricht: Steh auf, meine Freundinn, meine Schöne, und komm. Der Winter ist vorbey, der Regen vorüber. Hin ist er! Blumen sprossen vom Boden, der Lenz ist gekommen, und der Turteltaube Stimme hört ihr im Lande. Der Feigenbaum knotet. Die Rebe duftet. Steh auf, meine Freundinn, meine Schöne, und komm. Meine Taube in den Steinrizzen im Hohlhort des Felshangs. Zeig mir dein Antlitz, tön' deine Stimme, denn lieblich ist deine Stimme, schön dein Antlitz. Fahet uns die Füchse, die kleinen Füchse die die Wingerte verderben, die fruchtbaren Wingerte.

*

Mein Freund ist mein, ich sein, der unter Lilien weidet. Biss der Tag athmet, die Schatten fliehen, wende dich, sey gleich, mein Freund, einer Hinde, einem Rehbock, auf den Bergen Bether.

*

Auf meiner Schlafstäte zwischen den Gebürgen sucht ich den meine Seele liebt, sucht ihn, aber fand ihn nicht. Aufstehen will ich und umgehen in der Stadt, auf den Märckten und Strasen. Suchen den meine Seele liebt, ich sucht ihn, aber fand ihn nicht. Mich trafen die umgehenden Hüter der Stadt: den meine Seele liebt, saht ihr ihn nicht? Kaum da ich sie vorüber war fand ich den meine Seele liebt, ich fass ihn, ich lass ihn nicht. Mit mir soll er in meiner Mutter Haus, in meiner Mutter Kammer.

*

Wer ist die herauf tritt aus der Wüsten wie Rauch Säulen, wie Gerauch Myrrhen und Weyrauch, köstlicher Spezereyen.

*

Schön bist du, meine Freundinn, ia schön, Taubenaugen die deinen zwischen deinen Locken.
Dein Haar eine blinckende Ziegenheerde auf dem Berge Gilead. Deine Zähne eine geschorene Heerde, aus der Schwemme steigend, all zwilings trächtig, kein Misfall unter ihnen. Deine Lippen eine rosinfarbe Schnur, lieblich deine Rede! Wie der Riz am Granatapfel deine Schläfe zwischen deinen Locken. Wie der Turn David dein Hals, gebauet zur Wehre, dran hängen Tausend Schilde, alles Schilde der Helden. Deine beyden Brüste, wie Rehzwillinge die unter Lilien weiden. Völlig schön bist, meine Freundinn, kein Flecken an dir.

*

Komm vom Libanon, meine Braut, Komm vom Libanon! Schau her von dem Gipfel Amana, vom Gipfel Senir und Hermon, von den Wohnungen der Löwen, von den Bergen der Parden.

*

Gewonnen hast du mich, Schwester, liebe Braut, mit deiner Augen einem, mit deiner Halsketten einer. Hold ist deine Liebe, Schwester, liebe Braut! Trefflicher deine liebe denn Wein, deiner Salbe Geruch über alle Gewürze.
Honig triefen deine Lippen, meine Braut, unter deiner Zunge sind Honig und Milch, deiner Kleider Geruch wie der Ruch Libanons. Schwester, liebe Braut, ein verschlossner Garten Bist du, eine verschlossne Quelle, ein versiegelter Born. Dein Gewächse ein Lustgarten Granatbäume mit der Würzfrucht, Cypern mit Narden, Narden und Saffran, Calmus und Cynnamen, allerley Weyrauch Bäume, Myrrhen und Aloe und all die trefflichsten Würzen. Wie ein Garten Brunn, ein Born lebendiger Wasser, Bäche vom Libanon. Hebe dich, Nordwind, komm, Südwind, durchwehe meinen Garten dass seine Würze triefen.

*

Er komme in seinen Garten mein Freund und esse die Frucht seiner Würze!
Schwester, liebe Braut, ich kam zu meinem Garten, brach ab meine Myrrhen, meine Würze. As meinen Seim, meinen Honig, Tranck meinen Wein, meine Milch. Esset, Gesellen! Trincket, werdet truncken in Liebe.

*

Ich schlafe, aber mein Herz wacht. Horch! Die Stimme meines klopfenden Freundes: Öffne mir, meine Schwester, meine Freundinn, meine Taube, meine Fromme, denn mein Haupt ist voll Thaus und meine Locken voll Nachttropfen. Bin ich doch entkleidet, wie soll ich mich anziehen? hab ich doch die Füsse gewaschen, soll ich sie wieder besudeln? Da reichte mein Freund mit der Hand durchs Schalter und mich überliefs. Da stund ich auf meinem Freunde zu öffnen, meine Hände troffen von Myrrhen, Myrrhen liefen über meine Hände an dem Riegel am Schloss. Ich öffnete meinem Freund aber er war weggeschlichen, hingegangen. Auf seine Stimme kam ich hervor, ich sucht ihn und fand ihn nicht, rief ihm, er antwortet nicht. Mich trafen die umgehenden Wächter der Stadt. Schlugen mich, verwundeten mich, nahmen mir den Schleier die Wächter der Mauern.

*

Ich beschwör euch, Töchter Jerusalems. Findet ihr meinen Freund, wollt ihr ihm sagen dass ich für Liebe kranck bin. Was ist dein Freund vor andern Freunden, du schönste der Weiber, was ist dein Freund vor andern Freunden, dass du uns so beschwörest? Mein Freund ist weis und roth auserkohren unter viel Tausenden. Sein Haupt das reinste Gold, seine Haarlocken schwarz wie ein Rabe. Seine Augen Taubenaugen an den Wasserbächen, gewaschen in Milch, stehend in Fülle. Würzgärtlein seine Wangen, volle Büsche des Weyrauchs, seine Lippen Rosen träufelnd, köstliche Myrrhen. Seine Hände Goldringe mit Türkisen besezzt, sein Leib glänzend Elfenbein geschmückt mit Sapphiren. Seine Beine wie Marmorsäulen auf güldenen Sockeln. Seine Gestalt wie der Libanon, auserwehlet wie Cedern. Seine Kehle voll Süsigkeit, er ganz mein Begehren. Ein solcher ist mein Liebster, mein Freund ist ein solcher, o Töchter Jerusalems.

*

Wohin ging dein Freund, du schönste der Weiber? Wohin wandte sich dein Freund, wir wollen ihn mit dir suchen. Mein Freund ging in seinen Garten hinab, zu den Würzbeeten, sich zu weiden im Garten, Lilien zu pflücken. Mein Freund ist mein und ich bin sein der unter Lilien sich weidet.

*

Schön bist du, meine Freundinn, wie Thirza! Herrlich wie Jerusalem! Schröcklich wie Heerspizzen. Wende deine Augen ab von mir, sie machen mich brünstig.

*

Sechzig sind der Königinnen, achzig der Kebsweiber, Jungfrauen unzählig. Aber Eine ist meine Taube, Eine meine Fromme. Die einzige ihrer Mutter, die köstliche ihrer Mutter. Sie sahen die Mädgen, sie priesen die Königinnen und Kebsweiber, und rühmten sie.

*

Wer ist die hervorblickt wie die Morgenröthe? Lieblich wie der Mond, rein wie die Sonne, furchtbaar wie Heerspizzen.

*

Zum Nussgarten bin ich gangen zu schauen das grünende Thal. Zu sehen ob der Weinstock triebe, ob die Granatbäume blühten.

*

Kehre! Kehre! Sulamith! Kehre! Dass wir dich sehen. Seht ihr nicht Sulamith wie einen Reihen Tanz der Engel? Schön ist dein Gang in den Schuen, o Fürstentochter, deiner Lenden gleiche Gestalt wie zwo Spangen, Spangen des Künstlers Meisterstück. Dein Nabel ein runder Becher der Fülle, dein Leib ein Weizenhaufen umsteckt mit Rosen. Dein Hals ein Elfenbeinerner Turn, deine Augen wie die Teiche zu Hesbon am Thore Bathrabbim, deine nase der Turn Libanon schauend gegen Damaskus. Dein Haupt auf dir wie Carmel, deine Haarflechten wie Purpur des Königs in Falten gebunden. Wie schön bist du, wie lieblich! du Liebe in Wollüsten. Deine Gestalt ist Palmengleich, Weintrauben deine Brüste. Ich will auf den Palmbaum steigen, sagt ich, und seine Zweige ergreifen. Lass deine brüste seyn wie Trauben am Weinstock, deiner Nasen ruch wie Äpfel. Dein gaum wie guter Wein, der mir glatt eingehe, der die schlafenden geschwäzzig macht.

*

Ich bin meinem Freunde, bin auch sein ganzes Begehren!

*

Komm, mein Freund, lass uns aufs Feld gehn, auf den Landhäusern schlafen. Früh stehn wir auf zu den Weinbergen, sehen ob er der Weinstock blühe, Beeren treibe, Blüten die Granatbäume haben. Da will ich dich herzen nach Vermögen.

*

Die Lilien geben den Ruch, vor unsrer Thür sind allerley Würze, heurige, fernige. Meine Liebe bewahrt ich dir!

*

Hätt ich dich wie meinen Bruder der meiner Mutter Brüste saugt. Fänd ich dich draus ich küsste dich, niemand sollte mich höhnen. Ich führte dich in meiner Mutter Haus dass du mich lehrtest! Tränckte dich mit Würzwein, mit Most der Granaten.

*

Wer ist die heraufgeht aus der Wüsten, sich gesellet zu ihrem Freund?

*

Unterm Apfelbaum weck ich dich wo deine Mutter dich gebahr, wo dein pflegte die dich zeugte.

*

Sezze mich wie ein Siegel auf dein Herz, wie ein Siegel auf deinen Arm. Denn starck wie der Todt ist die Liebe. Eifer gewaltig wie die Hölle. Ihre Glut feuer Glut, eine fressende Flamme. Viel Wasser können die Liebe nicht löschen, Ströme sie nicht ersäufen. Böt einer all sein Haab und Gut um Liebe man spottete nur sein.

BIBLIOGRAPHY

Primary Sources

A. Johann Gottfried Herder

Manuscripts

Lieder der Liebe, MSS(1), (2), (3) and (a), as well as fragments, in Herder's *Nachlaß*, Kapsel VI, Konvolute 1-24 and 61-62, and Kapsel XX, Konvolute 120-23 (Handschriftenabteilung, Staatsbibliothek Preußischer Kulturbesitz, Berlin).

Collected Works

Sämmtliche Werke (ed. Bernhard Suphan; 33 vols.; Berlin: Weidmann, 1877–1913). For a list of the main primary texts used from this edition, see the Introduction to this study.

Werke (ed. Heinrich Meyer; 10 vols.; published as Deutsche National-Litteratur 74–77 [ed. Joseph Kürschner; Stuttgart: Union Deutsche Verlagsgesellschaft, 1893]).

Werke (ed. Theodor Matthias; 5 vols.; Meyers Klassiker-Ausgaben; Leipzig and Vienna: Bibliographisches Institut, n.d.).

Werke (ed. Martin Bollacher *et al.*, 10 vols.; especially vol. III, *Volkslieder, Übertragungen, Dichtungen* [ed. Ulrich Gaier]; and vol. V, *Schriften zum Alten Testament* [containing *Über die ersten Urkunden des Menschlichen Geschlechts: Einige Anmerkungen, Älteste Urkunde des Menschengeschlechts* and *Vom Geist der Ebräischen Poesie*] [ed. Rudolf Smend, Bibliothek deutscher Klassiker, 93; Frankfurt am Main: Deutscher Klassiker Verlag, 1990]).

Letters

Aus Herders Nachlaß: Ungedruckte Briefe (ed. Heinrich Düntzer and Ferdinand Gottfried Herder; 3 vols.; Frankfurt am Main: Meidinger, 1856–57).

Briefwechsel mit seiner Braut Caroline Flachsland, in Düntzer and Herder (eds.), *Aus Herders Nachlaß: Ungedruckte Briefe*, III.

Von und an Herder: Ungedruckte Briefe aus Herders Nachlaß (ed. Heinrich Düntzer and Ferdinand Gottfried Herder; 3 vols.; Leipzig: Dyk, 1861–62).

Herders Briefe in einem Band (ed. Regine Otto; Bibliothek deutscher Klassiker; Berlin and Weimar: Aufbau-Verlag, 1970).

Briefe an Hamann/Herders Briefwechsel mit Nicolai (ed. Otto Hoffmann; Berlin: Gaertner, 1889, repr. Hildesheim: Georg Olms, 1975).

Briefe: Gesamtausgabe 1763–1803 (ed. Wilhelm Dobbek and Günter Arnold; 9 vols.; (Weimar: Böhlau, 1977–88).

Lieder der Liebe

Lieder der Liebe. Ein Biblisches Buch. Nebst zwo Zugaben, 1776, printed in *SWS*, VIII, pp. 589-658.

Lieder der Liebe: Die ältesten und schönsten aus Morgenlande. Nebst vier und vierzig alten Minneliedern, 1778, printed in *SWS*, VIII, pp. 485-588.

Lieder der Liebe: Die ältesten und schönsten aus Morgenlande. Nebst vier und vierzig alten Minneliedern (Leipzig: Weygand, 1778).

Lieder der Liebe: Die ältesten und schönsten aus Morgenlande. Nebst vier und vierzig alten Minneliedern (Leipzig: Weygand, 2nd edn, 1781).

Lieder der Liebe (Nördlingen: Franz Greno Verlag, 1987).

Lieder der Liebe: Die ältesten und schönsten aus Morgenlande, in Bollacher *et al.* (eds.), *Werke.* III. *Volkslieder, Übertragungen, Dichtungen* (ed. Ulrich Gaier); = Bibliothek deutscher Klassiker, 60; Frankfurt am Main: Deutscher Klassiker Verlag, 1990).

Lieder der Liebe: Die ältesten und schönsten aus Morgenlande. Nebst vier und vierzig alten Minneliedern (ed. Regine Otto; Zürich: Manesse, 1992).

B. Others

Aquinas, Thomas, 'In Canticum Canticorum expositio altera', in *idem, Opera Omnia ad fidem optimarum editionum accurate recognita* (25 vols.; Parma: Fiaccadori, 1852–73), XIV, pp. 387-426.

Arvieux, Laurent D', *Hinterlassene merkwürdige Nachrichten, worinnen er sowol seine Reise nach Constantinopel, in Asien, Syrien, dem gelobten Lande, Egypten, und der Barbarei, als auch die Beschaffenheit dieser Länder, die Religion, Sitten, Gebräuche, und Handlung dieser Völker, nebst der Regierungsart, der natürlichen Historie, und den besondern in diesen Gegenden vorgefallenen Begebenheiten, genau und richtig beschreibet, im Französischen herausgegeben von dem Herrn Labat, und ietzt ins Deutsche übersetzt* (6 vols.; Copenhagen and Leipzig: Ackermann, 1753–56).

Bernard de Clairvaux, *Cantica Canticorum: Eighty-six Sermons on the Song of Solomon* (ed. and trans. Samuel J. Eales; London: Kegan Paul, 1895).

Biblia, das ist die ganze Heilige Schrift (The Weimar Bible; Nuremberg: Endter, 1768).

Biblia, das ist die ganze Heilige Schrift (ed. D. Gotthilf August Francken; The Canstein Bible; Halle: Verlag der Waysenhäusischen Buchhandlung, 2nd edn, 1770).

Biblia Sacra Vulgatae Editionis (London: Bagster, n.d.).

Blackwell, Thomas, *An Enquiry into the Life and Writings of Homer* (London: n.pub., 1735).

Blair, Hugh, *A Critical Dissertation on the Poems of Ossian, the Son of Fingal* (London: Becket and De Hondt, 1763).

Bodmer, Jakob, and Johann Jacob Breitinger, *Der Mahler der Sitten* (2 vols.; Zürich: Orell, 1746; repr. Hildesheim: Georg Olms, 1972).

Bossuet, Jacques Bénigne, *Canticum canticorum Salomonis*, in Gabriel Louis Calabre-Pérau (ed.), *Oeuvres complètes* (12 vols.; Paris: Coignard and Boudet, 1748), I, pp. 463-500.

Boysen, Friedrich Eberhard, *Kritische Erläuterungen des Grundtextes der Heiligen Schriften Altes Testaments* (Halle: Hemmerde, 1760–64).

—*Beyträge zu einem richtigen System der hebräischen Philologie [...]* (Leipzig and Chemnitz: Stössel, 1762–63).

Breithaupt, Johann Friedrich, 'Praefatio R. Salomonis Jarchi in Canticum Canticorum', in *R. Salomonis Jarchi [...] Commentarius Hebraicus in librr. Josuae [...] et Canticum Canticorum latine versus* (Gotha: Schall, 1714), pp. 915-84.

Breitinger, Johann Jacob, *Critische Dichtkunst* (2 vols.; Reihe Texte des 18. Jahrhunderts; ed. Paul Böckmann and Friedrich Sengle; Zürich: Orell; Leipzig: Gleditsch, 1740; repr. Stuttgart: Metzler, 1966).

Brenton, Sir Launcelot Lee, *The Septuagint Version of the Old Testament, with an English Translation* (London: Bagster, n.d.).

Calmet, Augustin, *Dissertations qui peuvent servir de prolégomènes de l'Ecriture Sainte* (Paris: Emery, 1720).

—*Dictionnaire historique, critique, chronologique, géographique et littéral de la Bible* (Paris: Emery, 1722–28).

Denis, Johann N.C. Michael (trans.), *Die Gedichte Ossians eines alten celtischen Dichters* (Vienna: von Trattrern, 1768–69).

Döderlein, Johann Christoph, *Salomons Prediger und Hohes Lied* (Jena: Cuno, 1784).

Eckermann, Johann Peter, *Gespräche mit Goethe in den letzten Jahren seines Lebens*, in Ernst Beutler (ed.), *Gedenkausgabe der Werke, Briefe und Gespräche* (24 vols.; Zürich: Artemis-Verlag, 1948), XXIV.

Ewald, Georg August Heinrich, *Das Hohelied Salomo's* (Göttingen: Deuerlich, 1826).

Gaspar Sanctius (Sanchez), *Commentarium in Canticum Canticorum* (Lyons: Cardon, 1616).

Gleim, Johann W.L., *Liebeslieder. Nach Salomon* (1779), in Wilhelm Körte (ed.), *Johann Wilhelm Ludewig Gleim's Lieder* (7 vols.; Halberstadt: Büreau für Literatur und Kunst, 1811), II, pp. 334-43.

Goethe, Johann Wolfgang von, *Sämtliche Werke* (ed. Ernst Beutler; 18 vols.; Zürich: Artemis Verlag, 1950; Munich: repr. Deutscher Taschenbuch Verlag, 1977).

—'Das Hohelied Salomons' (1775), *WW*, XXXVII, pp. 299-310.

—*Briefe an Sophie von La Roche und Bettina Brentano mit dichterischen Beilagen* (ed. Gustav von Loeper; Berlin: Hertz, 1879).

—*Briefe an Charlotte von Stein* (ed. Julius Petersen; 2 vols.; Leipzig: Insel-Verlag, 1923).

—*Gedenkausgabe der Werke, Briefe und Gespräche* (ed. Ernst Beutler; 24 vols.; Zürich: Artemis-Verlag, 1948).

—*Briefe an Charlotte von Stein* (ed. Jonas Fränkel; 3 vols.; Berlin: Akademie Verlag, 1960).

—*Briefe* (ed. Karl Robert Mandelkow, with Bodo Morawe; 4 vols.; Hamburg: Wegner, 1962–67).

Gottsched, Johann Christoph, *Ausführliche Redekunst, nach Anleitung der alten Griechen und Römer* (1743), in Joachim Birke, Brigitte Birke and P.M. Mitchell (eds.), *Ausgewählte Werke* (10 vols.; Berlin: W. de Gruyter, 1975), VII/1, VII/2 and VII/3.

—*Versuch einer Critischen Dichtkunst* (1751), in Joachim Birke, Brigitte Birke and P.M. Mitchell (eds.), *Ausgewählte Werke* (10 vols.; Berlin: W. de Gruyter, 1975), VI/1 and VI/2.

Graetz, Hirsch, *Schir Ha-Schirim [...] oder das Salomonische Hohelied übersetzt und kritisch erläutert* (Vienna and Leipzig: pub., 1871).

Grotius, Hugo (de Groot), 'Annotata ad Canticum Canticorum', in *idem*, *Annotata ad Vetus Testamentum* (3 vols.; Paris: S. and G. Cramoisy, 1644), I, pp. 541-48.

Hamann, Johann Georg, *Schriften* (ed. Friedrich Roth; 8 vols.; Berlin: Reimer, 1821–43).

—*Sämtliche Werke* (ed. Josef Nadler; 5 vols.; Vienna: Thomas-Morus-Presse im Verlag Herder, 1953).

—*Das Lied der Lieder*, in Nadler (ed.), *Sämtliche Werke*, IV, pp. 251-56).

—*Briefwechsel* (ed. Walther Ziesemer and Arthur Henkel; 7 vols.; Wiesbaden: Insel-Verlag, 1955–79).

Harmar, Thomas, *Beobachtungen über den Orient aus Reisebeschreibungen, zur Aufklärung der heiligen Schrift* (trans. Johann Ernst Faber; 3 vols.; Hamburg: Bohn, 1772–79).

—*Observations on Divers Passages of Scripture, Placing Many of Them in a Light Altogether New [...] Grounded on Circumstances Incidentally Mentioned in Books of Voyages and Travels into the East* (London: Field, 1764).

—*Outlines of a New Commentary on Solomon's Song* (London: Buckland, 1768).

Harris, James, *Three Treatises: The First Concerning Art, the Second Concerning Music, Painting, and Poetry, the Third Concerning Happiness* (London: Nourse and Vaillant, 1774).

Hartley, David, *Observations on Man, his Frame, his Duty, and his Expectations* (London and Bath: Leake and Frederick, 1749).

Hase, Christian Gottfried, *Versuch einer richtigern Auslegung des Hohenliedes Salomonis, worin das zuverläßige, schöne und göttliche dieses heiligen Buchs gezeiget wird* (Leipzig: J.W. and J.S. Halle, 1765).

Hasselquist, Fredrik, *Reise nach Palästina 1749 bis 1752* (ed. Carl Linnäus; trans. Theodor H. Gadebusch; Rostock: Koppe, 1762).

—*Voyages and Travels in the Levant in the Years 1749–1752* (London: Davis and Reymers, 1766).

Herder, Maria Caroline von, *Erinnerungen aus dem Leben Johann Gottfried's von Herder* (ed. Johann Georg Müller; 2 vols.; Tübingen: Cotta, 1820).

Hufnagel, Wilhelm Friedrich, *Salomo's Hohes Lied, geprüft, übersetzt, erläutert* (Erlangen: Palm, 1784).

Hume, David, *Vermischte Schriften* (4 vols.; Hamburg and Leipzig: Grund, 1754–55).

Jones, Sir William, *Abhandlung über die Litteratur des Orients* (trans. H.A.O. Reichard; Gotha: Ettinger, 1773).

—*Poeseos asiaticae commentariorum libri sex, cum appendice. Recudi curavit Io. Gottfried Eichhorn* (Leipzig: Weidemann and Reich, 1777 [1774]).

Kennicott, Benjamin, *The State of the Printed Hebrew Text of the Old Testament* (Oxford: Clements and Fletcher, 1753–59).

—*Vetus Testamentum Hebraicum cum variis lectionibus [...]* (2 vols.; Oxford: Clarendon Press, 1776–80).

Kleuker, Johann Friedrich, *Salomo's Schriften* (2 vols.; Leipzig: Weygand, 1777–80).

—*Sammlung der Gedichte Salomons, sonst das Hohelied oder Lied der Lieder genannt* (Hamm: Perrenon, 1780).

Klopstock, Friedrich Gottlieb, *Sämmtliche Werke* (10 vols.; Leipzig: Göschen, 1854–55).

Lessing, Gotthold Ephraim, *Sämtliche Schriften* (ed. Karl Lachmann; 23 vols.; Leipzig: Göschen, 3rd edn [ed. Franz Muncker], 1886–1907).

Lessing, Johann Gottlieb, *Eclogae Regis Salomonis* (Leipzig: Dyk, 1777).

Liscow, Christian Ludwig, *Vitrea Fracta oder, des Ritters Robert Clifton Schreiben an einen gelehrten Samojeden betreffend die seltsamen und nachdencklichen Figuren welche derselbe [...] auf einer gefrornen Fenster-Scheibe wahrgenommen* (Frankfurt and Leipzig: n.pub., 1732).

Locke, John, *An Essay Concerning Human Understanding* (London: Holt, 1689).

—*Some Thoughts Concerning Education* (London: A. and J. Churchill, 1693).

Lowth, Robert, *De sacra poesi Hebraeorum praelectiones academicae Oxonii habitae [...]* *subjicitur metricae Harianae brevis confutatio: et oratio Crewiana* (Oxford: Clarendon Press, 2nd edn, 1763).

—*Lectures on the Sacred Poetry of the Hebrews [...] to Which are Added the Principal Notes of Professor Michaelis* (trans. G. Gregory; 2 vols.; Anglistica & Americana, 43; London: J. Johnson, 1787; repr. Hildesheim: Georg Olms, 1969).

—*Auszug aus Dr. R. Lowth's [...] Vorlesungen über die heilige Dichtkunst der Hebräer, mit Herders und Jones's Grundsätzen verbunden* (Danzig: Troschel, 1793).

Luther, Martin, *Luther's Works* (ed. Jaroslav Pelikan and Helmut T. Lehmann; 55 vols.; St Louis: Concordia Publishing House, vols. 1–29; Philadelphia: Fortress Press, vols. 30–54, n.d.).

—*Das Hohe Lied Salomo* (1524), and *Das Hohelied Salomo* (1545), *WKGB*, X/2, pp. 134-47.

—*Ein Sendbrief von Dolmetschen*, *WKG*, XXX/2, pp. 627-46.

—*Summarien über die Psalmen und Ursachen des Dolmetschens (1531–33)*, *WKG*, XXXVIII, pp. 1-69.

—*Vorrede auf die Bücher Salomonis* (1534 and 1545), *WKGB*, X/2, pp. 6-11.

—*Vorlesung über das Hohelied: In Cantica Canticorum brevis, sed admodum dilucida enarratio*, *WKG*, XXXI/2, pp. 586-769.

—*Lectures on the Song of Solomon: A Brief but Altogether Lucid Commentary on the Song of Songs* (trans. Ian Siggins), in Pelikan and Lehmann (eds.), *Luther's Works*, XV, pp. 189-264.

Lyra, Nicolaus de, *Postilla super Psalterium et Cantica Canticorum* (Lyons: Dupré, 1488).

Macpherson, James, *Fragments of Ancient Poetry Collected in the Highlands of Scotland* (Edinburgh: Hamilton and Balfour, 1760).

—*The Works of Ossian, the Son of Fingal* (London: Becket and De Hondt, 3rd edn, 1765).

Mallett, Paul Henri, *Introduction à l'histoire de Dannemarc, où l'on traite de la religion, des loix, des moeurs et des usages des anciens Danois* (Copenhagen: Berling, 1755).

—*Northern Antiquities: Or, a Description of the Manners, Customs, Religion and Laws of the Ancient Danes, and other Northern Nations; including those of our own Saxon Ancestors [...]* (trans. Thomas Percy; London: Carnan, 1770).

Meinhard, Johann Nicolaus, *Versuche über den Charakter und die Werke der besten italienischen Dichter* (3 vols.; Brunswick: Fürstliche Waysenhaus-Buchhandlung, 1774).

Michaelis, Johann David, *Beurtheilung der Mittel, welche man anwendet, die ausgestorbene Hebräische Sprache zu verstehen* (Göttingen: Van den Hoek, 1757).

—*Roberti Lowth [...] de Sacra Poesi Hebraeorum Praelectiones [...] Notae et Epimetra* (Göttingen: Dieterich, 2nd edn, 1770).

—*Deutsche Uebersetzung des Alten Testaments, mit Anmerkungen für Ungelehrte* (Göttingen: Dieterich, 1773–90).

Michaelis, Johann Heinrich, *Biblia Hebraica ex aliquot manuscriptis et compluribus impressis codicibus, item Masora tam edita, quam manuscripta aliisque hebraeorum criticis diligenter recensita [...]* (Halle: Waysenhaus Verlag, 1720).

—*Erleichterte hebräische Grammatica: Richtige Anführung zur hebräischen Sprache zu mehrerem Nutzen der Jugend in teutscher Sprache [...]* (Halle: Waysenhaus Verlag, 8th edn, 1745).

Montagu, Lady Mary Wortley, *Letters Written during her Travels in Europe, Asia and Africa between 1763 and 1800* (3 vols.; London: Becket and De Hondt, 1763).

Niebuhr, Carsten, *Reisebeschreibung nach Arabien und andern umliegenden Ländern* (ed. J.N. Gloyer and J. Olshausen; 3 vols.; Copenhagen and Hamburg: Möller, 1774).

Opitz, Martin, *Salomons des Hebreischen Königes Hohes Liedt; Vom Martin Opitz in deutsche Gesänge gebracht* (Breslau: D. Müller, 1627).

Percy, Thomas, *The Song of Solomon, Newly Translated from the Original Hebrew with a Commentary and Annotations* (ed. R. Dodsley; London: n.pub., 1764).

—*Reliques of Ancient English Poetry* (ed. H.B. Wheatley; 3 vols.; New York: Dover Publications, 1966 [1765]).

Pococke, Richard, *Beschreibung des Morgenlandes und einiger andern Länder* (trans. Christian Ernst von Windheim; 3 vols.; Erlangen: Breitkopf, 1754–55).

Priestley, Joseph, *Essay on a Course of Liberal Education* (London: J. Johnson and Davenport, 1765).

—*Lectures on History and General Policy* (London: J. Johnson, 1788).

Richardson, John, *Abhandlung über Sprache, Literatur und Gebräuche morgenländischer Völker* (Leipzig: Weygand, 1779).

Sanctius, Gaspar, *Commentarium in Canticum Canticorum* (Lyons: Cardon, 1616).

Schiller, Friedrich von (ed.), *Die Horen* (Tübingen: Cotta, 1795–97).

Schöber, David Gottfried (ed.), *Das Hohelied Salomonis aus zwoen alten deutschen Handschriften [...]* (Augsburg: Klaffschenkels, 1752).

Schottelius, Justus Georgius, *Teutsche Sprachkunst* (Brunswick: Grubern, 1641).

—'Wie man recht verteutschen soll' (1663), in Wolfgang Hecht (ed.), *Ausführliche Arbeit von der Teutschen HaubtSprache* (2 vols.; Deutsche Neudrucke, 12; Tübingen: Niemeyer, 1967), II, Book 5, Tract 5, pp. 1217-68.

Seebach, Christoph, *Erklärung des Hohen Liedes Salomonis* (Berlin: Schlechtigern, 1706).

Semler, Johann Salomo, *Kurze Vorstellung wider die dreyfache Paraphrasin über das hohe Lied* (Halle: Hemmerde, 1757).

—*Abhandlung von freyer Untersuchung des Canon* (Halle: Hemmerde, 1776).

Shaw, Thomas, *Travels, or Geographical, Physical and Miscellaneous Observations Relating to Several Parts of Barbary and the Levant* (Oxford: Theatre, 1738).

—*Reisen, oder Anmerkungen, verschiedne Theile der Barbarey und der Levante betreffend. Nach der zweiten englischen Ausgabe ins Deutsche übersetzt* (trans. Johann Heinrich Merck; Leipzig: Breitkopf, 1765).

Spinoza, Benedictus de, *Tractatus theologico-politicus continens dissertationes aliquot, quibus ostenditur libertatem philosophandi non tantum salva pietate, & reipublicae pace posse concedi: sed eandem nisi cum pace reipublicae, ipsaque pietate tolli non posse* (Hamburg: Künraht, 1670).

Tytler, Alexander Fraser, Lord Woodhouselee, *Essays on the Principles of Translation* (Everyman's Library; London: Cadell and Creech, 1797; repr. London: Dent; New York: Dutton, 1907).

Umbreit, Friedrich Wilhelm Carl, *Lied der Liebe: Das älteste und schönste aus dem Morgenlande. Übersetzt und ästhetisch erklärt* (2nd edn; Heidelberg: Mohr, 1828).

Wachter, Georg, *Das Hohe Lied des Salomo, [...] samt einer vorgesetzten Einleitung und Abtheilung desselben als eines geistlichen Singspiels [...]* (Memmingen, 1722).

Whiston, William, *A Supplement to Mr. Whiston's Late Essay: Towards Restoring the True Text of the Old Testament, Proving that the Canticles is not a Sacred Book of the Old Testament* (London: Senex and Taylor, 1723).

Wiedeburg, Basilius, *Ausführliche Nachricht von einigen alten teutschen poetischen Manuscripten aus dem dreyzehenden und vierzehenden Jahrhunderte welche in der Jenaischen akademischen Bibliothek aufbehalten werden* (Jena: Melchiors, 1754).

Wilcox, Thomas, *An Exposition uppon the Booke of the Canticles* (London: Man, 1585).

Wood, Robert, *An Essay on the Original Genius of Homer* (London: Payne and Elmsly, 1769; repr. Washington, DC: McGrath, 1973).

Young, Edward, *Conjectures on Original Composition: In a Letter to the Author of Sir Charles Grandison* (London: A. Millar; R. and J. Dodsley, 1759).

Zesen, Philipp von, 'Das Hohe Lied des Weisen Königes Salomons: Nach Art einer Unterredung in unterschiedliche Lieder gebracht', in *idem, Deutsches Helicons Erster und Ander Theil* (Wittenberg: Röhnern, 1641), Part 2, Book 3, pp. 110-42; repr. as 'Salomons des Hebräischen Königs Geistliche Wollust, oder Hohes Lied. In Dactylische und Anapästische Verse gebracht', in Ulrich Maché and Volker Meid (eds.), *Sämmtliche Werke* (16 vols.; Berlin: W. de Gruyter, 1971), IX, pp. 355-88.

Secondary Sources

Abrams, Meyer H., *The Mirror and the Lamp: Romantic Theory and the Critical Tradition* (New York: Galaxy Books, 1953).

—*Natural Supernaturalism: Tradition and Revolution in Romantic Literature* (London: W.W. Norton, 1971).

—*A Glossary of Literary Terms* (Fort Worth: Holt, Rinehart, & Winston, 5th edn, 1985).

Abukhater, Lesley C., *German Orientalism in Herder, Goethe and Schlegel* (Lexington, KY: [n.pub.], 1983).

Adler, Emil, *Herder und die deutsche Aufklärung* (Vienna and Frankfurt am Main: Europa Verlag, 1968).

—'Über den Katalog von Johann Gottfried Herders handschriftlichem Nachlaß', in Johann Gottfried Maltusch (ed.), *Bückeburger Gespräche über Johann Gottfried Herder 1975* (Schaumburger Studien, 37; Rinteln: Bosendahl, 1976), pp. 85-98.

—'Johann Gottfried Herder und das Judentum', in Kurt Mueller-Vollmer (ed.), *Herder Today: Contributions from the International Herder Conference, Nov. 5–8, 1987, Stanford, California* (Berlin: W. de Gruyter, 1990), pp. 382-401.

Adler, Frederick H., *Herder and Klopstock: A Comparative Study* (New York: Stechert, 1914).

Albrecht, Erich A.G., *Primitivism and Related Ideas in Eighteenth-Century German Lyric Poetry 1680–1740* (Baltimore: The Johns Hopkins University Press, 1950).

Alter, Robert, *The Art of Biblical Narrative* (New York: Basic Books, 1981).

—*The Art of Biblical Poetry* (New York: Basic Books, 1985).

Apel, Friedmar, *Literarische Übersetzung* (Realien zur Literatur, Sammlung Metzler, 206; Stuttgart: Metzler, 1983).

Arminjon, Blaise, *The Cantata of Love: A Verse-by-Verse Reading of the Song of Songs* (trans. Nelly Marans; San Francisco: Ignatius Press, 1988).

Arnold, Günter, *Johann Gottfried Herder* (Leipzig: Bibliographisches Institut, 1979).

—'Ideale und reale Bedingungen für Editionen und die geplante Fortführung der Herder-Briefausgabe', in Günter Martens and Winfried Woesler (eds.), *Edition als Wissenschaft: Festschrift für Hans Zeller* (Beihefte zu Editio, 2; Tübingen: Niemeyer, 1991), pp. 53-61.

Atkins, George D., and Laura Morrow, (eds.), *Contemporary Literary Theory* (New York: Macmillan, 1989).

Atkins, Henry Gibson, *A History of German Versification: Ten Centuries of Metrical Evolution* (London: Methuen, 1923).

Bach, Rudolf, *Der Aufbruch des deutschen Geistes: Lessing–Klopstock–Herder* (Markkleeberg bei Leipzig: Rauch, 1940).

Badt, Benno, 'Goethe als Übersetzer des Hohenliedes', *Neue Jahrbücher für Philologie und Pädagogik, oder kritische Bibliothek für das Schul- und Unterrichts-Wesen* 27 (1881), pp. 346-57.

Baete, Ludwig, *Johann Gottfried Herder: Der Weg, das Werk, die Zeit* (Stuttgart: Hirzel, 1948).

Baildam, John D., ' *"Lieder der Liebe"*: Herder as Translator of the Song of Songs' (doctoral dissertation, University of London, 1994).

—' "Im vollen Kreise des Volks entsprungen?": Kultur, Nation und Herders *Lieder der Liebe*', in Regine Otto (ed.), *Nationen und Kulturen: Zum 250. Geburtstag Johann Gottfried Herders* (Würzburg: Königshausen & Neumann, 1996), pp. 435-47.

Banús, Enrique, *Untersuchungen zur Rezeption Johann Gottfried Herders in der Komparatistik: Ein Beitrag zur Fachgeschichte* (Europäische Hochschulschriften, Series XVIII, 82; Frankfurt am Main: Peter Lang, 1996).

Barnard, Frederick M., 'The Hebrews and Herder's Political Creed', *MLR* 54 (1959), pp. 533-46.

—'Herder's Treatment of Causation and Continuity in History', *JHI* 24 (1963), pp. 197-212.

—*Zwischen Aufklärung und Politischer Romantik: Eine Studie über Herders soziologisch-politisches Denken* (Philologische Studien und Quellen, 17; Berlin: E. Schmidt, 1964).

—*Herder's Social and Political Thought: From Enlightenment to Nationalism* (Oxford: Clarendon Press, 1965).

Barnard, Frederick M. (ed. and trans.), *J.G. Herder on Social and Political Culture* (Cambridge Studies in the History and Theory of Politics; Cambridge: Cambridge University Press, 1969).

Barr, James, *The Semantics of Biblical Language* (Oxford: Oxford University Press, 1962 [1961]).

—*Comparative Philology and the Text of the Old Testament* (Oxford: Clarendon Press, 1968).

Bartholmä, Johann Georg (ed.), *Das hohe Lied Salomonis in drei und vierzig Minneliedern aus dem 13ten und 14ten Jahrhundert* (Nuremberg and Leipzig: [n. pub.], 1827).

Bassnett-McGuire, Susan, and André Lefevere (eds.), *Translation, History and Culture* (London and New York: Pinter, 1990).

Bassnett-McGuire, Susan, *Translation Studies* (New Accents Series; London: Routledge, rev. edn, 1991).

Bea, Augustinus, Cardinal, *Canticum Canticorum: Novam Interpretationem Latinam cum Textu Masoretico et Notis Exegeticis* (Scripta Pontificii Instituti Biblici, 104; Rome: Pontificio Instituto Biblico, 1953).

Becker, Bernhard, *Herder-Rezeption in Deutschland: Eine ideologiekritische Untersuchung* (Saarbrücker Beiträge zur Literaturwissenschaft, 14; St Ingbert: Röhrig, 1987).

Begenau, Siegfried H., *Grundzüge der Ästhetik Herders* (Weimar: Böhlau, 1956).

Berger, Arnold E., *Der junge Herder und Winckelmann* (Studien zur deutschen Philologie: Festgabe der Germanistischen Abteilung der 47. Sammlung deutscher Philologen und Schulmänner; Halle: Niemeyer, 1903).

Berlin, Isaiah, 'Herder and the Enlightenment', in Earl R. Wasserman (ed.), *Aspects of the Eighteenth Century* (Baltimore: The Johns Hopkins University Press, 1965).

—*Vico and Herder: Two Studies in the History of Ideas* (New York: Vintage Books, 1977).

Berlin, Isaiah (ed.), *The Age of Enlightenment: The Eighteenth-Century Philosophers* (London: New English Library, 1956).

Betteridge, Harold T., 'The Ossianic Poems in Herder's *Volkslieder*', *MLR* 30 (1935), pp. 334-38.

—'Herder's Letters to Klopstock', *PMLA* 69 (1954), pp. 1213-32.

Bianchi, Lorenzo, *Hamann und Herder* (Bologna: Mareggiani, 1930).

Blackall, Eric A., 'Hamann in the Doldrums', *GLL* 10 (1957), pp. 258-62.

—'The Language of Sturm und Drang', in Paul Böckmann (ed.), *Stil- und Formprobleme in der Literatur: Vorträge des VII. Kongresses der Internationalen Vereinigung für moderne Sprachen und Literaturen in Heidelberg* (Heidelberg: Winter, 1959), pp. 272-83.

—*The Emergence of German as a Literary Language 1700–1775* (Ithaca, NY: Cornell University Press, 2nd edn, 1978).

—'The Imprint of Herder's Linguistic Theory on his Early Prose Style', *PMLA* 76 (1961), pp. 512-18.

Bleich, David, *Subjective Criticism* (Baltimore: The Johns Hopkins University Press, 1978).

Blochmann, Elisabeth, 'Die deutsche Volksdichtungsbewegung in Sturm und Drang und Romantik', *DVjs* 1 (1923), pp. 419-52.

Bluhm, Heinz S., *Martin Luther: Creative Translator* (St Louis: Concordia Publishing House, 1965).

—'Herders Stellung zu Luther', *PMLA* 64 (1949), pp. 158-82.

Bock, Claus V., 'A Tower of Ivory?' (Inaugural Lecture delivered at Westfield College, University of London, 30 April 1970).

Boening, John, 'Herder and the White Man's Burden: The *Ideen zur Philosophie der Geschichte der Menschheit* and the Shaping of British Colonial Policy', in Wulf Koepke (ed.), *Johann Gottfried Herder: Language, History, and the Enlightenment* (Studies in German Literature, Linguistics, and Culture, 52; Columbia, SC: Camden House, 1990), pp. 236-45.

Böker, Uwe, 'The Marketing of Macpherson: The International Book Trade and the First Phase of German Ossian Reception', in Howard Gaskill (ed.), *Ossian Revisited* (Edinburgh: Edinburgh University Press, 1991), pp. 73-93.

Bollacher, Martin (ed.), *Johann Gottfried Herder: Geschichte und Kultur* (Vorträge der Konferenz der Internationalen Herder-Gesellschaft, die vom 10.–13.6.1992 an der Ruhr-Universität Bochum gehalten wurden; Würzburg: Königshausen & Neumann, 1994).

Booth, Andrew D. *et al.*, *Aspects of Translation* (ed. A.H. Smith; London: Secker & Warburg, 1958).

Boyarin, Daniel, 'The Song of Songs: Lock or Key? Intertextuality, Allegory and Midrash', in Regina M. Schwartz (ed.), *The Book and the Text: The Bible and Literary Theory* (Oxford: Basil Blackwell, 1990), pp. 214-30.

Bran, Friedrich A., *Herder und die deutsche Kulturanschauung* (Berlin: Junker and Dünnhaupt, 1932).

Brislin, Richard W. (ed.), *Translation: Applications and Research* (New York: Gardner, 1976).

Bromiley, Geoffrey W., 'Herder's Contribution to the Romantic Philosophy of History, with Special Reference to the Theological Implications' (doctoral dissertation, University of Edinburgh, 1943).

Brower, Reuben A. (ed.), *On Translation* (Harvard Studies in Comparative Literature, 23; New York: Oxford University Press, 1966).

Brown, Francis, Samuel R. Driver and Charles A. Briggs (eds.), *A Hebrew–English Lexicon of the Old Testament with an Appendix Containing the Biblical Aramaic, Based on the Lexicon of William Gesenius as Translated by Edward Robinson* (Oxford: Clarendon Press, 1955).

Browne, Alice, *The Eighteenth-Century Feminist Mind* (Brighton: Harvester Press, 1987).

Bruford, Walter H., *Culture and Society in Classical Weimar, 1775–1806* (Cambridge: Cambridge University Press, 1962).

—*Germany in the Eighteenth Century: The Social Background of the Literary Revival* (Cambridge: Cambridge University Press, 1965).

Buber, Martin, and Franz Rosenzweig, *Die Schrift und ihre Verdeutschung* (Berlin: Schocken, 1936).

—'Zu einer neuen Verdeutschung der Schrift', in Hans Joachim Störig (ed.), *Das Problem des Übersetzens* (Wege der Forschung, 8; Darmstadt: Wissenschaftliche Buchgesellschaft, 2nd edn, 1973), pp. 322-62.

Budde, Karl, 'Was ist das *Hohelied?*', *Preußische Jahrbücher* 78 (1894), pp. 92-117.

Bunge, Marcia, 'Human Language of the Divine: Herder on Ways of Speaking about God', in Kurt Mueller-Vollmer (ed.), *Herder Today: Contributions from the International Herder Conference, Nov. 5–8, 1987, Stanford, California* (Berlin: W. de Gruyter, 1990), pp. 304-18.

—'Text and Reader in Herder's Interpretations of the New Testament', in Wulf Koepke (ed.), *Johann Gottfried Herder: Language, History, and the Enlightenment* (Studies in German Literature, Linguistics, and Culture, 52; Columbia, SC: Camden House, 1990), pp. 138-50.

Burgard, Peter J., 'Literary History and Historical Truth: Herder–"Shakespeare"–Goethe', *DVjs* 65 (1991), pp. 636-52.

Bürkner, Richard, *Herder: Sein Leben und Wirken* (Biographien-Sammlung Geisteshelden, 45; Berlin: Hofmann, 1904).

Butler, Elsie M., *The Tyranny of Greece over Germany* (Cambridge: Cambridge University Press, 1935).

Cassirer, Ernst, *Language and Myth* (trans. Suzanne K. Langer; New York and London: Dover Publications, 1946).

—*The Philosophy of the Enlightenment* (trans. Fritz C.A. Koelln and James P. Pettegrove; Boston: Beacon Press, 1965).

Castle, Eduard, 'Herder als Wiedererwecker des deutschen Volksliedes', in *In Goethes Geist: Vorträge und Aufsätze* (Vienna and Leipzig: Österreichischer Bundesverlag für Unterricht, Wissenschaft und Kunst, 1926), pp. 57-67; repr. from *Zeitschrift für die österreichischen Gymnasien* 55 (1904), pp. 193-202.

Ceillier, Remi, *Histoire générale des auteurs sacrés et ecclésiastiques [...]*, II (Paris: Vivès, 2nd edn, 1858–63).

Chadwick, Norah Kershaw, *Poetry and Prophecy* (Cambridge: Cambridge University Press, 1942).

Cheyne, Thomas K., *Founders of Old Testament Criticism* (London: Methuen, 1893).

Christ, Carol P., 'Why Women Need the Goddess: Phenomenological, Psychological, and Political Reflections', in Marilyn Pearsall (ed.), *Women and Values: Readings in Recent Feminist Philosophy* (Belmont, CA: Wadsworth Publishing Co., 1986), pp. 211-20.

Clark, Robert T., 'Herder's Conception of "Kraft" ', *PMLA* 57 (1942), pp. 737-52.

—'Herder, Percy, and the *Song of Songs*', *PMLA* 61 (1946), pp. 1087-1100.

—*Herder: His Life and Thought* (Berkeley: University of California Press, 1955).

Closs, August, 'Wurzeln der Romantik bei Herder', *MLQ* 2 (1941), pp. 611-18.

—'Gedanken zur Auslegung von Gedichten', *DVjs* 27 (1953), pp. 268-88.

—*Reality and Creative Vision in German Lyrical Poetry* (Colston Papers, 15; London: Butterworth, 1963).

—'The Art of Translating', *GLL* 22 (1969), pp. 210-19.

Coggins, Richard J., and James L. Houlden, *A Dictionary of Biblical Interpretation* (London: SCM Press, 1990).

Cohen, Abraham (ed.), *The Five Megilloth: Hebrew Text and English Translation* (13th impression, Soncino Books of the Bible; New York: Soncino Press, 1977).

Cohen, Ralph (ed.), *New Directions in Literary Theory* (London: Routledge & Kegan Paul, 1974).

Collier, Peter, and Helga Geyer-Ryan (eds.), *Literary Theory Today* (Oxford: Polity Press, 1990).

Cotterell, Peter, and Max Turner, *Linguistics and Biblical Interpretation* (London: SPCK, 1989).

Crane, R.S., *The Languages of Criticism and the Structure of Poetry* (Toronto: University of Toronto Press, 1953).

Cross, Frank L., and Elizabeth A. Livingstone (eds.), *The Oxford Dictionary of the Christian Church* (Oxford: Oxford University Press, 2nd edn, 1978).

Daly, Mary, *Beyond God the Father: Toward a Philosophy of Women's Liberation* (Boston: Women's Press, 1973).

—'The Qualitative Leap Beyond Patriarchal Religion', in Marilyn Pearsall (ed.), *Women and Values: Readings in Recent Feminist Philosophy* (Belmont, CA: Wadsworth Publishing, 1986), pp. 198-210.

Danby, Herbert (trans.), *The Mishnah: Translated from the Hebrew with Introduction and Brief Explanatory Notes* (Oxford: Clarendon Press, 1933).

Davidson, Benjamin, *The Analytical Hebrew and Chaldee Lexicon* (London: Bagster, [n.d.]).

Davidson, Samuel, *Sacred Hermeneutics Developed and Applied, Including a History of Biblical Interpretation from the Earliest of the Fathers to the Reformation* (Edinburgh: T. & T. Clark, 1843).

Dechent, Hermann, *Herder und die ästhetische Betrachtung der Heiligen Schrift* (Giessen: Ricker, 1904).

Delitzsch, Franz, *Commentary of the Song of Songs and Ecclesiastes* (trans. M.G. Easton; Edinburgh: T. & T. Clark, 1877).

Dietze, Walter, *Johann Gottfried Herder: Abriß seines Lebens und Schaffens* (Berlin and Weimar: Aufbau-Verlag, 1983).

Dobbek, Wilhelm, *Johann Gottfried Herders Mohrunger Jugendjahre in ihrer Bedeutung für seine Persönlichkeit und sein Werk* (Königsberg: Kanter, 1944).

—*J.G. Herders Humanitätsidee als Ausdruck seines Weltbildes und seiner Persönlichkeit* (Brunswick: Westermann, 1949).

—*Johann Gottfried Herder* (Weimar: Thüringer Volksverlag, 1950).

—*Johann Gottfried Herders Weltbild: Versuch einer Deutung* (Cologne and Vienna: Böhlau, 1969).

Doerne, Martin, *Die Religion in Herders Geschichtsphilosophie* (Leipzig: Meiner, 1927).

Döring, Heinrich, *Johann Gottfried Herder's Leben* (Weimar: Hoffmann, 1829).

Draper, John W., 'The Theory of Translation in the Eighteenth Century', *Neophilologus* 6 (1921), pp. 241-50.

Dreengel, Hans, *Herder, Schiller, Goethe und die Religion* (Göttingen: Vandenhoeck & Ruprecht, 1926).

Driver, Samuel R., *An Introduction to the Literature of the Old Testament* (Edinburgh: T. & T. Clark, 1892).

Dyson, Anthony O., 'Theological Legacies of the Enlightenment: England and Germany', in Stephen W. Sykes (ed.), *England and Germany: Studies in Theological Diplomacy* (Studien zur interkulturellen Geschichte des Christentums, 25; Frankfurt am Main and Bern: Peter Lang, 1982), pp. 45-62.

Eagleton, Terry, *Literary Theory: An Introduction* (Oxford: Basil Blackwell, 1983).

Eco, Umberto, *The Role of the Reader: Explorations in the Semiotics of Texts* (Bloomington: Indiana University Press, 1984).

Eliade, Mircea (ed.), *The Encyclopedia of Religion* (New York: Macmillan, 1987).

Elledge, Scott (ed.), *Eighteenth-Century Critical Essays* (Ithaca, NY: Cornell University Press, 1961).

Embach, Michael, *Das Lutherbild Johann Gottfried Herders* (Trierer Studien zur Literatur, 14; Frankfurt am Main: Peter Lang, 1987).

Epstein, Isidore (ed.), *The Babylonian Talmud* (Anniversary Edition in English; London: Soncino Press, 1935), especially *Seder Nezikin* (4 vols.): II (*Baba Bathra*) and III (*Sanhedrin*).

Ergang, Robert R., *Herder and the Foundations of German Nationalism* (New York: Columbia University Press; London: King, 1931; repr. New York: Octagon Books, 1976).

Ernst, Fritz, 'Die Entdeckung der Volkspoesie im 18. Jahrhundert', in Fritz Ernst and Kurt K.T. Wais (eds.), *Forschungsprobleme der vergleichenden Literaturgeschichte* (Tübingen: Niemeyer, 1958), pp. 1-6.

Esselborn, Hans, and Werner Keller (eds.), *Geschichtlichkeit und Gegenwart: Festschrift für Hans Dietrich Irmscher zum 65. Geburtstag* (Kölner germanistische Studien, 34; Cologne, Weimar and Vienna: Böhlau, 1994).

Falk, Marcia L., *Love Lyrics from the Bible: A Translation and Literary Study of the Song of Songs* (Bible and Literature Series, 4; Sheffield: Almond Press, 1982).

Federlein, Wilhelm-Ludwig (ed.), *Sein ist im Werden: Essays zur Wirklichkeitskultur bei Johann Gottfried Herder anläßlich seines 250. Geburtstages* (Frankfurt am Main: Peter Lang).

Feyerabend, Karl, *Langenscheidt's Pocket Hebrew Dictionary to the Old Testament: Hebrew–English* (Berlin and Munich: Hodder & Stoughton, n.d).

Fink, Gonthier-Louis, 'Herder, Bossuet und die Philosophen: Auch eine Theologie der Geschichte?', in Hans Esselborn and Werner Keller (eds.), *Geschichtlichkeit und*

Gegenwart: Festschrift für Hans Dietrich Irmscher zum 65. Geburtstag (Kölner germanistische Studien, 34; Cologne, Weimar and Vienna: Böhlau, 1994), pp. 66-92.

Fischer, Bernd, *Das Eigene und das Eigentliche: Klopstock, Herder, Fichte, Kleist–Episoden aus der Konstruktionsgeschichte nationaler Intentionalitäten* (Berlin: Schmidt, 1995).

Fish, Stanley E., *Is There a Text in This Class? The Authority of Interpretive Communities* (Cambridge, MA: Harvard University Press, 1980).

—*Doing What Comes Naturally: Change, Rhetoric, and the Practice of Theory in Literary and Legal Studies* (Oxford: Clarendon Press, 1989).

Fletcher, Robert (ed.), *The Prose Works of John Milton* (London: Westley and Davis, 1834).

Forster, Leonard (ed.), *The Penguin Book of German Verse* (Harmondsworth: Penguin Books, 1967 [1957]).

Frank, Luanne, 'Herder, Jauß, and the New Historicism: A Retrospective Reading', in Wulf Koepke (ed.), *Johann Gottfried Herder: Language, History, and the Enlightenment* (Studies in German Literature, Linguistics, and Culture, 52; Columbia, SC: Camden House, 1990), pp. 246-88.

Fränzel, Walter F.A., *Geschichte des Übersetzens im 18. Jahrhundert* (Beiträge zur Kultur und Universalgeschichte, 25; Leipzig: Voigtländer, 1914).

Frawley, William (ed.), *Translation: Literary, Linguistic, and Philosophical Perspectives* (Newark, London and Toronto: University of Delaware Press, 1984).

Frommholz, Rüdiger, *Wirkungen der Sprache und Dichtung: Studien am Werk Herders* (Bielefelder Hochschulschriften, 3; Bielefeld: Pfeffer, 2nd edn, 1972).

Fugate, Joe K., *The Psychological Basis of Herder's Aesthetics* (Studies in Philosophy, 10; The Hague: Mouton, 1966).

Gadamer, Hans-Georg, *Volk und Geschichte im Denken Herders* (Frankfurt am Main: Klostermann, 1942).

—*Wahrheit und Methode: Grundzüge einer philosophischen Hermeneutik* (Tübingen: J.C.B. Mohr, 2nd edn, 1965).

Gaertner, Johannes A., *Johann Gottfried Herders Anschauungen über eine christliche Kunst* (Heidelberg: n.pub., 1938).

Gaier, Ulrich, *Herders Sprachphilosophie und Erkenntniskritik* (Problemata, 118; Stuttgart-Bad Cannstatt: Frommann-Holzboog, 1988).

Gaskill Howard (ed.), *Ossian Revisited* (Edinburgh: Edinburgh University Press, 1991).

Gaskill, Howard, ' "Ossian" Macpherson: Towards a Rehabilitation', *Comparative Criticism* 8 (1986), pp. 113-46.

—'German Ossianism: A Reappraisal?', *GLL* 42 (1989), pp. 329-41.

Gay, Peter, *The Enlightenment: An Interpretation* (2 vols.; London: Wildwood House, 1969–70).

Gaycken, Hans-Jürgen, *Johann Gottfried Herder und seine zeitgenössischen Kritiker: Herderkritik in der Allgemeinen Deutschen Bibliothek* (Europäische Hochschulschriften, Series I, 853; Frankfurt am Main: Peter Lang, 1985).

Gentzler, Edwin, *Contemporary Translation Theories* (Translation Studies Series; London: Routledge, 1993).

Gesche, Astrid, *Johann Gottfried Herder: Sprache und die Natur des Menschen* (Epistemata: Reihe Literaturwissenschaft, 97; Würzburg: Königshausen & Neumann, 1993).

Gillies, Alexander, *Herder und Ossian* (Arbeiten zur Geistesgeschichte der germanischen und romanischen Völker, NS 19; Berlin: Junker and Dünnhaupt, 1933).

—'Herder's Essay on Shakespeare: "Das Herz der Untersuchung"', *MLR* 32 (1937), pp. 262-80.

—'Herder's Approach to the Philosophy of History', *MLR* 35 (1940), pp. 193-206.

—'Herder's Preparation of Romantic Theory', *MLR* 39 (1944), pp. 252-61.

—*Herder* (Oxford: Basil Blackwell, 1945).

—'The Heritage of Johann Gottfried Herder', *University of Toronto Quarterly* 16 (1947), pp. 399-410.

—'Herder and Goethe', in *German Studies Presented to Leonard Ashley Willoughby by Pupils, Colleagues and Friends on his Retirement* (Oxford: Basil Blackwell, 1952), pp. 82-97.

—*A Hebridean in Goethe's Weimar: The Reverend James Macdonald and the Cultural Relations between Scotland and Germany* (Oxford: Basil Blackwell, 1969).

Ginsburg, Christian D., *The Song of Songs: Translated from the Original Hebrew, with a Commentary, Historical and Critical* (London: Longman, Brown, Green, Longmans and Roberts, 1857); ed. and repr. by Sheldon H. Blank (New York: Ktav, 1970).

Giran, Etienne, *Sébastien Castellion et la réforme Calviniste: Les deux réformes* (Haarlem: Boissevain, 1913; repr. Geneva: Slatkine Reprints, 1970).

Goebel, Martin, *Die Bearbeitung des Hohen Liedes im 17. Jahrhundert: Nebst einem Ueberblick über die Beschäftigung mit dem Hohen Liede in früheren Jahrhunderten* (Halle: John, 1914).

Goldstein, David, 'On Translating God's Name', in William Radice and Barbara Reynolds (eds.), *The Translator's Art: Essays in Honour of Betty Radice* (Harmondsworth: Penguin Books, 1987), pp. 72-80.

Gollancz, Hermann (trans.), *The Targum to 'The Song of Songs'* (London: Luzac, 1908).

Gorman, John C. (ed.), *William of Newburgh's Explanatio Sacri Epithalamii in Matrem Sponsi: A Commentary on the Canticle of Canticles (Twelfth Century)* (Spicilegium Friburgense, 6; Fribourg: Fribourg University Press, 1960).

Grawe, Christian, *Herders Kulturanthropologie: Die Philosophie der Geschichte der Menschheit im Lichte der modernen Kulturanthropologie* (Abhandlungen zur Philosophie, Psychologie und Pädagogik, 35; Bonn: Bouvier, 1967).

Gray, George B., *The Forms of Hebrew Poetry, Considered with Special Reference to the Criticism and Interpretation of the Old Testament* (New York: Ktav, 1972).

Green, Jay (ed. and trans.), *The Interlinear Hebrew/Greek/English Bible* (3 vols.; Evansville, IN: Associated Publishers and Authors, 1978).

Green, Otis H., *Spain and the Western Tradition: The Castilian Mind in Literature from 'El Cid' to Calderón* (3 vols.; Madison and Milwaukee: University of Wisconsin Press, 1963–65).

Greenslade, Stanley L. (ed.), *The Cambridge History of the Bible* (3 vols.; Cambridge: Cambridge University Press, 1963).

Grohmann, Wilhelm, *Herders nordische Studien* (Leipzig: Süsserott, 1899).

Gundolf, Friedrich [F. Gundelfinger], *Shakespeare und der deutsche Geist* (Berlin: Küpper, 11th edn, 1959).

Günther, Gottfried, Albina Volgina and Siegfried Seifert, *Herder-Bibliographie* (Berlin and Weimar: Aufbau-Verlag, 1978).

Häfner, Ralph, *Johann Gottfried Herders Kulturentstehungslehre: Studien zu den Quellen und zur Methode seines Geschichtsdenkens* (Hamburg: Meiner, 1995).

Hampson, Norman, *The Enlightenment* (Harmondsworth: Penguin Books, 1968).

Harrison, Roland K., *Introduction to the Old Testament* (London: Tyndale Press, 1970).

Hartlich, Christian, and Walter Sachs, *Der Ursprung des Mythosbegriffs in der modernen Bibelwissenschaft* (Tübingen: J.C.B. Mohr, 1952).

Hatch, Irvin C., *Der Einfluß Shaftesburys auf Herder* (Berlin: Duncker, 1901).

Hatfield, Henry C., *Aesthetic Paganism in German Literature, from Winckelmann to the Death of Goethe* (Cambridge, MA: Harvard University Press, 1964).

Haupt, Josef (ed.), *Das Hohe Lied, übersetzt von Willeram, erklärt von Rilindis und Herrat, Äbtissinen zu Hohenburg im Elsasz 1147–1196* (Vienna: Braumüller, 1864).

Haupt, Paul, *Biblische Liebeslieder: Das sogenannte Hohelied Salomos unter steter Berücksichtigung der Übersetzungen Goethes und Herders* (Leipzig: J.C. Hinrichs; Baltimore: The Johns Hopkins University Press, 1907).

Haussmann, Johannes F., 'Der junge Herder und Hamann', *JEGP* 6 (1907), pp. 606-48.

—*Untersuchungen über Sprache und Stil des jungen Herder* (Leipzig: Noske, 1907).

Hawthorn, Jeremy, *A Glossary of Contemporary Literary Theory* (London: E. Arnold, 1992).

Haym, Rudolf, *Herder nach seinem Leben und seinen Werken dargestellt* (2 vols.; Berlin: Gaertner, 1877–85).

Hazard, Paul, *European Thought in the Eighteenth Century* (trans. J. Lewis May; Harmondsworth: Penguin Books, 1965).

Hebrew–English Lexicon (London: Bagster, 27th edn, n.d.).

Hecht, Hans, *T. Percy, R. Wood und J.D. Michaelis* (Stuttgart: W. Kohlhammer, 1933).

Heinz, Marion (ed.), *Herder und die Philosophie des deutschen Idealismus* (Fichte-Studien-Supplementa, 8; Amsterdam: Rodopi, 1997).

Heinz, Marion, *Sensualistischer Idealismus: Untersuchungen zur Erkenntnistheorie [und Metaphysik] des jungen Herder (1763–1778)* (Hamburg: Meiner, 1994).

Heizmann, Bertold, *Ursprünglichkeit und Reflexion: Die poetische Ästhetik des jungen Herder im Zusammenhang der Geschichtsphilosophie und Anthropologie des 18. Jahrhunderts* (Europäische Hochschulschriften, Series I, 373; Frankfurt am Main: Peter Lang, 1981).

Herder, Emil Gottfried, *Johann Gottfried von Herder's Lebensbild: Sein chronologisch geordneter Briefwechsel* (3 vols.; Erlangen: Bläsing, 1846).

Hermans, Theo (ed.), *Second Hand: Papers on the Theory and Historical Study of Literary Translation* (ALW-Cahier, 3; Wilrijk: Vlaamse Vereniging voor Algemene en Vergelijkende Literatuurwetenschap, 1985).

—*The Manipulation of Literature: Studies in Literary Translation* (London and Sydney: Croom Helm, 1985).

Herz, Andreas, *Dunkler Spiegel, helles Dasein: Natur, Geschichte, Kunst im Werk Johann Gottfried Herders* (Heidelberg: Winter, 1996).

Herzog, Johann Jakob, *Realencyklopädie für protestantische Theologie und Kirche* (ed. Albert Hauck; 24 vols.; Leipzig: J.C. Hinrichs, 3rd edn, 1896–1913).

Hettner, Hermann, *Geschichte der deutschen Literatur im achtzehnten Jahrhundert* (2 vols.; Berlin: Aufbau-Verlag, 1961).

Hewson, Lance, and Jacky Martin, *Redefining Translation: The Variational Approach* (London: Routledge, 1991).

Hintzenstern, Herbert von, 'Herders Lutherbild', in Brigitte Poschmann (ed.), *Bückeburger Gespräche über Johann Gottfried Herder 1983* (Schaumburger Studien, 45; Rinteln: Bosendahl, 1984), pp. 159-73.

—*'Immerdar auf Gottes Spur': Herder in Weimar* (Weimar and Jena: Wartburg-Verlag, 1994).

Hoffmann, H., *Willirams Uebersetzung und Auslegung des Hohenliedes* (Breslau: Grass, Barth, 1827).

Holub, Robert C., *Reception Theory: A Critical Introduction* (New Accents Series; London: Methuen, 1984).

Honour, Hugh, *Neo-Classicism* (Harmondsworth: Penguin Books, 1968).

Hornig, Gottfried, *Die Anfänge der historisch-kritischen Theologie: Johann Salomo Semlers Schriftverständnis und seine Stellung zu Luther* (Forschungen zur systematischen Theologie und Religionsphilosophie, 8; Göttingen: Vandenhoeck & Ruprecht, 1961).

Huber, Thomas, *Studien zur Theorie des Übersetzens im Zeitalter der deutschen Aufklärung 1730–1770* (Studien zur deutschen Literaturgeschichte, 7; Meisenheim am Glan: Hain, 1968).

Huyssen, Andreas, *Die frühromantische Konzeption von Übersetzung und Aneignung: Studien zur frühromantischen Utopie einer deutschen Weltliteratur* (Zürcher Beiträge zur deutschen Literatur- und Geistesgeschichte, 33; Zürich: Atlantis Verlag, 1969).

Inbar, Eva Maria, 'Zum Englischstudium im Deutschland des XVIII. Jahrhunderts', *Arcadia* 15 (1980), pp. 14-28.

Ingarden, Roman, *The Literary Work of Art: An Investigation on the Borderlines of Ontology, Logic, and Theory of Literature* (trans. George G. Grabowicz; Northwestern University Studies in Phonomenology and Existential Philosophy; Evanston, IL: Northwestern University Press, 1973).

Irmscher, Hans Dietrich, and Emil Adler, *Der handschriftliche Nachlaß Johann Gottfried Herders in Berlin* (Staatsbibliothek Preussischer Kulturbesitz, Kataloge der Handschriftenabteilung; ed. Tilo Brandis; Zweite Reihe: Nachlässe, vol. I; Wiesbaden: Harrassowitz, 1979).

Irmscher, Hans Dietrich, 'Mitteilungen aus Herders Nachlaß', *Euphorion: Zeitschrift für Literaturgeschichte* 54 (1960), pp. 281-94.

—'Der handschriftliche Nachlaß Herders und seine Neuordnung', in Walter Wiora (ed.), *Herder-Studien* (Marburger Ostforschungen, 10; ed. E. Keyser, Würzburg: Holzner, 1960), pp. 1-15.

—'Probleme der Herder-Forschung', *DVjs* 37 (1963), pp. 266-317.

—'Grundzüge der Hermeneutik Herders', in J.G. Maltusch (ed.), *Bückeburger Gespräche über Johann Gottfried Herder 1971* (Schaumburger Studien, 33; Bückeburg: Grimme, 1973), pp. 17-57.

—'Herder über das Verhältnis des Autors zum Publikum', in J.G. Maltusch (ed.), *Bückeburger Gespräche über Johann Gottfried Herder 1975* (Schaumburger Studien, 37; Rinteln: Bosendahl, 1976), pp. 99-138.

—'Beobachtungen zur Funktion der Analogie im Denken Herders', *DVjs* 55 (1981), pp. 64-97.

—'Goethe und Herder im Wechselspiel von Attraktion und Repulsion', *Goethe Jahrbuch* 106 (1989), pp. 22-52.

—'Nationalität und Humanität im Denken Herders', *Orbis litterarum* 49.4 (1994), pp. 189-215.

Isaacsen, Hertha, *Der junge Herder und Shakespeare* (Germanische Studien, 93; Berlin: Ebering, 1930).

Iser, Wolfgang P., *The Implied Reader: Patterns of Communication in Prose Fiction from Bunyan to Beckett* (Baltimore: The Johns Hopkins University Press, 1974).

—*Der Akt des Lesens: Theorie ästhetischer Wirkung* (Munich: Fink, 1976).

—*The Act of Reading: A Theory of Aesthetic Response* (Baltimore: The Johns Hopkins University Press, 1978).

—*Der implizite Leser: Kommunikationsformen des Romans von Bunyan bis Beckett* (Munich: Fink, 1979).

Jacoby, Günther, *Herders und Kants Aesthetik* (Leipzig: Dürr, 1907).

Jauß, Hans R., *Literaturgeschichte als Provokation* (Frankfurt am Main: Suhrkamp, 1970).

—'Literary History as a Challenge to Literary Theory', in Ralph Cohen (ed.), *New Directions in Literary History* (London: Routledge & Kegan Paul, 1974), pp. 11-41.

—*Toward an Aesthetic of Reception* (trans. Timothy Bahti; Brighton: Harvester Press, 1982).

Joret, Charles, *Herder et la renaissance littéraire en Allemagne au XVIIIᵉ siècle* (Paris: Hachette, 1875).

—*La littérature allemande au 18ᵉ siècle dans ses rapports avec la littérature française et la littérature anglaise* (Aix: Makaire, 1876).

Kaiser, Gerhard, *Pietismus und Patriotismus im literarischen Deutschland: Ein Beitrag zum Problem der Säkularisation* (Wiesbaden: Steiner, 1961).

—*Geschichte der deutschen Literatur von der Aufklärung bis zum Sturm und Drang, 1730–85* (ed. H. Rüdiger; Gütersloh: Gerd Mohn, 1966).

Kantzenbach, Friedrich W., *Johann Gottfried Herder: mit Selbstzeugnissen und Bilddokumenten* (Reinbek: Rowohlt, 1970).

Kathan, Anton, *Herders Literaturkritik: Untersuchungen zu Methodik und Struktur am Beispiel der frühen Werke* (Göppinger Arbeiten zur Germanistik, 6; Göppingen: Kümmerle, 2nd edn, 1970).

Keil, Karl F., and Franz J. Delitzsch, *Biblischer Commentar über das alte Testament* (Leipzig: Dörffling and Francke, 1861–75).

Kelletat, Andreas F., *Herder und die Weltliteratur: Zur Geschichte des Übersetzens im achtzehnten Jahrhundert* (Europäische Hochschulschriften, Series I, 760; Frankfurt am Main: Peter Lang, 1984).

Kelly, James Fitzmaurice, *A Short History of Spanish Literature*, in Edmund Gosse (ed.), *Short Histories of the Literatures of the World* (15 vols.; London: Heinemann, 1898), V.

Kelly, Louis G., *The True Interpreter: A History of Translation Theory and Practice in the West* (Oxford: Basil Blackwell, 1979).

Keyser, Erich (ed.), *Im Geiste Herders* (Marburger Ostforschungen, 1; Kitzingen am Main: Holzner, 1953).

Kircher, Erwin, 'Volkslied und Volkspoesie in der Sturm- und Drangzeit: Ein begriffsgeschichtlicher Versuch', *Zeitschrift für deutsche Wortforschung* 4 (1903), pp. 1-57.

Kluckhohn, Paul, *Die Auffassung der Liebe in der Literatur des achtzehnten Jahrhunderts und in der deutschen Romantik* (Halle: Niemeyer, 1922).

Knight, Dorothy, 'J.D. Bodmer's Contribution to the Knowledge and Appreciation of Middle High German Literature' (masters thesis, University of London, 1949).

Knoll, Renate, 'Herder als Promoter Hamanns: Zu Herders früher Literaturkritik', in Kurt Mueller-Vollmer (ed.), *Herder Today: Contributions from the International Herder Conference, Nov. 5–8, 1987, Stanford, California* (Berlin: W. de Gruyter, 1990), pp. 207-27.

Knox, Ronald A., *The Trials of a Translator* (New York: Sheed & Ward, 1949).

Koepke, Wulf, *Johann Gottfried Herder* (Twayne's World Authors Series, 786; Boston: Twayne, 1987).

Koepke, Wulf (ed.), *Johann Gottfried Herder: Academic Disciplines and the Pursuit of Knowledge* (Columbia, SC: Camden House, 1996).

—*Johann Gottfried Herder: Language, History, and the Enlightenment* (Studies in German Literature, Linguistics, and Culture, 52; Columbia, SC: Camden House, 1990).

Koepke, Wulf (ed.), in cooperation with Samson B. Knoll, *Johann Gottfried Herder: Innovator through the Ages* (Modern German Studies, 10; Bonn: Bouvier, 1982).

Koester, Albert, *Die deutsche Literatur der Aufklärungszeit* (Heidelberg: Winter, 1925).

Kohl, Katrin Maria, 'The Origins and Structure of Klopstock's Early "Hymns" in Free Rhythms' (doctoral dissertation, University of London, 1988).

Kohlhagen, Norgand, and Siegfried Sunnus, *Eine Liebe in Weimar: Caroline Flachsland und Johann Gottfried Herder* (Stuttgart: Quell, 1993).

Kohlschmidt, Werner, *Herder-Studien: Untersuchungen zu Herders kritischem Stil und zu seinen literaturkritischen Grundeinsichten* (Arbeiten zur Geistesgeschichte der germanischen und romanischen Völker, NS 4; Berlin: Junker and Dünnhaupt, 1929).

Kommerell, Max, *Der Dichter als Führer in der deutschen Klassik: Klopstock, Herder, Goethe, Schiller, Jean Paul, Hölderlin* (Berlin: Bondi, 1928).

Korff, Hermann A., *Der Geist der Goethezeit: Versuch einer ideellen Entwicklung der klassisch-romantischen Literaturgeschichte* (Leipzig: Koehler & Amelang, 2nd edn, 1953).

Kosmala, Hans, 'Form and Structure in Ancient Hebrew Poetry', *VT* 14 (1964), pp. 423-45.

Kraeling, Emil G., *The Old Testament since the Reformation* (London: Lutterworth Press, 1955).

Kraus, Hans Joachim, *Geschichte der historisch-kritischen Erforschung des Alten Testaments von der Reformation bis zur Gegenwart* (Neukirchen: Verlag der Buchhandlung des Erziehungsvereins, 1956).

—'Herders alttestamentliche Forschungen', in J.G. Maltusch (ed.), *Bückeburger Gespräche über Johann Gottfried Herder 1971* (Schaumburger Studien, 33; Bückeburg: Grimme, 1973), pp. 59-75.

Kriewald, Walter W.A., *Herders Gedanken über die Verbindung von Religion und Volkstum* (Ohlau: Eschenhagen, 1935).

Kronenberg, Moritz, *Herders Philosophie nach ihrem Entwickelungsgang und ihrer historischen Stellung* (Heidelberg: Winter, 1889).

Kugel, James L., *The Idea of Biblical Poetry: Parallelism and its History* (New Haven: Yale University Press, 1981).

Kuhn, Hugo, and Kurt Schier (eds.), *Märchen, Mythos, Dichtung: Festschrift zum 90. Geburtstag Friedrich von der Leyens am 19. August 1963* (Munich: Beck, 1963).

Kühnemann, Eugen, *Herders Persönlichkeit in seiner Weltanschauung: Ein Beitrag zur Begründung der Biologie des Geistes* (Berlin: Dümmler, 3rd edn, 1893).

—*Herders Leben* (Munich: Beck, 1895).

—*Herder und das deutsche Wesen* (Munich: Beck, 1914).

—*Herder* (Munich: Beck, 3rd edn, 1927).

Küntzel, Gerhard, *J.G. Herder zwischen Riga und Bückeburg: die Ästhetik und Sprachphilosophie der Frühzeit nach ihren existentiellen Motiven* (Frankfurter Quellen und Forschungen, 10; Frankfurt am Main: Diesterweg, 1936).

Land, Stephen K., *From Signs to Propositions: The Concept of Form in Eighteenth-Century Semantic Theory* (Longman Linguistics Library, 16; London: Longman, 1974).

—'Universalism and Relativism: A Philosophical Problem of Translation in the Eighteenth Century', *JHI* 35 (1974), pp. 597-610.

Landy, Francis, *Paradoxes of Paradise: Identity and Difference in the Song of Songs* (Sheffield: Almond Press, 1983).

Langen, August, 'Der Wortschatz des 18. Jahrhunderts', in Friedrich Maurer and Heinz Rupp (eds.), *Deutsche Wortgeschichte* (3 vols.; Berlin: W. de Gruyter, 3rd edn, 1974–78), II, pp. 31-244.

Lefevere, André, *Translating Poetry: Seven Strategies and a Blueprint* (Approaches to Translation Studies, 3; Assen: Van Gorcum, 1975).

Lefevere, André (ed.), *Translating Literature: The German Tradition from Luther to Rosenzweig* (Approaches to Translation Studies, 4; Assen: Van Gorcum, 1977).

—*Translation/History/Culture: A Sourcebook* (Translation Studies Series; London: Routledge, 1992).

—'Theory and Practice—Process and Product', *Modern Poetry in Translation* 41–42 (1981), pp. 19-27.

—*Translation, Rewriting, and the Manipulation of Literary Fame* (Translation Studies Series; London: Routledge, 1992).

—*Translating Literature: Practice and Theory in a Comparative Literature Context* (New York: Modern Language Association of America, 1992).

Lehrman, S.M., 'The Song of Songs: Introduction and Commentary', in Abraham Cohen (ed.), *The Five Megilloth: Hebrew Text and English Translation* (13th impression, Soncino Books of the Bible; London: Soncino Press, 1977), pp. i-xiii and 1-32.

Leuser, Claudia, *Theologie und Anthropologie: die Erziehung des Menschengeschlechts bei Johann Gottfried Herder* (Frankfurt am Main: Peter Lang, 1996).

Leventhal, Robert, *The Disciplines of Interpretation: Lessing, Herder, Schlegel and Hermeneutics in Germany 1750–1800* (Berlin: W. de Gruyter, 1994).

Litt, Theodor, *Kant und Herder als Deuter der geistigen Welt* (Leipzig: Quelle & Meyer, 1930).

Littledale, Richard F., *A Commentary on the Song of Songs: From Ancient and Mediaeval Sources* (London: Masters; New York: Pott and Amery, 1869).

Lohmeier, Dieter, *Herder und Klopstock: Herders Auseinandersetzung mit der Persönlichkeit und dem Werk Klopstocks* (Ars Poetica: Texte und Studien zur Dichtungslehre und Dichtkunst, 4; Bad Homburg: Gehlen, 1968).

Lohre, Heinrich, *Von Percy zum Wunderhorn: Beiträge zur Geschichte der Volksliedforschung in Deutschland* (Palaestra: Untersuchungen aus der deutschen und englischen Philologie und Literaturgeschichte, 22; Berlin: Mayer & Müller, 1902).

Lowrie, Walter, *J.G. Hamann: An Existentialist* (Princeton, NJ: Princeton University Press, 1950).

Luke, David, trans., *Johann Wolfgang von Goethe: Erotic Poems* (The World's Classics; Oxford: Oxford University Press, 1997).

Lüttgens, Donald, *Der 'Ursprung' bei Johann Gottfried Herder: Zur Bedeutung und Kontinuität eines Begriffs* (Europäische Hochschulschriften, Series I, 1260; Frankfurt am Main: Peter Lang, 1991).

Lutz, Emilie, *Herders Anschauungen vom Wesen des Dichters und der Dichtkunst in der ersten Hälfte seines Schaffens (bis 1784)* (Erlangen: Doros, 1925).

Maclean, Norman, 'From Action to Image: Theories of the Lyric in the Eighteenth Century', in R.S. Crane (ed.), *Critics and Criticism Ancient and Modern* (London: Cambridge University Press; Chicago: University of Chicago Press, 1952), pp. 408-60.

Magnus, Eduard Isidor, *Kritische Bearbeitung und Erklärung des Hohen Liedes Salomo's* (Halle: Lippert, 1842).

Malsch, Wilfried, and Wulf Koepke (eds.), *Herder Jahrbuch/Herder Yearbook: Publications of the International Herder Society*, II (Stuttgart and Weimar: Metzler, 1994).

Malsch, Wilfried, Hans Adler and Wulf Koepke (eds.), *Herder Jahrbuch/Herder Yearbook: Publications of the International Herder Society*, III (Stuttgart and Weimar: Metzler, 1997).

Manuel, Frank (ed.), *Johann Gottfried von Herder: Reflections on the Philosophy of the History of Mankind* (trans. T.O. Churchill; London, 1800; Chicago: University of Chicago Press, 1968).

Markworth, Tino, *Johann Gottfried Herder: A Bibliographical Survey 1977–1987* (Hürth-Efferen: Gabel, 1990).

Marschall, Amy Horning, 'Oral Poetry—Written Prose: "Throwing Light On" Johann Gottfried Herder's "Von den Lebensaltern einer Sprache"', *Michigan Germanic Studies* 16 (1990), pp. 1-20.

Marshall, M.E. Sandbach, 'Herder's Contribution to Nineteenth-Century Thought', *Church Quarterly Review* 103 and 104 (1927), pp. 298-315.

Mathews, Henry J., *Abraham Ibn Ezra's Commentary on the Canticles after the First Recension* (London: Trübner, 1874).

Max, Hugo, *Martin Opitz als geistlicher Dichter* (Beiträge zur neueren Literaturgeschichte, 17; Heidelberg: Winter, 1931).

Mayo, Robert S., *Herder and the Beginnings of Comparative Literature* (University of North Carolina Studies in Comparative Literature, 48; Chapel Hill: University of North Carolina Press, 1969).

McEachran, Frank, *The Life and Philosophy of Johann Gottfried Herder* (Oxford: Clarendon Press, 1939).

Meek, Theophile J., Hugh T. Kerr and Hugh T. Kerr Jr, 'The Song of Songs', *IB*, V.

Meier, John, *Werden und Leben des Volksepos* (Halle: Niemeyer, 1909).

—*Volksliedstudien* (Strasbourg: Trübner, 1917).

Meinecke, Friedrich, *Historism: The Rise of a New Historical Outlook* (trans. J.E. Anderson; rev. H.D. Schmidt; London: Routledge & Kegan Paul, 1972).

Menges, Karl, Wulf Koepke and Wilfried Malsch, *Herder Jahrbuch/Herder Yearbook: Publications of the International Herder Society*, I (Columbia, SC: Camden House, 1992).

Menze, Ernest A. and Karl Menges (eds.), *Johann Gottfried Herder: Selected Early Works 1764–1767. Addresses, Essays, and Drafts; 'Fragments on Recent German Literature'* (trans. Ernest A. Menze with Michael Palma, University Park, PA: Pennsylvania State University Press, 1992).

Menze, Ernest A., 'On Herder as a Translator and on Translating Herder', in Wulf Koepke (ed.), *Johann Gottfried Herder: Language, History, and the Enlightenment* (Studies in German Literature, Linguistics, and Culture, 52; Columbia, SC: Camden House, 1990), pp. 151-62.

Michel, Ernst, *Der Weg zum Mythos: Zur Wiedergeburt der Kunst aus dem Geiste der Religion* (Jena: Diederich, 1919).

Minor, Jakob, *Johann Georg Hamann in seiner Bedeutung für die Sturm- und Drangperiode* (Frankfurt am Main: Rütten & Loening, 1881).

Morgan, Robert C., with John Barton, *Biblical Interpretation* (Oxford: Oxford University Press, 1989).

Mücke, Dorothea von, 'Language as the Mark of the Soul: Herder's Narcissistic Subject', in Kurt Mueller-Vollmer (ed.), *Herder Today: Contributions from the International*

Herder Conference, Nov. 5–8, 1987, Stanford, California (Berlin: W. de Gruyter, 1990), pp. 331-44.

Mueller-Sievers, Helmut, ' "Gott als Schriftsteller": Herder and the Hermeneutic Tradition', in Kurt Mueller-Vollmer (ed.), *Herder Today: Contributions from the International Herder Conference, Nov. 5–8, 1987, Stanford, California* (Berlin: W. de Gruyter, 1990), pp. 319-30.

Mueller-Vollmer, Kurt (ed.), *Herder Today: Contributions from the International Herder Conference, Nov. 5–8, 1987, Stanford, California* (Berlin: W. de Gruyter, 1990).

Muir, Edwin and Willa Muir, 'Translating from the German', in Reuben A. Brower (ed.), *On Translation* (Harvard Studies in Comparative Literature, 23; New York: Oxford University Press, 1966), pp. 93-96.

Müller, Johann Georg, *Aus dem Herder'schen Hause* (ed. Jakob Baechtold; Berlin: Weidmann, 1881).

Munro, Jill M., *Spikenard and Saffron: A Study in the Poetic Language of the Song of Songs* (JSOTSup, 203; Sheffield: Sheffield Academic Press, 1995).

Muthesius, Karl, *Herders Familienleben* (Berlin: Mittler, 1904).

Needham, Harold A., *Taste and Criticism in the Eighteenth Century* (London: Harrap, 1952).

Newald, Richard, 'Von Klopstock bis zu Goethes Tod, 1750–1832: Ende der Aufklärung und Vorbereitung der Klassik', in Helmut de Boor and Richard Newald (eds.), *Geschichte der deutschen Literatur von den Anfängen bis zur Gegenwart* (Munich: Beck, 1957), VI/1.

Nicolai, Christoph Friedrich (ed.), *Allgemeine Deutsche Bibliothek* (118 vols.; Berlin, Stettin and Kiel: Bohn, 1765–96), especially X/1, p. 64; XVII/2, p. 438; and XXXVII/2, pp. 478-83.

Nicolson, Harold G., *The Age of Reason, 1700–1789* (London: Granada, 1960).

Nida, Eugene A., *God's Word in Man's Language* (New York: Harper, 1952).

—*Toward a Science of Translating, with Special Reference to Principles and Procedures Involved in Bible Translating* (Leiden: E.J. Brill, 1964).

—'Principles of Translation as Exemplified by Bible Translating', in Reuben A. Brower (ed.), *On Translation* (Harvard Studies in Comparative Literature, 23; New York: Oxford University Press, 1966), pp. 11-31.

Nida, Eugene A., and C.R. Taber, *The Theory and Practice of Translation* (Helps for Translators Prepared under the Auspices of the United Bible Societies, 8; Leiden: E.J. Brill, 1969).

Nisbet, Hugh B. (ed.), *German Aesthetic and Literary Criticism: Winckelmann, Lessing, Hamann, Herder, Schiller, and Goethe* (Cambridge: Cambridge University Press, 1985).

Nisbet, Hugh B., *Herder and the Philosophy and History of Science* (MHRA Dissertation Series, 3; Cambridge: Modern Humanities Research Association, 1970).

—'Zur Revision des Herder-Bildes im Lichte der neueren Forschung', in J.G. Maltusch (ed.), *Bückeburger Gespräche über Johann Gottfried Herder 1971* (Schaumburger Studien, 33; Bückeburg: Grimme, 1973), pp. 101-17.

—'Goethes und Herders Geschichtsdenken', in Hans Esselborn and Werner Keller (eds.), *Geschichtlichkeit und Gegenwart: Festschrift für Hans Dietrich Irmscher zum 65. Geburtstag* (Kölner germanistische Studien, 34; Cologne, Weimar and Vienna: Böhlau, 1994), pp. 93-115.

Norton, Robert E., *Herder's Aesthetics and the European Enlightenment* (Ithaca, NY: Cornell University Press, 1991).

Nufer, Wolfgang, *Herders Ideen zur Verbindung von Poesie, Musik und Tanz* (Germanische Studien, 74; Berlin: Ebering, 1929).

Nunlist, Rene, *Homer, Aristoteles und Pindar in der Sicht Herders* (Studien zur Germanistik, Anglistik und Komparatistik, 9; Bonn: Bouvier, 1971).

O'Flaherty, James C., 'J.D. Michaelis: Rational Biblicist', *JEGP* 49 (1950), pp. 172-81.

—*Johann Georg Hamann* (Twayne's World Authors Series, 527; Boston: Twayne, 1979).

Ohly, Friedrich, *Hohelied-Studien: Grundzüge einer Geschichte der Hohenliedauslegung des Abendlandes bis um 1200* (Schriften der wissenschaftlichen Gesellschaft der Johann Wolfgang Goethe-Universität Frankfurt am Main, Geisteswissenschaftliche Reihe, 1; Wiesbaden: Steiner, 1958).

Oppel, Arnold, *Das Hohelied Salomonis und die deutsche religiöse Liebeslyrik* (Abhandlungen zur mittleren und neueren Geschichte, 32; Berlin and Leipzig: Rothschild, 1911).

Otto, Regine (ed.), *Nationen und Kulturen: Zum 250. Geburtstag Johann Gottfried Herders* (Würzburg: Königshausen & Neumann, 1996).

Pascal, Roy, *Shakespeare in Germany, 1740–1815* (Cambridge: Cambridge University Press, 1937).

—*The German Sturm und Drang* (Manchester: Manchester University Press, 1953).

Pearsall, Marilyn (ed.), *Women and Values: Readings in Recent Feminist Philosophy* (Belmont, CA: Wadsworth Publishing, 1986).

Peyer, Heinz, *Herders Theorie der Lyrik* (Winterthur: Keller, 1955).

Pfeiffer, Johannes S., *Über das Dichterische und den Dichter: Beiträge zum Verständnis deutscher Dichtung* (Hamburg: Meiner, 2nd edn, 1956).

Pope, Marvin H., *The Song of Songs* (AB, 7C; Garden City, NY: Doubleday, 1977).

Price, Lawrence M. and Mary B. Price, *The Publication of English Literature in Germany in the Eighteenth Century* (University of California Publications in Modern Philology, 17; Berkeley: University of California Press, 1934).

—*English Literature in Germany* (University of California Publications in Modern Philology, 37; Berkeley: University of California Press, 1953).

Price, Lawrence M., *English–German Literary Influences* (University of California Publications in Modern Philology, 9; Berkeley: University of California Press, 1919).

—*The Reception of English Literature in Germany* (Berkeley: University of California Press, 1932).

Prickett, Stephen (ed.), *Reading the Text: Biblical Criticism and Literary Theory* (Oxford: Basil Blackwell, 1991).

Purdie, Edna (ed.), *Von deutscher Art und Kunst* (Oxford: Clarendon Press, 1924).

Purdie, Edna, 'Some Problems of Translation in the Eighteenth Century in Germany', *English Studies: A Journal of English Letters and Philology* 30 (1949), pp. 191-205.

—*Studies in German Literature of the Eighteenth Century: Some Aspects of Literary Affiliation* (London: Athlone Press, 1965).

—'Some Word Associations in the Writings of Hamann and Herder', in *German Studies Presented to Leonard Ashley Willoughby by Pupils, Colleagues and Friends on his Retirement* (Oxford: Basil Blackwell, 1952), pp. 144-58.

—'Hamann, Herder and *Hamlet*', *GLL* 10 (1957), pp. 198-209.

Radice, William, and Barbara Reynolds (eds.), *The Translator's Art: Essays in Honour of Betty Radice* (Harmondsworth: Penguin Books, 1987).

Radjai-Bokarai, Ali, 'Die Bedeutung der Poesie des Orients bei Johann Gottfried Herder' (doctoral dissertation, University of Tübingen, 1973).

Rasch, Wolfdietrich, *Herder: Sein Leben und Werk im Umriß* (Hanbücherei der Deutschkunde, 1; Halle: Niemeyer, 1938).

Redeker, Martin, *Humanität, Volkstum, Christentum in der Erziehung: Ihr Wesen und gegenseitiges Verhältnis an der Gedankenwelt des jungen Herder für die Gegenwart dargestellt* (Arbeiten zur Geistesgeschichte der germanischen und romanischen Völker, NS 23; Berlin: Junker and Dünnhaupt, 1934).

Reed, Eugene E., 'Herder, Primitivism and the Age of Poetry', *MLR* 60 (1965), pp. 553-67.

Reinke, Joseph, *J.G. Herder als Übersetzer altdeutscher Gedichte* (Herder Studies, 1; Münster: Westfälische Vereinsdruckerei, 1902).

Reisiger, Hans, *Johann Gottfried Herder: Sein Leben in Selbstzeugnissen, Briefen und Berichten* (Berlin: Propyläen-Verlag, 1942; repr. Hildesheim: Georg Olms, 1970).

Richter, Lutz (ed.), *Johann Gottfried Herder im Spiegel seiner Zeitgenossen: Briefe und Selbstzeugnisse* (Berlin: Vandenhoeck & Ruprecht, 1978).

Riedel, Wilhelm, *Die Auslegung des Hohenliedes in der jüdischen Gemeinde und der griechischen Kirche* (Leipzig: Deichert, 1898).

Ringgren, Helmer, and Otto Kaiser, 'Das Hohelied', in *Das Alte Testament Deutsch* (25 vols.; Neues Göttinger Biblewerk, 3rd edn; Göttingen: Vandenhoeck & Ruprecht, 1981), XVI/2.

Ritshl, Dietrich, 'Johann Salomo Semler, 1725–1791: The Rise of the Historical-Critical Method in Eighteenth-Century Theology on the Continent', in Robert Mollenauer (ed.), *Introduction to Modernity: A Symposium on Eighteenth-Century Thought* (Austin: University of Texas Press, 1965).

Robbins, Keith (ed.), *Protestant Evangelicalism: Britain, Ireland, Germany and America, C. 1750–C. 1950: Essays in Honour of W.R. Ward* (Studies in Church History, Subsidia, 7; Oxford: Basil Blackwell, 1990).

Robertson, John G., 'Shakespeare on the Continent', in A.W. Ward and A.R. Waller (eds.), *The Cambridge History of English Literature* (15 vols.; Cambridge: Cambridge University Press, 1907–16, repr. 1933–34), V, pp. 283-308.

—*Studies in the Genesis of Romantic Theory in the Eighteenth Century* (Cambridge: Cambridge University Press, 1923).

Robinson, Douglas, *The Translator's Turn* (Baltimore: The Johns Hopkins University Press, 1991).

Robinson, Theodore H., *The Poetry of the Old Testament* (Studies in Theology, 49; London: Duckworth, 1969 [1947]).

Robscheit, Hellmuth, 'Herder als Ausleger des Alten Testamentes (dargestellt an seiner Schrift *Vom Geist der Ebräischen Poesie*)', in Eva Schmidt (ed.), *Herder im geistlichen Amt: Untersuchungen, Quellen, Dokumente* (Leipzig: Koehler & Amelang, 1956), pp. 26-38.

Robson-Scott, William D., *The Literary Background of the Gothic Revival in Germany: A Chapter in the History of Taste* (Oxford: Clarendon Press, 1965).

Rogerson, John, *Old Testament Criticism in the Nineteenth Century: England and Germany* (London: SPCK, 1984).

Rosenzweig, Franz, 'Die Schrift und Luther', in Hans Joachim Störig (ed.), *Das Problem des Übersetzens* (Wege der Forschung, 8; Darmstadt: Wissenschaftliche Buchgesellschaft, 2nd edn, 1973), pp. 194-222.

Roston, Murray, 'The Influence of Lowth's *De sacra poesi Hebraeorum* on Verse-Forms of the Eighteenth Century' (masters thesis, University of London, 1956).

—*Prophet and Poet: The Bible and the Growth of Romanticism* (London: Faber & Faber, 1965).

Rowley, Harold, 'The Interpretation of the Song of Songs', in *idem*, *The Servant of the Lord and Other Essays on the Old Testament* (Oxford: Basil Blackwell, 2nd edn, 1965).

Rundgren, Frithiof, *The Word and the Text* (Uppsala: Acta Universitatis Upsaliensis, 1992).

Said, Edward W., *The World, the Text and the Critic* (London: Vintage Books, 1991).

—*Orientalism: Western Conceptions of the Orient* (Harmondsworth: Penguin Books, 1991).

Salmon, Paul, 'Herder's Essay on the Origin of Language and the Place of Man in the Animal Kingdom', *GLL* 22 (1968), pp. 59-70.

Sapir, Edward, 'Herder's "Ursprung der Sprache"', *MP* 5 (1907–1908), pp. 109-42.

Sasse, H.-C., 'Michael Denis as a Translator of Ossian', *MLR* 60 (1965), pp. 547-52.

Sauder, Gerhard (ed), *Johann Gottfried Herder 1744–1803* (Studien zum achtzehnten Jahrhundert, 9; Hamburg: Meiner, 1984).

Sauter, Michael J., *Kant, Herder and the Enlightenment Public Sphere: Universal Morality versus Cultural Plurality in Eighteenth-Century Germany* (Chapel Hill: University of North Carolina Press, 1993).

Savory, Theodore, *The Art of Translation* (London: Cape, 1957).

Scheel, Heinrich (ed.), *Johann Gottfried Herder: Zum 175. Todestag am 18. Dezember 1978* (Sitzungsberichte der Akademie der Wissenschaften der DDR: Gesellschafts-wissenschaften, 8/G; Berlin: Akademie-Verlag, 1978).

Schenk, Hans G., *The Mind of the European Romantics: An Essay in Cultural History* (Oxford: Oxford University Press, 1979).

Scherpe, Klaus R., *Gattungspoetik im achtzehnten Jahrhundert: Historische Entwicklung von Gottsched bis Herder* (Studien zur allgemeinen und vergleichenden Literatur-wissenschaft, 2; Stuttgart: Metzler, 1968).

Schick, Edgar B., *Metaphorical Organicism in Herder's Early Works: A Study of the Relation of Herder's Literary Idiom to his World-View* (Series Practica, 20; The Hague: Mouton, 1971).

Schleypen, Georg von, 'Herders Theorie des Übersetzens', *Die Deutsche Höhere Schule* 5 (1938), pp. 283-90.

Schmidt, Erich, *Lessing: Geschichte seines Lebens und seiner Schriften* (Berlin: Weid-mann, 1923; repr. Hildesheim: Georg Olms, 1983).

Schmidt, Eva (ed.), *Herder im Geistlichen Amt: Untersuchungen, Quellen, Dokumente* (Leipzig: Koehler & Amelang, 1956).

Schmidt, Nathaniel, *The Messages of the Poets: The Books of Job and Canticles* (The Messages of the Bible 7; London: J. Clarke, 1911).

Schmitz, Reta, *Das Problem 'Volkstum und Dichtung' bei Herder* (Arbeiten zur Geistes-geschichte der germanischen und romanischen Völker, NS 31; Berlin: Junker and Dünnhaupt, 1937).

Schnebli-Schwegler, Brigitte, *Johann Gottfried Herders Abhandlung über den Ursprung der Sprache und die Goethe-Zeit* (Wintherthur: Keller, 1965).

Schneider, Jost (ed.), *Herder im 'Dritten Reich'* (Bielefeld: Aisthesis, 1994).

Schneider, Karl L., *Klopstock und die Erneuerung der deutschen Dichtersprache im acht-zehnten Jahrhundert* (Heidelberg: Winter, 1960).

Schnur, Harald, *Schleiermachers Hermeneutik und ihre Vorgeschichte im 18. Jahrhundert: Studien zur Bibelauslegung, zu Hamann, Herder und F. Schlegel* (Stuttgart and Weimar: Metzler, 1994).

Schöffler, Herbert, *Deutscher Geist im achtzehnten Jahrhundert: Essays zur Geistes- und Religionsgeschichte* (ed. Götz von Selle; Göttingen: Vandenhoeck & Ruprecht, 1956).

Schönlank, Bruno, *Hartley und Priestley, die Begründer des Associationismus in England* (Halle: Hendel, 1991 [1882]).

Schork, Luise, *Herders Bekanntschaft mit der englischen Literatur* (Beiträge zur Erforschung der Sprache und Kultur Englands und Nordamerikas: Beiheft; Breslau: Selbstverlag des Englischen Seminars der Universität Breslau, 1928).

Schumacher, Douglas, 'Herder's Treatment of his English Sources in the Volkslieder' (masters thesis, University of London, 1937).

Schütze, Martin, 'The Fundamental Ideas in Herder's Thought', *MP* 18.2 (1920), pp. 1-14; and 18.6 (1920), pp. 57-70; 19.2 (1921), pp. 13-30 and 361-82; 21.1 (1923), pp. 29-48; and 21.2 (1923), pp. 113-32.

Schwartz, Regina M. (ed.), *The Book and the Text: The Bible and Literary Theory* (Oxford: Basil Blackwell, 1990).

Schwarz, Werner, 'Theory of Translation in Sixteenth-Century Germany', *MLR* 40 (1945), pp. 289-99.

—'Luther's Translation of the Bible in the Light of Humanistic Scholarship' (doctoral dissertation, University of London, 1949).

—*Principles and Problems of Biblical Translation: Some Reformation Controversies and Their Background* (Cambridge: Cambridge University Press, 1970 [1955]).

—*Schriften zur Bibelübersetzung und mittelalterlichen Übersetzungstheorie* (Publications of the Institute of Germanic Studies, 39; Hamburg: Wittig, 1986).

Sdun, Winfried, *Probleme und Theorien des Übersetzens in Deutschland vom achtzehnten bis zum zwanzigsten Jahrhundert* (Munich: Hueber, 1967).

Sears, Richard A., *Hebrew Poetry for the Eighteenth Century: Johann Gottfried Herder's 'The Spirit of Hebrew Poetry'* (Newton Centre, MA: Andover Newton Theological School, 1992).

Seemüller, Joseph (ed.), *Willirams deutsche Paraphrase des Hohen Liedes, mit Einleitung und Glossar* (Quellen und Forschungen zur Sprach- und Culturgeschichte der germanischen Völker, 28; Strasbourg and London: Trübner, 1878).

Segal, M.H., 'The Song of Songs', *VT* 12 (1962), pp. 470-90.

Selden, Raman (ed.), *The Theory of Criticism: From Plato to the Present* (London: Longman, 1988).

Senger, Anneliese, *Deutsche Übersetzungstheorie im achtzehnten Jahrhundert* (Abhandlungen zur Kunst-, Musik- und Literaturwissenschaft, 97; Bonn: Bouvier, 1971).

Shichiji, Yoshinori, 'Johann David Michaelis und Johann Gottfried Herder', in Hans Esselborn and Werner Keller (eds.), *Geschichtlichkeit und Gegenwart: Festschrift für Hans Dietrich Irmscher zum 65. Geburtstag* (Kölner germanistische Studien, 34; Weimar: Böhlau, 1994), pp. 55-65.

Siegel, Carl, *Herder als Philosoph* (Stuttgart and Berlin: Cotta, 1907).

Simon, Ralph, *Das Gedächtnis der Interpretation: Gedächtnistheorie als Fundament für Hermeneutik, Ästhetik und Interpretation bei Johann Gottfried Herder* (Studien zum achtzehnten Jahrhundert, 23; Hamburg: Meiner, 1998).

Paradisal Love

Simpson, Georgina R., *Herder's Conception of 'Das Volk'* (doctoral dissertation, University of Chicago; private edn, University of Chicago Libraries, 1921).

Smith, Ronald G., *J.G. Hamann: A Study in Christian Existence* (London: Collins, 1960).

Solbrig, Ingeborg, 'Herder and the "Harlem Renaissance" of Black Culture in America: The Case of the "Neger-Idyllen" ', in Kurt Mueller-Vollmer (ed.), *Herder Today: Contributions from the International Herder Conference, Nov. 5–8, 1987, Stanford, California* (Berlin: W. de Gruyter, 1990), pp. 402-14.

Sørensen, Bengt A., *Symbol und Symbolismus in den ästhetischen Theorien des achtzehnten Jahrhunderts und der deutschen Romantik* (Scandinavian University Books; Copenhagen: Munksgaard, 1963).

Sparks, Hedley F.D., *On Translations of the Bible* (E.M. Wood Lecture, University of London; London: Athlone Press, 1973).

Stadelmann, Rudolf, *Der historische Sinn bei Herder* (Halle: Niemeyer, 1928).

Stamm, Israel S., 'Herder and the Aufklärung: A Leibnizian Context', *GR* 38 (1963), pp. 197-208.

Steiner, George, *After Babel: Aspects of Language and Translation* (London: Oxford University Press, 1975).

Stellmacher, Wolfgang, *Herders Shakespeare-Bild: Shakespeare-Rezeption im Sturm und Drang—Dynamisches Weltbild und Bürgerliches Nationaldrama* (Berlin: Rütten & Loening, 1978).

Stemmrich-Köhler, Barbara, *Zur Funktion der orientalischen Poesie bei Goethe, Herder, Hegel: Exotische Klassik und ästhetische Systematik in den 'Noten und Abhandlungen zu besserem Verständnis des West-östlichen Divans' Goethes, in Frühschriften Herders und in Hegels Vorlesungen zur Ästhetik* (Bochumer Schriften zur deutschen Literatur, 31; Frankfurt am Main: Peter Lang, 1992).

Stephan, Horst, *Herder in Bückeburg und seine Bedeutung für die Kirchengeschichte* (Tübingen: J.C.B. Mohr, 1905).

Sternberg, Meir, *The Poetics of Biblical Narrative: Ideological Literature and the Drama of Reading* (Bloomington: Indiana University Press, 1985).

Stolpe, Heinz, *Die Auffassung des jungen Herder vom Mittelalter: ein Beitrag zur Geschichte der Aufklärung* (Weimar: Arion Verlag, 1955).

Störig, Hans Joachim (ed.), *Das Problem des Übersetzens* (Wege der Forschung, 8; Darmstadt: Wissenschaftliche Buchgesellschaft, 2nd edn, 1973).

Strand, Kenneth A., *German Bibles before Luther: The Story of Fourteen High-German Editions* (Grand Rapids: Eerdmans, 1966).

—*Early Low-German Bibles: The Story of Four Pre-Lutheran Editions* (Grand Rapids: Eerdmans, 1967).

Sunnus, Siegfried, 'Der Pastoraltheologe Herder: Zum 250. Geburtstag von Johann Gottfried Herder am 25. August 1994', in *Pastoraltheologie: Monatsschrift für Wissenschaft und Praxis in Kirche und Gesellschaft* 83 (1994).

Suphan, Bernhard, 'Meine Herder-Ausgabe', *Revue germanique* 3 (1907), pp. 233-40.

Taylor, Irmgard, *Kultur, Aufklärung, Bildung, Humanität und verwandte Begriffe bei Herder* (Giessen, 1938), repr. by Alfred Götze and Karl Viëtor (eds.) (Gießener Beiträge zur deutschen Philologie, 62; Amsterdam: Swets & Zeitlinger, 1968).

Terrot, Charles H., *Principles of Biblical Interpretation, Translated from the Institutio Interpretis of J.A. Ernesti* (2 vols.; Edinburgh: T. & T. Clark, 2nd edn, 1843–48).

Timm, Hermann (ed.), *Das Hohe Lied Salomos: Nachdichtungen und Übersetzungen aus sieben Jahrhunderten* (Frankfurt am Main: Insel Verlag, 1982).

Tombo, Rudolph, *Ossian in Germany* (Columbia University Germanic Studies, 1; New York: Columbia University Press, 1901; repr. New York: AMS Press, 1966).

Tomkins, J.P., *Reader-Response Criticism: From Formalism to Post-Structuralism* (Baltimore: The Johns Hopkins University Press, 1986).

Trabant, Jürgen, 'Herder's Discovery of the Ear', in Kurt Mueller-Vollmer (ed.), *Herder Today: Contributions from the International Herder Conference, Nov. 5–8, 1987, Stanford, California* (Berlin: W. de Gruyter, 1990), pp. 345-66.

Ullmann, Karl Theodor, 'Friedrich Wilhelm Carl Umbreit: Blätter der Erinnerung', *Theologische Studien und Kritiken: Eine Zeitschrift für das gesammte Gebiet der Theologie* (1862), pp. 437-79.

Ulrich, Gisela, *Herders Beitrag zur Deutschkunde unter besonderer Berücksichtigung seiner literaturwissenschaftlichen Theorie* (Arbeiten aus dem germanischen Seminar der Universität Berlin, 11; Würzburg: Triltsch, 1943).

Unger, Rudolf, *Hamann und die Aufklärung* (2 vols.; Halle: Niemeyer, 2nd edn, 1925).

Van Tieghem, Paul, *Ossian en France* (Paris: Rieder, 1917; repr. 2 vols.; Geneva: Slatkine Reprints, 1967).

—*Ossian et l'ossianisme dans la littérature européenne au 18ème siècle* (Neophilologiese bibliotheek, 4; Groningen and The Hague: Wolters, 1920).

—*Le préromantisme: Etudes d'histoire littéraire européenne* (Paris: SFELT, 1948).

Via, Dan O., *The Ethics of Mark's Gospel—in the Middle of Time* (Philadelphia: Fortress Press, 1985).

Vulliaud, Paul, *Le Cantique des cantiques d'après la tradition juive* (Paris: Presses Universitaires de France, 1925).

Waag, Albert, *Über Herders Übertragungen englischer Gedichte* (Beilage zum Jahresbericht der Höheren Mädchenschule zu Heidelberg vom Jahre 1891/1892; Heidelberg: Hörning, 1892).

Wackernell, Joseph E., *Das deutsche Volkslied* (Hamburg: Verlagsanstalt und Druckerei A.-G., 1890).

Wagener, Haucke F., *Das Eindringen von Percy's Reliques in Deutschland* (Heidelberg: Pfeffer, 1897).

Wagner, Fritz, *Herders Homerbild: Seine Wurzeln und Wirkungen* (Cologne: n. pub., 1960).

Waldberg, Max von, *Goethe und das Volkslied* (Berlin: Hertz, 1889).

Watson, Wilfred G.E., *Classical Hebrew Poetry: A Guide to its Techniques* (JSOTSup, 26; Sheffield: JSOT Press, 1984).

Weber, Gottfried, *Herder und das Drama: Eine literarhistorische Untersuchung* (Forschungen zur neueren Literaturgeschichte, 56; Weimar: Duncker, 1922; repr. Hildesheim: Gerstenberg, 1978).

Weddigen, Friedrich H. Otto, *Geschichte der deutschen Volkspoesie seit dem Ausgange des Mittelalters bis auf die Gegenwart* (Munich: Callwey, 1884).

Wehrli, Max, 'Sacra Poesis: Bibelepik als europäische Tradition', in Siegfried Gutenbrunner *et al.* (ed.), *Die Wissenschaft von deutscher Sprache und Dichtung: Methoden, Probleme, Aufgaben* (Festschrift für Friedrich Maurer zum 65. Geburtstag am 5. Januar 1963; Stuttgart: Klett, 1963), pp. 262-83.

Weingreen, J., *A Practical Grammar for Classical Hebrew* (repr.; Oxford: Clarendon Press, 2nd edn, 1985).

Welldon, James E.C., *S. Aurelii Augustini Episcopi Hipponensis De Civitate Dei Contra Paganos Libri XXII* (2 vols.; London: SPCK; New York: Macmillan, 1924).

Wellek, René, *A History of Modern Criticism, 1750–1950* (New Haven: Yale University Press, 1958).

Wells, George A., *Herder and After: A Study in the Development of Sociology* (Anglica Germanica: British Studies in Germanic Languages and Literatures, 1; 'S-Gravenhage: Mouton, 1959).

Wendel, François, *Calvin: Sources et évolution de sa pensée religieuse* (Etudes d'Histoire et de Philosophie Religieuses, publiées par la Faculté de Théologie Protestante de l'Université de Strasbourg, 41; Paris: Presses Universitaires de France, 1950).

Werner, August, *Herder als Theologe: Ein Beitrag zur Geschichte der protestantischen Theologie* (Berlin: Henschel, 1871).

Werner, Josef Maria, *Herders Völkerpsychologie unter besonderer Berücksichtigung ihres religionsphilosophischen Blickpunktes* (Düsseldorf: Nolte, 1934).

Wielandt, Rudolf, *Herders Theorie von der Religion und den religiösen Vorstellungen* (Naumburg: Lippert, 1903).

Wiese, Benno von, 'Dichtung und Geistesgeschichte des 18. Jahrhunderts: Eine Problem- und Literaturschau', *DVjs* 12 (1934), 430-78; and 13 (1935), pp. 311-55.

—*Volk und Dichtung von Herder bis zur Romantik* (Erlangen: Palm & Enke, 1938).

—*Deutsche Dichter des achtzehnten Jahrhunderts* (Berlin: E. Schmidt, 1977).

Wigram, George V. (ed.), *The Englishman's Hebrew and Chaldee Concordance of the Old Testament* (2 vols.; London: Bagster, 3rd edn, 1874).

Willey, Basil, *The Eighteenth-Century Background: Studies in the Idea of Nature in the Thought of the Period* (London: Chatto & Windus, 1953).

Willi, Thomas, *Herders Beitrag zum Verstehen des Alten Testaments* (Beiträge zur Geschichte der biblischen Hermeneutik, 8; Tübingen: J.C.B. Mohr, 1971).

—'Die Metamorphose der Bibelwissenschaft in Herders Umgang mit dem Alten Testament', in Martin Bollacher (ed.), *Johann Gottfried Herder: Geschichte und Kultur* (Vorträge der Konferenz der Internationalen Herder-Gesellschaft, die vom 10.–13.6.1992 an der Ruhr-Universität Bochum gehalten wurden; Würzburg: Königshausen & Neumann, 1994), pp. 239-56.

Willinsky, Margarete, *Bischof Percys Bearbeitung der Volksballaden und Kunstgedichte seines Folio-Manuskriptes* (Beiträge zur englischen Philologie, 22; Leipzig: Tauchnitz, 1932).

Wimsatt, William K., and Cleanth Brooks, *Literary Criticism: A Short History* (London: Routledge & Kegan Paul, 1957).

Wisbert, Rainer, *Das Bildungsdenken des jungen Herder: Interpretation der Schrift 'Journal meiner Reise im Jahr 1769'* (Europäische Hochschulschriften, Series XI, 297; Frankfurt am Main: Peter Lang, 1987).

Wittig, Susan, 'Theory of Multiple Meanings', *Semeia* 9 (1977), pp. 75-103.

Wolf, Herman, 'Die Genielehre des jungen Herder', *DVjs* 3 (1925), pp. 401-30.

Wolff, Hans M., 'Der junge Herder und die Entwicklungsidee Rousseaus', *PMLA* 57 (1942), pp. 753-819.

Wood, Rheaman P., *Herder as a Translator of Shakespeare* (Chapel Hill: University of North Carolina Press, 1973).

Würthwein, Ernst, *Der Text des Alten Testaments: Eine Einführung in die Biblia Hebraica* (Stuttgart: Württembergische Bibelanstalt, 4th edn, 1973).

Young, Edward J., *An Introduction to the Old Testament* (Grand Rapids: Eerdmans, 1963).

Young, Robert, *Analytical Concordance to the Holy Bible* (London: Lutterworth Press, 8th edn, 1977).

Zart, Gustav, *Der Einfluß der englischen Philosophen seit Bacon auf die deutsche Philosophie des 18. Jahrhunderts* (Berlin: Dummler, 1881).

Zeitlin, Solomon, *An Historical Study of the Canonization of the Hebrew Scriptures* (Philadelphia: Jewish Publication Society of America, 1933).

Zeller, Bernhard (ed.), *Weltliteratur: Die Lust am Übersetzen im Jahrhundert Goethes* (Eine Ausstellung des Deutschen Literaturarchivs im Schiller-Nationalmuseum Marbach am Neckar, Marbacher Kataloge, 37; Munich: Deutsche Schiller-gesellschaft; Kösel, 1982).

Zinkernagel, Franz A.A., *Herders Shakespear-Aufsatz in dreifacher Gestalt* (Bonn: Marcus and Weber, 1912).

Zippert, Thomas, *Bildung durch Offenbarung: das Offenbarungsverständnis des jungen Herder als Grundmotiv seines theologisch-philosophisch-literarischen Lebenswerks* (Marburger theologische Studien, 39; Marburg: Elwert, 1994).

INDEXES

INDEX OF REFERENCES

OLD TESTAMENT

INDEX OF NAMES